Theodore Roosevelt and Japan

THEODORE ROOSEVELT AND JAPAN

RAYMOND A. ESTHUS

University of Washington Press   *Seattle and London*

Second printing, 1967
Copyright © 1966 by the University of Washington Press
Library of Congress Catalog Card Number 66-19567
Manufactured by North Central Publishing Company, St. Paul, Minnesota

To Paul Hibbert Clyde

Preface

OF all the Presidents of the United States none has been more admired and respected in Japan than Theodore Roosevelt. The greatest statesman of Japan's modern history, Hirobumi Ito, who was a contemporary of Roosevelt, hung Roosevelt's portrait in a place of honor second only to that of the Meiji Emperor. Yet no President of the United States has found his foreign policy so dominated by troubles with Japan. Near the end of his seven years in the White House, Roosevelt could write without exaggeration that the problems of Japanese-American relations had given him more concern than "any of the other rather stormy incidents during my career as President." The Roosevelt period therefore constitutes an important chapter in the history of United States Far Eastern policy.

Roosevelt's Japanese policy has attracted the interest and efforts of some of America's better known historians. Tyler Dennett, the Pulitzer-prize-winning biographer of John Hay, published a volume on Roosevelt and the Russo-Japanese War in 1925. A decade later the prolific pen of Thomas A. Bailey set down a study of Roosevelt and the Japanese-American crises which came in the period after the war. Also, A. Whitney Griswold included two provocative chapters dealing with Roosevelt and Japan in his classic study of United States Far Eastern policy which appeared in 1938. The accounts of these writers were, of necessity, incomplete and on many points speculative, for there were available the records of only one side, the United States. Now, as a result of victory in the Japanese-American war that Roosevelt feared might one day come, the United States has gained access to the records of the Japanese Ministry of Foreign Affairs and has microfilmed these for the benefit of scholars of history. The Japanese records of the Roosevelt period are particularly fruitful, the most important collection being the Telegram Series. Tokyo, being far from other major capitals of the world, sent virtually all its important diplomatic communications in telegraphic form, and in the 1901–09 period the Telegram Series contains over eighty thousand pages of telegrams. It is therefore possible to re-examine Japanese-American relations in the era of Theodore Roosevelt with full records on both sides.

In writing the present study I have had the able assistance of the staffs of the Library of Congress, the National Archives, the Houghton Library, Harvard University, the Albert R. Mann Library, Cornell University, and the Howard Tilton Library, Tulane University. I am indebted to the editors of the *Journal of Modern History* and the *Mississippi Valley Historical Review* (now the *Journal of American History*) for permission to use materials previously published in those journals. Grateful acknowledgement is also made to the Harvard University Press for permission to quote passages from *The Letters of Theodore Roosevelt*, edited by Elting E. Morison. My greatest indebtedness is to Paul H. Clyde, whose pioneering work in the history of Far Eastern international relations has made an inestimable contribution to the present study.

RAYMOND A. ESTHUS

Tulane University

Contents

Theodore Roosevelt and Japan

CHAPTER ONE

The Russo-Japanese War Begins

THE Russo-Japanese War marked a turning point in Japanese-American relations. For fifty years the contacts between the two countries had been characterized by a cordiality and intimacy seldom witnessed in international affairs. Commodore Matthew Perry and Townsend Harris had laid well the foundations of friendship, and the American diplomats who followed them to Japan continued to implement a policy which was considerate and helpful. During the crucial years of treaty revision in the 1890's, the United States stood sympathetically by Japan. A decade later this friendship reached its culmination in the policy of President Theodore Roosevelt during the Russo-Japanese War. With the Peace of Portsmouth, however, Japanese-American relations entered upon a new course. The cordiality of the years from Perry to Portsmouth was to be no more. The new road led from Portsmouth to Pearl Harbor.

It was by no means inevitable that the march of events beginning in 1904–05 would lead to Pearl Harbor, but it was certain that a change would come in the relationship between Tokyo and Washington. A readjustment was dictated by the changed international status of the two powers. While Japan and the United States were yet minor powers, the conflicts of interest did not loom large. Within the short period of a decade, however, both the United States and Japan stepped forth upon the stage of international politics in the role of major powers. The United States, caught up in the surge of imperialism of the 1890's, extended its domain and its responsibilities far across the Pacific to the Philippine archipelago. Japan defeated China in 1895, allied herself with England, the world's mightiest naval power, in 1902 and a few years later con-

3

founded the world by defeating the colossus of the Far East, Tsarist Russia. The Russo-Japanese War left the United States and Japan as the two major powers on the Pacific Ocean, while at the same time it gave Japan strategic interests on the continent of Asia which might conflict with American commercial interests there. Even more important, during the years that the Russo-Japanese War was being fought, a new and difficult problem was arising with the increasing immigration of Japanese into the United States.

America's rise to major power status was the natural culmination of a long period of development by a nation with great inherent strength. Japan's rise to power, on the other hand, was a phenomenal development which was both unexpected and fraught with great significance for Far Eastern power relationships. It came at a time when international rivalries in the Far East were at a peak. In 1895 Japan was sufficiently strong to defeat China, the great Middle Kingdom, but not so powerful that she could ignore the "friendly," though none the less humiliating, advice of Germany, Russia, and France to forego taking Port Arthur from China. Then only a few years later, Japan was obliged to watch the spectacle of those very powers scrambling for naval bases and spheres of influence in China.

In 1897 Germany seized Kiaochow in Shantung province and in subsequent negotiations with China gained not only the right to use that port as a naval base but also a monopoly for capitalistic investment in that province. In 1898 Russia secured a lease on Port Arthur in South Manchuria. St. Petersburg had already received from Peking in 1896 the right to construct the Trans-Siberian railroad across Manchuria and to operate that road through a Russian-dominated Chinese Eastern Railway company. Now, along with the lease of Port Arthur, Russia secured the right to connect that port by rail with the main line of the Chinese Eastern Railway. Russia hoped to convert all Manchuria into an exclusive investment area, or sphere of influence, just as Germany had achieved in Shantung. France, in 1898, acquired a naval base at Kwangchow-wan and sought to make southern China a French sphere of influence.

Japan could not view those events with equanimity. The newspapers of Japan exhibited much irritation over the German occupation of Kiaochow, and when the Russians appeared at the very port from which Japan had been barred by the Triple Intervention, the press became violent in its denunciation. Some of Japan's diplomats, such as Tadasu Hayashi and Takaaki Kato, favored an arrangement with England, for only from that country could Japan expect any aid in opposing the Russian advance. France was tied to Russia in the Dual Alliance, and though not enthusiastic about Russia's Far Eastern ventures, the French government would not put itself in opposition to them. Germany, on the other hand, was eager to see Russia heavily committed in the Far East, for this weakened the Franco-Russian Alliance as it touched Europe. With England, however, it was quite another matter. The British public had a keen sense of the danger of losing part of the Chinese market, and they viewed the apparently irresistible descent of Russia upon north China with alarm.

It was during the Far Eastern crisis of 1897–98 that the first soundings occurred in the direction of an Anglo-Japanese Alliance, but they proved to be premature. The prevailing mood, both at Tokyo and London, was that of compromise with Russia. The leading Japanese statesmen, such as Hirobumi Ito and Kaoru Inouye, still hoped to come to an agreement with Russia. The Russian Foreign Minister, Count Michael Muraviev, was at the same time disposed to buy off the Japanese by making concessions in Korea. In the Nishi-Rosen Agreement of April 25, 1898, Russia agreed not to hinder the development of Japanese commercial and industrial enterprises in Korea. Britain was unable to get compensation from Russia, but found "cartographic consolation" in the form of a sphere of influence in the Yangtze Valley and a leasehold on Weihaiwei, a port just across the Gulf of Pechili from Port Arthur.[1]

The Far Eastern crisis ended with Russian interests firmly established in Manchuria and with the other powers, in varying degrees, entrenched in China south of the Great Wall. It was against this background that the American Secretary of State, John Hay,

1 William L. Langer, *The Diplomacy of Imperialism, 1890–1902*, 2nd ed., 2 vols. in 1, New York, 1951, II, 445–480.

sent out his famous open door notes on September 6, 1899, asking
the powers to accord equal commercial opportunity within their
spheres of influence. Hay was convinced that the spheres were so
well developed that it was hopeless to secure equal rights for capitalistic investment in such things as railroads and mining, but he
hoped to preserve equal opportunity for ordinary commerce. The
replies to Hay's notes were qualified and Russia's response was a
virtual rejection, but he nevertheless announced that he considered the replies as satisfactory and as "final and definitive."

The inadequacy of Hay's notes as an effective protection for
American commercial interests was soon shown when in the summer of 1900 the Boxer Rebellion precipitated another scramble
for concessions in China. Hay, fearing that the partitioning of
China was imminent, sent a circular to the powers announcing
that the United States aimed at a solution of the Boxer troubles
which would preserve Chinese territorial and administrative entity. Thus another major principle was added to Hay's policy. For
four decades American Far Eastern policy was to revolve around
these twin principles of the open door and the integrity of China.[2]

During the Boxer Rebellion Russia put fifty thousand troops in
Manchuria, and in the months that followed, the St. Petersburg
government refused to consent to their withdrawal except in return for an agreement which would add greatly to Russia's exclusive rights within the Manchurian sphere and would deny even
commercial equality to the other powers. This China refused to
grant, and the troops remained in Manchuria.

The continuation of the Russian military occupation of Manchuria led directly to the signing of the Anglo-Japanese Alliance on
January 30, 1902. The agreement effected a complete revolution
in the Far Eastern balance of power and set the stage for the Russo-
Japanese War. By its terms the two powers declared their support
for the open door and the integrity of China and recognized the
respective special interests of both powers in China and the special
interests of Japan "politically as well as commercially and indus-
trially" in Korea. The alliance pledged each signatory to neutrality

2 A. Whitney Griswold, *The Far Eastern Policy of the United States*, New York,
1938, ch. ii; Tyler Dennett, *John Hay: From Poetry to Politics*, New York. 1922. chs.
xxiv–xxv.

if the other was at war and to come to the other's assistance if attacked by more than one power.[3]

Only four months before the conclusion of the Anglo-Japanese
Alliance, the death of President William McKinley had brought
Theodore Roosevelt to the White House. The new President entered office with little knowledge of Far Eastern affairs. During the
campaign of 1900 when he was running for the vice presidency, he
confessed his ignorance to William W. Rockhill, John Hay's chief
adviser on Far Eastern questions: "I have not any but the most
muddled idea as to what is to happen in China and as I will have
to take the stump I shall be very grateful for any hints you can give
me."[4] During that year, however, Roosevelt watched closely the
events in China as the Boxer Expedition fought its way to the relief of foreigners besieged in Peking. He was greatly impressed by
the fighting abilities of the Japanese, who, according to many reports reaching him, were the best soldiers among the troops of the
expeditionary force.[5] During the fall of 1900 Roosevelt formed some
ideas which were later to reach fruition. He became convinced
that it would be bad for all the powers if China were sliced up into
colonies. But, he thought Japan should have Korea in order that
she might be a check upon Russia.[6]

Once in the presidency, Roosevelt took no decisive steps in the
Far East for more than two years. Though he soon implemented a
vigorous foreign policy in the Caribbean — a policy in tune with
his own pugnacious personality — he followed a course in the Far
East characterized by caution and restraint. The architect of that
policy was John Hay, whom Roosevelt kept on as Secretary of State.
At the time Roosevelt became President, Hay had already mapped
out the broad outlines of that policy. As Russia strengthened her
hold on Manchuria, Hay abandoned the position of his July, 1900,
circular, the integrity of China, and retreated to his first open door

[3] Text in G. P. Gooch and Harold Temperley, *British Documents on the Origins of the War, 1898–1914*, 11 vols., London, 1926–38, II, 115–120.

[4] Roosevelt to Rockhill, July 21, 1900, Elting E. Morison, ed., *The Letters of Theodore Roosevelt*, 8 vols., Cambridge, 1951–54, II, 1359.

[5] Roosevelt to Cecil Spring Rice, November 19, 1900, Morison, *Roosevelt Letters*, II, 1422–24.

[6] Roosevelt to Speck von Sternberg, August 28, 1900, Morison, *Roosevelt Letters*, II, 1394.

notes, hoping to salvage equal commercial opportunity in Manchuria by dealing with Russia. Hay's policy had first become manifest when in February, 1901, Japan had sounded the United States
regarding aid in opposing Russia. The Secretary replied that "we
were not at present prepared to attempt singly, or in connection
with other Powers, to enforce these views [as to China's integrity]
in the east by any demonstration which could present a character
of hostility to any other Power." [7]

Hay's policy — now Roosevelt's — at times appeared successful
in achieving its limited objective. In April, 1902, Russia signed an
agreement with China providing for a three-stage withdrawal of
her troops from Manchuria, and it appeared that equal opportunity
in the area would be assured even though Russia retained certain
other advantages. Hay sent a letter to Roosevelt defining the policy
of the United States and expressing the hope that its objective had
been achieved:

We are not in any attitude of hostility towards Russia in Manchuria. On the
contrary, we recognize her exceptional position in northern China. What we
have been working for two years to accomplish, and what we have at last accomplished, if assurances are to count for anything, is that, no matter what
happens eventually in northern China and Manchuria, the United States shall
not be placed in any worse position than while the country was under the
unquestioned domination of China. [8]

Acquiring equal commercial opportunity in Manchuria proved
an elusive goal. Time and again Hay thought he had the matter
nailed down only to see it come loose. When the time came for the
second stage of the Russian evacuation in April, 1903, the Russian
troops did not withdraw. Instead, St. Petersburg presented new demands to China, among them that China employ only Russians as
advisers in north China and that no new cities be opened to trade in
Manchuria. Hay and Roosevelt were disgusted. "Dealing with a
government with whom mendacity is a science is an extremely difficult and delicate matter," Hay wrote the President. [9] Both agreed,

[7] Alfred L. P. Dennis, *Adventures in American Diplomacy, 1896–1906*, New York,
1928, p. 242.

[8] Hay to Roosevelt, May 1, 1902, Roosevelt Papers, Library of Congress, Washington,
D.C.

[9] Hay to Roosevelt, May 12, 1903, Hay Papers, Library of Congress, Washington,
D.C.

nevertheless, that the United States could do little to stop Russia. Hay's letters to Roosevelt were filled with despair. "I am sure you will think it out of the question," he wrote on April 25, "that we should adopt any scheme of concerted action with England and Japan which would seem hostile to Russia. Public opinion in this country would not support such a course, nor do I think it would be to our permanent advantage." [10] Three days later he expressed similar views:

I take it for granted that Russia knows as well as we do that we will not fight over Manchuria, for the simple reason that we cannot. . . . If our rights and our interests in opposition to Russia in the far East were as clear as noonday, we could never get a treaty through the Senate the object of which was to check Russian aggression.[11]

Roosevelt agreed, though he felt great discomfort at having to pursue a weak policy. "The bad feature of the situation from our standpoint," he wrote Hay, "is that as yet it seems that we cannot fight to keep Manchuria open. I hate being in the position of seeming to bluster without backing it up." [12]

Roosevelt and Hay undertook one project to counter the Russians in Manchuria. In 1903 they opened negotiations with China for a new commercial treaty which would have as one of its provisions the opening of more Manchurian cities to trade. At the time only one city there, the port of Newchwang, was open. During the negotiations Washington put pressure on Peking to agree to the opening of more cities, while Russia at the same time warned China not to open them. Though St. Petersburg continually denied that it was opposing the proposed Sino-American treaty, Roosevelt and Hay were under no illusions about the brutal pressure being exerted by Russia at Peking. In a letter to Henry White in May, 1903, Hay realistically summed up the matter:

The Chinese, as well as the Russians, seem to know that the strength of our position is entirely moral, and if the Russians are convinced that we will not fight for Manchuria — as I suppose we will not — and the Chinese are convinced that they have nothing but good to expect from us and nothing but a beating from Russia, the open hand will not be so convincing to the poor

10 Hay to Roosevelt, April 25, 1903, Hay Papers.
11 Hay to Roosevelt, April 28, 1903, Hay Papers.
12 Roosevelt to Hay, May 22, 1903, Morison, *Roosevelt Letters*, III, 478.

devils of chinks as the raised club. Still, we must do the best we can with the means at our disposition.[13]

In June, while Russian pressure at Peking continued to hold up the conclusion of the Sino-American treaty, Roosevelt undertook to publicize the Hay-Roosevelt policy. In letters to Albert Shaw, editor of the American *Review of Reviews*, and Lyman Abbott, editor of the *Outlook*, he explained that the United States recognized Russia's exceptional position in Manchuria but that it wanted Manchurian cities open to trade: "All we ask is that our great and growing trade shall not be interrupted and that Russia shall keep its solemn promises. Russia has not only declined to keep these promises but has declined in that most irritating way — by persistent lying." He then added a comment which had been drafted by Hay:

We have always recognized the exceptional position of Russia in relation to Manchuria. We have done nothing to interfere with her progress and her legitimate aspirations. We have only insisted upon that freedom of access and of opportunity for our commerce which has been guaranteed to us by the agreement of the whole civilized world including Russia, and confirmed to us repeatedly by the voluntary and unsolicited assurances of the Russian Government.[14]

On July 1 Roosevelt executed a more dramatic move. He issued a strong statement condemning Russia's treatment of the Jews — the Kishinev massacre having recently occurred — and criticizing Russian policy in Manchuria.[15] Hay was not in Washington at this time, and Roosevelt took the step without consulting him. "I felt it was just as well to show our teeth," he later explained to Hay.[16]

The move may have had some effect. In mid-July St. Petersburg sent to Washington a categorical denial that it was opposing the opening of cities in Manchuria. Roosevelt and Hay immediately

[13] Hay to White, May 22, 1903, Hay Papers. Most of the records of the effort to get Manchurian cities opened are in the Hay Papers and in United States, Department of State, *Papers Relating to the Foreign Relations of the United States, 1903*, Washington, 1904, pp. 46–78, 91–101.

[14] Roosevelt to Shaw, June 22, 1903, Morison, *Roosevelt Letters*, III, 497–498. A similar letter went to Abbott on the same day. Morison, *Roosevelt Letters*, III, 500–502. Hay's draft of the statement is in Hay to Roosevelt, June 22, 1903, Hay Papers.

[15] New York *Herald*, July 2, 1903.

[16] Roosevelt to Hay, July 29, 1903, Hay Papers.

seized upon the Russian assurance, published it, and presented Peking with a firm demand that the treaty of commerce be signed with the United States. Though Russia continued to threaten China with retaliation if she did sign, in mid-August China reluctantly promised to conclude the treaty on a future date, October 8, the new date Russia had fixed for the withdrawal from Manchuria.

While the struggle for the treaty was going on, Roosevelt's own impatience with the mild policy he was pursuing reached a zenith. On July 18 he wrote to Hay: "I have not the slightest objection to the Russians knowing that I feel thoroughly aroused and irritated at their conduct in Manchuria; that I don't intend to give way and that I am year by year growing more confident that this country would back me in going to an extreme in the matter." [17] At the end of July, in another letter to Hay, Roosevelt's belligerent mood was even more apparent:

Of course your public announcement of what they had promised makes future treachery *more* difficult for them; but after all they never find any treachery *really* difficult. And I wish, in Manchuria, to go to the very limit I think our people will stand. If only we were sure neither France nor Germany would join in, I should not in the least mind going to "extremes" with Russia! [18]

But despite Roosevelt's evident desire to take action against Russia, in the succeeding months nothing was done. In the end, it was left to Japan to meet the Russian challenge.

Throughout the controversy with Russia, Japan watched American policy closely. Japan's ally Britain also took great interest in Washington's diplomatic moves. As Hay explained to Roosevelt, the British appreciated fully the American attitude of independent action but were ready to do everything in their power to support the United States and to adopt any line of action the United States decided upon. The Japanese government was in the same position, said Hay, but it was "painfully anxious to know what we propose to do." Hay believed the Japanese would accept the slightest hint of

17 Roosevelt to Hay, July 18, 1903, Morison, *Roosevelt Letters*, III, 520. He sent similar views to Brooks Adams, July 18, 1903, Roosevelt Papers.
18 Roosevelt to Hay, July 29, 1903, Hay Papers.

support, "and if we gave them a wink, would fly at the throat of Russia in a moment." Hay told Roosevelt, however, that he had constantly told the Japanese Minister, Kogoro Takahira, that the United States must pursue an independent course.[19] In early September, Hay made it still clearer that the United States could not be relied upon for military aid against Russia. After a long talk with Takahira, Hay sent the following account to Roosevelt:

Takahira fears the worst from Russian aggression in Korea. But he said, in a tone of quiet resolution, "if she goes any farther, we shall have something to say." I thought proper not to leave him with any illusions, and so told him plainly that we could not take part in any use of force in that region, unless our own interests were directly involved.

And it was a hard thing to say.

I believe those little people will fight, if they are crowded too far.[20]

Later in September, the Japanese attempted to draw the United States more actively into the diplomatic struggle with Russia. In that month Russia presented new proposals to China and indicated that the scheduled evacuation of Manchuria would not be carried out on October 8 unless China capitulated to the new demands. A week after Russia's *démarche*, Takahira brought a copy of the Russian demands to the State Department and asked for an expression of views.[21] Roosevelt and Hay did not wish to reopen the dispute with Russia at this juncture, however, for to do so might interfere with getting China's assent to the new Sino-American treaty of commerce, which Peking had committed itself to sign on October 8. Hay, who was in New Hampshire, wrote to Alvey A. Adee, the Second Assistant Secretary of State, that "we can fight Russian aggression in Manchuria better after our treaty is signed than we can now." [22] When Takahira sent the Japanese First Secretary, Hirokichi Mutsu, to the Department to get the response to his overture, Adee told the Secretary that the United States was not disposed to consider any collateral questions until the main question was fixed

19 Hay to Roosevelt, May 12, 1903, Hay Papers.

20 Hay to Roosevelt, September 3, 1903, Hay Papers.

21 Note handed to Alvey A. Adee, Second Assistant Secretary of State, by Takahira, September 12, 1903, *Foreign Relations, 1903*, pp. 617–618.

22 Hay to Adee, September 18, 1903, Hay Papers.

by the signing of the treaty on October 8. "Ah," said Mutsu, "Mr. Takahira will understand that." [23]

As it turned out, the United States treaty project had no decisive influence on the struggle over Manchuria. China signed the treaty on October 8, but since the Manchurian cities were not to be opened until after ratifications were exchanged, the United States-Russian showdown could not take place for many months. Before that time arrived, Japan had cut the Gordian knot by force of arms.

The reluctance of the United States to pursue a strong policy toward Russia and the willingness of Japan to resort to arms was owing to a fundamental difference between American and Japanese interests. The interest of the United States was primarily commercial, while Japan's interest was almost entirely strategic. Washington concentrated its attention upon Russia and Manchuria; Tokyo had its eyes fixed upon Russia and Korea. Rightly or wrongly, Japanese leaders felt that their nation's safety depended upon predominance in Korea. Russia's position in Manchuria assumed importance in Japanese thinking primarily because of Manchuria's propinquity to Korea. Though Japan unquestionably intended to gain domination over Korea in one form or another, she had no fixed designs upon Manchuria. True, as a result of the Russo-Japanese War Japan would get a naval base, a railway, and the beginnings of a sphere of influence in South Manchuria, but these came as incidental by-products of the principal war aim of eliminating Russian influence in Korea and in Chinese territory adjacent to Korea. After the war, Japan's imperial ambitions would expand, and ultimately Japanese leaders would put a high value on her position in South Manchuria. But in the summer of 1903 when Japan opened comprehensive negotiations with Russia, Tokyo's thoughts were centered on Korea, which lay just one hundred miles across the sea from Japan. [24]

By July of 1903 the Russian military occupation of Manchuria

[23] Adee to Hay, September 26, 1903, Hay Papers.

[24] Japan's paramount concern over Korea is revealed in the record of the cabinet decision of June 23, 1903, when the Japanese proposal to Russia was formulated. Collection of Cabinet Decisions (Kakugi kettei-sho shūroku), PVM 9-55, pp. 616–629, Japanese Ministry of Foreign Affairs Archives, microfilm collection, Library of Congress, Washington, D.C.

had persisted for three years. During that time Japan's leaders had waited patiently but vainly for a change in Russian policy. In the summer of 1903 matters took a turn for the worse. The Tsar fell under the influence of an adventurous group headed by Alexander Bezobrazov which had designs not only on Manchuria but on Korea as well. At this juncture Tokyo resolved to force a showdown. In July the Japanese Minister at St. Petersburg, Shinichiro Kurino, opened negotiations with the Russian Foreign Minister, Vladimir Lamsdorff. Thus began the crucial negotiations that were destined to last for six months and end in war. The American Minister at Tokyo, Lloyd C. Griscom, was kept *au courant* of the negotiations by Henry W. Denison, the American adviser to the Japanese Foreign Office, and Griscom in turn kept Washington informed. Several months were to pass before Roosevelt and Hay discerned the importance of these negotiations, but from the outset Griscom fully realized their significance. He reported to Hay July 22:

> In the event of Russia refusing to admit of a discussion of the question, it is impossible to predict the course which the Japanese Government will pursue. I am inclined to think that if the present Government continues in power, it would take some decided action. Public opinion in Japan, without being bellicose, is strong for some settlement of the disturbed situation in the Far East. The Japanese press is practically unanimous on the subject.[25]

Japan presented to Russia the first definite draft for an understanding on August 12, 1903. It was proposed that both powers respect the independence and territorial integrity of the Chinese and Korean Empires and that they undertake to maintain the principle of equal opportunity for the commerce and industry of all nations in those countries. More specifically — and somewhat out of tune with these high principles — Japan proposed a reciprocal recognition of Japan's "preponderating interests" in Korea and Russia's "special interests in railway enterprises" in Manchuria. Both powers would be entitled to send troops to their respective areas temporarily, but Japan would have more freedom of action in Korea than Russia would have in Manchuria. Japan would have the exclusive right to give advice and assistance in the interest of

[25] Griscom to Hay, July 22, 1903, *Foreign Relations, 1903*, pp. 616–617.

reform and good government in Korea, including necessary military assistance.[26]

On the same day that this proposal was presented by Kurino, the Russian government took a step which was greatly to complicate the Russo-Japanese negotiations. A special vice-regency was established for the Amur and Kwantung areas, and Admiral Eugene Alexieff was appointed Viceroy of the Far East. He was given supreme power over the civil administration of these territories, with the command of the naval forces in the Pacific and of all the troops in the areas. Even more important, he was to manage all diplomatic affairs concerning these regions. The Viceroy was released from the jurisdiction of the ministers at St. Petersburg and was subject only to the control of a special committee presided over by the Tsar. In order to facilitate the new system, the Russian government insisted that the Russo-Japanese negotiations be transferred from St. Petersburg to Tokyo, a proposition to which Japan agreed most reluctantly. Foreign Minister Lamsdorff, who opposed the adventurous policy in the Far East, was thus by-passed.

Later in August a further development shook Japan's hopes for a peaceful settlement. Finance Minister Sergius Witte, the strongest opponent of the reckless Far Eastern policy, was ousted from office.[27] These political changes caused policy making in the Russian government to become more muddled than ever. A month after Witte's removal, Tokyo had not yet received an answer to its proposal of August 12. When Griscom inquired at the Foreign Office concerning the negotiations in late September, Foreign Minister Jutaro Komura told him that the only desire of the Russian government seemed to be to delay matters. "Baron Komura," Griscom wrote to Hay, "evidently wished to give me the impression

26 Foreign Minister Jutaro Komura to Kurino, telegrams, August 3 and 6, 1903, *Correspondence Regarding the Negotiations Between Japan and Russia, 1903–1904,* Tokyo, London, and Washington, 1904, pp. 7–10. The negotiations can be followed from the Japanese side in this "White Book" and in K. Asakawa, *The Russo-Japanese Conflict: Its Causes and Issues,* Boston and New York, 1904, pp. 296–362. An account from the Russian side is given in Andrew Malozemoff, *Russian Far Eastern Policy, 1881–1904: With Special Emphasis on the Causes of the Russo-Japanese War,* Berkeley and Los Angeles, 1958, pp. 237–249.

27 Malozemoff, *Russian Far Eastern Policy,* pp. 224–226.

that his Government is determined on a firm line of action, and that its patience is nearly exhausted." [28]

After two months of waiting, Japan finally received a reply from Russia on October 3. By that date Bezobrazov's influence in the Russian government had declined,[29] but the Russian communication made it evident that he and his adventurous group had left an indelible imprint on Russian policy. The Russian counter proposal, which Baron Roman Rosen presented at Tokyo after conferring with Admiral Alexieff at Port Arthur, made no mention of China's integrity or the open door for commerce. The only mention of Manchuria came in Russia's request that Japan recognize "Manchuria and its littoral as in all respects outside her sphere of interest." Thus Russia would have a completely free hand in Manchuria. At the same time Russia proposed that definite restrictions be placed on Japan's freedom of action in Korea. The most serious restriction would be that the area north of the thirty-ninth parallel be designated a neutral zone. Japan might give advice and assistance to Korea on civil administration but no part of the territory of Korea was to be used for strategical purposes.[30]

The Russian communication gave scant hope that the negotiations would be successful. Also, while it was being considered, the October 8 date for the Russian withdrawal from Manchuria came and passed with no move on the part of the Russians to evacuate. Japan nevertheless formulated a reply to the Russian proposal. The Japanese counter proposal went far toward an even trade on Korea and Manchuria. It repeated Japan's demand for recognition of her preponderating interests in Korea, but now Japan offered to recognize Russia's special interests in Manchuria and the right of Russia to take such measures as might be necessary for the protection of those interests. Regarding Russia's proposal for a neutral buffer zone in north Korea, Japan proposed that the zone be shifted northward so as to be fifty kilometers on each side of the Korean-Manchurian border. Retained from Japan's original proposal was

[28] Griscom to Hay, September 21, 1903, *Foreign Relations, 1903*, p. 618. See also Lloyd C. Griscom, *Diplomatically Speaking*, New York, 1940, p. 234.

[29] Malozemoff, *Russian Far Eastern Policy*, pp. 221–222.

[30] Komura to Kurino, telegram, October 5, 1903, *Correspondence Regarding the Negotiations Between Japan and Russia*, pp. 22–24.

the provision that both powers would respect the independence and territorial integrity of China and Korea. Japan would, as in her original proposal, have the right to give military assistance to Korea.[31] This provision would give Japan slightly more freedom of action in Korea than Russia would have in Manchuria, but overall the Japanese proposal of October 30 came close to a fifty-fifty bargain.

The next Russian proposal, which Rosen presented to Komura on December 11, did not even approach a balancing of concessions. It repeated most of the previous Russian proposals on Korea, including the neutral zone north of the thirty-ninth parallel, and — what was most remarkable — it made absolutely no mention of Manchuria.[32] The omission of Manchuria from the Russian communication caused consternation at Tokyo. As Komura told Griscom, "the original basis of negotiations proposed by Japan was lost sight of." [33] With this unfortunate turn in the negotiations, Komura now undertook to reveal officially to the United States the details of the negotiations. He sent long telegrams to Washington on December 21 and 23 recounting the exchanges with Russia and instructing Takahira to present the telegrams to Hay. Komura made no effort to hide the seriousness of the situation. "Japan," he said frankly, "finds it impossible to acquiesce in an exceedingly abnormal and precarious condition which would inevitably result from Russia's remaining indefinitely in the flank of Korea." [34] On the same day that the first of the two telegrams was sent to Washington, Komura gave Rosen a counter proposal in which Japan reinjected Manchuria into the negotiations,[35] but there now remained little hope that Russia would agree to terms that Japan could accept.

At Washington, Hay was ill, and Komura's explanatory tele-

31 Komura to Kurino, telegram, October 30, 1903, *Correspondence Regarding the Negotiations Between Japan and Russia*, pp. 28–29.
32 Komura to Kurino, telegram, December 12, 1903, *Correspondence Regarding the Negotiations Between Japan and Russia*, pp. 41–42.
33 Griscom to Hay, December 24, 1903, *Foreign Relations, 1903*, pp. 621–622.
34 Komura to Takahira, telegrams, December 21 and 23, 1903, *Foreign Relations, 1903*, pp. 619–621.
35 Komura to Kurino, telegram, December 21, 1903, *Correspondence Regarding the Negotiations Between Japan and Russia*, pp. 42–43.

grams were given directly to Roosevelt. The President, evidencing his first interest in the negotiations, telegraphed the American legation at Tokyo for further information.[36] Griscom's response gave little hope for peace. In his last conversation with Komura, he reported, the Foreign Minister had stated that Japan would not wait more than a reasonable time for a Russian reply. "The whole tenor of his conversation," wrote Griscom, "implies that war is now almost inevitable." [37] When Hay returned to the Department a few days later, Roosevelt had him sound French Ambassador Jules Jusserand on the possibilities of disinterested powers offering good offices,[38] but when Tokyo indicated it wanted no mediation, Hay immediately dropped the project.[39] Japan believed that a lasting agreement could be secured only by direct negotiations between Russia and Japan and, furthermore, that Russia would only use the time gained by mediation efforts to carry on military preparations. Roosevelt and Hay were not disposed to question the wisdom of Japan's position. Hay told Takahira on January 12 that the steps taken by Japan in the negotiations constituted a wise course which would meet the sympathy of the civilized world.[40] Many diplomats agreed with this assessment. Griscom reported from Tokyo: "It is the opinion of all fairminded observers here that Japan has indeed exercised great moderation and patience." [41]

Though the Roosevelt administration sympathized with Japan, it was careful not to become involved in the controversy. In Decem-

---

[36] Francis B. Loomis, First Assistant Secretary of State, to Griscom, telegram, December 30, 1903, Instructions: Japan, V, Department of State Records, National Archives, Washington, D.C. Until the Department of State adopted the Numerical File system in 1906, the correspondence between the United States and Japan was filed in four classifications: (1) Instructions, Japan, (2) Despatches, Japan, (3) Notes to the Japanese Legation, (4) Notes from the Japanese Legation.

[37] Griscom to Hay, telegram, December 31, 1903, *Foreign Relations, 1903*, p. 622.

[38] Hay diary, January 4, 1904, and Hay to Roosevelt, January 5, 1904, Hay Papers.

[39] Telegram from Komura left at the Department of State, January 4, 1904, Notes from: Japan, VIII; Griscom to Hay, telegram, January 5, 1904, Despatches: Japan, LXXVIII; Hay diary, January 5 and 11, 1904, Hay Papers; Takahira to Komura, January 12, 1904, Telegram Series, XLI, 1789, Japanese Ministry of Foreign Affairs Archives, microfilm collection, Library of Congress, Washington, D.C.

[40] Takahira to Komura, January 12, 1904, Telegram Series, XLI, 1904.

[41] Griscom to Hay, January 11, 1904, Despatches: Japan, LXXVIII. (Printed in Payson J. Treat, *Diplomatic Relations Between the United States and Japan, 1895–1905*, Stanford, 1938, pp. 188–191).

ber Komura had questioned Griscom concerning what the United
States was going to do to get the treaty ports opened in Manchuria
as provided for in the new Sino-American treaty, and Griscom gave
him no encouragement. "I am giving them no handle here to draw
us in," he reported to Hay.[42] When the Russian counter proposal
arrived on January 6, a similar incident occurred. The Russian
note included nothing regarding China's sovereignty in Manchuria,
but it did offer not to impede Japan or other powers in the en-
joyment of their rights under existing treaties with China, *exclusive
of the establishment of foreign settlements*.[43] Komura had Takahira
sound Hay on the matter of foreign settlements at the new treaty
ports, and Hay betrayed no inclination to go into the matter. Takahira concluded that the indifferent attitude of the United States
regarding settlements was owing to a desire not to become involved in the Russo-Japanese controversy.[44]

Japan received from her ally Britain even less support than was
forthcoming from the United States. At London Foreign Secretary
Henry Lansdowne favored bringing pressure on Japan to agree to
Russian terms. Faced with the possibility of involvement in war,
Lansdowne and other British leaders showed much less enthusiasm
for the alliance than they had when it was concluded in 1902. Prime
Minister Arthur Balfour opposed Lansdowne's proposal to attempt to prevent the outbreak of hostilities, but not because he
had any enthusiasm for the alliance with Japan or because he favored Japan. On the contrary, he believed that the outcome of the
impending war would be a limited Russian victory and that such a
development would be to the advantage of Britain. After over-
running Korea, he conjectured, Russia would be over-extended and
thus weaker on the border of India, in Persia, and in Europe. When
on December 29 Hayashi sounded Lansdowne on what support
Britain might render Japan, he received no encouragement whatever. Balfour had already concluded that Britain should do noth-

[42] Griscom to Hay, December 8, 1903, Hay Papers.
[43] Komura to Kurino, telegram, January 7, 1904, *Correspondence Regarding the
Negotiations Between Japan and Russia*, pp. 46–47.
[44] Takahira to Komura, January 15, 1904, Telegram Series, XLI, 1791–93; Hay diary,
January 9, 1904, Hay Papers; Hay to Griscom, telegram, January 18, 1904, Instructions:
Japan, V; Hay to Takahira, January 18, 1904, Notes to: Japan, II.

ing to aid Japan except under the letter of the treaty.[45] Thus Japan was left to face Russia virtually alone. Washington and London provided no significant diplomatic support, and the Anglo-Japanese alliance would be useful militarily only in preventing the entrance of another power into a Russo-Japanese war on the side of Russia. And it was apparent that Britain would fill even that limited role with reluctance.

Tokyo was undaunted by lack of support from Washington and London. Japanese leaders met on January 11 at the home of Prime Minister Taro Katsura to consider the Russian proposal of January 6, and their attitude was one of firmness. It was apparent that the negotiations were foundering on two crucial items: (1) Russia's insistence upon a neutral zone in Korea north of the thirty ninth parallel, and (2) Russia's refusal to recognize China's integrity vis-à-vis Manchuria. If Japan's demands on these issues were not met, it was believed that Russia would remain free to annex Manchuria and extend Russian influence into north Korea. Komura was ready to break off the negotiations and go to war. The navy leaders pointed out, however, that the concentration of transport vessels had not been accomplished and that more time was needed for preparations. It was decided, therefore, that one more proposal would be submitted to Russia which would repeat Japan's position on the crucial items.[46]

Komura presented the final Japanese proposal to Baron Rosen on January 13.[47] On the same day Komura gave Griscom a copy of the communication and confided to him that if no reply was forthcoming from Russia within a reasonable time, Japan would "decide what measures it may have to take to protect its rights and interests." [48] Griscom knew the meaning of the Foreign Minister's words. He wrote to Hay:

45 George Monger, *The End of Isolation: British Foreign Policy, 1900–1907*, London, 1963, pp. 147–153.

46 Tatsuji Takeuchi, *War and Diplomacy in the Japanese Empire*, New York, 1935, p. 142; Atsushi Hiratsuka, ed., *Ito Hakubun Hiroku*, 2 vols., Tokyo, 1929–30, p. 234; Collection of Cabinet Decisions, PVM 9–55, pp. 630–641.

47 Komura to Kurino, telegram, January 13, 1904, *Correspondence Regarding the Negotiations Between Japan and Russia*, pp. 47–49.

48 Griscom to Hay, telegram, January 13, 1904, Despatches: Japan, LXXVIII.

The Japanese nation is now worked up to a high pitch of excitement, and it is no exaggeration to say that if there is no war it will be a severe disappointment to the Japanese individual of every walk of life. The people are under such a strain that the present condition cannot last long. Nothing but the most complete backdown by the Russian Government will satisfy the public feeling, and even then it would require the most skilful handling on the part of the Japanese Government to mollify the war spirit which is now rampant.[49]

To his brother he wrote that the Japanese were "pluck personified" and that he rather expected a complete backdown from Russia.[50]

By the end of January, Japanese military preparations were completed, and the government feared that further delay would be detrimental to Japan. Russia might gain an advantage either through military preparations or through diplomatic interference by other powers. Several times Komura instructed Kurino to request Lamsdorff to accelerate the Russian reply, but still no word was forthcoming from St. Petersburg. "The delay," Griscom telegraphed Hay at the end of January, "is straining the patience of the Japanese Government lately almost to the breaking point." [51] As tension mounted, Peking evidenced concern about the fate of Manchuria in the impending war, and Tokyo sent categorical assurance that Japan would not take the area from China at the end of the war.[52]

At St. Petersburg a conference of high-ranking officials took place on January 28 to formulate the reply to Japan's proposal. The decision was made not to permit a discussion of "Chinese territorial integrity in Manchuria" in the Russian reply. The conference decided, however, to give up completely the demand for a neutral zone in north Korea.[53] This was a significant change in Russian policy, but now a strange incident occurred which canceled out

---

[49] Griscom to Hay, January 21, 1904, Despatches: Japan, LXXVIII. (Printed in Treat, *Diplomatic Relations Between the United States and Japan*, pp. 191–194).

[50] Griscom to Rodman E. Griscom, January 29, 1904, Lloyd C. Griscom Papers, Library of Congress, Washington, D.C.

[51] Griscom to Hay, January 31, 1904, Despatches: Japan, LXXVIII.

[52] Uchida to Komura, January 26, 1904, and Komura to Uchida, January 27, 1904, Telegram Series, XLIII, 4018–19, 4291.

[53] Malozemoff, *Russian Far Eastern Policy*, p. 248.

any good results from that change. After the conference was over, Rear Admiral A. M. Abaza, who was director of the Secretariat of the Special Committee for Far Eastern Affairs and, incidentally, the cousin of Bezobrazov, went to Kurino and deliberately misrepresented the decisions of the conference. He told the Minister that the Russian reply would contain nothing on the integrity of China — which was correct — and that Russia would insist upon some kind of neutral zone in north Korea — which was totally incorrect. Kurino immediately telegraphed this information to Tokyo, and Japanese leaders concluded that the Russian reply would be negative on the two crucial items.[54]

Events now raced toward war. On February 3 Komura instructed Kurino to make no further attempt to secure a reply from Russia.[55] The next day the cabinet and Genro met before the Emperor and made the decision for war.[56] On the afternoon of the following day (February 5), Kurino was instructed to sever relations. In doing so he was to give Lamsdorff a note which should have left the Russians under no illusions concerning Japan's intentions. Japan, said the communication, reserved the right to take such independent action as it deemed best to consolidate and defend its menaced position.[57] Later on the same day (February 5), Kurino sent a telegram to Tokyo which must have removed any lingering doubts, if indeed any remained among Japan's leaders. Kurino had conferred with Lamsdorff, and the Foreign Minister had talked in earnest about the need for a buffer zone in Korea.[58] Thus Lamsdorff unwittingly gave substantiation to the erroneous information which Abaza had given to Kurino. Griscom reported to Hay that this telegram from Kurino "made clear to the Japanese Government that from their point of view war was inevitable." [59]

On February 6 Kurino carried out the severance of relations at

---

[54] Kurino to Komura, January 28, 1904, Telegram Series, XLI, 2238. This episode was also related by Witte to Emile Dillon. See Emile Joseph Dillon, *The Eclipse of Russia*, New York, 1918, pp. 286–287.

[55] Komura to Kurino, February 3, 1904, Telegram Series, XLI, 2285.

[56] Collection of Cabinet Decisions, PVM 9-55, pp. 974–976.

[57] Komura to Kurino, February 5, 1904, Telegram Series, XLI, 2289–95.

[58] Kurino to Komura, February 5, 1904, Telegram Series, XLI, 2253–54.

[59] Griscom to Hay, February 8, 1904, Despatches: Japan, LXXVIII. (Printed in Treat, *Diplomatic Relations Between the United States and Japan*, pp. 194–196).

St. Petersburg. On the same day, Komura called in Griscom and gave him a full account of the recent developments.[60] The next day Takahira asked Hay if the United States would assume the protection of Japanese interests in Russia, a proposal to which the Roosevelt administration readily agreed.[61] On the evening of February 8 came the Japanese attack on the Russian fleet at Port Arthur, and the formal declarations of war followed on February 10. The opening of hostilities came as no surprise to the capitals of the world — except to one, St. Petersburg. Up to the end the Tsar remained convinced that little Japan would never attack mighty Russia.

[60] Griscom to Hay, telegram, February 6, 1904, Despatches: Japan, LXXVIII. Griscom's report of this conference later caused a stir. He reported that Komura told him that a declaration of war would be issued before the commencement of hostilities. In 1905 when the Department of State released to the press galley proofs of *Foreign Relations* for the year 1904, Griscom's despatch was included, and it was given some publicity. Takahira reported this to Komura, who denied having given any such assurance. On Griscom's recommendation the Department deleted the despatch from the published volume. When Griscom later wrote his memoirs, however, he asserted that Komura gave the assurance. It is likely that Komura was under such a strain in February, 1904, that his memory did not accurately record events. Griscom relates an amusing story of how Komura forgot to tell the British Minister that Japan was breaking relations with Russia. Takahira to Komura, April 15, 1905, Telegram Series, LXII, 3110–11; Komura to Takahira, April 21, 1905, Telegram Series, LXIII, 3240; Griscom to Hay, telegram, April 21, 1905, Despatches: Japan, LXXX; Griscom, *Diplomatically Speaking*, pp. 240–241.

[61] United States efforts on behalf of Japanese interests and nationals in Russia and Russian occupied Manchuria are recounted in Treat, *Diplomatic Relations Between the United States and Japan*, pp. 198–201, 224–227.

CHAPTER TWO

Maintaining China's Neutrality

RUSSIAN conduct in Manchuria in the years 1900–03 had created so much resentment against St. Petersburg that world leaders and world opinion at the outset of the war generally sided with Japan. Nowhere was this attitude more apparent than among Roosevelt and his associates. When news came of the Japanese naval victory at Port Arthur, Roosevelt wrote to his son, Theodore Roosevelt, Jr., ". . . between ourselves — for you must not breathe it to anybody — I was thoroughly well pleased with the Japanese victory, for Japan is playing our game." [1] Oscar S. Straus, who was later to become a member of Roosevelt's cabinet, wrote the President: "Japan is certainly battling on the side of civilization — may Wisdom and Victory be on her side." [2] Henry White, one of Roosevelt's favorite members of the diplomatic service, joined in the praise: "How wonderfully the Japanese have succeeded so far." [3] Elihu Root, Roosevelt's former Secretary of War and future Secretary of State, expressed the general feeling with perhaps the best Rooseveltian style: "Was not the way the Japs began the fight bully?" [4] But despite this prevailing partiality of thought, Roosevelt and Hay determined to pursue a policy of strict neutrality in deed. Concurrently they undertook to maintain, insofar as possible, the neutrality of China. At the beginning of the war, this second objective constituted the most immediate problem.

Even before the outbreak of hostilities, efforts were underway to keep China out of the war and to persuade Russia and Japan to

[1] Roosevelt to Theodore Roosevelt, Jr., February 10, 1904, Morison, *Roosevelt Letters*, IV, 724.

[2] Straus to Roosevelt, February 11, 1904, Roosevelt Papers.

[3] White to Roosevelt, February 20, 1904, Roosevelt Papers.

[4] Root to Roosevelt, February 15, 1904, Roosevelt Papers.

respect China's neutrality. Manchuria and Korea were obviously to be the seat of war and nothing could conceivably be done to prevent this. It was to the interests of all the neutral powers, however, to limit the effects of the war to those areas. In the final analysis, even the belligerents would deem it to their advantage to keep China from further involvement in the war.

Germany took the initiative in the matter. On the day that Japan severed relations with Russia (February 6), Ambassador Speck von Sternberg, a long-time friend of Roosevelt, gave the President a memorandum from his government proposing that the United States take the lead in getting the cooperation of the powers in localizing the impending war. Specifically the proposal suggested that Chinese territory south of the latitude of Talienwan, except the Liaotung peninsula, be declared neutral and its neutrality be put under the safeguarding of the powers.[5]

Hay was in Georgia resting from an illness when the German proposal arrived, and Roosevelt sent it to Rockhill, who was still serving as Hay's adviser on Far Eastern affairs. Rockhill felt that the German plan would be prejudicial to Japan's interests, for it would preclude China from joining forces with Japan when her aid might bring the final defeat of Russia. In this regard Rockhill was placing a confidence in China's military power which Japan apparently did not share, for throughout the war Japan was to hold resolutely to the policy of keeping China out of the war. Rockhill also felt that the German proposition might be interpreted as a tacit acknowledgment of Russia's right to continue in military occupation of Manchuria. This was, however, a moot question. Japan was going to war to end the Russian military administration in Manchuria. If Japanese forces were victorious, that objective would be accomplished. If Russia won, St. Petersburg would work its will in Manchuria as it pleased, and no amount of note writing would have much effect upon Russian policy. Rockhill did discern, however, two aspects of the German proposal that deserved considera-

5 Memorandum by Sternberg, n.d., Notes from: Germany, XXIV. The text of the proposal in the original German is found in Chancellor Bernhard von Bülow to Baron Mumm von Schwarzenstein, telegram, February 5, 1904, Germany, Auswärtige Amt., *Die Grosse Politik der Europäischen Kabinette, 1871–1914*, 40 vols., Berlin, 1922–27, XIX, pt. 1, pp. 98–99.

tion. The line of latitude that Germany proposed would leave outside the neutral area not only Manchuria but all of Outer Mongolia and most of Inner Mongolia and Sinkiang. This would leave Russia freedom of action in a vast area on China's borderlands. The memorandum also proposed that China's neutrality be under the safeguard of the powers. This raised dangerous possibilities. If the proposal meant that foreign troops would enter north China in great numbers to protect that neutrality, it would have a disturbing influence upon the people of China and upon the Imperial Court at Peking.[6]

Hay arrived back in Washington on Sunday, February 7, and conferred with Roosevelt that evening. Despite Rockhill's lack of enthusiasm, they decided to proceed with the project. They agreed, though, to modify the proposal. No attempt would be made to fix a definite line between the war area and the neutral territory. It was nevertheless understood that Manchuria would be the seat of war and would not be in the neutral area. No suggestion for the use of neutral armed forces to safeguard the neutral area would be included. Hay himself formulated the final and deliberately ambiguous phraseology to be used. Notes would be sent to the neutral powers urging them to join with the United States in using "good offices" with Russia and Japan to induce them "to respect the neutrality of China and in all practicable ways her administrative entity."[7]

Later that evening Hay put the finishing touches on the notes that would be sent to the powers. The next morning Sternberg was at his house before breakfast, and Hay showed him the draft. Sternberg made no objection to the change. Later in the day Hay showed it to Roosevelt, Rockhill, and high officers at the Department of State. The draft was also shown to the Chinese Minister, who was "greatly pleased."[8] On that same day (February 8), Hay telegraphed his proposal to the neutral capitals, London, Paris,

[6] Rockhill to Roosevelt, ca. February 6, 1904, and Memorandum by Rockhill, ca. February 6, 1904, Roosevelt Papers.

[7] Hay diary, February 7, 1904, Hay Papers; United States, Department of State, *Papers Relating to the Foreign Relations of the United States, 1904*, Washington, 1905, p. 327.

[8] Hay diary, February 8, 1904, Hay Papers.

and Berlin. The action was none too soon. The Japanese navy
was at that very time making its surprise attack on the Russian fleet
at Port Arthur. German concurrence arrived in the evening of February 9.[9] The next day, without waiting for replies from London
and Paris, Hay sent his own representations to St. Petersburg,
Tokyo, and Peking.[10] He then sent his original proposal to Italy,
Austria, the Netherlands, Belgium, Denmark, Spain, and Portugal, all signatories of the Boxer Protocol of 1901, urging that they
use their good offices in similar fashion.[11]

Within ten days all the neutral powers concurred in the neutrality proposal, but there was much confusion regarding the exact
meaning of Hay's notes. Austria asked whether the neutrality to
be respected included Manchuria.[12] Belgium accepted on the condition that "administrative entity" did not include Manchuria.[13]
The Netherlands agreed to accept the proposal if it related to
China "in its restricted sense, and not affecting in any way Manchuria." [14]

Roosevelt and Hay were not greatly concerned about the reactions of the minor neutral powers, but the responses of Paris and
London were crucial. On February 13 the favorable French reply
arrived. The only important reservation was that Manchuria as the
actual theater of war should be excluded from the neutral territory
during the military operations.[15] Since Germany had indicated
concurrence at the outset, this left only England among the major
neutral powers. "This makes the whole business safe," Hay wrote to
Roosevelt. "With Germany and France both favorable I do not see
how any other power should hold back, nor how Russia should sus-
pect the good faith of the step you have taken." [16]

9 Ambassador Charlemagne Tower to Hay, telegram, February 9, 1904, *Foreign Relations, 1904*, pp. 309–310.

10 *Foreign Relations, 1904*, pp. 118, 418, 722–723.

11 *Foreign Relations, 1904*, pp. 42, 95, 258, 405, 521, 700, 806.

12 Minister Bellamy Storer to Hay, telegram, February 12, 1904, *Foreign Relations, 1904*, p. 42.

13 Minister Lawrence Townsend to Hay, telegram, February 16, 1904, *Foreign Relations, 1904*, p. 96.

14 Minister Stanford Newel to Hay, February 19, 1904, *Foreign Relations, 1904*, pp. 522–523.

15 Ambassador Horace Porter to Hay, February 13, 1904, *Foreign Relations, 1904*, p. 302.

16 Hay to Roosevelt, February [13], 1904, Hay Papers.

Actually London had also given its concurrence by February 13, but this was not clear to Washington. The vagueness of Hay's notes had caused a flurry of telegrams between Washington and London and between London and Tokyo. When the American note arrived in London on February 9, the British Foreign Secretary, Lord Lansdowne, immediately took up the question with the Japanese Minister, Tadasu Hayashi. Hayashi said it would be disagreeable to Japan to establish any precedent that Manchuria was excluded from China, but on the other hand, it would also be disagreeable to include Manchuria in the neutral sphere, since it must be the theater of war.[17] Hayashi promised to get immediate instructions from Tokyo, and Lansdowne meanwhile proceeded to question Washington on the extent of the neutral territory. Hay telegraphed a clarification to London, but it failed to clarify. "The proposal of this government," he explained to Lansdowne, "does not contemplate definition of neutral limits but aims to secure the smallest possible area of hostilities and the largest possible area of neutrality compatible with the military necessities of the two belligerents in their hostile operations against each other."[18]

The next day (February 11) Hayashi brought to Lansdowne a message from Tokyo in which Japan approved the neutrality proposal on the condition that the neutrality not extend to territory in adverse possession by Russia.[19] Lansdowne thereupon sent to Washington Britain's agreement "in principle" to the neutrality proposal with a further request for a description of the area to be neutralized.[20] On the same day, Takahira was instructed to inform Hay that Japan would accept the neutralization proposal on the understanding that the area occupied by Russia was excluded and on the condition that Russia accepted it.[21] If Japan had any qualms about accepting the neutrality proposal, they were doubtless dispelled the next day. The First Assistant Secretary of State, Francis B. Loomis, assured Takahira that there was "no suggestion or disposition anywhere to except Manchuria or Korea from the field

[17] Hayashi to Komura, February 10, 1904, Telegram Series, XL, 1418–19, 1420.
[18] Hay to Ambassador Joseph H. Choate, February 10, 1904, Roosevelt Papers.
[19] Komura to Hayashi, February 11, 1904, Telegram Series, XL, 1630–31.
[20] Choate to Hay, telegram, February 11, 1904, *Foreign Relations, 1904*, p. 328.
[21] Komura to Takahira, February 11, 1904, Telegram Series, XL, 2025.

of war-like action, and," said Loomis, "I think the general understanding is clear on this point." [22]

Britain's agreement "in principle" of February 11 was the London government's final reply, and on that basis Britain proceeded to make the appropriate representations to the belligerents. Lansdowne's subsequent questions, however, led Roosevelt and Hay to believe that Britain had not given assent and was holding back. For several days telegrams continued to fly between Washington and London. Hay informed Ambassador Joseph H. Choate on February 12 that it would be unwise to attempt a strict delimitation of the area of hostilities because the friends of the respective combatants would never agree on any such concurrent representation. [23] On the same day, Choate relayed a question from Lansdowne as to whether "administrative entity" extended to Manchuria, where there was still to a certain extent a Chinese administrative entity in spite of the Russian occupation. [24] To this, Hay replied: "We certainly wish Chinese administrative entity everywhere to suffer as little violation as possible, but if we attempt the specification of metes and bounds we should never get the powers to agree." [25]

Roosevelt called Hay to the White House on February 13 to express his concern over Lansdowne's questions and hesitations. Hay was confident, however, that the matter would turn out all right. "We all have the same view as to neutrality of Manchuria," Hay noted in his diary, "but they [the British] seem very dull in taking the fact that it is unnecessary to state in a note like this the notorious fact that there is war in Manchuria and in Korea." [26] Hay's optimism was well founded. On February 14 the diplomatic skies suddenly cleared. Griscom sent to Washington Japan's formal acceptance of the neutrality proposal, thus making official the assurance Takahira had already given to Hay. [27] A telegram also arrived from Choate indicating — to Hay's amazement — that Brit-

22 Loomis to Takahira, February 12, 1904, Notes to: Japan, II.
23 Hay to Choate, telegram, February 12, 1904, Hay Papers.
24 Choate to Hay, telegram, February 12, 1904, Despatches: Britain, CCIX.
25 Hay to Choate, telegram, February 13, 1904, Roosevelt Papers.
26 Hay diary, February 13, 1904, Hay Papers.
27 Griscom to Hay, telegram, February 13, 1904, Despatches: Japan, LXXVIII.

ain had accepted the proposal on February 11 and that all the telegraming since had been "purely academic." [28]

Actually, Hay's *démarche* in support of China's neutrality was very much in accord with the prevailing mood at London. Indeed, British leaders were contemplating even stronger measures to support China. Prime Minister Balfour believed that Russia would win the war and that when she came within sight of victory would pick a quarrel with China. He lamented to Lansdowne on February 11 that a Russo-Chinese war would lead to the annexation of Manchuria and other serious consequences. When these dangers materialized, he said, he hoped that the United States might join with Britain in going to war to defend China's integrity. He even urged Lansdowne to begin the process of persuasion that would bring the United States into such military cooperation with Britain.[29] Balfour's hope that the United States would use armed forces to support its policy regarding China's integrity was, of course, detached from reality. The views he expressed nevertheless indicate that the London government possessed a keen interest in protecting China. Roosevelt's concern over what he believed to be British hesitation over the neutrality proposal thus had no foundation.

The last reply to Hay's neutrality proposal to arrive in Washington was — predictably — from St. Petersburg. It was the usual vague, equivocal diplomatic communication. It accepted Hay's proposal on the condition that Manchuria be excepted and that Japan "observe the engagements entered into with the powers, as well as the principles generally recognized by the law of nations." [30] Hay told Takahira that the Russian reply appeared from its tone to invite further discussion but that he would not allow it and considered the question settled.[31] As Hay noted in his diary, he accepted "at once and finally the answer of Russia as responsive to our note." Two days later he conferred with Roosevelt and found him "much pleased" at the outcome of the China neutrality correspondence.[32]

28 Hay diary, February 14, 1904, Hay Papers. See also Choate to Hay, February 17, 1904, Hay Papers.

29 Monger, *The End of Isolation*, p. 155.

30 Ambassador Robert S. McCormick to Hay, telegram, February 19, 1904, *Foreign Relations, 1904*, p. 724.

31 Takahira to Komura, February 20, 1904, Telegram Series, XLI, 1827.

32 Hay diary, February 19 and 21, 1904, Hay Papers.

What it all meant was not entirely clear. Roosevelt and Hay obviously expected Manchuria to be excepted from the area of China to which neutrality applied. This was approximately what Hay meant when he told Choate on February 10 that he aimed "to secure the smallest possible area of hostilities and the largest area of neutrality compatible with the military necessities." [33] This is further substantiated by another letter to Choate in which Hay explained that he did not specifically mention Manchuria and Korea in his note because it would prevent getting the assent of all the powers.[34] Also, Loomis was doubtless reflecting the views of Roosevelt and Hay when he assured Takahira on February 12 that there was "no disposition anywhere" to include Manchuria and Korea in the neutral area.[35] Thus A. Whitney Griswold's assertion that the Hay neutrality note was a "flat failure" because the Japanese and Russian replies excepted Manchuria from the neutral area misses the point.[36] Roosevelt and Hay never entertained the slightest illusion that the neutrality of the Manchurian territory would be recognized. This much was clear. But what about the second element in Hay's note, China's administrative entity? Was this to be respected in Manchuria?

On this vital point Hay remained conspicuously silent. He did not even make explicit the wish to see China's administrative entity in Manchuria respected after the war was over. When, during the correspondence, Italy sent in a laudable suggestion that Manchuria be mentioned in such a way as to allow the combatants to fight there but not to lessen the ultimate sovereignty of China, Hay remained unresponsive. "I leave them to struggle with that problem," Hay noted in his diary. "I did not want such an apple of discord in my note." [37] Hay doubtless favored the restoration of China's administrative entity in Manchuria, but he was unwilling to raise that issue when it might interfere with the immediate and limited objective of getting China's neutrality respected in areas other than Manchuria. Before the war was over, the restoration of

33 Hay to Choate, telegram, February 10, 1904, Roosevelt Papers.
34 Hay to Choate, February 27, 1904, Hay Papers.
35 Loomis to Takahira, February 12, 1904, Notes to: Japan, II.
36 Griswold, Far Eastern Policy, p. 94.
37 Hay diary, February 15, 1904, Hay Papers.

Manchuria to China was to become a cardinal principle of American policy, but this was a later development. The note of February, 1904, was not the beginning of the campaign in support of China's integrity.[38]

Roosevelt's analysis of the neutrality proposal, which he sent to Root, implied that Hay's note supported China's integrity in Manchuria whereas the original German proposal had not done so:

Yes, it was on the suggestion of "Bill the Kaiser" that we sent out the note on the neutrality of China. But the insertion of the word "entity" was ours. His suggestion originally was in untenable form; that is, he wanted us to guarantee the integrity of China south of the latitude of the Great Wall, which would have left Russia free to gobble up what she really wanted. We changed the proposal by striking out the limitation, and Germany cheerfully acceded! It is a good thing to give Germany all credit for making the suggestion. As a matter of fact, in this instance Germany behaved better than any other power, for in England Lansdowne drove us half crazy with thick-headed inquiries and requests about our making more specific exactly what it was highly inexpedient to make specific at all.[39]

Roosevelt was claiming too much, however, for Hay's vague phraseology insofar as China's integrity was concerned. Actually the German proposal did not call for guaranteeing China's "integrity" or "administrative entity." Thus on this aspect the only difference between the Hay note and the original German proposal was that the German memorandum left the matter unmentioned, while Hay merely mentioned "administrative entity" and left unmentioned the vital question of whether it applied to Manchuria. Overall the only important difference between the Hay note and the German proposal was the delimitation of the war area. Though Roosevelt and Hay would not specifically delimit the war area, they expected that as a result of their *démarche* it would be limited roughly to Manchuria and Korea. Germany had proposed, on the other hand, that a vast area of China's borderlands be open to the belligerents.

Roosevelt's critics have dealt with him rather harshly for his belief that Germany supported the Hay neutrality note. True, Roose-

[38] Griswold again misses the mark, therefore, when he characterizes Hay's neutrality note as the reaffirmation of Hay's policy of 1899–1900 in its "pristine form." Griswold, *Far Eastern Policy*, pp. 93–94.

[39] Roosevelt to Root, February 16, 1904, Morison, *Roosevelt Letters*, IV, 730–732.

velt did not fully appreciate the Kaiser's schemes to get Russia mired in the Far East and thus relieve the pressure on Germany's eastern frontier. But it is equally true that Germany gave support to the American neutralization proposal. However much Berlin may have preferred its own proposal, and however devious may have been its motives in initiating the neutrality proposal, the German government nevertheless accepted the Hay note without question and strongly urged Russia to adhere to the proposal.[40] Berlin not only made representations at St. Petersburg, the German Kaiser himself told the Russian ambassador at great length that it was "most important" for Russia to accept the neutrality proposal.[41] In persuading Russia to accept the neutralization proposal, Germany assured the Russian government that it still regarded Manchuria as outside the neutral area, but this was in line with Hay's own interpretation of his note.

Roosevelt's own role in the drafting of the neutrality note is a matter of controversy, and since there is no definitive evidence on the question, it will probably remain so. In July, 1905, after the death of Hay, Roosevelt wrote a long letter to Henry Cabot Lodge in which he belittled Hay's work as Secretary of State and claimed that he wrote the note:

When, for instance, the Kaiser made the excellent proposition about the integrity of China, Hay wished to refuse and pointed out where the Kaiser's proposition as originally made contained what was inadvisable. I took hold of it myself, accepted the Kaiser's offer, but at the same time blandly changed it so as to wholly remove the objectionable feature (that is, I accepted it as applying to all of China outside of Manchuria, whereas he had proposed in effect that we should allow Russia to work her sweet will in all northern China) and had Hay publish it in this form.[42]

Roosevelt's use of the words "integrity of China" raises the possibility that in this letter he was referring to a later proposal of the Kaiser in January, 1905, which also resulted in a Hay note. However, Roosevelt's statement that it applied to China "outside of

40 Bülow to Count von Alvensleben (St. Petersburg), telegrams, February 9 and 11, 1904, and Alvensleben to the Foreign Minister, telegram, February 12, 1904, *Die Grosse Politik*, XIX, pt. 1, pp. 102–107.
41 M. A. De Wolf Howe, *George von Lengerke Meyer, His Life and Public Services*, New York, 1920, pp. 85–87.
42 Roosevelt to Lodge, July 11, 1905, Morison, *Roosevelt Letters*, IV, 1271–72.

Manchuria" makes it more likely that he was writing of the neutrality proposal of February, 1904. If he was referring to the earlier episode, his account may have some truth in it, but not the whole truth. Possibly Hay voiced some initial opposition to carrying through the Kaiser's proposal, just as Rockhill had done, but it is unlikely that Roosevelt actually authored the neutrality note alone. When Roosevelt described the event to Root just a few days after the dispatch of the note, he said "we changed the proposal" of the Kaiser. Hay's diary, which recorded the event the very day it occurred (February 7), states that Hay suggested the wording. It is probable that the drafting of the note was a joint venture, with Roosevelt suggesting the broad outline of the project and Hay providing the exact — or perhaps one should say the inexact — phraseology.

In the months following the issuance and acceptance of the neutrality note, the United States took the lead in counseling China to maintain neutrality. In mid-March China was warned to observe strict neutrality and give no provocation of any sort to either of the belligerents. Peking responded with an expression of appreciation for the friendly interest of the United States and gave assurance that it was resolved to maintain neutrality.[43] This information was passed on to the Japanese government, which immediately informed Washington that it was "highly gratified."[44] When Hay informed the Russian Ambassador, Arturo Cassini, of China's assurance, however, Cassini was not convinced that China would maintain neutrality. He told Hay that the Chinese army was being organized and drilled with great energy by the Japanese and that the "Yellow Peril" should not be laughed off.[45] Hay soon became convinced that Cassini, in addition to being an inveterate liar as Hay had previously discerned, was the possessor of a very overactive imagination. When Hay discussed the China issue with Takahira a few days after the conference with Cassini, the Japanese Minister told him categorically that Japan did not wish China

[43] Hay to Conger, telegram, March 12, 1904, Conger to Hay, telegram, March 15, 1904, *Foreign Relations, 1904*, pp. 130–131.

[44] Hay to Griscom, telegram, March 15, 1904, *Foreign Relations, 1904*, pp. 422–423; Griscom to Hay, telegram, March 17, 1904, Despatches: Japan, LXXVIII.

[45] Hay diary, March 17, 1904, Hay Papers.

to enter the war. Hay passed this information along to Cassini, but the Russian Ambassador remained in a state of great anxiety about the "dangerous situation" in China.[46]

A month later Cassini was more agitated than ever. He told Hay that Russia was "in terror of some aggression from the Chinese," and he urged Hay to again counsel China to remain neutral. Hay said he would, but he pointed out that it would grow absurd if the admonitions were repeated too frequently. "The Russians seem singularly excited about China," Hay noted in his diary, "or does it mean that they are looking for a pretext." [47] Whatever the Russian motive may have been in raising the issue, there is no question about Japan's position. The Japanese Minister at Peking, Yasuya Uchida, told the American Minister, Edwin Conger, on May 7 that it was far from Japan's wish to see China depart from her attitude of neutrality.[48] Three days later Komura instructed Uchida to tell the Chinese government that Japan desired that it maintain neutrality.[49] Several weeks later, Sir Robert Hart, the head of the Chinese Maritime Customs Administration, questioned Uchida regarding what Japan expected from China, and the Japanese Minister told him that Japan expected nothing but the maintenance of neutrality.[50]

While championing China's neutrality, the Roosevelt administration itself pursued a policy of strict neutrality. In addition to the usual neutrality proclamation, Roosevelt issued a special presidential order on March 10 warning all officials of the government to abstain from either action or speech which could legitimately cause irritation to either of the combatants. Takahira reported to Tokyo with much accuracy that the order had been issued in anticipation of too frequent indulgence of government officials in expression of partial feeling in favor of Japan.[51] But despite the prevalence of this sympathy for Japan, the proclamation had been issued with the unanimous approval of Roosevelt's cabinet. The Presi-

46 Hay diary, March 24, 1904, Hay Papers.

47 Hay diary, April 29, 1904, Hay Papers.

48 Uchida to Komura, May 7, 1904, Telegram Series, XLIII, 1223–24.

49 Komura to Uchida, May 10, 1904, Telegram Series, XLIII, 4338. Takahira gave Hay a copy of the instructions on May 12. *Foreign Relations, 1904*, pp. 423–424.

50 Uchida to Komura, June 1, 1904, Telegram Series, XLIII, 4259.

51 Takahira to Komura, March 19, 1904, Telegram Series, XLI, 1863–64.

dent, Hay noted in his diary, "is determined to do his duty by Russia and not be swerved from strict neutrality. . . ."[52]

During the month of March the policy of strict neutrality was given practical application. Japan's request for permission to lay a cable between Japan and Guam was rejected on the ground that it would not be consonant with strict neutrality.[53] This request was refused despite the opinion of Acting Attorney General Henry M. Hoyt that granting the permission could not be justly construed as a violation of neutral obligations.[54] The policy of neutrality was also evidenced when Japan proposed to send a good will mission to the United States. Takahira came to Hay with a proposal from Tokyo to send Prince Arisugawa Takehito to the United States on a visit, and when Roosevelt learned of the matter he was deeply concerned. Hay noted in his diary: "He was a good deal troubled over the matter — but could not see any way of escaping the visit without giving grave offense."[55] Roosevelt evinced such lack of enthusiasm for the visit that Takahira counseled his government to defer the project, advice which Tokyo wisely accepted.[56]

Russian Ambassador Cassini was little impressed with Roosevelt's "strict neutrality." He knew that the personal sympathies of American leaders were on the side of Japan, and both he and his government resented this fact. He admitted to Hay that the attitude of the United States was "technically correct," but he continued to exhibit bitterness.[57] On one of the many occasions when he came to Hay to complain, Hay lectured him bluntly, concluding with the remark, "You have nothing to complain of at our hands."[58] A few days after this incident, Hay wrote to Spencer Eddy at St. Petersburg: "Every time the Russians get a kick from the Japanese, they turn and swear at us."[59]

[52] Hay diary, March 8 and 9, 1904, Hay Papers.
[53] Hay to Takahira, March 5, 1904, Notes to: Japan, II.
[54] Hoyt to Roosevelt, February 24, 1904, Roosevelt Papers.
[55] Hay diary, March 6, 1904, Hay Papers.
[56] Takahira to Komura, March 8 and 9, 1904, and Komura to Takahira, March 12, 1904, Telegram Series, XLI, 1857–61, 2057.
[57] Hay diary, February 12, 1904, Hay Papers.
[58] Hay diary, June 2, 1904, Hay Papers.
[59] Hay to Spencer Eddy, June 7, 1904, Hay Papers.

While Hay busied himself with the day-to-day implementation of the policies of neutrality — neutrality for the United States and neutrality for China — Roosevelt turned his thoughts to the wider implications of the gigantic struggle that was underway in the Far East. The spectacular victories of the Japanese forces in the early months of the war brought a reappraisal of Japan in the major capitals of the world. Of all those re-evaluations, Roosevelt's was perhaps the most searching. There was considerable justification for his initial reaction to the Japanese victories, the belief that Japan was playing the game of civilized mankind in driving the Russians from Manchuria. Russia had shown every intention of staying in Manchuria and organizing it into an exclusive preserve; and, if Japan had lost the war, there is little doubt that the Russians would have annexed Manchuria.[60]

Roosevelt was nevertheless aware that while Japan was playing the game of civilized mankind, it was also rising to a new position in the Far East. What this would mean for the future of the Far East was uncertain, and it gave Roosevelt much substance for contemplation. If the Japanese won, he wrote to his British friend Cecil Spring Rice in March, 1904, not only Russia but all the powers would have to reckon with a "great new force in eastern Asia." Furthermore, he continued, if Japan seriously started to reorganize China and made any headway, "there will result a real shifting of the center of equilibrium as far as the white races are concerned." He then went on to express a view — indeed a hope — which would recur in his thoughts many times during the course of the war: "It may be that the two powers will fight until both are fairly well exhausted, and that then peace will come on terms which will not mean the creation of either a yellow peril or a Slav peril." [61]

Running parallel to Roosevelt's wish to see a balance of power established in the Far East was his desire to prevent Japan from being robbed of the fruits of victory. As long as Russian power in eastern Asia was not decisively destroyed, these two objectives would not conflict but rather would coincide. Roosevelt was par-

60 Edward H. Zabriskie, *American-Russian Rivalry in the Far East, 1895–1914*, Philadelphia, 1946, p. 129.
61 Roosevelt to Spring Rice, March 19, 1904, Morison, *Roosevelt Letters*, IV, 759–761.

ticularly concerned that Germany and France might intervene,
either during the war or in the peace settlement, to dislodge Japan
from the Asian continent, as they had done by the Triple Intervention in 1895. Whether Roosevelt actually warned Germany and
France against intervention remains uncertain. Eighteen months
after the beginning of the war, he told Spring Rice:

As soon as this war broke out I notified Germany and France in the most
polite and discreet fashion that in the event of a combination against
Japan to try to do what Russia, Germany, and France did to her in 1894
[sic], I should promptly side with Japan and proceed to whatever length
was necessary on her behalf.[62]

It is entirely possible that Roosevelt voiced such sentiments to
Sternberg and Jusserand. But if he did, he apparently did it in such
polite terms that they did not discern its significance and did not
report the statement to their governments. No records of such warnings have yet been uncovered. However that may be, there is no
question that Roosevelt's concern was genuine. When Sternberg
assured him in March, 1904, that Germany was following a policy
of "absolute neutrality," Roosevelt was "visibly reassured." [63]

Roosevelt's concern that Japan should acquire the fruits of victory appeared and reappeared in his talks and correspondence
during the war, but it would be easy to overestimate his sympathy
for Japan. His realistic appraisal of balance of power factors always
outweighed his personal feelings in favor of Japan. Concern for
the balance of power dominated his thoughts throughout the war,
a fact that was abundantly clear in his talks with diplomats at
Washington. In March, 1904, he told "Specky": "It is to our interest that the war between Russia and Japan should drag on, so
that both powers may exhaust themselves as much as possible
and that their geographical area of friction should not be elimi-
nated after the conclusion of peace. . . ." [64] Some months later,
he told French Ambassador Jules Jusserand the same. "From my

[62] Roosevelt to Spring Rice, July 24, 1905, Morison, *Roosevelt Letters*, IV, 1283–87.

[63] Sternberg to the Foreign Minister, telegram, March 21, 1904, *Die Grosse Politik*,
XIX, pt. 1, pp. 112–113. (Translated in Dennis, *Adventures in American Diplomacy*,
p. 364).

[64] Sternberg to the Foreign Minister, telegram, March 21, 1904, *Die Grosse Politik*,
XIX, pt. 1, pp. 112–113.

point of view," he said, "the best would be that the Russians and the Japanese should remain face to face balancing each other, both weakened." [65]

Where the line of friction between Russia and Japan should be established at the conclusion of the war, could not be anticipated with precision. The outcome of the battles in Manchuria would have a decisive influence on this question. By early May, 1904, when Roosevelt again discussed the issue with Sternberg, the Japanese had won every engagement, but no decisive battle had yet been fought. Russian forces had been driven out of Korea, and Japanese forces had landed in South Manchuria, but the siege of Port Arthur and the massive battles of Liaoyang and Mukden further to the north were still many months in the future. At this early stage of the war, Roosevelt envisaged a postwar line of friction along the Korean-Manchurian border. He told Sternberg that Korea should belong to Japan and that Russia should retain a "leading position" in Manchuria but surrender Port Arthur as a fortress and observe the open door for commerce there.[66]

Later, as Japanese victories continued, Roosevelt would shift the "line of friction" northward and westward in favor of Japan, but there were limits to how far he wished to shift the line. In June, 1904, when future military developments could be only dimly foreseen, Roosevelt told Japanese leaders that in the event they were victorious in South Manchuria he hoped their armies would not go north of Mukden.[67] Thus, while Roosevelt was sympathetic toward Japan and wished to prevent Japan from being robbed of the fruits of victory, it is apparent that even in the early months of the war his sympathy and support would be forthcoming only as long as those "fruits of victory" were not north of Mukden.

[65] Jean Jules Jusserand, *What Me Befell: the Reminiscences of J. J. Jusserand*, Boston, 1933, pp. 300–301.

[66] Sternberg to the Foreign Minister, May 9, 1904, *Die Grosse Politik*, XIX, pt. 1, pp. 113–114. (Partially translated in Dennis, *Adventures in American Diplomacy*, p. 365).

[67] Takahira to Komura, June 9, 1904, Telegram Series, XLI, 1959–62.

CHAPTER THREE

Roosevelt Counsels Japan

FROM the outset of the war, Roosevelt contemplated taking a leading role in peacemaking. His principal preoccupations during the struggle were to prepare a foundation for his own peace efforts, and as a part of that endeavor, to give counsel to Japan looking toward the peace negotiations. Roosevelt well knew that he could not take the lead in bringing peace unless his participation was acceptable to Russia as well as to Japan. The policy of strict neutrality was dictated therefore not only by traditional rules of international law but also by this consideration. But while outwardly pursuing strict neutrality, Roosevelt gave his friendly counsel to the Japanese.

Roosevelt's role as adviser to Japan was facilitated by the arrival in Washington of Baron Kentaro Kaneko in March, 1904. Roosevelt and Kaneko had been at Harvard together, and because of this personal connection the Japanese government had dispatched Kaneko to the United States to establish liaison with the President and to influence American public opinion. Shortly before Kaneko arrived, Hay received a letter from Griscom giving an uncomplimentary appraisal of the special envoy. He was, said Griscom, rather a "lightweight." [1] Whether Roosevelt saw this characterization is not known. If he did, he ignored it, for he took the Baron into his confidence completely. It is known, however, that Takahira did not hold Kaneko in high esteem. Takahira doubtless resented the intrusion of this special agent into his own diplomatic preserve. [2]

[1] Griscom to Hay, February 23, 1904, Hay Papers.
[2] The unfriendly relationship between Takahira and Kaneko is evident in Takahira to Komura, March 29, 1905, Telegram Series, LXII, 3102–03. Witte's secretary at the Portsmouth Peace Conference noted that Kaneko "was not on good terms with Takahira, who resents his interference." J. J. Korostovetz, *Pre-War Diplomacy: The Russo-Japanese Problem, Treaty Signed at Portsmouth, U. S. A. 1905, Diary of J. J. Korostovetz*, London, 1920, p. 86.

Takahira first brought his unwanted colleague to the Department of State on March 26. Kaneko talked volubly about the gratitude of Japan for American sympathy. Hay noted in his diary: "I had to remind him that we were neutral." [3] On the same day Kaneko had an interview with Roosevelt at the White House. The discussion was general, but the President expressed confidence that Japan would win the war and establish herself as the great civilizing force of the entire East.[4] In the subsequent weeks Kaneko spent most of his time outside of Washington pursuing his publicity activities, but while doing so he sent to Roosevelt books and articles about Japan.

In June, Kaneko reappeared in Washington, and on June 6 he and Takahira lunched with the President. On this occasion Roosevelt expressed his views candidly and at great length. He told his Japanese visitors that he believed Japan's chief danger was that she might get the "big head" and enter into a general career of "insolence and aggression." Takahira and Kaneko both said, however, that there was no danger of the Japanese becoming intoxicated with victory because the upper and influential class would not permit this. All talk of Japan's even thinking of seizing the Philippines, they assured Roosevelt, was nonsense. Roosevelt agreed but threw in the thought that if aggression toward the Philippines came from any quarter, "we would be quite competent to defend ourselves."

On Japan's future role in the Far East, Roosevelt spoke in expansive terms. He said he hoped Japan would take her place among the great nations, "with, of course, a paramount interest in what surrounds the Yellow Sea, just as the United States has a paramount interest in what surrounds the Caribbean. . . ." The importance of this statement, which conceded a kind of Monroe Doctrine to Japan, apparently was not discerned by Takahira and Kaneko at the time, for their report to Tokyo made no mention of this remarkable Rooseveltian enunciation. When Roosevelt expressed this idea again in July, 1905, however, Kaneko did not miss its importance. Shortly after the Portsmouth Conference he asked Roosevelt whether he might make public the President's

[3] Hay diary, March 26, 1904, Hay Papers.
[4] Takahira to Komura, March 29, 1904, Telegram Series, XLI, 1877–79.

view, a request that Roosevelt denied on the ground that it would invite suspicion among the powers.[5]

Roosevelt discussed in detail with his Japanese luncheon guests the territorial dispositions which he hoped would come at the end of the war. Korea, he said frankly, should be entirely within Japan's sphere of interest. Manchuria should be returned to China. As to who should maintain order and peace there, he had no easy solution. The presence of a Japanese army there would be resented by the Western powers. Perhaps a Chinese army with a staff of Japanese advisers might be used, but Roosevelt felt that the competence of the Chinese army was questionable. Regarding the rest of China, Roosevelt told his listeners that he would welcome any part played by Japan which would tend to bring China forward along the road Japan had traveled. He pointed out, however, that unless everyone was mistaken about the Chinese character, the Japanese would have their hands full in mastering it.[6] At this point Roosevelt was jumping ahead of Japan's own ambitions. Takahira and Kaneko told him that the Japanese were already aware of the difficulty they were going to have even in Korea and were satisfied with that job.

The problem of getting the belligerents together in peace talks was the last item Roosevelt took up with Takahira and Kaneko. A week earlier rumors had circulated that the United States was considering offering its good offices. At that time Hay had told Takahira that the rumors were unfounded but that the United States

[5] Kaneko diary, July 7 and 8, September 10, 1905, Documents Relating to the Despatch of Barons Suematsu and Kaneko to Europe and the United States for the Purpose of Enlightening Public Opinion in Various Countries Regarding the Russo-Japanese War (Nichi-Ro Sen'eki kankei kakkoku yoron keihatsu no tame Suematsu, Kaneko ryō-Danshaku Obei e haken ikken), MT5.2.18.33, reel 804, pp. 422–439, 591–598, Japanese Ministry of Foreign Affairs Archives, microfilm collection, Library of Congress, Washington, D. C.; Kentaro Kaneko, "A 'Japanese Monroe Doctrine' and Manchuria," *Contemporary Japan*, I (1932–33), 175–184. Kaneko asserts in his diary and in his later article that Roosevelt promised in 1905 that he would publicly proclaim Japan's Monroe Doctrine after he left the Presidency. If Roosevelt made such a promise, which is highly doubtful, he changed his mind by the time he left the White House.

[6] There were limits to Roosevelt's wish that Japan assist China. He told Sternberg that a "permanent establishment of Japan in China was positively undesirable." Sternberg to the Foreign Minister, telegram, May 9, 1904, *Die Grosse Politik*, XIX, pt. 1, pp. 113–114.

would be glad, if occasion offered, to help bring about peace.[7] Roosevelt now discussed the question at length. He said he knew the time was not yet right, but when the proper season came he would try to perform good offices for Japan. That, he explained, was why he was maintaining strict neutrality. Furthermore, said Roosevelt, he would exercise his influence to afford Japan the full fruits of her victory. He cautioned Takahira and Kaneko, however, that Japan should not expand her war aims; and it was on this occasion that he expressed the hope that Japanese armies would not go north of Mukden.[8]

A week after this conversation, Roosevelt sent a long account of it to Spring Rice with the injunction that he be very careful not to let anyone see it. "I am perfectly well aware that if they win out it may possibly mean a struggle between them and us in the future, but I hope not and believe not." He confessed that he did not anticipate that Tokyo would show a superior morality to that which existed in the other world capitals, but he saw "nothing ruinous to civilization in the advent of the Japanese to power among the great nations."[9] Several weeks later he wrote to Hay: "The Japs have played our game because they have played the game of civilized mankind. . . . We may be of genuine service, if Japan wins out, in preventing interference to rob her of the fruits of her victory."[10]

In Tokyo, Roosevelt's views were warmly received. Komura telegraphed Takahira that the Japanese government highly appreciated the President's remarks, and he told Takahira that it was of the utmost importance to have the good will and sympathy of the United States "and especially of the President." Komura even wondered whether the appreciation of the Imperial government should be formally expressed to Roosevelt, but Takahira reminded him that Roosevelt was giving his views in a personal conversation and that an official recognition of the conversation would place

7 Hay diary, May 29, 1904, Hay Papers; Takahira to Komura, May 29, 1904, Telegram Series, XLI, 1949–50.

8 Roosevelt to Spring Rice, June 13, 1904, Morison, *Roosevelt Letters*, IV, 829–833; Takahira to Komura, June 9, 1904, Telegram Series, XLI, 1959–62; Kaneko diary, June 6, 1904, Documents Relating to the Despatch of Barons Suematsu and Kaneko to Europe and the United States, MT5.2.18.33, reel 804, pp. 265–280.

9 Roosevelt to Spring Rice, June 13, 1904, Morison, *Roosevelt Letters*, IV, 829–833.

10 Roosevelt to Hay, July 26, 1904, Morison, *Roosevelt Letters*, IV, 865.

the President in an embarrassing position. Takahira nevertheless did convey orally the appreciation of his government during a talk with Hay, and he asked the Secretary to give the message to Roosevelt "if he found it proper." [11]

In the weeks that followed, the issues discussed at the White House luncheon of June 6 were further explored in conversations between Takahira and Hay. On June 23 Hay explained to the Japanese minister that when Roosevelt said Japan should not expand her war aims, he did not mean that Japan should be confined to what she declared before the war. Rather, Tokyo might modify and increase its demands in such form as might be looked upon as just and reasonable in the eyes of the world in order to secure a guarantee of peace in the Far East. In another conversation, Hay said that Roosevelt would be disposed to "mediate" the war. In saying this, Hay doubtless was going beyond Roosevelt's ideas, for the President had suggested only "good offices," which merely meant providing a channel of communication between the two belligerents. But even if Roosevelt's efforts were limited to "good offices," Takahira was confident that the President's friendly influence could be counted upon. He reported to Komura that he believed the United States government was fully convinced of the justice and reasonableness of Japan and would endeavor to shape its attitude and action to suit the desire of the Japanese government. [12]

In the Hay-Takahira talks the question of Germany came up again and again. Since the beginning of the war, Takahira had evidenced great concern over Germany's possible moves. By the summer of 1904 it was clear that this question bothered the Tokyo government more than any other. France and Britain, the allies of the belligerents, were known quantities. When peace was concluded they could be expected to give diplomatic support to their respective allies. There had been some concern during the first weeks of the war that those powers might be drawn into the conflict, but the conclusion of the Anglo-French Entente in April, 1904, greatly lessened that danger. Furthermore, relations between Paris and

[11] Komura to Takahira, June 13, 1904, and Takahira to Komura, June 22 and 27, 1904, Telegram Series, XLI, 2123, 1974, 1986–88; Hay diary, June 23, 1904, Hay Papers.
[12] Takahira to Komura, June 15 and 27, 1904, Telegram Series, XLI, 1880–81, 1986–88.

Tokyo were generally friendly, despite France's alliance with Russia. This left Germany as the one great question mark. In the early months of the war, Berlin had made no effort to hide its partiality for Russia, and Tokyo lived in almost constant fear that Germany would intervene either in the war or in the peacemaking. Hay noted in his diary after a conference with Takahira on June 23: "He is much preoccupied as to the attitude of Germany." After another talk on July 9, when they talked about the danger that a conference of powers might try to dictate a peace settlement, Hay noted: "He seemed specially anxious about Germany." [13] A week later Hay wrote to Roosevelt: "Takahira was here yesterday and talked for some time on several matters, among them the preoccupation, amounting to dread, which they seem to have of the possible action of Germany when the time comes for making peace. I could not give him very much comfort." [14]

The danger of German intervention haunted Roosevelt almost as much as it did the Japanese leaders. This factor is crucial to an understanding of Roosevelt's dealings with Germany during the war. Roosevelt's critics have had much sport ridiculing his elaborate show of friendliness toward the Kaiser. Certainly Roosevelt made many statements to his friend Specky that appear ridiculous when read by themselves. But his relations with the Kaiser do not appear so ludicrous when due consideration is given to the fact that Roosevelt had one central and abiding aim: to win the Kaiser's friendship and to use that friendship to keep him from interfering in the war and in the peace settlement. Roosevelt may have overestimated his influence with the Kaiser, but Japanese leaders considered his efforts valuable. "I am inclined to think," Takahira reported to Tokyo, "that the voice of the U. S. Gov't. may be respected by Germany more than that of any other Gov't. in case she should attempt to meddle with conclusion of war." [15]

During the summer and fall of 1904, Roosevelt undertook a concerted effort to keep Germany out of the Russian camp and to improve the relations between Berlin and Tokyo. At his luncheon with Takahira and Kaneko on June 6, Roosevelt had warned that

13 Hay diary, June 23 and July 9, 1904, Hay Papers.
14 Hay to Roosevelt, July 15, 1904, Hay Papers.
15 Takahira to Komura, June 27, 1904, Telegram Series XLI, 1986–88.

Germany was worried over its position in Shantung, and he told them that Japan should not give Germany the slightest chance to get a charge against Japan. In the Hay-Takahira talks that followed, the Japanese Minister asserted repeatedly that Japan had no designs on German interests in Shantung. "They must know there is no danger from us; that we will not interfere with their holdings," Takahira told Hay on July 15.[16] Takahira doubtless made such statements in good faith, not knowing that a decade later Japan's ambition would have outgrown such a pledge.

On August 9 Roosevelt relayed Takahira's assurance to Sternberg, though he presented it as his own view. He told his friend Specky that it would be to the interest of Germany to allow Japan to obtain the full fruits of victory and that in his judgment there was no doubt that Japan would respect Germany at Kiaochow. He said further that there must not be another coalition of powers to deprive Japan of the results of her victory.[17]

Roosevelt's primary objective in his conference with Sternberg on August 9 was to get Germany committed to his views and thereby to remove the question mark that surrounded German policy. He presented his own ideas for the postwar settlement and said that if Germany did not agree with his views he wished to resolve the differences. He then outlined his conception of the peace settlement. Korea, he believed, should be under a Japanese protectorate, "which may be tantamount to control." As to Manchuria, the powers should guarantee its neutralization and it should be under the control of a Chinese viceroy. In an obvious attempt to win German assent to his plans, he suggested that Germany select the Chinese viceroy. Regarding the disposal of Port Arthur and other conditions of peace, Roosevelt did not comment, for, as he later told Takahira, such questions "should be considered according so the course of events may take hereafter." [18]

The reaction in Berlin to Roosevelt's views indicated that Germany was in no mood to have its hands tied at this early date. When Chancellor Bernhard von Bülow relayed Sternberg's report

16 Hay to Roosevelt, July 15, 1904, Hay Papers.
17 Takahira to Komura, August 17, 1904, Telegram Series, LV, 18149–50; Hay diary, August 10, 1904, Hay Papers.
18 Takahira to Komura, August 17, 1904, Telegram Series, LV, 18149–50.

to the Kaiser, the latter noted in the margin: "One must not divide the hide of the bear before he has been shot." Neither was he enticed by Roosevelt's proposal that he appoint the viceroy for Manchuria. "Simple nonsense! Quite impossible!" were his only comments.[19]

The official German reply to Roosevelt's overtures, which arrived at the end of September, was friendly but vague. Sternberg had on his own initiative assured Roosevelt and Hay that Germany would not interfere to deprive Japan of her legitimate fruits of victory,[20] but Berlin made no such commitment. "His Majesty fully agrees," said the German message, "to our maintaining the closest possible touch with the President and the United States in the Far East." Germany was in favor of the open door and was "hand in hand" with America in carrying it through. Regarding peace terms, the communication merely said that if Russia was defeated, Manchuria "would be most likely" to fall to China and Korea would go to Japan with the reservation of the open door.[21]

Roosevelt thought his endeavor more successful than it actually was. When Sternberg presented the German reply, he read it to the President and did not leave it in written form. Either Sternberg said more than he was authorized to say or Roosevelt inferred too much, for Roosevelt believed the German reply to be satisfactory. He told Takahira on October 8 that he had received a communication from the Kaiser and that Germany would do nothing to interfere with the result of the war. He explained that he had nothing in writing but that there could not be much doubt of the honorable character of the German statement. He said further that the Kaiser was concerned that England would violate the open door in the Yangtze region but so long as England observed the open door there, the German communication could be regarded "as a pledge for the attitude of Germany."[22]

19 Bülow to the Kaiser, August, 31, 1904, *Die Grosse Politik*, XIX, pt. 2, pp. 535–537.

20 Takahira to Komura, August 14 and 17, 1904, Telegram Series, LV, 18071, 18149–50.

21 Bülow to Sternberg, telegram, September 5, 1904, and Sternberg to the Foreign Minister, telegram, September 27, 1904, *Die Grosse Politik*, XIX, pt. 2, pp. 541–542. (Translated in E. T. S. Dugdale, *German Diplomatic Documents, 1871–1914*, 4 vols., London, 1930, III, 200–201).

22 Takahira to Komura, October 8, 1904, Telegram Series, LVI, 19918–20. Takahira's

While Roosevelt was striving to allay the threat of German interference against Japan, he was continuing to give counsel to Japan on other matters. In the summer of 1904 Japan's detention of newspaper correspondents in Tokyo raised a ticklish problem. Many American correspondents had gone to Japan after the outbreak of war hoping to go to the front lines to observe the military operations. The Japanese military, unlike their Russian counterparts, put a high value upon secrecy, and the correspondents were kept in Tokyo week after week. The hands of the civilian leaders in the government were tied, and all they could do was attempt to appease the correspondents with promises that the delay would be only a little longer. Griscom made heroic efforts to make the correspondents comfortable in Tokyo — for which he won their high praise — but the newspapermen were very importunate and caused him much trouble. "I would not mind the legal questions if you would recall the correspondents to the U. S.," he wrote Hay in a personal letter. "We have not even extraterritoriality here. In Turkey and Persia I could have clapped them into jail or deported them!" [23]

Japan's manner of handling the correspondents had unfortunate consequences. Many of them became bitterly anti-Japanese. "They came here their friends," Richard Harding Davis wrote to Roosevelt, "but the authorities have made them their enemies." [24] Roosevelt became so worried about the matter that he made known to the Japanese government his interest in seeing the correspondents get to the front. Komura could only reply, however, that the moment had not yet arrived when this could be done. He explained to Griscom that it was quite impossible for the civil branch of the government to interfere with the military authorities in a matter involving such vital national interests.[25]

Throughout the summer of 1904 both Roosevelt and Hay con-

---

despatch repeating the information in this telegram was on a ship which was captured by the Russians. The despatch must have caused raised eyebrows in St. Petersburg. Hay diary, October 13, 1904, Hay Papers.

23 Griscom to Hay, April 28, 1904, Hay Papers.

24 Davis to Roosevelt, May 26, 1904, Roosevelt Papers.

25 Hay to Griscom, telegram, June 22, 1904, Instructions: Japan, V; Griscom to Hay, June 30, 1904, Despatches: Japan, LXXVIII.

tinued to urge Japan to give better treatment to the correspondents. Hay wrote to Roosevelt on July 21:

I went over the whole thing with Takahira again the day before I left Washington, telling him how short sighted it was of the Japanese Government to convert these clever and friendly fellows, who have the ear of the people of this country, into hostile and resentful critics — when absolutely nothing is to be gained by it. He agreed with me, and said he had cabled his Gov't. in that sense, and would do it again.[26]

Later in the summer the Japanese government allowed the correspondents to go to the armies in Manchuria, but they were allowed to see so little of the action that they remained discontented. In September many of them left the Japanese armies in disgust, vowing to use their influence against Japan.[27] Unfortunately for Japan, that influence was to reach even the White House.

Japan again betrayed little inclination to accept Roosevelt's advice in the *Ryeshitelui* incident, which occurred in August, 1904. In this instance Japan's actions were to bring a noticeable cooling of Roosevelt's pro-Japanese sympathies. The incident came as a by-product of an important Japanese naval victory. On August 10 the Russian Port Arthur squadron, which had been inactive for many months, steamed out to do battle with Admiral Heihachiro Togo's fleet. The Russian force was promptly defeated, and its remnants scattered in all directions. Most of the ships got back into Port Arthur, but many headed for refuge in neutral ports. The Russian destroyer *Ryeshitelui* sought asylum in the Chinese port of Chefoo just across the Gulf of Pechili from Port Arthur. A Japanese destroyer came into the harbor in pursuit of the ship, which at that moment was in the process of disarming. A Japanese officer was sent to parley with the Russian captain but was unceremoniously thrown overboard by the Russians. Thereupon the Japa-

---

26 Hay to Roosevelt, July 21, 1904, Hay Papers.

27 Midzuno (Chefoo) to Komura, September 13, 1904, Uchida (Peking) to Komura, September 14, 1904, and Segawa (Yinkow) to Komura, September 17, 1904, Telegram Series, LVI, 19421, 19444–45, 19546. In telegrams to Tokyo both Hayashi at London and Takahira at Washington bemoaned the consequences. Hayashi to Komura, September 14 and 17, 1904, and Takahira to Komura, September 19, 1904, Telegram Series, LVI, 19459–60, 19537–38, 19596–97.

nese attacked and captured the Russian ship and took it out of Chinese waters.[28]

The incident caused a stir in all the major capitals. At Washington Hay's reaction was typical of both the official and the public response: "The cutting out exploit of the Japanese at Chefoo promises to be a troublesome matter. Unless explained by later facts, it looks like a breach of the neutrality of China." The next day Hay told Takahira that if a violation of international law had been committed, Japan ought in its own interest to make immediate reparation.[29] A few days later Roosevelt himself took the matter in hand. He invited Takahira to lunch and proceeded to urge the surrender of the Russian ship to Chinese jurisdiction. He said he did not doubt that Japan had sufficient reasons for upholding the action of its naval forces but he could not help doubting the wisdom of such a course. Could Japan not turn over the ship to China and clear the record beyond any shadow of error?[30]

Takahira strongly urged his government to accept Roosevelt's advice, and he sent a long telegraphic report giving the unfavorable reaction of the American press.[31] London, upon learning of the American action, joined in urging Japan to surrender the Russian ship.[32] But all the entreaties sent to Tokyo were in vain. Despite the fact that Japan's two leading elder statesmen, Hirobumi Ito and Aritomo Yamagata, favored the acceptance of Roosevelt's advice,[33] the Katsura ministry refused to give in. On August 19 Takahira brought to Hay a long telegram from Komura thanking Roosevelt for his kindly intention but refusing his advice. The Tokyo government took the ground that to give way in this instance would set a precedent dangerous to Japan. If Russia gained the impression it could use Chinese ports for refuge and after a pretence of disarmament still remained in a position to take to the sea, it would be highly advantageous to Russia. In the present critical condition

28 Komura to Takahira, August 17, 1904, and Midzuno to Komura, August 24, 1904, Telegram Series, LV, 18743, 18331.

29 Hay diary, August 12 and 13, 1904, Hay Papers.

30 Takahira to Komura, August 17, 1904, Telegram Series, LV, 18149-50.

31 Takahira to Komura, August 18, 1904, Telegram Series, LV, 18171-73.

32 Hayashi to Komura, August 22, 1904, Telegram Series, LV, 18310-11; Choate to Hay, August 25, 1904, Hay Papers.

33 Griscom to Hay, October 12, 1904, Hay Papers; Hay diary, December 30, 1904, · Hay Papers.

of military operations at Port Arthur, said Komura, the entire Russian fleet might take refuge in Chinese ports.[34]

Takahira believed his government had made a grievous mistake, and he continued to urge the acceptance of Roosevelt's advice. He telegraphed Komura on August 20 that he had talked with the President again and found him irritated. "I think Japan may be technically right," the President had told him; "still I believe Japan will lose nothing but gain much by restoring that worthless boat to China." Takahira told Komura bluntly that if the Imperial government did not take some steps to meet the desire of the President, he feared greatly that there would be some changes in Roosevelt's personal attitude towards Japan.[35] Komura's only response was another long telegraphic explanation which Takahira was instructed to present to Hay.[36]

When Takahira saw Hay, his anxieties were not allayed, despite Hay's endeavor to put the best face on the matter. In their previous meeting Hay had remarked that the question of asylum in international law was very vague,[37] and he now assured Takahira that the suggestion of the President was an entirely informal one and that the Japanese government was in the best position to decide how to shape its conduct. Takahira nevertheless discerned that Hay was far from agreeing with Tokyo's position. He reported to Komura that Hay was the author of the plan for the neutralization of China, and the impression prevailed in Washington that the Secretary of State was keenly disappointed by the present developments — and that the President strongly shared the feeling. Takahira thus urged Tokyo again to reconsider its position.[38]

34 Komura to Takahira, August 19, 1904, Telegram Series, LV, 18785–86; Memorandum by Hay, August 19, 1904, Notes from: Japan, VIII.

35 Takahira to Komura, August 20, 1904, Telegram Series, LV, 18224–26.

36 Komura to Takahira, August 20, 1904, Telegram Series, LV, 18813; Telegram from Komura handed to Hay, August 20, 1904, Notes from: Japan, VIII.

37 Takahira to Komura, August 20, 1904, Telegram Series, LV, 18224–26.

38 Takahira to Komura, August 21, 1904, Telegram Series, LV, 18254–55. Hay's position regarding the legalities is not clear. In his diary on August 16 he said the Japanese action was a glaring violation of international law and the neutrality of China, but in a memorandum for Roosevelt two days later he found the issue "not clearly defined." Memorandum by Hay, August 18, 1904, Roosevelt Papers. When Choate wrote that Britain assumed Hay believed Japan to be in the wrong, Hay replied: "I did not give Japan the advice to return the Reshitiliu because I was convinced they had no case, but on general grounds I felt it would be better for Japan,

Takahira's pleas now brought a slight concession. At the insistence of Ito, Komura telegraphed on August 26 that as soon as the military necessity ceased, the Imperial government would be prepared to modify their attitude without endangering their military position.[39] In the succeeding months, however, the ship was not restored to China.

The *Ryeshitelui* incident produced mixed results. It unquestionably generated ill feeling in both Tokyo and Washington. Roosevelt was irritated, as Takahira noted, and the Japanese government was also miffed. Griscom wrote to Hay that the Japanese Foreign Office was "a little sore about your advice to restore the Reshitelui."[40] The consequences, nevertheless, were not all bad. During the remainder of the war, Japan used utmost caution not to violate China's neutrality in the areas outside of Manchuria. When Port Arthur fell in January, 1905, four Russian destroyers took refuge in Chefoo, and Japan left them unmolested. Griscom wrote to Hay: "The position you took in the [*Ryeshitelui*] case is remembered and they are now restraining themselves in order not to displease you and the President."[41]

During August, while the *Ryeshitelui* issue was running its course, other Russian ships took refuge at Kiaochow and Shanghai. Much to the surprise and gratification of Tokyo, when the Russian ships appeared at Kiaochow, the German authorities interned the ships in accordance with strict neutrality. The Russian ships were not seriously damaged and had a plentiful supply of ammunition. "It seems her officers behaved like cowards," Sternberg observed to Roosevelt.[42] At Shanghai only the weak authority of China existed to enforce internment upon the Russian cruiser and destroyer which appeared there. When the Russian ships refused to

as well as for Russia and China. . . ." Choate to Hay, August 22, 1904, and Hay to Choate, September 1, 1904, Hay Papers.

39 Komura to Takahira, August 26, 1904, Telegram Series, LV, 18921; Memorandum by Adee of interview with Takahira, August 27, 1904, Roosevelt Papers. Takahira asked if this meant the Russian destroyer might later be restored to China, and Komura said it did. Takahira to Komura, August 26, 1904, and Komura to Takahira, August 27, 1904, Telegram Series, LV, 18427, 18934.

40 Griscom to Hay, October 12, 1904, Hay Papers.

41 Griscom to Hay, January 3, 1905, Hay Papers.

42 Sternberg to Roosevelt, October 29, 1904, Roosevelt Papers.

disarm and began effecting repairs, the danger was raised that Japanese warships might go in and attack them.

The Shanghai crisis caused much alarm among American leaders. Hay was ready to throw up in despair the whole business of China's neutrality in her ports. He thought it might be best for China simply to make the ports "spheres of hostility" and to let the belligerents fight it out. The United States had two battleships and five destroyers at Shanghai, but Hay was convinced that the United States should not interfere if hostilities developed. "It would be a mistake to let the impression get abroad," he wrote to Roosevelt, "that we stand ready to enforce Chinese neutrality against all comers." [43] After some initial indecision, Roosevelt came to the same conclusion and sent orders to the navy not to interfere.[44] Fortunately, the crisis ended the day after Roosevelt sent these orders, when Russia agreed to disarm and intern the ships.

The remaining months of 1904 witnessed no major developments in United States-Japanese relations, though some minor events occurred. In September the Russian cruiser *Lena* appeared at San Francisco, and when found to be unseaworthy without extensive repairs, it was interned and disarmed. All the arrangements were made to the satisfaction of Japan. In October the claim of the American Tobacco Company against the Japanese government was settled. For property taken over when the tobacco industry was made a government monopoly, Japan paid five and one-half million dollars — over a million more than the company had expected.[45] Then in November, shortly after Roosevelt's landslide reelection to the Presidency, the long-delayed Japanese good will visit took place with much felicitation but no political discussions. Prince Sadanaru of the House of Fushimi, who was next in rank to the Emperor in the Imperial Councils, visited the White House and the Louisiana Purchase Exposition in St. Louis.

[43] Hay to Roosevelt, August 23 and 25, 1904, Hay Papers. In deference to Russian sensibilities Roosevelt kept most of the United States naval vessels out of China's northern waters during the war. William R. Braisted, *The United States Navy in the Pacific, 1897–1909*, Austin, 1958, ch. iv.
[44] Roosevelt to Hay, August 24, 1904, Morison, *Roosevelt Letters*, IV, 904.
[45] Griscom to Hay, October 12, 1904, Hay Papers. Roosevelt had made his interest in the claim known to the Japanese government. Takahira to Komura, May 5, 1904, Telegram Series, XLI, 1922–23.

Thus as the end of 1904 approached, all the outward signs indicated a growing intimacy between Tokyo and Washington. But appearances were deceptive. There was still a residue of irritation in Roosevelt's mind over Japan's refusal to accept his advice in the *Ryeshitelui* incident. Even more important, Roosevelt was receiving disturbing reports from the disgruntled correspondents and military attachés who had been with the Japanese forces. The anxieties growing in Roosevelt's thoughts were revealed when he told Sternberg on December 5 that he still wanted Japan to succeed "but not too overwhelmingly." [46] On the very day Roosevelt expressed this wish to the German Ambassador, Tokyo received an indication of Roosevelt's views. From London, Hayashi reported that he learned from a friend who was acquainted with Roosevelt that at a private interview the President had evidenced a strong aversion to the Japanese and had expressed the wish to see the two powers exhausted as a result of the war.[47] Though this report gave Roosevelt's views in exaggerated and partially inaccurate form, it nevertheless contained a large element of truth. How much credence Tokyo gave the report is unknown.

Roosevelt's anxieties reached a high point in late December. On December 23 he called in Takahira and gave him a strong lecture about the arrogance the Japanese reportedly manifested after the victory of Liaoyang in September. Such an attitude, he told the Japanese Minister, was extremely mischievous in defending Japan's cause, and it would handicap the friendly action he was contemplating in favor of Japan.[48] The next day Roosevelt sent for Hay and told him of his concern. After the conference Hay noted in his diary: "He is very much exercised by the reports brought back by the newspaper correspondents and by March and Fortescue [military attachés] as to Japanese hostility to the white race in general and especially to Americans." [49] Three days later in a long letter to Spring Rice, Roosevelt expressed deep misgivings:

The Japanese, as a government, treated us well and what they contended for was what all civilized powers in the East were contending for. But I wish I

46 Hay diary, December 6, 1904, Hay Papers.
47 Hayashi to Komura, December 5, 1904, Telegram Series, LVIII, 22336.
48 Takahira to Komura, December 26, 1904, Telegram Series, LIX, 22743–44.
49 Hay diary, December 24, 1904, Hay Papers.

were certain that the Japanese down at bottom did not lump Russians, English, Americans, Germans, all of us, simply as white devils inferior to themselves not only in what they regard as the essentials of civilization, but in courage and forethought, and to be treated politely only so long as would enable the Japanese to take advantage of our various national jealousies, and beat us in turn.

Thus, as the new year approached, a year that would bring further Japanese victories, Roosevelt was more than ever convinced that a balance of power should be established in East Asia with a line of friction between Russia and Japan. In establishing that balance of power, he hoped to play a key role. And beyond that, he confided to "Springy," he intended to "trust in the Lord and keep our powder dry." [50]

[50] Roosevelt to Spring Rice, December 27, 1904, Morison, *Roosevelt Letters*, IV, 1084–88.

CHAPTER FOUR

The Road to Portsmouth

THE year 1905 opened with the fall of Port Arthur to General Maresuke Nogi's forces on January 2. The Russian garrison had put up such a stubborn defense that the Japanese had won the fortress only after a siege of five months and at a cost of twenty thousand lives. At the moment it fell, Japan had made no final determination to retain the Russian base, but it was obvious to many observers that having gained it at so great a cost Japan would likely not give it up. The day after its capture, Griscom sent to Hay the opinion of Denison, the American adviser to the Foreign Ministry, that Japanese leaders were getting more and more disposed to hold Port Arthur permanently.[1]

The fall of the Russian fortress caused peace rumors to fly in all directions. In Berlin the rumors roused something akin to panic. Throughout 1904 Tokyo and Washington had been greatly concerned that Germany would interfere to bring a peace settlement favorable to Russia. Now, ironically, it was the German Kaiser who most feared the intervention of some power or powers. The explanation for Germany's anxieties is found in the shifting power balance in Europe. The rise of the German navy had led Britain to sign the Entente Cordiale with France in April, 1904, and though the agreement related largely to colonial questions, its significance, as Berlin well knew, lay in the fact that Britain was taking the first decisive step toward entering the Franco-Russian camp. During 1904 the Kaiser struggled desperately to reverse the trend of events but with little success. He tried to reopen the line to St. Petersburg which had been cut when the Reinsurance

[1] Griscom to Hay, January 3, 1905, Hay Papers. The Russian and Japanese reactions to the fall of Port Arthur are discussed in John A. White, *The Diplomacy of the Russo-Japanese War*, Princeton, 1964, pp. 185–189.

Treaty was allowed to lapse in 1890. He urged his cousin, Tsar Nicholas, to sign an alliance with Germany which would relegate France to a junior partnership in a German-Russian-French alliance. When in October, 1904, the Russian Baltic Fleet fired on British fishing trawlers on the Dogger Bank (thinking them to be Japanese torpedo boats), the danger of an Anglo-Russian war panicked the Tsar into taking up the alliance project with the Kaiser. But the pact was not concluded.[2] French Foreign Minister Théophile Delcassé bent all efforts to compose the Dogger Bank incident, and it was referred to a commission of inquiry at The Hague for settlement.[3] At St. Petersburg, Lamsdorff successfully opposed the alliance with Germany. When news arrived in Berlin that the alliance project had collapsed, the Kaiser was deeply dejected.

In his despondency, the Kaiser began to imagine all kinds of schemes being concocted against Germany's interests. The specter that haunted him most was an Anglo-French mediation of the war in which Britain and France might take vast areas of Chinese territory. The chief conspirator in the plot, according to the Kaiser's wild thoughts, was Foreign Minister Delcassé. Actually, the Kaiser's fears had no foundation, for Delcassé was scrupulously avoiding even suggesting peace to Russia.[4] Nevertheless, the Kaiser's fears appear to have been genuine rather than feigned, as some historians have supposed. They reached a high point in December, 1904, when he learned that Lamsdorff had told the German Ambassador at St. Petersburg that "France alone knows our conditions." He complained to his cousin "Nicky" that he preferred being informed of Russia's peace conditions directly instead of in a round about way through other agencies.[5]

Such was the background of the Kaiser's overture to Washington in January, 1905, which was to result in another famous diplomatic circular by John Hay. At the same time that the Kaiser wrote

[2] Bernhard von Bülow, *Memoirs of Prince von Bülow*, trans. by F. A. Voigt, 4 vols., Boston, 1931, II, 148–149; Sidney B. Fay, "The Kaiser's Secret Negotiations with the Tsar, 1904–05," *American Historical Review*, XXIV (1918), 48–72.

[3] Maurice Paléologue, *Three Critical Years (1904–05–06)*, New York, 1957, pp. 100–105; White, *Diplomacy of the Russo-Japanese War*, pp. 179–182.

[4] Paléologue, *Three Critical Years*, pp. 179–186.

[5] Kaiser William to Tsar Nicholas, January 2, 1905, *Die Grosse Politik*, XIX, pt. 2, pp. 404–405.

his complaining letter to the Tsar, he unburdened himself to Roosevelt. As he had done at the beginning of the war, he now again
suggested an American diplomatic initiative. In the message, which
was sent through Sternberg, who happened to be in Berlin at the
time, the Kaiser said that a powerful coalition headed by France
was under formation which was directed against the integrity of
China and the open door. The coalition, he said, aimed to convince the belligerents that peace without compensation to the neutral powers was impossible. The compensation would be in the form
of Chinese territory. The Kaiser went on to suggest that Roosevelt
ask the neutral powers to pledge that they would not demand compensation in China or elsewhere. He believed, however, that the
request should go only to the neutral powers, for he thought that
"a grant of a certain portion of territory to both belligerents, eventually in the north of China, is inevitable." [6]

Roosevelt and Hay immediately agreed that it was advisable to
take up the project. After conferring with Roosevelt on the evening
of January 9, Hay noted in his diary: "I found him full of the proposition of the German Emperor. He had come to the same conclusion at which I had arrived the day before: that it would be best to
take advantage of the Kaiser's proposition, 1st. to nail the matter
with him and 2nd. to ascertain the views of the other powers." [7]
Roosevelt and Hay accepted the Kaiser's suggestion that only the
neutral powers be sounded, but no specific reservation in favor of
the belligerents was included. It is uncertain, however, whether
the Kaiser wanted such a reservation. Some historians have concluded that the Kaiser was attempting to extract from Roosevelt
and the other neutrals an admission that Russia was free to take
Chinese territory, but it is unlikely that he had such a large objective in mind. The wording of the messages sent through Sternberg suggests that the German ruler merely wished to leave the

[6] Sternberg to Roosevelt, telegram, January 5, 1905, Roosevelt Papers. A week later
a letter from Sternberg arrived in Washington giving the same views. Sternberg to
Roosevelt, December 29, 1904, Roosevelt Papers. The Kaiser later told Ambassador
Tower that M. Doumer, President of the French Chamber of Deputies, had sounded
the German Ambassador at Paris regarding Germany's participation in the projected
coalition. Tower to Roosevelt, February 4, 1905, Roosevelt Papers.

[7] Hay diary, January 9, 1905, Hay Papers.

question of compensation to the belligerents open for the future.[8] Roosevelt and Hay were willing to pass over this question for the present, though they certainly had no desire to see either Russia or Japan take Chinese territory in the peace settlement.

On January 13, after securing Roosevelt's approval of his draft, Hay dispatched to the neutral powers his circular note on the integrity of China.[9] The communication, which was addressed to Germany, France, Britain, Austria, Belgium, Italy, and Portugal, was a simple disclaimer on the part of the United States of any desire for Chinese territory. It reminded the powers of the United States policy regarding the open door and the integrity of China and invited an "expression of views thereon."[10] Within two days London and Rome pledged concurrence with the American policy.[11] Hay was already convinced that the project would be successful. "The answers from England and Italy," he noted in his diary, "show clearly the extent of the Kaiser's illusion."[12] On the nineteenth Paris gave assent, and eventually all the powers sounded replied favorably. Of all the responses, only the one from Berlin left a loophole. Germany stated that its policy corresponded to that of the United States but went on to say that its position was defined in the Anglo-German Agreement of October 16, 1900.[13] Since this agreement had been interpreted by Germany as not including Man-

8 Griswold states that the Kaiser "fabricated from whole cloth" a French plot to partition China. He goes on to say that the Kaiser "was still trying manfully to save Manchuria for the Czar and with it his own chance for a share in the partitioning of north China." Griswold, *Far Eastern Policy*, p. 103. This interpretation rests upon the theories that the Kaiser's fears of a coalition were feigned and that Germany favored the partition of China at this time. The evidence on these questions is not conclusive, but the greater weight of evidence is on the side that the Kaiser's fears were genuine and that Germany did not favor the partitioning of China below the Great Wall for the obvious reason that Britain and France would make off with far more territory than Germany.

9 Hay diary, January 10 and 11, 1905, Hay Papers.

10 Hay to the ambassadors and ministers to Austria, Belgium, France, Germany, Great Britain, Italy, and Portugal, telegrams, January 13, 1905, United States, Department of State, *Papers Relating to the Foreign Relations of the United States, 1905*, Washington, 1906, p. 1.

11 Choate to Hay, telegram, January 14, 1905, and Meyer to Hay, telegram, January 14, 1905, *Foreign Relations, 1905*, p. 4.

12 Hay diary, January 18, 1905, Hay Papers.

13 Tower to Hay, telegram, January 20, 1905, Despatches: Germany, LXXXII; Bülow to Tower, January 18, 1905, *Foreign Relations, 1905*, p. 3.

churia as a part of China, Germany remained unpledged regarding China's integrity in Manchuria.

As soon as the outcome of the American diplomatic move was known, Hay informed Takahira and Cassini of the project. Takahira was gratified, though he still feared that Germany would demand compensation if Japan retained Port Arthur.[14] Cassini's reaction is not known, but Hay later concluded that Russia disapproved of his action. Though the belligerents had not been committed, the support the neutrals had pledged for China's integrity would make it more difficult for the belligerents to claim Chinese territory. As was said in a clipping from the Russian newspaper *Novosti* which came into Hay's possession: "We cannot say that it promises the belligerents agreeable prospects."[15]

The Kaiser's primary objective of smoking out the intentions of France and Britain had been achieved, but the German ruler's plan to leave the field free for Russia to acquire Chinese territory had suffered an obvious setback. There is no evidence that Roosevelt gave the matter much thought, but for several weeks Hay continued to ponder the meaning of it all. He noted in his diary on January 20: "What the whole performance meant to the Kaiser it is difficult to see. But there is no possible doubt that we have scored for China."[16] A few weeks later he discerned that Germany must have regretted starting the project. He wrote to Choate on February 10: "Our venture in sending out the circular of the 13th of January has turned out very well — perhaps too well to suit the views of some of those who were most enthusiastically in favor of it."[17]

The Kaiser's fear of China's partitionment by France and Britain had obviously been groundless. The Paris government had not conspired in that direction, and the thoughts of British leaders were running directly opposite to what the Kaiser suspected. In January, 1905, the British Foreign Office took up the project for renewal of the Anglo-Japanese alliance, and Prime Minister Balfour contem-

14 Takahira to Komura, January 20, 1905, Telegram Series, LXII, 3045–46.
15 Hay to Roosevelt, January 31, 1905, Hay Papers.
16 Hay diary, January 20, 1905, Hay Papers.
17 Hay to Choate, February 10, 1905, Hay Papers.

plated inviting the United States to join in a renewed alliance which would be modified to protect China from partitionment. The Prime Minister, who had betrayed no enthusiasm for the Anglo-Japanese alliance as then constituted, hesitated to commit future ministries by renewing it, but a triple alliance including the United States appeared more attractive. "If we could bring in the Americans," he wrote to Under Secretary Earl Percy, "that would be a new arrangement, and, as part of it, an extension of the Japanese Treaty would clearly be legitimate." Balfour even drafted a letter for Spring Rice to send to Roosevelt proposing an alliance, but the letter apparently was never sent. There was, of course, no chance that Roosevelt would bring the United States openly into the alliance. At the end of January, however, he informed British leaders through Ambassador Durand that he considered the interests of the two countries identical in the Far East and he wished Britain and the United States to stand together. But he cautioned that in order to avoid exciting criticism they should do so by their actions rather than by an "open evident agreement." [18]

Meanwhile the rumors of peace continued to circulate. There was much speculation in the press about a possible move for peace by Washington, but both Roosevelt and Hay knew that the time was not ripe. Cassini kept insisting that Russia must go on with the war, and there seemed little prospect of changing St. Petersburg's attitude.[19] The issue of peace was nevertheless much on Roosevelt's mind, and in mid-January he called in Takahira to counsel him on peace conditions. He told him that Japan had earned Port Arthur and had a right to hold it. As to Manchuria, he hoped to see it restored to China under the guidance of the powers.[20] A few weeks later, Roosevelt expressed similar views to George von Lengerke Meyer, who would shortly be sent to St. Petersburg as ambassador: "Of course the military situation may alter, but if peace should come now, Japan ought to have a protectorate over Korea (which has shown its utter inability to stand by itself) and ought

18 Monger, *The End of Isolation*, pp. 180–182.
19 Hay diary, January 3 and 6, 1905, Hay Papers.
20 Meyer to Roosevelt, January 20, 1905, Roosevelt Papers.

to succeed to Russia's rights in and around Port Arthur, while I should hope to see Manchuria restored to China." [21]

Roosevelt's outline of peace conditions was substantially in accord with the views of the Tokyo government. After Takahira telegraphed Roosevelt's remarks to Tokyo, Komura sent to Washington for the first time an outline of Japan's plans for peace. Regarding Korea there was no difference in views. Komura stated that Japan must have full predominance of influence. At Port Arthur, said the Foreign Minister, Japan could accept nothing less than succeeding to the Russian rights. This was no more than Roosevelt himself had suggested. It was only on the question of Manchuria that any divergence occurred between Roosevelt's views and those of Tokyo, and here the difference was minor. Komura said that Japan adhered to her engagements favorable to the open door and wished to have the administrative entity restored to China. Japan did not agree, however, with the President's idea to put Manchuria under some kind of international neutralization or guidance. Such a scheme, said Komura, might open the door to regrettable complications.[22] Roosevelt had no definite plans on the matter, and in subsequent weeks he dropped the idea entirely. Thus by February, 1905, Roosevelt and Japan were in complete agreement on peace terms.

Japanese leaders were left in no doubt concerning Roosevelt's support of their peace plans. In addition to the assurance transmitted through Takahira, he made his views known through an indirect channel. In February he voiced his opinions to Richard Barry, a writer for *Collier's*, who was to relay them to George Kennan in Tokyo. There Kennan could communicate the President's views to "a few men of influence." Roosevelt expressed himself to Barry in unequivocal terms. When Barry mentioned the danger that the powers would again prevent Japan from retaining Port Arthur, Roosevelt exclaimed: "Retain Port Arthur! If in no other way, I would *make* her hold Port Arthur. She has won it, and it is hers, never to be surrendered again. Japan must hold Port Arthur and she must hold Korea. These two points are already settled."

21 Roosevelt to Meyer, February 6, 1905, Morison, *Roosevelt Letters*, IV, 1115–16.
22 Hay diary, January 26, 1905, Hay Papers.

In March, 1905, Kennan read a verbatim account of Roosevelt's interview to Katsura.[23]

The strong support which Roosevelt gave to the Japanese peace plans did not, however, blind him to the need for a balance of power in Eastern Asia. It did shift the line of friction between Russia and Japan from the Manchurian-Korean border to somewhere in Manchuria. But Roosevelt was still anxious that the Japanese not proceed too far to the north in Manchuria. In early February he unofficially conveyed advice to the Russian government to make peace before the Japanese took Mukden. This advice, which was transmitted to Cassini through John Callan O'Laughlin, a correspondent of the *Chicago Tribune*, was prompted as much by the desire to halt further Japanese conquests as by the wish to assure Japan possession of what she held at the time. Roosevelt said that if the Baltic fleet, which was then on its way to the Pacific, had a chance of success and if Russia could keep six hundred thousand men in Manchuria, then it was all right and he had nothing to say. If not, he advised, it was in Russia's own interest to make peace, for if Japan took Mukden and got north of Harbin, the peace terms would certainly be worse for Russia.[24]

Russia disdained Roosevelt's advice, and the Russian military defeat of which he warned soon came. At the gigantic Battle of Mukden, February 23-March 10, the Russian forces were routed with a loss of 97,000 men. It was the largest and last land battle of the war. Unknown to Roosevelt, the balance of power for which he longed had now been established. The Japanese had won the biggest battle in the history of modern warfare before the First World War, but they had done so only by straining their material and financial resources to the limit. Roosevelt's fears that the Japanese would advance north of Mukden never materialized for the simple reason that Japan had reached the limit of its capacity. This fact was appreciated by the Japanese military leaders even more than by the civilian leaders in Tokyo. Following the Battle of Mukden

23 Barry to Kennan, February 21, 1905, George Kennan Papers, Library of Congress, Washington, D.C.; Kennan to Roosevelt, March 30, 1905, Roosevelt Papers.

24 Memorandum by O'Laughlin, February 9, 1905, Roosevelt Papers; Roosevelt to George Otto Trevelyan, March 9, 1905, and Roosevelt to Edward VII, March 9, 1905, Morison, *Roosevelt Letters*, IV, 1132–35, 1135–36.

Marshal Aritomo Yamagata, the chief of staff, Marshal Iwao Oyama, the commander of the Japanese expeditionary forces, and General Gentaro Kodama, the chief of staff of the expeditionary forces, all advocated peace.[25]

Griscom, at Tokyo, soon learned of the military's desire for peace, but the episode through which he heard this information almost caused a mixup. At a dinner party on March 8, General Masatake Terauchi, the Minister of War, told Griscom to tell President Roosevelt that in his opinion the fighting should stop. The next day Griscom told Denison of Terauchi's statement, and Denison pleaded with him not to telegraph the General's message to Roosevelt. Denison said he was certain that Prime Minister Katsura and Foreign Minister Komura had no knowledge of the matter and that they would be deeply offended if they learned of Terauchi's action. Griscom agreed not to telegraph the General's message, but he felt obliged to sound Komura in order to make sure that the cabinet was not putting out a feeler for peace. When he saw Komura that evening, Griscom was convinced that Terauchi had given only his personal view. Komura told Griscom that Japan's detailed terms had been formulated but would be made known to the President only when Japan was assured that the inquiry came from Russia. He also told Griscom that in his opinion Russia would not be ready to make peace until the Baltic Fleet had arrived and been dealt with.[26]

Griscom's brief telegraphic reports to Washington caused much perplexity. The confusion was compounded when, after another conversation with Denison, Griscom reported that Japan planned to ask Roosevelt to be the peacemaker when the proper moment arrived.[27] Roosevelt feared that Griscom had put him forward as peacemaker, and he had Hay immediately telegraph Griscom telling him to make it clear to Komura that the President was not offering his services and that if any other agency should seem more practicable and appropriate he hoped it would be chosen. The

---

25 Takeuchi, *War and Diplomacy*, p. 149.

26 Griscom to Hay, March 13, 1905, Despatches: Japan, LXXX (Printed in Treat, *Diplomatic Relations Between the United States and Japan*, pp. 238–241); Griscom to Hay, March 15, 1905, Hay Papers.

27 Griscom to Hay, telegrams, March 9 and 10, 1905, Despatches: Japan, LXXX.

"other agency," Hay later explained to Takahira, meant some power which might be more acceptable to Russia, such as France.[28] Actually, there had been no misunderstanding in Tokyo regarding Roosevelt's position, and Komura hastened to telegraph Washington giving assurance that there had been none.[29]

Though Roosevelt did not wish to put himself forward as peacemaker until called upon by one or both of the belligerents, he did not hesitate to press both sides to make peace after the Battle of Mukden. Before he left Washington at the end of March for a hunting trip in the West, he conferred at length with Cassini, Takahira, Jusserand, Sternberg, and British Ambassador Sir Mortimer Durand. He urged upon all the diplomats the advisability of peace. To Cassini he stated that it was eminently to Russia's interest to make peace, for each delay, if it meant another Japanese victory, would mean more unfavorable terms for Russia.[30] Rumors were already circulating that Japan would now demand an indemnity, in addition to the other terms, and when Cassini said Russia would never consider paying an indemnity, Roosevelt replied that it was merely a question of paying it now or waiting until the Japanese had taken Harbin and Vladivostok.[31]

When Roosevelt talked with Takahira, he found that the rumors regarding an indemnity were indeed true. Takahira told him that in addition to the points already mentioned, Japan would insist upon an indemnity. To this Roosevelt replied that while he was in hearty accord with Japan on the terms contemplated before the Battle of Mukden, he would reserve judgment on the matter of an indemnity.[32] He then gave Takahira a clear hint that he was quite unenthusiastic about an indemnity. He said that a few months of extra war would eat up all the indemnity Japan could expect Russia to pay. Furthermore, if there were any doubt about the outcome of the approaching naval battle with the Baltic Fleet, he be-

28 Hay to Griscom, March 11, 1905, Despatches: Japan, LXXX. (Original copy missing from Instructions: Japan, V). Hay diary, March 11, 1905, Hay Papers.

29 Telegram from Komura, March 14, 1905, Notes to: Japan, IX.

30 Roosevelt to Sternberg, March 31, 1905, Morison, *Roosevelt Letters*, IV, 1155.

31 Roosevelt to Hay, April 2, 1905, Morison, *Roosevelt Letters*, IV, 1156–58.

32 Roosevelt to Hay, April 2, 1905, Morison, *Roosevelt Letters*, IV, 1156–58.

lieved Japan should build a bridge of gold for the beaten enemy.[33] Tokyo, however, was not persuaded. A week later Takahira confided that Japan also felt justified in demanding cession of the island of Sakhalin, the large island that lay directly north of the Japanese home islands.[34]

Roosevelt's lack of enthusiasm for the new Japanese peace terms was due primarily to balance of power considerations. He was concerned that the higher terms would prolong the war and lead to the destruction of Russia's power in the Far East. This was an eventuality that he feared throughout the war. He believed that Britain also shared this fear. He wrote to Hay in March that he had an idea that "the English would be by no means overjoyed if the Japs took Vladivostok." [35] He may have been right. Ambassador Durand told Takahira at this time that it was only natural for Russia to wish to retain Vladivostok and that Japan should be moderate in her peace terms.[36]

Roosevelt's counsel for peace was rejected in St. Petersburg.[37] He believed his advice was also rejected in Tokyo, but his understanding of the situation in Japan was not altogether accurate. He thought Japan was continuing the war because of the existence of a "war party" that wanted to fight on for an indemnity and territory.[38] Actually, there was unanimity of opinion at Tokyo on the need for peace. When in April, 1905, the cabinet drafted terms, only the pre-Mukden items were listed as mandatory. The indemnity and the cession of Sakhalin were listed merely as items which were not absolutely necessary but were to be achieved if possible.[39] The reason Japan did not respond to Roosevelt's entreaties for peace was not because of a "war party" but because, since the beginning of the war, the government had believed that no peace negotiations would likely succeed unless St. Petersburg was con-

[33] Roosevelt to Spring Rice, May 13, 1905, and Roosevelt to Lodge, May 15, 1905. Morison, *Roosevelt Letters*, 1178–79, 1179–82.

[34] Taft to Roosevelt, April 5, 1905, Roosevelt Papers.

[35] Roosevelt to Hay, March 30, 1905, Morison, *Roosevelt Letters*, IV, 1150–51.

[36] Takahira to Komura, March 17, 1905, Telegram Series, LXII, 3086–88.

[37] O'Laughlin to Roosevelt, April 9, 1905, Roosevelt Papers.

[38] Roosevelt to Lodge, May 15, 1905, Morison, *Roosevelt Letters*, IV, 1179–82.

[39] Prospective Articles of Peace, April 21, 1905, Collection of Cabinet Decisions. PVM9-55, pp. 1024-26.

vinced it needed peace. Russia, therefore, must make the first move for peace.

The conferences of March, 1905, were not entirely in vain. While conferring with Cassini and Takahira, Roosevelt had carried on simultaneous talks with Durand, Jusserand, and Sternberg. As a result of these discussions, the ghost of intervention was finally laid. During the winter and spring of 1905, the Kaiser had continued to bombard Roosevelt with wild reports of British and French schemes to intervene in peacemaking in order to partition China. Roosevelt had been much reassured when Spring Rice visited Washington in late January and told him that Britain was willing to follow his lead in the Far East.[40] Now, after talking with the ambassadors at Washington, Roosevelt became convinced that the Kaiser was suffering from hallucinations. His confidence in the German ruler was nearly destroyed. What remained was shattered when, at the end of March, the Kaiser made his dramatic landing at Tangier openly challenging France's ascendancy in Morocco. As the Moroccan question escalated into a major world crisis, Roosevelt hastened to assure his associates that he no longer trusted the Kaiser. On April 2 he sent a letter to Hay, who had gone to Europe in a futile effort to regain his health. "The Kaiser," he wrote, "has become a monomaniac about getting into communication with me every time he drinks three pen'orth of conspiracy against his life and power." [41] To Lodge he confided that "nothing would persuade me to follow the lead of or enter into close alliance with a man who is so jumpy." [42]

In April, while Roosevelt journeyed west to hunt bears in Colorado, French Foreign Minister Delcassé briefly took over the role of peacemaker. Until this time, Delcassé had avoided urging peace upon Russia, fearing that France would share the blame for a humiliating peace.[43] But now with the Moroccan crisis threaten-

[40] Hay diary, January 30 and February 2, 1905, Hay Papers; Stephen Lucius Gwynn, ed., *The Letters and Friendships of Sir Cecil Spring Rice*, 2 vols., Boston and New York, 1929, I, 447–450.

[41] Roosevelt to Hay, April 2, 1905, Morison, *Roosevelt Letters*, IV, 1156–58.

[42] Roosevelt to Lodge, May 15, 1905, Roosevelt Papers. See also Roosevelt to Spring Rice, May 13, 1905, Morison, *Roosevelt Letters*, IV, 1177–79, and Jusserand, *What Me Befell*, p. 267.

[43] Paléologue, *Three Critical Years*, p. 180.

ing war between Germany and France, he was anxious to free Russia from the war in the East in order to help redress the balance of power in Europe. On April 5 he made his first definite overture to the Japanese Minister, Ichiro Motono. He told Motono that he was convinced he could bring Japan and Russia together if Japan would consent to eliminate from the negotiations the questions of an indemnity and cession of territory.

Five days later, on instructions from Tokyo, Motono asked Delcassé whether he could confirm Russia's desire for peace. The Japanese government was eager to know, of course, whether Delcassé was transmitting a peace feeler from Russia or merely expressing his own views. Motono got no adequate answer. Delcassé merely replied that *he* had a firm conviction of Russia's sincere desire for peace. A few days later, after receiving instructions from Tokyo again, Motono told the French Foreign Minister that Japan could not go into a conference pledged to reserve any demands while Russia remained unpledged to accept any demands.[44]

At this point Tokyo brought Roosevelt into the matter. With Hay in Europe and Roosevelt in Colorado, Takahira sought out the Secretary of War, William Howard Taft, who had been left in Washington "to sit on the lid." Takahira gave to Taft the full story of the Delcassé-Motono talks, and Taft immediately telegraphed the information to Roosevelt. Roosevelt's return telegram made it clear that he agreed with the Japanese position completely. He said he favored direct negotiations between the belligerents which would include *all possible terms of peace.* The only thing he wished to have Japan committed to before the conference was the open door in Manchuria and the restoration of that area to China.[45] As to whether Japan should get an indemnity and cession of Sakhalin in those negotiations, Roosevelt himself remained uncommitted. In a letter to Taft sent on the same day as his telegram, he said he heartily approved of Japan's getting control over Korea,

[44] B. F. Barnes to William Loeb, Jr. (Taft to Roosevelt), telegram, April 18, 1905, Roosevelt Papers. (Printed in Tyler Dennett, *Roosevelt and the Russo-Japanese War,* New York, 1925, pp. 176–177).

[45] Roosevelt to Taft, telegram, April 20, 1905, Roosevelt Papers. (Printed in Dennett, *Roosevelt and the Russo-Japanese War,* p. 178).

possession of Port Arthur and the Port Arthur-Harbin railroad, but on the other issues he did not wish to commit himself.[46]

The Japanese government was gratified that Roosevelt agreed with its position that it should not enter negotiations with prior commitments to Russia on peace terms, and Komura hastened to give the commitment which Roosevelt sought. In a telegram on April 25 he declared that Japan adhered to the position of maintaining the open door in Manchuria and of restoring that province to China. The telegram also revealed Tokyo's desire for the opening of peace negotiations — and its perplexity about what to do when Russia would not take the first step. Komura asked Roosevelt to advise him in regard to the steps to be taken in order to pave the way for the inauguration of negotiations.[47]

When Roosevelt received this message, he was almost as confused as Tokyo. He telegraphed Taft that he was "a good deal puzzled" by the Japanese communication but that he would cut short his hunt and return to Washington. He suggested that Taft, in the meantime, confer with Takahira, and, if agreeable with Takahira, Taft should sound Cassini on peace. Taft was to tell Cassini merely that the President, on his own motion, wished to ascertain if the two combatants could come together and negotiate.[48]

Within a few days the Japanese government indicated that it did not wish to sound Russia through Cassini, whose views and temperament Komura regarded as being unfavorably disposed toward peace. Japan informed Roosevelt that it would submit another plan of procedure to him on his return to Washington. Takahira confided to Taft that he thought his government overcautious, and he revealed that he did not approve of its position in claiming an indemnity or cession of territory. He even urged that Roosevelt advise the Japanese government to relinquish these claims.[49] When Roosevelt returned to Washington, however, he refused to tender

[46] Roosevelt to Taft, April 20, 1905, Morison, *Roosevelt Letters*, IV, 1161–65.

[47] Barnes to Loeb (Taft to Roosevelt), telegram, April 25, 1905, Roosevelt Papers. (Printed in Dennett, *Roosevelt and the Russo-Japanese War*, pp. 179–180).

[48] Roosevelt to Taft, telegram, April 27, 1905, Morison, *Roosevelt Letters*, IV, 1167–68.

[49] Taft to Roosevelt, telegram, May 2, 1905, Roosevelt Papers. (Printed in Dennett, *Roosevelt and the Russo-Japanese War*, pp. 183–185).

such advice. He had already intimated to Tokyo through Takahira that a continuation of the war would likely consume any indemnity Japan could hope to get, and he did not wish to press the Japanese government further on the matter. However, he privately confided to Meyer, his new Ambassador to Russia, that if he were a Russian he would not accept Japan's terms.[50]

There is no doubt that the Japanese government had committed a grievous error in letting it become known that an indemnity and cession of territory would be demanded at the peace conference. Japan had very cautious and capable leaders during the Russo-Japanese War who made few mistakes. But they did make this one colossal blunder. Both military and civilian leaders realized that peace was needed and that these items, at best, could be classified only as terms which Japan hoped to get but which could not be insisted upon. Yet, once these demands became known, Russia was even more reluctant to make peace. Furthermore, when it later developed that these aims could not be fully achieved at the peace conference, the Japanese public would be given the erroneous impression that Japan had suffered a diplomatic defeat at the conference. It is unlikely, however, that the error could have been undone once the demands had become public knowledge in the spring of 1905. If they had been withdrawn in May, 1905, as Takahira wished, it would have been a sure sign of weakness. Japanese leaders were fully aware that in Manchuria their forces had reached the limit of their capability, and they were very fearful that Russia would sense Japan's weakness. They firmly believed — and with good reason — that any indication of weakness would be disastrous to Japan. Thus Japan's apparent intransigence in May, 1905, probably was caused more by a feeling of weakness than by intoxication over military victories.

By the time Roosevelt returned to Washington in mid-May, it was apparent that Russia had no desire for peace until the outcome of the approaching naval battle was known. Roosevelt wrote to Spring Rice on May 13: "Just at the moment Russia is riding a high horse and will not talk peace." [51] During the days that fol-

[50] Roosevelt to Meyer, May 24, 1905, Morison, *Roosevelt Letters*, IV, 1190–91.
[51] Roosevelt to Spring Rice, May 13, 1905, Morison, *Roosevelt Letters*, IV, 1178–79.

lowed he anxiously awaited news of the naval battle as the Russian Baltic Fleet approached the Japanese home islands. He thought Japan would win, but he was not without doubts. Sternberg was more confident. He wrote to Roosevelt: "The Russians are on the big horse again, but Togo is bound to knock them out of the saddle. Suppose the smashing up of the Russian battleship fleet will occur near the bases of Japan." [52]

Sternberg's prediction could hardly have been more accurate. On May 28 near the island of Tsu-shima in the Korean Strait, the Russian fleet was destroyed. All eight battleships were sunk or captured. Japan lost not a single ship. "Neither Trafalgar nor the defeat of the Spanish Armada was as complete — as overwhelming," Roosevelt wrote elatedly to Kaneko.[53] In Tokyo the happy excitement did not overshadow the need for peace. Despairing of Russia's ever making the first move for peace, Japan, now at the moment of victory, took the decisive step. On May 31 Takahira brought Roosevelt a telegram from Komura requesting that the President "directly and entirely on his own motion and initiative" invite Russia and Japan to open direct negotiations.[54]

Roosevelt immediately acted on the Japanese request. He saw Cassini and told him he wished Russia and Japan to get together to discuss peace. If Russia would agree, he would sound Japan without telling of Russia's assent, and he felt sure Japan would respond favorably to his proposal.[55] In the meantime Takahira confided to Sternberg that Roosevelt was making a move for peace. Kaiser William immediately telegraphed Roosevelt that he would "silently

[52] Sternberg to Roosevelt, April 21, 1905, Roosevelt Papers.

[53] Roosevelt to Kaneko, May 31, 1905, Morison, *Roosevelt Letters*, IV, 1198. Some of the smaller Russian ships took refuge in Manila Bay after the battle. They were promptly interned. During the voyage to the Far East, the fleet had taken on supplies and trained off Madagascar and French Indochina. While Japan bombarded Paris with protests, the French government sent instructions to colonial officials to order the fleet away. The Russian fleet ignored the orders, and France took no effective steps. The whole matter caused considerable anxiety at the Foreign Ministry in Paris. When the ships were in French waters, Delcassé would ask every morning when he arrived at the Foreign Office, "Well, have they gone yet?" Paléologue, *Three Critical Years*, p. 163.

[54] Komura to Takahira, telegram, May 31, 1905, Morison, *Roosevelt Letters*, IV, 1221–22.

[55] Roosevelt to Lodge, June 5, 1905, Morison, *Roosevelt Letters*, IV, 1202–06.

support" his efforts.[56] The next day the Kaiser confided to Ambassador Charlemagne Tower that he had urged the Tsar to accept Roosevelt as peacemaker and had told him the President was the right person to appeal to "with the hope that he may be able to bring the Japanese down to reasonable proposals." [57]

When Roosevelt learned of the Kaiser's action, he decided to send a message directly to the Tsar through Ambassador Meyer. He was not certain he could trust Cassini to relay his views faithfully; and furthermore, he wished to make it clear that he was not offering mediation but only "good offices" to arrange the conference. "I do not desire to be asked to squeeze out of Japan favorable terms to Russia," Roosevelt wrote to Lodge.[58]

The telegram to Meyer arrived in St. Petersburg on June 5, and an audience was arranged for the following afternoon. When Meyer met with the Tsar, he presented the proposal for the belligerents to meet "without intermediaries," and he then set forth at length Roosevelt's argument about the hopelessness of Russia's position in the war. After an hour's persuasion, the Tsar reluctantly assented. Meyer thereupon hastily departed before Nicholas could change his mind.[59]

Roosevelt moved rapidly to close the matter before anything could go awry. There was, of course, no need to sound Japan. So when Meyer's report arrived in Washington, Roosevelt sent identic notes to Tokyo and St. Petersburg formally proposing that they appoint delegates without intermediary "in order to see if it is not possible for these representatives of the two powers to agree to terms of peace." [60] Meanwhile, Cassini, who had been left uninformed by his government, was making a fuss. He accused Meyer of misrepresenting the Tsar's words and said that Roosevelt was

56 Sternberg to Roosevelt, June 3, 1905, Roosevelt Papers.

57 Tower to Roosevelt, telegram, June 4, 1905, Morison, *Roosevelt Letters*, IV, 1203.

58 Roosevelt to Lodge, June 5, 1905, Morison, *Roosevelt Letters*, IV, 1202–06.

59 Department of State to Meyer, telegram, June 5, 1905, and Meyer to the Secretary of State, telegram, June 7, 1905, Morison, *Roosevelt Papers*, IV, 1203–04, 1223; Meyer to Roosevelt, June 9, 1905, Howe, *Meyer*, pp. 157–162. The British Ambassador at St. Petersburg, Sir Charles Hardinge, believed that the Russian reply through Cassini to Roosevelt's first suggestion of peace negotiations would have been negative. Hardinge to Lansdowne, June 20, 1905, *British Documents*, IV, 89–90.

60 Roosevelt to Meyer, telegram, June 8, 1905, Morison, *Roosevelt Letters*, IV, 1224; Loomis to Griscom, telegram, June 8, 1905, *Foreign Relations, 1905*, p. 808.

rushing his government into negotiations too quickly.[61] In Japan there was no irritation over Roosevelt's haste. Griscom sent the President's formal proposal to the Japanese Foreign Ministry at 11:30 P.M. the evening it arrived, and at 1 A.M. he had Japan's reply giving unequivocal assent! [62]

The formal Russian reply was not received until June 12, and was something less than satisfactory when it did arrive. In the closing paragraph Lamsdorff seized upon the hazy wording that Roosevelt had used in his identic notes. The Russian note read: "With regard to the eventual meeting of Russian and Japanese plenipotentiaries, 'In order to see if it is not possible for the two powers to agree to terms of peace,' the Imperial Government has no objection in principle to this endeavor if the Japanese Government expresses the desire." [63] This wording naturally infuriated Japanese leaders. They suspected that Russia would send delegates lacking plenipotentiary powers who would merely receive the Japanese terms.[64] Roosevelt agreed that the Russian reply exhibited "a certain slyness and an endeavor to avoid anything like a definite committal." [65] Ambassador Meyer characterized it perhaps even more accurately when he noted that the response had a tone of "superior indifference." [66]

[61] Roosevelt to Lodge, June 16, 1905, Morison, Roosevelt Letters, IV, 1221–33.

[62] Griscom to Roosevelt, telegram, June 10, 1905, Morison, Roosevelt Letters, IV, 1224; Griscom to the Secretary of State, June 10, 1905, Despatches: Japan, LXXX. For some unknown reason, Roosevelt's telegram to Japan was delayed fifteen to twenty hours in transmission.

[63] Meyer to the Secretary of State, telegram, June 12, 1905, Foreign Relations, 1905, p. 811. The copy printed in Morison, Roosevelt Letters, IV, 1225, incorrectly says "expresses a like desire."

[64] Telegram received by the Japanese legation from Komura, June 14, 1905, Roosevelt Papers.

[65] Roosevelt to Lodge, June 16, 1905, Morison, Roosevelt Letters, IV, 1221–33.

[66] Meyer to Roosevelt, July 1, 1905, Howe, Meyer, pp. 173–175. The Russian attitude was also noted in a report sent to London by the British Ambassador at St. Petersburg: "Count Lamsdorff's statement to me on the 14th instant, which I hear he made to other Ambassadors on the same day, to the effect that the Emperor in accepting the proposal to enter into pourparlers with Japan had only been actuated by humanitarian principles, that Russia did not want peace unless Japan expressed a desire for it and was prepared to continue the war indefinitely, was quite in consonance with the arrogant tone in which it is customary in the press and in St. Petersburg to speak of the Japanese and which hardly corresponds with the actual achievements and relative positions of the two belligerents in the Far East." Hardinge to Lansdowne, June 20, 1905, British Documents, IV, 89–90.

Within a few days, however, Roosevelt wrung from Cassini an oral assurance that the Russian delegates would have full powers, and he urged the Japanese not to argue the matter further. Tokyo reluctantly acceded.[67] Fortunately, when the delegates were appointed, they were vested with full power to conclude peace.

Before the delegates were named in early July much jockeying for position occurred as each side sought to reassure itself that the other would appoint men of caliber equal to its own. Finally on July 2 Roosevelt was able to announce that Japan had appointed Komura and Takahira and Russia had designated N. V. Muravieff and Baron Rosen. Two weeks later Sergius Witte was appointed in place of Muravieff, the latter being reluctant to undertake the unpleasant duty of making peace with a victorious enemy. Owing to personal antipathy the Tsar had been averse to sending Witte, but both in Russia and Japan he was regarded as the best man for the task. Witte himself was not overjoyed at receiving the honor. He commented to Finance Minister V. N. Kokovtsov: "When a sewer has to be cleaned, they send Witte; but as soon as work of a cleaner and nicer kind appears, plenty of other candidates spring up." [68]

Meanwhile the site of the conference had been agreed upon. At the outset Japan had suggested Chefoo with Washington as a second choice. Russia wanted Paris but also named Washington as a second preference. Roosevelt suggested The Hague, but Tokyo stated categorically that it would not go to Europe. As soon as Roosevelt learned of this, he publicly announced Washington as the chosen site, without further consultation. Russia tried to reopen the issue, now expressing a preference for The Hague, but Roosevelt refused to reverse his action.[69] After two heated conferences between Meyer and Lamsdorff, the Foreign Minister reluctantly assented to Washington. "I am not," remarked Lamsdorff,

---

[67] Roosevelt to Griscom, telegram, June 16, 1905, Morison, *Roosevelt Letters*, IV, 1228–29; Griscom to the Secretary of State, telegram, June 18, 1905, *Foreign Relations, 1905*, pp. 811–812.

[68] Count V. N. Kokovtsov, *Out of My Past: The Memoirs of Count Kokovtsov, Russian Minister of Finance, 1904–1914, Chairman of the Council of Ministers, 1911–1914*, ed. by H. H. Fisher, trans. by L. Matveev, Stanford, 1935, pp. 52–53.

[69] Telegram received by the Japanese legation from Komura, June 14, 1905, Roosevelt Papers; Roosevelt to Meyer, telegram, June 16, 1905, Morison, *Roosevelt Letters*, IV, 1227–28.

"accustomed to be hustled so, and cannot see the need of such terrible haste!" [70]

Russian leadership was in such a state of confusion that it actually could not decide whether it wanted haste or delay. At the same time that Cassini and Lamsdorff were criticizing Roosevelt's haste, the Russian government was pressing for the early opening of the peace conference. Japanese forces had not yet occupied any Russian territory, and St. Petersburg feared an attack upon Sakhalin Island before the conference could assemble. When Tokyo suggested that the conference convene in the first ten days of August, the Tsar telegraphed Roosevelt that he agreed, but found the date "rather distant." [71] As it turned out, it was too distant to save Sakhalin. In hope of staving off the Japanese attack, Russia had Roosevelt sound Tokyo "on his own initiative" regarding an armistice, but Japan refused.[72] As Russia feared, in July Japan attacked and captured the island.

By mid-July all the official arrangements for the peace conference had been completed. By that time the nerves of the diplomats were frayed and the summer heat was bearing down upon Washington. Amid all the political disagreements, there was one practical matter upon which all could agree. Washington would be a terrible place for a peace conference in the month of August. Thus it was proposed that the site be moved to New England, the usual summer retreat of Washington's diplomatic corps. The United States had a naval base at Kittery, Maine, adjacent to Portsmouth, New Hampshire, and it was agreed that the negotiations would take place there where a cooler climate might engender calm deliberation. As the time for the conference approached, Roosevelt was not overly optimistic about success. He wrote to Griscom in late July: "Before you receive this the peace negotiations will have come to an end and I rather think they will end in failure." [73]

70 Meyer to Roosevelt, June 18, 1905, Howe, *Meyer*, pp. 167–170.

71 Secretary of State to Meyer, telegram, June 24, 1905, *Foreign Relations, 1905*, p. 813; Meyer to Roosevelt, telegram, June 26, 1905, Roosevelt Papers.

72 Meyer to the Secretary of State, telegrams, July 1 and 2, 1905, and Roosevelt to Meyer, telegram, July 11, 1905, Despatches: Russia, LXIII.

73 Roosevelt to Griscom, July 27, 1905, Roosevelt Papers. (Printed in Dennett, *Roosevelt and the Russo-Japanese War*, p. 241).

CHAPTER FIVE

The Portsmouth Peace Conference

THE key to an understanding of Roosevelt's role in peacemaking is found in his concept of *Realpolitik*. Roosevelt firmly believed that the creation of a balance of power in East Asia would be best for Russia and Japan, best for the European powers, and — most of all — best for the United States. By the middle of June, 1905, though still fundamentally pro-Japanese, the President was convinced that his diplomatic intervention to bring peace would save Russia from being driven out of the vast area east of Lake Baikal and help establish that balance of power. "I should be sorry to see Russia driven out of East Asia," he wrote to Ambassador Whitelaw Reid at London, "and driven out she surely will be if the war goes on." [1] To Lodge he confided that "while Russia's triumph would have been a blow to civilization, her destruction as an eastern Asiatic power would also in my opinion be unfortunate." "It is best," he concluded, "that she be left face to face with Japan so that each may have a moderative action on the other." [2]

While engaged in making arrangements for the peace conference in the summer of 1905, Roosevelt exerted his influence upon both Russia and Japan to put them in a frame of mind for peace. He sent a long letter to Ambassador Meyer on June 16 with instructions to show it to Lamsdorff or the Tsar. Meyer, knowing where the seat of power was located, saw that the letter got to Nicholas himself. [3] In giving his views, Roosevelt did not spare Russian sensitivities. "The Japanese," he said, "have won an overwhelming triumph." If Russia continued to fight in hope of escaping payment of an indemnity, all eastern Siberia would be lost and Russia

[1] Roosevelt to Reid, June 5, 1905, Roosevelt Papers.
[2] Roosevelt to Lodge, June 16, 1905, Morison, *Roosevelt Letters*, IV, 1221–33.
[3] Meyer to Roosevelt, July 18, 1905, Howe, *Meyer*, pp. 181–183.

would never get it back. It would be far better, he said, to make peace by paying a reasonable indemnity and surrendering Sakhalin, for Russia could never redeem herself in this war.[4] While sending such views to St. Petersburg, Roosevelt concurrently urged moderation upon Japan. He told Takahira that Japan had Port Arthur and Korea and dominance in Manchuria, and the less she asked for in addition the better it would be.[5]

At the same time that Roosevelt was urging peace upon St. Petersburg and Tokyo, he was endeavoring to get the other powers to exert pressure on the belligerents. His efforts with England greatly disappointed him. When he asked the London government to influence Japan to make the terms moderate, Lansdowne replied coolly that he did not know Japan's terms and that it would be useless for him to express an opinion on them. Roosevelt had the State Department telegraph Ambassador Reid: "President desires you to find out whether the English Government really does wish peace or not." [6] When Reid saw the Foreign Secretary again, Lansdowne insisted that nothing would be more abhorrent to Britain than a continuation of the bloodshed, but he said again that his government would not put pressure on Japan.[7]

In the subsequent weeks Roosevelt continued to send entreaties to London, using Spring Rice to transmit his views. He revealed to the British leaders that he had undertaken his peace effort at the request of Japan, and he argued that it would be better for Britain

4 Roosevelt to Meyer, June 19, 1905, Morison, *Roosevelt Letters*, IV, 1241–42.

5 Roosevelt to Lodge, June 16, 1905, Morison, *Roosevelt Letters*, IV, 1221–33. What Roosevelt meant by "dominance in Manchuria" is not clear. It was probably another instance of loose, expansive language. He may have meant that with Port Arthur and the railway in South Manchuria, Japan's influence in Manchuria was now dominant over that of Russia, it being understood that Chinese sovereignty existed in Manchuria. If he meant more than that, the Japanese did not assume so. Tokyo never lost sight of the commitment given to Roosevelt in April, 1905, that Manchuria would be restored to Chinese administration. This was to be one of Japan's cardinal peace terms at Portsmouth.

6 Telegram from the Marquis of Lansdowne, June 3, 1905, and Loomis to Reid, telegram, June 15, 1905, Roosevelt Papers.

7 Reid to the Secretary of State, telegram, June 16, 1905, and Reid to Roosevelt, June 17, 1905, Roosevelt Papers. King Edward suggested to Reid that Japan might capture Vladivostok and return it to Russia as a magnanimous gesture. Roosevelt thought that any such waste of blood and treasure would be conduct warranting a *commission de lunatico*. Memorandum by Reid, June 22, 1905, and Reid to Roosevelt, June 23, 1905, Roosevelt Papers; Roosevelt to Reid, July 7, 1905, Morison, *Roosevelt Letters*, IV, 1265.

if peace came now and left Russia face to face with Japan in East Asia.[8] Despite these pleas, London continued to hold aloof from the peace endeavor. In early August, however, Ambassador Durand came to see Roosevelt at Oyster Bay and showed him draft copies of the Anglo-Japanese Alliance which was in the process of being renewed.[9] At this time Roosevelt did not discern the importance of this development, but later he would come to realize that by renewing the alliance, Britain made a major contribution toward the success of the Portsmouth Peace Conference.

From Berlin, Roosevelt received full cooperation. In early June the Kaiser had urged the Tsar to accept Roosevelt's proposal for a conference, and in the succeeding weeks he continued to urge peace upon St. Petersburg. Roosevelt appreciated very much the Kaiser's efforts, though he confessed his bafflement concerning the Kaiser's motives. "There is one thing I am a little puzzled at," he wrote to Spring Rice, "and that is why excepting on distinterested grounds the German Emperor should want Russia and Japan to make peace; he has done all he could to bring it about." Roosevelt was on the right track, however, when he added that perhaps the German ruler feared a continuation of the war might bring the break up of Russia.[10] The Kaiser had told Ambassador Tower some weeks before that if the war continued, he feared for the life of the Tsar, and with an infant heir to the throne a situation would be created which would be dangerous to Russia and to the rest of the world.[11]

While appreciating the Kaiser's efforts for peace, Roosevelt nevertheless felt somewhat harassed by his continued accusations against the other European powers and by his repeated insistence that Roosevelt exact favorable terms from Japan. Delcassé, having resigned during the Moroccan crisis, could no longer be the object

8 Roosevelt to Spring Rice, June 16 and July 24, 1905, Morison, *Roosevelt Letters*, IV, 1233–34, 1283–87; Spring Rice to the American Secretary of State, July 10, 1905, Spring Rice to Lansdowne, August 6, 1905, Spring Rice to Mrs. Roosevelt, August 10, 1905, Gwynn, *Letters and Friendships of Sir Cecil Spring Rice*, I, 474–485; Lansdowne to Spring Rice, August 7, 1905, Roosevelt Papers.

9 Roosevelt to Reid, August 3, 1905, Morison, *Roosevelt Letters*, IV, 1298.

10 Roosevelt to Spring Rice, July 24, 1905, Morison, *Roosevelt Letters*, IV, 1283–87.

11 Tower to Roosevelt, June 9, 1905, Roosevelt Papers (Printed in Dennett, *Roosevelt and the Russo-Japanese War*, pp. 218–219).

of the Kaiser's suspicions. Now Britain was cast in the role of villain. In mid-July, Tower relayed to Roosevelt the Kaiser's charges that Britain hoped the peace negotiations would fail because it hoped to settle the war by Anglo-French diplomatic intervention. This, said the Kaiser, was a revival of "Delcassé's plan of indemnifying Belligerent and Mediator at the expense of China." Roosevelt placed no credence in the accusation, but to quiet the volatile Kaiser he sent assurance that he would "absolutely refuse to submit to such action by any of the Powers." [12]

The day after Roosevelt sent this message, the German ruler dispatched a telegram to him from Björkö, where he was meeting with the Tsar. The Tsar hoped, said the Kaiser, that the President's "powerful personality and genial statesmanship" would lower the exorbitant Japanese demands to a sensible level.[13] By this time the Kaiser had such confidence in Roosevelt that he even considered telling him of the secret treaty of alliance he had just signed with the Tsar. It took the combined opposition of Bülow and Baron Friedrich von Holstein to restrain the German ruler from confiding in "his friend" Roosevelt.[14] As it turned out, it did not matter. The alliance project again proved abortive, and the episode had no discernible effect upon peace negotiations.

Throughout July and early August as the time for the peace conference approached, Roosevelt continued to occupy the central position in the peacemaking project. During this time Elihu Root became Secretary of State, following the death of John Hay, but this brought no change in Roosevelt's activities. The President had all matters relating to the peace conference in his hands, and, as Root later stated, "He kept them in his hands." [15] At Oyster Bay,

12 Tower to Roosevelt, July 13, 1905, Roosevelt Papers. (Printed in Dennett, *Roosevelt and the Russo-Japanese War*, pp. 233–235). Roosevelt to Tower, July 27, 1905, Morison, *Roosevelt Letters*, IV, 1288. The Kaiser's support did not significantly restore Roosevelt's confidence in the German ruler. In the summer of 1905 he told Ambassador Durand that a year ago he thought the Kaiser was nothing more than "inconvenient" in his ways but now he thought he was "really dangerous." Sir Percy M. Sykes, *The Right Honourable Sir Mortimer Durand, K.C., G.C.M.G., K.C.S.I., K.C.I.E., A Biography*, London, 1926, p. 287.

13 Mühlberg to Bussche, telegram, July 28, 1905, *Die Grosse Politik*, XIX, pt. 2, p. 614.

14 Bülow to the Foreign Minister, telegrams (nos. 24 and 25), July 26, 1905, and Holstein to Bülow, July 26, 1905, *Die Grosse Politik*, XIX, pt. 2, pp. 466–470.

15 Philip C. Jessup, *Elihu Root*, 2 vols., New York, 1938, II, 4.

where Roosevelt was spending the summer, he entertained the Russian and Japanese delegations as each arrived. Then on August 5 he brought the two delegations together at a festive ceremony on board the yacht *Mayflower*. Thereupon the envoys journeyed to Portsmouth, where the first meeting would take place on August 9. Roosevelt remained at Oyster Bay, keeping in touch with the proceedings through the Third Assistant Secretary of State, Herbert Peirce, who was the official host at Portsmouth. He also maintained contact with the Japanese through Baron Kaneko, who was in New York City. He had no comparable liaison with the Russian delegation, though John Callan O'Laughlin, who was acquainted with the Russians, sent daily letters and many telegrams to Oyster Bay.

Komura and Witte brought to the peace conference instructions that did not necessarily conflict. The Japanese instructions designated only three conditions that were absolutely imperative: (1) a free hand in Korea, (2) withdrawal of the Russian army from Manchuria, and (3) transference to Japan of the Liaotung leasehold and the railway line running from Harbin to Port Arthur at the southern tip of the leasehold. Komura was told to work for some additional concessions, but they were not considered absolutely necessary. These were: (1) surrender of Russian warships interned in neutral ports, (2) fishing rights along the coast of the Maritime Province, (3) cession of Sakhalin, and (4) payment of an indemnity. Two other items were added to the Japanese conditions merely for bargaining purposes: (1) restriction of the size of the Russian navy in the Far East, and (2) demilitarization of Vladivostok.[16] Witte's instructions would allow him to concede all three of Japan's imperative demands. But trouble would come when the bargaining centered on the items in the next category, for Witte had categorical instructions to cede no land and to pay no money.[17]

The first session of the conference was held on August 9 as scheduled, and within a week agreement had been reached on many of the terms. Russia recognized Japan's paramount political, military,

[16] These instructions had been drafted by the cabinet June 30, approved by the Genro and cabinet July 4, and sanctioned by the Emperor July 5. Collection of Cabinet Decisions, PVM 9-55, pp. 1029–33.

[17] Sergius Witte, *The Memoirs of Count Witte*, trans. and ed. by Abraham Yarmolinsky, New York, 1921, p. 135; Baron Rosen, *Forty Years of Diplomacy*, 2 vols., New York, 1922, I, 263; White, *Diplomacy of the Russo-Japanese War*, pp. 250–254.

and economic interests in Korea. Both Russia and Japan agreed to evacuate Manchuria and restore that area to China's administration. At Japan's insistence, Russia declared that it had no concessions in Manchuria in impairment of Chinese sovereignty or inconsistent with the principle of equal opportunity. Russia agreed to transfer to Japan the Liaotung leasehold, which included the naval base at Port Arthur. Russia was to retain the railway stretching across north Manchuria to Vladivostok (the Chinese Eastern Railway), but most of the branch line running from Harbin to Port Arthur was to go to Japan. Komura sought to get all of this branch line, but at Witte's insistence he agreed that Russia would retain the small section between Changchun and Harbin which was still in the possession of Russian troops. Russia also agreed to arrange fishing rights in a subsequent treaty with Japan. Komura had decided not to present the demand for the demilitarization of Vladivostok, so by August 18 only four Japanese demands remained unfulfilled: (1) surrender of interned Russian ships, (2) limitation of the Russian navy in the Far East, (3) cession of Sakhalin, and (4) payment of an indemnity. But by that date the negotiations appeared hopelessly deadlocked over the questions of the indemnity and the cession of Sakhalin.

At this juncture Roosevelt decided to intervene in the negotiations — in a private and unofficial capacity, as he characterized it. On Friday, August 18, he conferred with Kaneko at Oyster Bay. They worked out a compromise proposal wherein Japan would relinquish her demands concerning limitation of the Russian navy in the Far East and the surrender of interned ships, Russia would cede Sakhalin to Japan, and the amount of indemnity to be paid would be submitted to arbitration which would not be binding. It was Roosevelt's thought that the arbitration would take a considerable period of time, at the end of which Japan would decide not to continue the war for money alone. That evening Roosevelt telegraphed Witte, asking him to send Baron Rosen to see him, and the next day he presented the scheme to the Russian emissary.[18]

18 Korostovetz, *Pre-War Diplomacy*, pp. 89–92; Rosen, *Forty Years of Diplomacy*, I, 269–270. Dennett asserts incorrectly that at this interview Roosevelt proposed the division of Sakhalin. He is confusing Roosevelt's initial proposal made to Rosen with

Roosevelt's first intervention proved abortive. The distance between Portsmouth and Oyster Bay and the imperfect liaison through Kaneko greatly handicapped his efforts. He soon learned that on the same day he conferred with Kaneko (Friday, August 18), Komura and Witte were together working out a compromise plan which differed from the Roosevelt-Kaneko plan. In the formal session on that day, Komura said Japan would yield on the demand for the interned ships and the limitation of Russian naval power in the Far East if Russia would give way on Sakhalin and the indemnity. Witte thereupon proposed private consultation between himself and Komura to explore further the possibilities of compromise. In that talk Witte proposed the division of Sakhalin with the southern part going to Japan. Komura then suggested a way to break the impasse over the indemnity. Japan would relinquish the demand for war costs if Russia would pay a considerable amount for the return of northern Sakhalin, which was then in Japan's possession. Komura stated the sum of twelve hundred million yen (six hundred million dollars) as the minimum Japan would accept.[19] Witte immediately telegraphed this plan to St. Petersburg, thus before the Roosevelt-Rosen meeting took place, and in the Russian capital, consideration of the Witte-Komura plan overshadowed Roosevelt's proposal.

The initial reaction to the Witte-Komura compromise proposal in St. Petersburg held forth little promise that it would be accepted. Lamsdorff telegraphed Witte the Tsar's judgment that the proposal did not alter his basic view: not an inch of land and not a ruble in repayment of expenses. Lamsdorff indicated, however, that the proposal would be submitted to the Ministers of War, Navy, and Finance, before a final decision was reached.[20] While

the Witte-Komura plan and with the later proposal that Roosevelt made to the Tsar in a message of August 21. Dennett, *Roosevelt and the Russo-Japanese War*, p. 252.

[19] Gaimusho, *Komura Gaikoshi*, 2 vols., Tokyo, 1953, II, 87–90. Witte told St. Petersburg that this compromise plan was proposed by Komura. Kaneko told Roosevelt it was proposed by Witte. The Japanese records make it clear that it was authored jointly by Witte and Komura. In his memoirs Baron Rosen indicates that both he and Witte were willing to give way regarding cession of Sakhalin and that Witte was even inclined to agree to payment of money. Rosen, *Forty Years of Diplomacy*, I, 263.

[20] Lamsdorff to Witte, telegram no. 132, August 7/20, 1905, Ministerstvo inostrannykh del, *Sbornik diplomaticheskikh dokumentov, Kasaiushchikhsia peregovorov*

this was being done, Witte telegraphed Roosevelt's proposal which had been given through Baron Rosen. Since this was less favorable to Russia than the Witte-Komura plan, it received scant consideration. The Tsar noted on Witte's telegram: "Anyway this measure will not lead to anything. The Japanese desperately need money and we will not give it to them, and on this we will never come to an agreement." [21]

Tokyo immediately telegraphed assent to the Witte-Komura proposal and even gave Komura discretion to adjust the amount of compensation for the return of northern Sakhalin.[22] St. Petersburg, however, rejected the plan. Lamsdorff informed Witte on August 21 that the proposal was unanimously considered unacceptable. He went on to say ominously that final instructions for ending the conference would be sent after his audience with the Tsar the following day.[23]

When Roosevelt learned of the Witte-Komura compromise plan — but before he knew of its rejection in St. Petersburg — he decided to inject himself into the negotiations in even more dramatic fashion. On Monday, August 21, he telegraphed a long personal message to Tsar Nicholas which Ambassador Meyer was to deliver directly to His Majesty. He told the Tsar that to his "surprise and pleasure" he found that Japan was willing to relinquish northern Sakhalin, "Russia of course in such case to pay a substantial sum for this surrender of territory." Such a peace, said Roosevelt, would be just and honorable. Then Roosevelt added a new variation to the Witte-Komura plan. He proposed that in the peace treaty Russia merely give agreement "in principle" to payment of this compensation and that the amount be left to later negotia-

---

mezhdu. Rossiei i Iaponiei o zakliuchenii mirnogo dogovora, 24 maia — 3 oktiabria, 1905, St. Petersburg, 1906, p. 144.

21 Witte to Lamsdorff, telegram no. 142, August 7/20, 1905, *Sbornik diplomaticheskikh dokumentov*, pp. 162–163. (Translated in Korostovetz, *Pre-War Diplomacy*, pp. 91–92). Rosen later sent Roosevelt a letter rejecting his proposal. Rosen to Roosevelt, August 23, 1905, Roosevelt Papers. By that time, however, the plan was outdated.

22 *Komura Gaikoshi*, II, 90.

23 Lamsdorff to Witte, telegram no. 144 bis., August 8/21, 1905, *Sbornik diplomaticheskikh dokumentov*, p. 164. Ironically, the navy minister, who now had no navy, was the strongest advocate of continuing the war. The views of the ministers are given in the above cited collection of documents, pp. 149–161.

tions.[24] Roosevelt went on to state that though it was to Japan's advantage to conclude peace, it was "infinitely more to the advantage of Russia." If the war went on, he warned, Russia would be shorn of the east Siberian provinces which she had held for centuries.[25] On the same day this message was sent to St. Petersburg, Roosevelt forwarded copies of it to Sternberg and Jusserand, urging their governments to support his plea. A copy was also sent to Witte at Portsmouth.[26]

When Roosevelt's message arrived in the Russian capital, the Tsar was away on maneuvers, and Meyer was not able to secure an audience until the afternoon of August 23. In the meantime the Tsar received a copy of Roosevelt's proposal through Witte.[27] Witte's telegram giving Roosevelt's message crossed with several telegrams from St. Petersburg instructing Witte to break up the peace conference.[28] Roosevelt's intervention thus came just in time to save the peace conference. Witte telegraphed Lamsdorff that he was not obeying his instructions to end the negotiations because the President's message required a personal answer from the Tsar.

24 Whether Komura approved of this variation is doubtful. Kaneko approved of the telegram before it was sent, but later developments strongly indicate that it did not have Komura's approval.

25 Roosevelt to Tsar Nicholas, telegram, August 21, 1905, Morison, *Roosevelt Letters*, IV, 1306–07.

26 Roosevelt to Sternberg, telegram, August 21, 1905, and Roosevelt to Jusserand, August 21, 1905, Morison, *Roosevelt Letters*, IV, 1306–07, 1307–08. While Germany gave vigorous support, France's attitude was lukewarm. Premier Maurice Rouvier contemplated giving full backing to Roosevelt's proposal but when reminded that Delcassé had consistently refrained from urging peace upon St. Petersburg, he decided to do nothing. Paléologue, *Three Critical Years*, pp. 277–278. French Ambassador Maurice Bompard did nevertheless offer France's assistance to effect the compromise or to find some other way out. This was apparently done on the suggestion of his friend Jusserand, who was then on vacation in Paris. Lamsdorff to Witte, telegram no. 166, August 12/25, 1905, *Sbornik diplomaticheskikh dokumentov*, pp. 182–183.

27 Witte to Lamsdorff, telegram no. 145, August 9/22, 1905, *Sbornik diplomaticheskikh dokumentov*, pp. 164–166. Meyer, not knowing that a copy had been sent to Witte, thought the Russians secured a copy by decoding his telegraphic instructions. The Russians did have the American diplomatic code, but whether it was used in this case is doubtful. Meyer also believed, probably correctly, that the message was held up in transmission by the Russians, so he would not get it in time to present it that afternoon (August 22) when he would have occasion to see the Tsar at the maneuvers. The Russians, he suspected, wanted time to consider the matter before Meyer confronted the Tsar. Meyer to Roosevelt, August 25, 1905, Howe, *Meyer*, pp. 197–202.

28 Lamsdorff to Witte, telegrams nos. 147, 148, 149, 150, August 9/22, 1905, *Sbornik diplomaticheskikh dokumentov*, pp. 167–170.

To break off the talks before that, he warned Lamsdorff, would drive the President to the side of Japan.[29]

In St. Petersburg, Japan's demand for twelve hundred million yen (six hundred million dollars) for the return of northern Sakhalin was viewed as a poorly disguised indemnity.[30] Roosevelt was inclined to agree. While Meyer was awaiting his audience with the Tsar, Roosevelt sent a strongly worded letter to Kaneko objecting to the size of the amount sought. "I do not think," he wrote, "that anything like the amount advanced by Japan as what she wants — that is, six hundred millions — should be asked or could possibly be obtained." If Japan continued the war for a money indemnity, he warned, there would be a considerable shifting of public opinion against her. The next day he sent another message arguing against an indemnity. In a sentence that revealed an unfortunate lapse of regard for China's sovereignty in Manchuria, he said: "It is Japan's interest now to close the war. She has won the control of Korea and Manchuria; she has doubled her own fleet in destroying that of Russia; she has Port Arthur, Dalny, the Manchurian railroad, she has Sakhalin." [31] In hope of securing British support for this position — a futile hope, it turned out — Roosevelt dispatched a letter to Ambassador Durand stating his judgment that "every true friend of Japan should tell it as I have already told it, that the opinion of the civilized world will not support it in continuing the war merely for the purpose of extorting money from Russia." [32]

The day Meyer was to meet with the Tsar (August 23), the telegrams being sent to Witte offered small promise that Meyer's audience would be successful. Lamsdorff told Witte that the Japanese

[29] Witte to Lamsdorff, telegram no. 152, August 9/22, 1905, *Sbornik diplomaticheskikh dokumentov*, pp. 170–171. Witte sent a letter to Roosevelt rejecting his proposal, but since the message was directed to the Tsar, Witte realized the final answer must come from St. Petersburg. Roosevelt sent a rejoinder to Witte arguing his case again. Roosevelt to Witte, August 23, 1905, Morison, *Roosevelt Letters*, IV, 1311–12.

[30] Dennett states incorrectly that Japan was demanding seven billion dollars. Dennett, *Roosevelt and the Russo-Japanese War*, p. 255.

[31] Roosevelt to Kaneko, August 22 and 23, 1905, Morison, *Roosevelt Letters*, IV, 1308–10, 1312–13.

[32] Roosevelt to Durand, August 23, 1905, Morison, *Roosevelt Letters*, IV, 1310–11. Lansdowne noted on Durand's telegram to London: "This is a suggestion that we should press the Japanese to make further concessions. Were we to do so our advice would not be taken and would be resented." *British Documents*, IV, 105.

proposal was regarded by Tsar Nicholas as payment of military costs only under a different form. The conditions were completely unacceptable, the Tsar had told him.[33] There is no doubt that the Tsar was not bluffing. In answer to an appeal from Kaiser William, he said that nothing would induce him to cede an inch of territory or pay one ruble of war indemnity.[34]

Meyer was received by Tsar Nicholas at Peterhof at 4 P.M. on August 23. At the outset Nicholas told Meyer that he would not pay any war indemnity whatever. Furthermore, he would not pay a substantial sum for the return of northern Sakhalin, for it would be interpreted as a war indemnity. For two hours Meyer urged Roosevelt's proposal, but he could not budge the Russian ruler on the money issue. He did, however, get the Tsar to agree to cede the southern half of Sakhalin, which Meyer insisted was not really Russian territory since Japan had held it until 1875.[35] This was a significant concession. Though Witte had talked of giving up southern Sakhalin and had urged the cession in telegrams to Lamsdorff, this was the first time the Tsar assented. Having gotten this concession, Meyer pressed further on the matter of paying for the return of northern Sakhalin. When Meyer insisted that the Japanese should at least be paid the real value of the area, the Tsar replied, "But how can that be ascertained?" This was the closest Nicholas came to any concession on the money issue.[36]

33 Lamsdorff to Witte, telegram no. 155, August 10/23, 1905, *Sbornik diplomaticheskikh dokumentov*, pp. 172–173.

34 Tsar Nicholas to Kaiser William, telegram, August 23, 1905, *Die Grosse Politik*, XIX, pt. 2, pp. 430–431. Finance Minister Kokovtsov telegraphed Witte: "The mood of the Tsar is very stubborn.'" Kokovtsov to Witte, August 8/21, 1905, "Portsmouth Correspondence of S. Y. Witte and Others," in Union of Soviet Socialist Republics, Tsentral'nvi Arkhiv, *Krasnyi Arkhiv*, 73 vols., Moscow, 1922–41, VI, 37–38. This collection of documents is from Kokovtsov's papers. Little information is given in this collection that is not recounted more fully in the *Sbornik diplomaticheskikh dokumentov*. For an account of Witte's role in the peace conference which uses these Kokovtsov papers as the principal documentary source see: Robert K. Godwin, "Russia and the Portsmouth Peace Conference," *American Slavic and East European Review*, IX (1950), 279–291.

35 In 1875 Japan had relinquished claim to southern Sakhalin in return for Russia's recognition of her claim to the Kurile Islands.

36 Meyer to Roosevelt, telegrams, August 23 and 24, 1905, Morison, *Roosevelt Letters*, V, 5–6; Meyer to Roosevelt, August 25, 1905, Howe, *Meyer*, pp. 197–202; Meyer diary, August 23, 1905, George von Lengerke Meyer Papers, Library of Congress, Washington, D. C. There is no evidence to support Dennett's statement that the Tsar

When Roosevelt received Meyer's telegraphic report, he correctly discerned that Meyer had not emphasized that under his plan the amount Russia was to pay for the return of northern Sakhalin was to be left to future negotiations. He therefore sent another message telling Meyer to make it clear that all he wanted was Russia's acceptance "in principle" of the payment for northern Sakhalin. The Portsmouth treaty could be signed now and the sum to be paid would be relegated to later negotiations. He also explained that he was not sure the Japanese would accept his plan but that he would try his best to get their approval.[37]

Meanwhile at Portsmouth the negotiations had been recessed while the delegates awaited instructions and the outcome of Roosevelt's efforts. No session was held between Friday, August 18, and Wednesday, August 23. On the twenty-third a futile session took place in which the Witte-Komura compromise plan of August 18 was reviewed. Since the Russian government had rejected the plan and the Japanese government had approved it, Komura now formally presented it as a Japanese proposal. Its features were the same as previously discussed: Japan would get southern Sakhalin and return northern Sakhalin, receiving compensation in the amount of twelve hundred million yen. The demands for the interned ships and the limitation of Russian naval power in the Far East were to be dropped. Komura did not propose, however, Roosevelt's scheme for leaving the amount of compensation to future negotiations. Witte ventured no formal reply to what was now the Komura compromise plan, but it was evident that his instructions precluded him from accepting it. Witte did make a tentative counter suggestion. He asked Komura how Japan would look upon the combination of Russia giving up *all* Sakhalin and Japan withdrawing the demand for reimbursement. Komura rejected this suggestion outright. If Witte was attempting to put Japan into the position of continuing the war for money alone, his stratagem was successful. He was nevertheless engaging in risky diplomacy, for at

agreed to pay a "substantial sum." Dennett, *Roosevelt and the Russo-Japanese War*, pp. 255–256.
[37] Roosevelt to Meyer, telegram, August 23, 1905, Morison, *Roosevelt Letters*, V, 6.

turned gray by dealing with the Russian and Japanese peace negotiators," Roosevelt confided to his son Kermit. "The Japanese
ask too much but the Russians are ten times worse. . . ." [44] With
all signs pointing to the imminent collapse of the conference,
Roosevelt decided to send a second appeal to Tsar Nicholas. In a
long telegram to St. Petersburg on August 25, he repeated his plan
for leaving to future negotiations the amount to be paid for the
return of northern Sakhalin, and he warned Russia again that if
the war continued eastern Siberia would be lost.[45]

On Saturday, August 26, Roosevelt received replies to his appeal
to Tokyo (through Baron Kaneko) and to his first appeal to St.
Petersburg. Japan thanked the President for his advice and agreed
to make still further concessions as to the amount of compensation.[46] The Russian reply was less satisfactory. Russia would cede
southern Sakhalin, as the Tsar had told Meyer on August 23, but
no other concession would be made.[47] Several days were to pass
before Roosevelt received a reply to his second appeal, but in St.
Petersburg the decision to reject it had already been reached. When
Lamsdorff presented it to the Tsar on August 26, Nicholas noted
simply: "I remain with my views." [48]

On the same day Roosevelt received the replies from Tokyo and
St. Petersburg (Saturday, August 26), the delegates at the peace
conference held the long-postponed session. Witte still presented
no formal reply to the Japanese compromise proposal, but he
said orally that it was rejected. Russia would cede southern Sakhalin but would pay no money for the return of northern Sakhalin.
He frankly told Komura and Takahira that no result could come
from prolonging the conference. In Russia the military leaders
wished to continue the war, he said, and he and the Foreign Office
could not prevail over their influence. He admitted that the Japanese delegates had put in much effort for peace, and he expressed
the hope that they could separate without ill feelings on either side.

[44] Roosevelt to Kermit, August 25, 1905, Morison, *Roosevelt Letters*, IV, 1316–17.
[45] Roosevelt to Meyer, telegram, August 25, 1905, Morison, *Roosevelt Letters*, IV,
1314–15.
[46] Kaneko to Roosevelt, August 26, 1905, Roosevelt Papers.
[47] Meyer to Roosevelt, telegram, August 26, 1905, Morison, *Roosevelt Letters*, V, 8.
[48] Lamsdorff to the Tsar, August 13/26, 1905, *Sbornik diplomaticheskikh documentov*, p. 187.

Komura said he understood Witte's position, and he made no attempt to argue the issues further. Had Komura known of his government's message to Roosevelt, which had been transmitted through Kaneko, he might have lowered the amount of compensation Japan was requesting, but he had not yet received a copy of that communication. He, like Witte, was ready to give up. He requested, however, that one more meeting be held in order that he might receive a formal Russian reply to the Japanese compromise proposal. It was agreed that the final session would be held on Monday.[49] That evening Komura telegraphed Tokyo his belief that to make further concessions would effect the honor of Japan and that the meeting on Monday would be the last.[50]

On Sunday Kaneko informed Roosevelt that Komura thought the last hope for peace was gone.[51] On the same day, the President received Russia's rejection of his second appeal to the Tsar.[52] Roosevelt was now ready to admit defeat. He sent word to Kaneko that it would be useless to add another word to what he had said to the Tsar.[53] Later that evening, however, Melville Stone of the Associated Press came to see Roosevelt, and at his suggestion the President decided to make one last attempt to save the conference. Stone had conferred with Kaneko, and he brought to Oyster Bay a new scheme. The amount of compensation Russia was to pay for the return of northern Sakhalin would be referred to a mixed commission, and the award would be binding on both sides. Instead of sending this proposal directly to St. Petersburg, Stone suggested that Kaiser William be asked to present it to Tsar Nicholas. That evening the plan was telegraphed to Berlin, but the project went no further. The next day Takahira told one of Stone's correspondents at Portsmouth that Kaneko had no authority to commit Japan to the plan. Upon learning this, Roosevelt had the German embassy telegraph Berlin and withdraw the message.[54]

49 Witte to Lamsdorff, telegram no. 177, August 13/26, 1905, Sbornik diplomaticheskikh documentov, p. 191; Komura Gaikoshi, II, 104–105; Korostovetz, Pre-War Diplomacy, p. 100.
50 Komura Gaikoshi, II, 105.
51 Kaneko to Roosevelt, August 27, 1905, Roosevelt Papers.
52 Meyer to Roosevelt, telegram, August 27, 1905, Morison, Roosevelt Letters, V, 8.
53 Memorandum of telephone message given to Kaneko's private secretary, August 27, 1905, Roosevelt Papers.
54 Roosevelt to the Kaiser, telegram, August 27, 1905, Morison, Roosevelt Letters,

By this time Komura had abandoned all hope of success, and he was firm in his belief that Japan should not yield to the Russians. On Sunday evening (August 27) he sent a long telegram to Tokyo again recommending that no further concession be made.[55] This message, however, crossed a telegram from Tokyo instructing Komura to secure a twenty-four hour postponement of the final meeting which was scheduled for the next day.[56] When Komura sent Takahira to ask Witte for the postponement, the forebodings of doom for the peace conference were confirmed. Witte said that he had no objection to delaying the session until Tuesday but that his instructions were final. If Japan presented any new proposal that did not meet Russia's announced position, he would reject it outright without even referring it to St. Petersburg.[57] When Komura learned of Witte's statement, he dispatched another long telegram to Tokyo urging that his government stand firm. He believed that Russia would not capitulate on either the indemnity or Sakhalin Island. It would be better to continue the war, he counseled, rather than give in to the Russians on both issues.[58] Though Roosevelt had no knowledge of Komura's telegrams, he probably would have sympathized with his views. He wrote to James Stillman at this time that the Russians had taken "an impossible position." [59]

In his conference with Takahira, Witte had not underestimated the Tsar's intentions. The Russian ruler had every intention of

IV, 1317; Roosevelt to Chargé d'Affaires Hilmar Bussche, August 28, 1905, Morison, *Roosevelt Letters*, IV, 1323; Bussche to Roosevelt, August 28, 1905, Roosevelt Papers; Melville E. Stone, *Fifty Years A Journalist*, New York, 1922, pp. 286–291. Roosevelt sent a sharp letter to Komura asking whether Kaneko was empowered to represent his views. Komura replied denying that Takahira had made a statement "containing the slightest suggestion that Baron Kaneko was not fully authorized to see you on my behalf." Roosevelt to Komura, August 28, 1905, Morison, *Roosevelt Letters*, IV, 1319–21; Komura to Roosevelt, August 29, 1905, Roosevelt Papers. It is likely, however, that Takahira did make the statement attributed to him. It is known that he did not like Kaneko's interference in the negotiations. Furthermore, it is very doubtful that Komura and Takahira approved of the mixed commission scheme. Komura sent word to Roosevelt through Kaneko on August 28 that he did not want Roosevelt to proceed with the matter. Kaneko to Roosevelt, August 28, 1905, Roosevelt Papers.

55 Komura to Katsura, telegram, August 27, 1905, *Komura Gaikoshi*, II, 107–108.

56 Katsura to Komura, telegram, August 27, 1905, *Komura Gaikoshi*, II, 106.

57 Witte to Lamsdorff, telegram no. 178, August 14/27, 1905, *Sbornik diplomaticheskikh dokumentov*, pp. 191–192. (Translation given in Witte, *Memoirs*, p. 158). See also Kaneko to Roosevelt, August 28, 1905, Roosevelt Papers.

58 Komura to Katsura, telegram, August 27, 1905, *Komura Gaikoshi*, II, 108–109.

59 Roosevelt to Stillman, August 28, 1905, Roosevelt Papers.

continuing the war. By Monday he did not even wish peace on the terms he had offered in his conference with Meyer four days before. On Monday, August 28, he had Lamsdorff order Witte to break off the conference no matter what Japan proposed. "Send Witte my order to end discussion tomorrow in any case," he told Lamsdorff; "I prefer to continue the war than to await gracious concessions on the part of Japan." [60]

Witte was not, however, to be handled so cavalierly. The next day (Tuesday, August 29) before the final session of the conference convened, Witte telegraphed Lamsdorff that he was not going to follow the Tsar's order. He used diplomatic and patriotic language to express his resolve, but his meaning was clear. If Japan accepted Russia's previous offer of southern Sakhalin with the retrocession of northern Sakhalin without payment, he was going to make peace. If he did otherwise, he said, Russia would be accepting in the eyes of the whole world the guilt for continuing the war.[61]

In Tokyo meanwhile the Katsura cabinet was engaged in long and painful deliberation. On the evening of August 27 the cabinet and Genro met at Ito's home until 1:30 A.M. considering Komura's recommendation that no further concessions be made to Russia. During the discussion, the Japanese leaders were under the mistaken impression that peace could be secured only if the demand for compensation were withdrawn and Japan returned *all* of Sakhalin to Russia. Roosevelt had been so intent on obtaining Russia's assent to the total compromise plan that he had neglected to inform the Japanese that he had the Tsar's commitment to cede southern Sakhalin.[62] He regarded the Japanese claim for the island so strong that it doubtless never entered his mind that Japan

60 Lamsdorff to Witte, telegram no. 180, August 15/28, 1905, *Sbornik diplomaticheskikh dokumentov*, p. 193. (Translation given in Witte, *Memoirs*, p. 178.)

61 Witte to Lamsdorff, telegram no. 182, August 16/29, 1905, *Sbornik diplomaticheskikh dokumentov*, pp. 193–194.

62 Roosevelt may have told Kaneko of the Tsar's concession when Kaneko saw him at Oyster Bay on August 25, but if he did, Kaneko did not note it in his diary. Kaneko diary, August 25, 1905, Documents Relating to the Dispatch of Barons Suematsu and Kaneko to Europe and the United States . . ., MT5.2.18.33, reel 804, pp. 554–556. Roosevelt's inclination to overlook the importance of this concession is evident in a letter he sent to Komura on August 28. He sent Komura copies of his messages to the Tsar and then stated: "The Czar has answered each by declining my suggestion, and asserting that he would neither cede any territory nor pay any indemnity under no matter what form." Roosevelt to Komura, August 28, 1905, Morison, *Roosevelt Letters*, IV, 1319–21.

might consider giving back the entire island to Russia. Komura had further confused the matter. Witte had definitely offered southern Sakhalin to Japan in the session of August 26, but the next day Komura was unsure whether Witte was still offering half of the island. In his telegrams to Tokyo, therefore, he said peace could be had only if Japan waived the money claim and returned Sakhalin.

On the morning of August 28 the cabinet and Genro met again, and that afternoon they met with high military and naval officials before the Emperor. It was unanimously agreed that Japan must make peace, even if it required the withdrawal of the money claim and the restoration of all Sakhalin to Russia. A telegram was immediately sent to Komura containing detailed instructions in accordance with this decision. He was first to withdraw the demand for reimbursement but to insist upon the cession of the entire island of Sakhalin to Japan. If Russia refused this proposal, he was secretly to ask Roosevelt to request Japan to withdraw the demand for land. If by any chance the President refused, Komura himself was to withdraw the demand.[63]

Komura was dejected, but was resigned to carrying out his unpleasant instructions. Before the final session on the morning of August 29, however, he received a rush telegram from Tokyo. Prime Minister Katsura had just learned through the British Ambassador, Sir Claude MacDonald, that the Tsar had agreed to the cession of southern Sakhalin in his conference with Meyer on August 23.[64] Komura was therefore instructed to hold out for the cession of the southern part of the island.[65]

Fortunately, Witte was in no mood to argue over southern Sakhalin. When the delegates met in the dramatic and crucial session of August 29, Witte formally rejected Japan's compromise proposal of August 23, but he offered to cede southern Sakhalin if Ja-

63 Katsura to Komura, telegram, August 28, 1905, Komura Gaikoshi, II, 125–126.

64 MacDonald had received a copy of a telegram from the British Ambassador in St. Petersburg to London giving this information. MacDonald revealed this important news to Kikujiro Ishii, the head of the commercial bureau of the Foreign Ministry, and Ishii in turn informed Katsura. Some Japanese leaders were sceptical, and Ishii was reportedly warned that he would be obliged to commit harakiri if his information proved incorrect and peace was lost as a consequence. Komura Gaikoshi, II, 126–127; Kikujiro Ishii, Gaiko Yoroku, Tokyo, 1931, pp. 82–83; White, Diplomacy of the Russo-Japanese War, pp. 307–308.

65 Katsura to Komura, telegram, August 29, 1905, Komura Gaikoshi, II, 126–127.

pan would restore the northern part of the island without payment by Russia. Komura immediately accepted.[66] Peace was now
assured. Several days were spent in completing the details of the
treaty, and the formal signing took place on September 5.

It is apparent that Roosevelt's intervention in the peace negotiations had been important largely because it kept the conference
going at a time when Russia had resolved to end it. The Russian
records leave no doubt that the Tsar had determined to break off
the negotiations just at the moment the President sent his appeal
of August 21. Roosevelt's intervention also won southern Sakhalin
for Japan, but this was not vital to the successful outcome of the
conference. It doubtless made Japan more willing to give up the
indemnity claim, but it is clear that by August 28 the Tokyo government would have made peace without southern Sakhalin if necessary. For his efforts in getting the conference convened and keeping it together until peace was concluded, Roosevelt well deserved
the Nobel Peace Prize he was awarded in 1906. But Roosevelt's
appeals to Tokyo and St. Petersburg during the negotiations were
not the most important influences in bringing peace. The peace
conference was a success primarily because: (1) Japanese leaders
in Tokyo were of the unanimous opinion that Japan must have
peace, and (2) Witte was willing to violate the direct order of the
Tsar to break off the negotiations.

Komura's sudden capitulation to Witte's terms on August 29
came as a surprise to Roosevelt. To Spring Rice he wrote: "I think
the Japanese gave up more than they need to have given up when
they returned the northern half of Sakhalin, which I am confident
I could have obtained for them — or at least which I think I could
have made Russia redeem for a small sum of money." [67] It was
some time before Roosevelt realized how necessary peace was for
Japan. "I did not appreciate quite how urgent their need of peace
was," he confessed to George Kennan in October, 1905.[68] The following summer Kennan called on Roosevelt and told him that Japan's leaders had admitted to him that they were bled white and
had to have peace.[69]

66 Korostovetz, *Pre-War Diplomacy*, pp. 106–108.
67 Roosevelt to Spring Rice, September 1, 1905, Roosevelt Papers.
68 Roosevelt to Kennan, October 15, 1905, Morison, *Roosevelt Letters*, V, 56–60.
69 Roosevelt to Kermit Roosevelt, June 9, 1906, Morison, *Roosevelt Letters*, V,

Still another factor weighed more heavily in the scales in favor of peace than Roosevelt's intervention. On August 12, 1905, Japan gained security for the future by the renewal of the Anglo-Japanese Alliance. The terms of the original alliance were revised so as to bring either signatory to the immediate assistance of the other in case any of its interests, as defined by the treaty, were attacked by a third power.[70] Thus, Japan was guaranteed against a Russian war of revenge. Roosevelt was notified of the conclusion of the treaty on September 5, and he recognized its significance. "I have no doubt," he wrote to British Ambassador Durand, "that the signing of that treaty between England and Japan was a powerful factor in inducing Japan to be wise and reasonable as to terms." [71]

Though Japan failed to secure an indemnity and northern Sakhalin, the Portsmouth peace settlement was by no means a diplomatic defeat. Her gains were real and substantial. Unfortunately, Japanese leaders had led their people to expect an indemnity, and the Japanese people accepted the Russian claim that the conference was a Russian victory. The result was riots in Tokyo. When on September 5 the Japanese police unwisely attempted to prevent a peaceful meeting of protest at Hibiya Park, riots ensued in which eleven people were killed and over a thousand were injured. The residence of the Minister for Home Affairs, who was the immediate superior of the Chief of Police, was attacked and only the timely arrival of troops prevented its destruction. On the following day the city was placed under martial law, and by September 9 order had been restored.

The American and European press immediately interpreted the riots in Tokyo as being directed against foreigners, and more particularly against President Roosevelt. This, however, was not the case. Griscom dispatched a long report from Tokyo making it clear that the riots were directed primarily against the police, secondarily against the Japanese government officials, and only incidentally

296. Hayashi confirms this in his memoirs: "Although a great deal of criticism has been published about the unsatisfactory conditions of peace signed at Portsmouth, those who know the real circumstances recognize that at the time the negotiations were in progress it was absolutely necessary for us to make peace. Tadasu Hayashi, *The Secret Memoirs of Count Tadasu Hayashi*, edited by A. M. Pooley, New York, 1915, p. 230.

70 Text in *British Documents*, IV, 165–169.

71 Roosevelt to Durand, September 8, 1905, Roosevelt Papers.

against foreigners.[72] Secretary of War Taft and Alice Roosevelt, the President's daughter, were in Japan at this time, and none of their party was subjected to any indignity. Taft telegraphed Roosevelt that "any effort to create the impression that there is an anti-foreign demonstration or anti-American sentiment in the great body of the people of Japan is unjust." [73]

It was only natural, however, that some of the resentment of the Japanese people was directed at Roosevelt because of his close connection with the peace negotiations. Griscom reported to Roosevelt that his popularity had received a "distinct check," as a result of the peace settlement.[74] Nevertheless, it would be easy to overestimate this factor. In the years that followed, even during the crises of 1906 and 1907, the Japanese newspapers continued to express great admiration and friendship for the American President and to regard him as a sincere friend of Japan.

As for Roosevelt, he remained fundamentally sympathetic to Japan. When the peace settlement was achieved, he wrote to Rockhill, who had recently been sent as minister to China: "I was pro-Japanese before, but after my experience with the peace commissioners I am far stronger pro-Japanese than ever." [75] Roosevelt's sympathies were, to be sure, moderated somewhat by the news of the riots in Tokyo. "The outbreak in Tokio," he wrote to Lodge, "is unpleasant evidence that the Japanese mob — I hope not the Japanese people — had its head completely turned; the peace is evidently a wise one from *our* standpoint too." [76] Nevertheless, he remained pro-Japanese. He wrote again to Lodge a few days later, saying: "I shall do everything I can to help Japan and have a most friendly feeling for her. . . ." [77] That friendly feeling he was destined to retain, even through the serious crises in Japanese-American relations which were to come in the years 1906–07.

[72] Griscom to Root, September 15, 1905, Roosevelt Papers.
[73] Taft to Roosevelt, telegram, September 17, 1905, Roosevelt Papers.
[74] Griscom to Roosevelt, September 21, 1905, Roosevelt Papers.
[75] Roosevelt to Rockhill, August 29, 1905, Morison, *Roosevelt Letters*, IV, 1326–27.
[76] Roosevelt to Lodge, September 6, 1905, Morison, *Roosevelt Letters*, V, 12–13.
[77] Roosevelt to Lodge, September 8, 1905, Henry Cabot Lodge, *Selections from the Correspondence of Theodore Roosevelt and Henry Cabot Lodge, 1884–1918*, 2 vols., New York, 1925, II, 192.

CHAPTER SIX

The Korean Withdrawal

WITHIN a fortnight of the outbreak of the Russo-Japanese War the United States was writing off the Hermit Kingdom as an independent state. "I cannot see any possibility of this Government using its influence 'to bolster up the Empire of Korea in its independence,'" wrote W. W. Rockhill to Minister Horace N. Allen at Seoul.

I fancy that the Japanese will settle this question when the present war is finished. The annexation of Korea to Japan seems to be absolutely indicated as the one great and final step westward of the extension of the Japanese Empire. I think when this comes about it will be better for the Korean people and also for the peace in the Far East.[1]

Virtually every high official in Washington was in agreement with Rockhill's views.

In Seoul the men who ruled Korea did not grasp so quickly the danger to Korea in a war between Russia and Japan. Just a few days before the outbreak of hostilities, the Emperor's Minister, Yi Yong Ik, told Frederick A. McKenzie, a British war correspondent, that Korea was in no danger, since her independence was guaranteed by America and Europe. When McKenzie questioned whether other nations would protect Korea when she would not protect herself, Yi replied: "We have the promise of America. She will be our friend whatever happens."[2]

The promise to which Yi referred was that in the treaty of 1882. When Commodore Robert W. Shufeldt negotiated that treaty between the United States and Korea, a clause was inserted in Article

[1] Rockhill to Allen, February 20, 1904, Rockhill Papers, Houghton Library, Harvard University, Cambridge, Massachusetts.
[2] Frederick A. McKenzie, *Korea's Fight for Freedom*, New York, 1928, pp. 77–78.

I providing that "If other Powers deal unjustly or oppressively with either Government, the other will exert their good offices, on being informed of the case, to bring about an amicable arrangement, thus showing their friendly feeling." [3] Korean leaders, having little understanding of western legal concepts such as "good offices," were inclined to interpret this provision broadly and to look upon the United States as an "Elder Brother." [4]

Minister Allen at Seoul found himself in a difficult position during the Russo-Japanese War, caught as he was between the Korean government's expectations and the known views of officials in Washington as expressed by Rockhill. Allen himself was partly responsible for his anomalous position, for he had encouraged Korea's leaders to look to the United States for support.[5] During his long career in Korea as missionary and then as diplomat, Allen had been a champion of Korean independence. During the years of Russian ascendance, he had favored the Japanese as the protectors of that independence. When Japan emerged as the greater threat to Korean independence, his sympathies switched to the Russians. While on leave in the United States in 1903, he had tried in vain to win Rockhill and Roosevelt over to his anti-Japanese views.[6] By the outbreak of the Russo-Japanese War, however, Allen's enthusiasm for Korean independence had cooled. Like so many other champions of Korea, he experienced disillusionment as a result of the corruption and intrigue of the Korean court. In January, 1904, he wrote Rockhill that he believed the United States would be making a big mistake if it allowed sentimental reasons to induce it to attempt to bolster up Korea in its independence. "These people cannot govern themselves," he frankly conceded.

---

[3] United States, *Statutes at Large*, XXIII, 720.

[4] The Korean King (later styled Emperor) told Allen in his first audience as American minister in 1897: "We feel that America is to us as our Elder Brother." Allen to Secretary of State John Sherman, September 13, 1897, Despatches: Korea, XIII.

[5] In August, 1900, Allen had assured the Korean Emperor that the United States and the other treaty powers would make it difficult for any nation to take away the independence of the Korean nation. Allen to Hay, August 31, 1900, Despatches: Korea, XVI.

[6] Fred Harvey Harrington, *God, Mammon and the Japanese: Dr. Horace N. Allen and Korean-American Relations, 1884–1905*, Madison, 1944, pp. 313–317.

Korea should belong to Japan, and it would be a mistake, he said, to try to have Japan continue the fiction of independence.[7]

It was not long before Allen could discern that Japan would take Korea. Before hostilities began, Japanese troops occupied Seoul, and soon the entire country was occupied. On February 23, 1904, a protocol was signed by which Korea agreed to place "full confidence" in the Japanese government and to "adopt the advice of the latter with regard to improvements in administration."[8] News of Russian losses in the first months of the war indicated that the Japanese had come to stay. As this Japanese purpose became apparent, the anxiety of the Korean Emperor increased. "He falls back in his extremity upon his old friendship with America," reported Allen. "It is my endeavor to sooth him all I can, at the same time pointing out to him how the course of his Government during the past years could not well lead to any other result than something like the alliance of February 23." Though Allen asserted that he had not encouraged the ruler to dispatch anyone to the United States to secure aid under the treaty, he wrote to Secretary Hay:

At the same time I may as well inform you that the Emperor confidently expects that America will do something for him at the close of this war, or when opportunity offers, to retain for him as much of his independence as is possible. He is inclined to give a very free and favorable translation of Article I of our treaty of Jenchuan of 1882. I trust to be able to prevent a direct invocation of this treaty, however, though I am obliged to assure His Majesty that the condition of Korea is borne in mind by the United States Government, who will use their good offices when occasion occurs.[9]

In the same month that Allen sent this dispatch, the Emperor's palace burned, and he moved into a library building adjoining the American legation. The Korean ruler did his best to create the impression that he was under Allen's care.[10] The following month

7 Allen to Rockhill, January 4, 1904, Rockhill Papers.

8 Text in Carnegie Endowment for International Peace, *Korea: Treaties and Agreements*, Washington, 1921, pp. 36–37.

9 Allen to Hay, April 14, 1904, United States, Department of State, *Occupation of Korea*, Message of the President of the United States transmitting in response to a Senate resolution of February 21, 1916, a report from the Secretary of State submitting copies of certain correspondence had between the official representatives of the United States and the representatives of Korea relative to the occupation of Korea, 64th Congress, 1st Session, Senate Document No. 342, pp. 12–13.

10 Harrington, *God, Mammon and the Japanese*, pp. 320–321.

the Emperor asked for asylum in the American legation, but Allen told the Emperor's messenger that if the Emperor scaled the walls of the compound, he would have to put him out.[11]

The protocol of February 23, 1904, was followed by additional agreements strengthening Japan's control over Korea. In August, 1904, Korea entrusted to Japan the appointment of advisers to the Korean finance and foreign affairs departments.[12] In that month Japan appointed Tanetaro Metega financial adviser and Durham W. Stevens, an American, adviser to the Department of Foreign Affairs. By the beginning of 1905 Japan had taken over the policing of the Korean capital and had placed a Japanese police inspector in every province.[13] Then in the following April the Japanese took over the control of postal, telegraph, and telephone services in Korea.[14]

Despite Allen's long advocacy of Korean independence, he voiced no objection to Japan's increasing control over Korea. On the contrary, he earnestly sought to convince both Tokyo and Washington that he was no longer anti-Japanese. Allen told the Japanese Minister at Seoul that he regretted that he was suspected of a pro-Russian bias and that he would gladly make known to the United States the just action of Japan in Korea.[15] To Hay he wrote that if Japan succeeded in the war, it would be best for Korea's foreign relations to be handled through Tokyo, where there was a "responsible government." [16] In another letter to Hay, he stated that he was entirely friendly to Japan in Korea, and that he recognized that Korea could not stand alone. "Japan," he stated, "is the rightful and natural overlord." [17]

Allen's pleas of friendship for Japan were prompted primarily by his desire to be retained at the Seoul post until the anticipated withdrawal of the legation took place. He undoubtedly correctly gauged the temper of the Roosevelt administration. When Baron Suyematsu visited Washington in March, 1904, while on his way

[11] Allen to Hay, January 5, 1905, Despatches: Korea, XXII.
[12] Text in *Korea: Treaties and Agreements*, p. 37.
[13] Allen to Hay, September 6 and December 16, 1904, Despatches: Korea, XXI.
[14] Text in *Korea: Treaties and Agreements*, pp. 38–40.
[15] Komura to Uchida, March 2, 1904, Telegram Series, XLIII, 4338.
[16] Allen to Hay, March 27, 1904, Despatches: Korea, XX.
[17] Allen to Hay, December 24, 1904, Hay Papers.

to England, Roosevelt told him that Japan should have a position with Korea "just like we have with Cuba." [18] In June, 1904, when Kaneko and Takahira lunched at the White House, Roosevelt told them that Korea should be entirely within Japan's sphere of interest.[19] He told Sternberg in August, 1904, that Korea should be a Japanese protectorate, which "may be tantamount to control." [20] Writing to Secretary Hay in January, 1905, Roosevelt made that much quoted statement: "We can not possibly interfere for the Koreans against Japan. They couldn't strike one blow in their own defence." [21] In February he wrote to Ambassador Meyer stating that Korea had shown its utter inability to stand by itself and Japan ought to have a protectorate over it.[22] The following month Roosevelt's views — including the view that Japan should hold Korea — were made known to Katsura by George Kennan.[23]

Allen's efforts to save himself from dismissal were unsuccessful. He convinced Tokyo of his friendship, but he failed to persuade Washington that he was no longer anti-Japanese. Roosevelt took the occasion of his second inauguration in March, 1905, to send new diplomatic representatives to many capitals of the world. Rockhill was sent to Peking. Robert McCormick, who was too pro-Russian, was transferred from St. Petersburg to Paris, thus opening the way for Meyer to go to the Russian capital. Whitelaw Reid went to London. Seoul did not escape the shuffle. Indeed, Roosevelt was intent that it did not. Edwin V. Morgan was appointed Minister to Korea to replace Allen.

The dismissed minister soon convinced himself that he had been ousted because Roosevelt thought him to be anti-Japanese, and he was right. Many observers even speculated that the Japanese government had urged Allen's dismissal at Washington, but there was no justification for this suspicion. Ironically, the opposite was true. Both Durham Stevens and Takahira intervened at Washing-

18 Hayashi to Komura, March 15, 1904, Telegram Series, XLI, 1465.

19 Takahira to Komura, March 15, 1904, Telegram Series, XLI, 1959–62.

20 Bülow to the Kaiser, August 31, 1904, *Die Grosse Politik*, XIX, pt. 2, pp. 535–537. (Partially translated in Dennis, *Adventures in American Diplomacy*, p. 390).

21 Roosevelt to Hay, January 28, 1905, Morison, *Roosevelt Letters*, IV, 1112.

22 Roosevelt to Meyer, February 6, 1905, Morison, *Roosevelt Letters*, IV, 1115–16.

23 Barry to Kennan, February 21, 1905, Kennan Papers; Kennan to Roosevelt, March 30, 1905, Roosevelt Papers.

ton in an attempt to save Allen.[24] Neither of these appeals nor one from the Korean Emperor prevented his ouster. Roosevelt was determined to be rid of the vacillating ex-missionary. In April Morgan received his commission as minister to Korea.

By the time Morgan arrived in Seoul in June, 1905, Japanese leaders were anticipating the end of the war and were busily engaged in the diplomatic field seeking to gain the approval of the powers for a full protectorate over Korea. When in the following month Secretary of War Taft appeared in Tokyo while on his way to the Philippines, Prime Minister Katsura seized the opportunity to elicit a statement from Taft on the Korean question. Thus occurred the famous Taft-Katsura conversation of July 27, 1905.

In the long conversation between Taft and the Japanese Prime Minister which took place on the morning of July 27, it was but natural that the Philippine Islands would be one of the topics of conversation. Taft had once been Governor General there and the islands were presently under his administration as Secretary of War. Taft remarked to Katsura that some pro-Russians in the United States would have the public believe that the victory of Japan would be a certain prelude to her aggression in the direction of the Philippines. But in his opinion, said Taft, Japan's only interest in the Philippines would be to have the islands governed by a strong and friendly nation like the United States. Katsura confirmed in the strongest terms the correctness of Taft's views and stated that Japan harbored no aggressive designs whatever on the Philippines.

Prime Minister Katsura then turned the discussion to a general consideration of how peace could be insured in the Far East after the conclusion of the war. In his opinion, he said, the only means for accomplishing that object would be to form a good understanding between the three governments of Japan, the United States, and Great Britain. He said that he understood that the traditional policy of the United States made it impossible for it to enter a formal alliance, but he thought "an alliance in practice if not in name" should be made between these three nations insofar as respects the affairs of the Far East. Taft assured the Prime Minister that the

24 Hay to Roosevelt, January 26, 1905, Hay Papers; Takahira to Komura, March 20, 1905, Telegram Series, LXII, 3094.

people of the United States were so fully in accord with the policy of Japan and Great Britain in the maintenance of peace in the Far East that cooperation could be counted on by those nations quite as confidently as if the United States were under treaty obligations.

Finally the discussion turned to Korea. Katsura stated that it was of absolute importance to Japan that a complete solution of the peninsular question should be made as the logical consequence of the war. If left alone after the war, Korea would certainly revert to her old habit of entering into agreements with other powers and Japan would be confronted with the same complications as existed before the war. In view of this, said Katsura, Japan felt constrained to take some definite steps with a view to precluding that possibility. In response to this, Taft said that in his personal opinion the establishment by Japanese troops of a suzerainty over Korea to the extent of requiring that Korea enter into no foreign treaties without the consent of Japan was the logical result of the war and would contribute to the permanent peace of the Far East. Further, said Taft, he believed President Roosevelt would concur in his views, although he had no authority to give assurance of this. Taft then explained that he felt much delicacy in advancing the views he did, for he had no mandate for the purpose from the President, and since he left Washington Mr. Root had been appointed Secretary of State, and he might seem thus to be trespassing on another's department.

Following the talk an "agreed memorandum of conversation" was drawn up, presumably by Katsura, embodying the important views exchanged. The title of the memorandum did not mean that it constituted an "agreement," but only that the two parties agreed that the memorandum was an accurate record of what had been said. This "agreed memorandum of conversation" was telegraphed to Root on July 29. Taft explained to the new Secretary of State that Katsura had been quite anxious for the interview and it would have been difficult to avoid a statement. "If I have spoken too freely or inaccurately or unwittingly, I know you can and will correct it." [25] Taft soon knew that he had spoken neither inaccurately

25 Taft to Root, telegram, July 29, 1905, Roosevelt Papers. Copy cited is reproduced in Tyler Dennett, "President Roosevelt's Secret Pact with Japan," Current History,

nor unwittingly. Root was not then at Washington, but on July 31 a telegram came from Roosevelt saying, "Your conversation with Count Katsura absolutely correct in every respect. Wish you would state to Katsura that I confirm every word you have said." [26]

The Taft-Katsura "agreed memorandum" has been interpreted as a "secret pact" or executive agreement whereby the United States approved Japan's suzerainty over Korea in return for a Japanese disavowal of any aggressive intentions toward the Philippines.[27] It is true that the conversation was not officially made public. It was not public knowledge in the United States until Tyler Dennett read it to a conference at Williamstown, Massachusetts, in August, 1924, characterizing it as a "secret pact." It can not be established, however, that the conversation and resulting "agreed memorandum" constituted a bargain in *Realpolitik* with a *quid pro quo*. Roosevelt put no such interpretation upon it. Shortly after the Portsmouth settlement, Minister Griscom telegraphed that rumors were current in Tokyo that such a bargain had been struck. The rumors emanated from the *Kokumin Shimbun*, a newspaper generally recognized as a government organ.[28] Roosevelt took exception to the suggestion that his Korean policy was the result of a bargain in which Japan guaranteed the Philippines. "I think that a sufficient answer," he wrote to Taft, "would be that we neither ask nor give any favor to anyone as a reward for not meddling with any American territory. We are entirely competent to prevent such meddling, and require no guaranty of assistance to preserve our territorial integrity."[29] After reading the "agreed memorandum" again, Roosevelt was even more sure of his interpretation.

The statement about the Philippines [he wrote to Taft] was merely to clear up Japan's attitude, which had been purposely misrepresented by pro-Rus-

XXI (1924–25), 15–21. Another copy is filed in the Department of State Archives, Miscellaneous Letters, July (Part III), 1905. This copy is reproduced in John Gilbert Reid, "Taft's Telegram to Root, July 29, 1905," *Pacific Historical Review*, IX (1940), 66–70. The two published copies are alike except that names of sender and recipient are deleted from the copy edited by Dennett.

26 Roosevelt to Taft, telegram, July 31, 1905, Morison, *Roosevelt Letters*, IV, 1293.
27 See Griswold, *Far Eastern Policy*, pp. 125–126, and Dennett, "President Roosevelt's Secret Pact with Japan," *Current History*, XXI (1924–25), 15–21.
28 Griscom to Root, telegram, October 4, 1905, Despatches: Japan, LXXXI.
29 Roosevelt to Taft, October 5, 1905, Morison, *Roosevelt Letters*, V, 46.

velt's approval of Japanese suzerainty over Korea. Roosevelt had
decided over a year before the Taft-Katsura conversation that he
would not object to Japanese control over Korea. He had expressed
those views to many people, including Takahira, and it is certain
that his views were made known to Katsura by George Kennan at
least four months before the conversation of July 27. At the same
time, it is unlikely that Roosevelt desired any *quid pro quo* for his
policy concerning Korea. He viewed Japanese control of Korea as a
good thing in itself. It was good for the balance of power in the
Far East and therefore good for the United States. Furthermore, a
guarantee of the Philippines was hardly necessary in Roosevelt's
view, for any such assurance was in substance a guarantee not to
make war on the United States. Such a guarantee Roosevelt considered superfluous.

Within two years after the Taft-Katsura conversation, Roosevelt
was indeed very much concerned over the possibilities of war with
Japan, and he came to realize that Japan could easily take the
Philippines in the opening stages of such a war. Nevertheless,
throughout the war scare of 1907 and during the subsequent period
of Roosevelt's administration — a time when anxiety over the safety
of the Philippines was ever on the minds of Roosevelt, Root, and
Taft — never was any mention made of the alleged "secret pact."
If this secret agreement had any reality, it is strange that not even
passing reference to it is found in the records of the Department of
State or in the private papers of Roosevelt, Taft, and Root during
the years 1906–09.

In any case, Roosevelt's letters to Taft of October 5 and 7 state
conclusively that the agreed memorandum did not represent a "secret pact" in any sense of the word. He stated emphatically to Taft
— and he was in no position to misrepresent the matter to Taft —
that it was not a bargain with a *quid pro quo*. Formal concurrence
in this interpretation was given by the Japanese Prime Minister.
The Taft-Katsura conversation was, then, an honest exchange of
views. Its value to Japan lay in the fact that she received another
verbal assurance from Roosevelt that he favored Japanese suzerainty over Korea, and that the cooperation of the United States
could be counted upon in the maintenance of peace in the Far

East. What form that cooperation would take was not specified, and nothing more than a community of interest with Japan and Britain in the Far East was implied.[32]

While Taft was in Tokyo giving renewed assurance that the United States would not oppose the establishment of a Japanese protectorate over Korea, the Korean Emperor was still looking to the United States to save him from the Japanese. An agent of the Emperor came to Morgan in July to ask whether an attempt on the part of Korea to gain admittance to the peace negotiations would receive the support of the United States. Failing this, would the United States use its good offices to obtain favorable terms for Korea? To this Morgan said that though he had no instructions on the question, it was his personal opinion that Korea's presence at the conference would be unwelcome. Though the United States had been instrumental in bringing Japan and Russia together, Morgan explained, the United States was no more able than other neutral powers to intimate its views in regard to the articles of peace. The Emperor, said Morgan, should "await calmly the result of the negotiations." [33]

When the peace terms were revealed six weeks later, the Emperor found them to be all that he had feared. Russia recognized Japan's paramount political, military, and economic interests in Korea and agreed not to place any obstacle in the way of any measure of "direction and protection and supervision" which Japan deemed necessary to adopt in Korea.[34] Within a short time Tokyo was making preparations to assume a full protectorate over the Hermit Kingdom.

Among the diplomats in Seoul witnessing the gradual extinction of Korean independence was a young American named Willard Straight. After service in the Imperial Chinese Maritime Customs Administration and a short career as war correspondent, he had come to Seoul as private secretary to Morgan and as Vice Consul. This adventurous American diplomat, whose later activities were

---

32 This interpretation of the Taft-Katsura conversation has been previously summarized in Raymond A. Esthus, "The Taft-Katsura Agreement — Reality or Myth," *Journal of Modern History*, XXXI (1959), 46–51.

33 Morgan to Root, July 20, 1905, Despatches: Korea, XXII.

34 Carnegie Endowment for International Peace, *Manchuria: Treaties and Agreements*, Washington, 1921, p. 70.

destined to leave a lasting imprint on American Far Eastern policy, was a keen but subjective observer of events at the Korean capital. He had not been at Seoul long before he decided he did not like the Japanese. "Under the guise of waging a war for the preservation of her national existence," he noted in his diary, "she [Japan] has carried on a war of aggression." Straight's strong anti-Japanese feelings nevertheless did not blind him to the faults of the Koreans. "Where the Japanese would fight and the Chinaman resist with his impassive obstinacy," he confided to his diary, "the Korean will beg an issue by duplicity and double dealing." [35]

The Korean propensity for underhanded intrigue was evidenced during the visit of Alice Roosevelt to Seoul. The President's daughter had come with the Taft party when the Secretary of War made a second visit to Tokyo in September, 1905. While in the Far East she came to the Korean capital accompanied by Senator and Mrs. Francis G. Newlands and Congressman Frederick H. Gillette. The Emperor made a great play for American sympathy by his lavish entertainment of the visitors. "These people are seeking for straws," noted Straight, "and the Roosevelt trip [looks] like a life preserver to their jaundiced imaginations." [36] During the course of the visit, the Emperor approached Senator Newlands and asked his aid in persuading the United States to use its good offices to save Korea from the Japanese. The Senator advised the Emperor to engage the services of an international lawyer and to draw up a dignified protest. This, of course, was just what the Emperor wished to avoid, for he was afraid to oppose the Japanese openly. What the Emperor had in mind, Straight observed, was some sort of backstairs proceeding such as he used with the Russians and the Japanese in the good old days when he was playing off one power against the other. [37]

As the end of Korean independence drew near, Roosevelt made

[35] Straight diary, June 22, 1905, Willard D. Straight Papers, Albert B. Mann Library, Cornell University, Ithaca, New York; Herbert Croly, *Willard Straight*, New York, 1924, pp. 169–171.

[36] Straight to Frederick Palmer, October 3, 1905, Straight Papers; Croly, *Willard Straight*, pp. 163–164.

[37] Straight diary, November 14, 1905, Straight Papers; Croly, *Willard Straight*, pp. 176–177.

one effort on behalf of the Koreans. Minister Griscom wrote to the President on October 12 saying that America ought to throw its "whole moral weight" into the scales to prevent the Japanese from abusing the Koreans. Griscom conceded that the Koreans did not deserve much good treatment, but he felt the United States should "try to prevent the Japanese from going too far." [38] Roosevelt immediately took up the matter with Takahira, who telegraphed Roosevelt's concern to Tokyo. Within a few days Katsura replied that the Japanese government would carefully watch over the conduct of the Japanese in Korea and would spare no effort to prevent ill treatment of the Koreans. He went on to confide to Roosevelt that Japan would shortly assume charge of Korea's external relations.[39]

On November 9, only three days after Katsura sent his assurances to Roosevelt, Marquis Ito, one of the leading members of the Genro, arrived in Seoul to negotiate the protectorate treaty. As Ito pressed the Korean government to sign a treaty, the Emperor sent renewed pleas to Morgan and Straight. When Morgan refused to relay a message to Roosevelt, Straight agreed that his decision was wise. "The chances were ten to one," Straight noted, "that in the same breath he had sent a message to the Japanese saying they could have anything they wanted. That would be his game. Then he'd sit on the side lines and see us fight it out." When a few days later the Emperor's agents pleaded with Straight, he reminded them that Senator Newlands had advised them to make an open appeal, but they had refused to follow this advice. The time for protesting, said Straight, had gone by. Korea had had a ten year chance to improve, he said frankly, and neither Emperor nor officials had shown the slightest inclination to take advantage of it.[40]

The Korean government capitulated to the Japanese demands on November 17. Morgan reported to Washington that there were many Japanese gendarmes around the palace during the negotiations, and, though it was improbable that physical force was em-

38 Griscom to Roosevelt, October 12, 1905, Roosevelt Papers.
39 Katsura to Takahira, telegram, November 6, 1905, Notes from: Japan, IX.
40 Straight diary, November 14 and 17, 1905, Straight Papers; Croly, *Willard Straight*, pp. 176–182.

ployed, the members of the cabinet could not be considered "to have acted entirely as free agents." [41] The new treaty gave Japan the complete control of Korea's foreign relations and provided for the appointment of a Resident General at Seoul "primarily" to take charge of diplomatic affairs. What other affairs he might take control of were not specified.[42]

To these terms Washington had no objection. Takahira informed Root of the treaty on November 23, and the very next day Root telegraphed Morgan ordering the withdrawal of the American legation from Seoul.[43] Within a week the ministers of the other powers were leaving the Korean capital. "It is like the stampede of rats from a sinking ship," observed Straight.[44] When in the subsequent weeks Homer B. Hulbert and Min Yeung-tchan, the Korean minister to France, brought secret appeals to Washington from the Korean Emperor, Root and Roosevelt turned deaf ears.[45]

President Roosevelt was the dominant force in the shaping of American policy toward Korean-Japanese relations during 1904–05, but that policy was approved by Root, Taft, Rockhill, Griscom, and even at times Minister Allen. Intervention, or even a moderate exertion of American influence on behalf of Korean independence was never considered seriously. The whole tenor of Roosevelt's policy indicates that he believed Japanese suzerainty in Korea would, under the existing conditions, be best for the Koreans as well as Japanese. Apart from this, however, there were other considerations which weighed heavily in the scales of policy making. Korea was powerless to strike a blow in her own defense, as Roosevelt had told Hay. Had the United States taken up the battle for Korean independence, it would have found itself arrayed against the combined power of the Anglo-Japanese Alliance, and

---

41 Morgan to Root, November 20, 1905, Despatches: Korea, XXII. The Japanese version of the negotiations is given in George T. Ladd, *In Korea with Marquis Ito*, New York, 1908, pp. 254–269. The Korean version is given in McKenzie, *Korea's Fight for Freedom*, pp. 88–94, and Homer B. Hulbert, *The Passing of Korea*, New York, 1906, pp. 221–222.

42 *Korea: Treaties and Agreements*, pp. 55–56.

43 Takahira to Root, November 23, 1905, and Root to Morgan, telegram, November 24, 1905, *Foreign Relations, 1905*, pp. 612–613, 631.

44 Croly, *Willard Straight*, p. 188.

45 Roosevelt to Root, November 25, 1905, Morison, *Roosevelt Letters*, V, 96; Root to Min Yeung-tchan, December 19, 1905, *Occupation of Korea*, pp. 20–21.

there was not the slightest chance that intervention could have met with success. Roosevelt's policy was not to place the United States in opposition to the Anglo-Japanese Alliance but rather to associate the United States with that dominant diplomatic combination. Roosevelt's Korean policy in 1905 was the first example of this larger policy which he was to pursue consistently throughout his second administration. Early in 1906 he confided to the British Ambassador, Sir Mortimer Durand, that the prompt withdrawal of the United States legation from Seoul was meant to show to the world his unreserved acceptance of the Anglo-Japanese Alliance and his intention to act loyally in support of it.[46]

The only alternative to Roosevelt's policy regarding Korea was a policy of nonrecognition. Such a policy of paper diplomacy was as alien to his conception of diplomacy as the doctrine of propinquity was pertinent. Had such a policy been followed, however, the results would probably have been unfortunate. The real choice in 1905 was not between Korean independence or a Japanese protectorate. Rather the choice was between a Japanese protectorate or outright annexation by Japan. Japan's decision in favor of a protectorate represented a victory by Marquis Ito over the Yamagata faction within the Japanese body politic, but it was a hard won victory. Had the United States opposed a Japanese protectorate in 1905, this would have served only to increase Japan's determination to make her position in Korea secure and would have played into the hands of the Yamagata faction. As it was, Korea was given a respite of five years, during which time Ito labored as Resident General at Seoul attempting to reform Korea — a thankless task that ultimately brought Ito's death at the hands of a Korean assassin.[47]

46 Sykes, *Durand*, p. 299.
47 On Ito's role as Resident General see Hilary Conroy, *The Japanese Seizure of Korea: 1868–1910*, Philadelphia, 1960, ch. vii.

CHAPTER SEVEN

The Open Door in Manchuria

DURING the first months following the Russo-Japanese War, the important issues in Japanese-American relations concerned Japan's new position on the continent of Asia. In the case of Korea, the adjustment of Japan's position to a new status raised no controversial issues in Japanese-American relations. There Ito's reform program had received the sanction of the powers and at least the temporary acquiescence of the Yamagata faction in Japan. In the case of Manchuria, however, Japan's policy was not so clearly defined, while at the same time innumerable controversial issues were inherent in the Manchurian question itself. Was Manchuria an integral part of the Chinese Empire? If so, how was Japan's position to be reconciled with China's sovereignty? How were the treaty rights and the commercial interests of the other powers to be affected by Japan's special position? In short, how was the new Japanese sphere of influence in South Manchuria to be reconciled with Hay's principles of the open door and the integrity of China?

The Treaty of Portsmouth had reaffirmed Hay's principles but had not resolved the complex problems relating to Manchuria. By its terms Japan and Russia agreed to restore the administration of that area to China, but this was not to be effected fully until the withdrawal of the two armies. Since the belligerents had allowed themselves eighteen months for the military evacuation, conditions in Manchuria would probably be unsettled for many months. In the treaty Russia asserted that it had no territorial concessions in impairment of Chinese sovereignty, but this, too, did not resolve the status of Manchuria. By other terms of the treaty, Russia transferred to Japan rights of such far-reaching character that they constituted in themselves a violation of China's integrity.[1] In the agreements of 1896 providing for the construction of the Chinese Eastern Railway across northern Manchuria, the Russian-controlled railway company was granted "the absolute and exclusive right of administration" over "the lands actually necessary for the construction, operation, and protection of the line." Under these provisions, which were to become a source of great dispute in 1908, Russia exercised extensive administrative powers in the railway zone. After 1898 Russia possessed the same rights over the branch line of the Chinese Eastern Railway which was constructed from Harbin to Port Arthur. In the Liaotung leasehold which Russia acquired that year, the rights were even more extensive. There Russia possessed complete civil and military control.[2] The Portsmouth treaty transferred to Japan the leasehold and the railway from Changchun to Port Arthur, and with this grant went all the extensive Russian rights. What interpretation Japan would accord to these rights remained to be determined.

In the first months following the peace settlement, Japan's leaders had no clear conception of what form the Japanese position in South Manchuria would take. It is evident that they had no definite plans for making South Manchuria a private preserve, as the Russians had attempted to do, for in October, 1905, the Katsura government came near to disposing of half its interests in the Manchurian railway to American capitalists. At the time the peace treaty was signed, E. H. Harriman was in Tokyo negotiating with Japanese leaders with a view to securing control of the southern branch of the Chinese Eastern Railway, which he planned to make a part of a projected round-the-world transportation line.[3]

[1] Text in *Manchuria: Treaties and Agreements*, p. 77.

[2] Texts in *Manchuria: Treaties and Agreements*, pp. 13–17, 41–44, 47.

[3] Harriman had come to the Far East at the invitation of Minister Griscom to further American commerce there and to implement his plan for a global transportation line. Harriman's plans were grandiose. He proposed to reconstruct the Japanese line with American capital and make it the eastern part of a trans-Asiatic line. Having secured this essential link, he intended to buy the Chinese Eastern, which he thought the Russians would sell, and then acquire transportation or trackage rights over the trans-Siberian and Russian government roads to the Baltic Sea. These acquisitions, in connection with the Pacific Mail Steamship Company and American railroad systems that he already controlled, would give him a continuous line more than three quarters of the way around the globe, and it would be an easy matter to complete the world

The Tokyo government was receptive to Harriman's proposal, and for several weeks he and Minister Griscom carried on negotiations with Katsura and other Japanese leaders. On October 12, 1905, a memorandum of preliminary understanding was drawn up by Katsura and Harriman providing for the formation of a Japanese corporation that would provide capital for the purchase of the southern branch of the Chinese Eastern Railway from the Japanese government. The Harriman interests and the Japanese government were to have equal ownership in the properties acquired. Harriman and his associates were also to have the right to an equal interest in the development of all industrial enterprises in Manchuria. With this preliminary, and as yet unsigned, agreement in his possession, Harriman sailed from Yokohama on October 12.[4]

If the Harriman-Katsura preliminary agreement had been carried to fulfillment, the United States would have joined hands with Japan in the commercial and industrial development of South Manchuria. But it was not to be. Three days after the departure of Harriman, Baron Komura returned to Tokyo from the United States bearing with him the Treaty of Portsmouth, and he immediately voiced opposition to the scheme. The Foreign Minister pointed out that the Japanese people were already so dissatisfied with the peace settlement that they resorted to mob violence and that their discontent would be greatly increased if they learned that their government had sold to a Japanese-American syndicate much of what Japan had gained in two years of successful war. A decisive debate within the Japanese government between the proponents and the opponents of the Harriman scheme followed.

The Elder Statesmen Ito and Count Kaoru Inouye argued in favor of the plan, pointing out Japan's desperate need for funds to rebuild the war-damaged railroad line. This was no empty argument, for Japan, having gotten no indemnity from Russia, was in serious financial difficulties, and the rebuilding of the railway line in South Manchuria would be expensive. When Japan captured the line not a single passenger car or locomotive was left, and only a

system by establishing a steamship line across the Atlantic. George Kennan, *E. H. Harriman: A Biography*, 2 vols., Boston, 1922, II, 1–3.

[4] Kennan, *Harriman*, II, 5–15.

few freight cars remained. Furthermore, all the railway bridges had been destroyed. But these considerations did not sway Komura. He asserted that funds could be secured elsewhere on terms which would not involve sharing control of the railroad.

The Minister of Communications, Oura Kanetake, strongly supported Komura's arguments, but the advocates of the Harriman scheme countered that there would be positive advantages in a sharing arrangement. They stated that an American interest in South Manchuria would help to create a buffer between Japan and Russia. This line of reasoning must have had a hollow ring for the military-oriented Yamagata faction. In the years preceding the Russo-Japanese War, Japan had learned that she could not rely upon the United States for military support — or even strong diplomatic support — in a contest with Russia. The arguments of Komura were decisive. With the Portsmouth settlement already under attack, the government could not afford to sell out for a few American dollars one of the few tangible fruits of a costly war. Within a week following Komura's return to Japan his colleagues accepted his position.

When Harriman arrived in San Francisco, he found waiting for him a telegram from Katsura asking that the agreement be held "in abeyance." Later, following the conclusion of the Sino-Japanese Treaty of December 22, 1905, Harriman was informed that Japan had found it necessary, in reaching agreement with China, to provide that the Manchurian railway be worked by a company composed exclusively of Japanese and Chinese shareholders.[5] Thus ended the Harriman scheme of 1905, though he was destined to renew his interest in South Manchuria later during the Dollar Diplomacy of the Taft administration.

The Treaty of Portsmouth had provided that the transfer to Japan of the Port Arthur leasehold and the railway in South Manchuria be conditioned upon the consent of the Chinese government. Accordingly, early in November Baron Komura left for the Chinese capital to secure the necessary consent and also to work

5 Kennan, *Harriman*, II, 17–21. For details concerning the cancellation of the agreement see Richard T. Chang, "The Failure of the Katsura-Harriman Agreement," *Journal of Asian Studies*, XXI (1961–62), 65–76. This article contains much speculation, but one point is clear: Komura's opposition killed the project.

out a basis of agreement for harmonizing conflicting Japanese and Chinese interests in South Manchuria.

In securing the transfer of Russian rights, Komura had the full support of the United States. Before Komura's arrival at Peking, Roosevelt had instructed Rockhill that if it became necessary he should state strongly to the Chinese government at the proper time that "China cannot with propriety question the efficacy of this transfer or hesitate to allow Japanese all the rights the Russians were exercising." [6] The Chinese government well knew that it could not defy the results of the Russo-Japanese War, and in the Treaty of Peking, signed December 22, 1905, China consented to all the transfers. China also agreed to open a number of cities in each of the Three Eastern Provinces (Manchuria) to international residence and trade, a provision that would be of great value to all the powers. Japan enhanced its own position in Manchuria by securing timber rights and the right to rebuild and operate the Antung-Mukden railway, which had been constructed for military purposes during the war.[7]

Certain "secret protocols" which were to figure prominently in the controversies that arose concerning the rights of other powers in Manchuria were also concluded at Peking. By one of the clauses of these protocols (actually signed minutes of the negotiations), the Chinese government engaged not to construct any main line in the neighborhood of and parallel to the South Manchuria Railway or any branch line which might be prejudicial to the interest of that railway.[8] The so-called "secret protocols" did not long remain a secret to the United States government. In February, 1906, the Japanese Foreign Office in strict confidence communicated the protocols to the American Chargé at Tokyo, F. M. Huntington Wilson. Wilson saw in them nothing of a sinister nature. On the contrary, he believed that one reason the Japanese government was eager to keep them secret was that both the Diet and the people

[6] Roosevelt to Rockhill, telegram, September 10, 1905, Morison, *Roosevelt Letters,* V, 18.

[7] Text in *Manchuria: Treaties and Agreements,* pp. 78–83. The negotiations are recounted at length in White, *Diplomacy of the Russo-Japanese War,* pp. 331–342, 364–368.

[8] Summary of the secret protocols is given in *Manchuria: Treaties and Agreements,* pp. 83–85.

believed the advantages gained at Peking to be greater than they actually were.[9]

The modest gains in the Peking Treaty could not counteract the dissatisfaction in Japan over the Portsmouth settlement. On January 8, 1906, the Katsura ministry accepted the verdict of the populace and resigned. Marquis Kimmochi Saionji, protégé of Ito and leader of the Seiyukai party, became premier. Takaaki Kato, who had served as Foreign Minister in the last Ito cabinet (1900–1901), returned to the Foreign Ministry. Three associates of Katsura were appointed to the cabinet, and thus the new ministry represented a compromise between the civilian (Ito-Saionji) and the military (Yamagata-Katsura) factions. The fall of the Katsura ministry was a setback for the military faction, but this was counterbalanced in part by Yamagata's elevation to the Presidency of the Privy Council in place of Ito, who became Resident General at Seoul. The formation of the new ministry did not resolve the many undecided questions regarding the policy Japan would follow in Manchuria, and Saionji and Kato soon found their power to make decisions seriously circumscribed by the military.

During the Russo-Japanese War, those powers having a substantial commercial stake in China looked forward to exploiting the Manchurian market when the war came to an end. Before the war almost all the trade of Manchuria had been handled at the treaty port of Newchwang, but in 1903 Japan and the United States had signed treaties with China providing for the opening of Mukden, Antung, and Tatungkau. Now with the return of peace, commercial interests wished to expand their trade to those cities and also to the many cities to be opened under the Treaty of Peking of December 22, 1905. The United States had a substantial interest in the Manchurian market. Only twenty Americans resided at Newchwang in March, 1906, but since most American trade was handled by Chinese agents, the small number was not indicative of the size of American commercial interests in Manchuria. In 1905 American products imported at Newchwang amounted to more than those of all other foreign nations combined.[10]

9 Wilson to Root, February 16, 1906, Despatches: Japan, LXXXI.
10 United States, Department of Commerce (Bureau of Manufactures), *Monthly Consular and Trade Reports*, Washington, nos. 306 (March, 1906) and 308 (May, 1906).

The Japanese military administration in Manchuria betrayed an exasperating indifference to the commercial ambitions of the foreign powers. Month after month the military authorities refused to open the interior of Manchuria to commercial agents, and they made it clear to the Japanese civilian leaders that they wanted no foreigners in Manchuria during the period of the evacuation. The Tokyo government was placed in an embarrassing position by the intransigence of the military leaders. There was apparently some genuine concern that Russian spies would come in disguised as commercial agents, but the idea that Russia would renew the war at that moment was so far-fetched that the Foreign Ministry was hesitant to advance this thesis to the powers. In February, 1906, Kato resigned as Foreign Minister, and though the principal reason for his resignation was his opposition to the ministry's bill for nationalization of the railroads, the Manchurian question was doubtless also a factor in his decision.

In March, 1906, both the United States and Britain made strong representations at Tokyo urging the opening of Manchuria to trade. On March 8 Chargé Huntington Wilson presented the American complaint directly to Prime Minister Saionji, who was serving temporarily as Foreign Minister following Kato's resignation. When Saionji said that foreigners could not be admitted because of the difficulties of withdrawing the troops, Wilson rejoined that he did not think the army would require a road so broad as the whole of Manchuria in order to march out. In making his report to the Department of State, Wilson observed:

It is well known here that the military authorities are so far quite out of sympathy with the policy in which the United States is interested and to which Japan is committed. Apparently they have an idea that there is to be a war of revenge, to prepare for which they desire to have a free hand in Manchuria. Meanwhile, they are inclined to look upon foreigners in Manchuria in the light of intruders, if not spies.

It was Wilson's opinion that Yamagata was even more influential than Ito and that the military faction was able to shape the government's attitude to its will. Only strong pressure, he said, would bring the Japanese government to overcome the opposition of the military and translate into practice the policy of the open door.[11]

[11] Wilson to Root, March 15, 1906, Despatches: Japan, LXXXI. (Printed in part in

On March 19 the British Ambassador, Sir Claude MacDonald, presented to Saionji the complaint of his government. British residents in Newchwang, it said, entertained serious misgivings with regard to the intentions of the Japanese government owing to the stumbling blocks placed by local officials in the way of British trade and enterprise. Among the specific complaints listed were the refusal to give facilities in regard to telegraph communication and railway transport, the refusal to allow representatives of the British-American Tobacco Company to proceed to Mukden, and the refusal to permit British ships to resume trade at Tatungkau. The note asked that immediate instructions be sent to the authorities in Manchuria calling for explanations.[12]

The British note of March 19 was concise and to the point, listing specific complaints and asking for satisfaction. More American notes soon followed which brought charges of a more sweeping nature. On March 24 Root telegraphed Wilson to tell the Japanese government that the United States was painfully impressed by the information that the action of Japanese authorities in Manchuria was so directed toward establishing Japanese commercial interests as to leave no opening for other foreign trade by the time the territory was evacuated.[13] A week later an even stronger note was sent. Root told Tokyo bluntly that while military exigencies might explain temporary restrictions, such an explanation did not meet "the rapidly developing situation of the absorption of a great part of the commercial and mining opportunities of Manchuria by the freely admitted Japanese." "If this condition continues," Root concluded, "China will find herself after the Japanese occupancy has ceased, the merely nominal sovereign of a territory the material advantages of which have been appropriated by the temporary occupants."[14]

Japan's refusal to open South Manchuria to trade gave the United States just cause for complaint. The charge that the Japa-

United States, Department of State, *Papers Relating to the Foreign Relations of the United States, 1906*, 2 pts., Washington, 1909, I, 171–172).

12 MacDonald to Saionji, March 19, 1906, enclosed in Wilson to Root, March 28, 1906, Despatches: Japan, LXXXI.

13 Root to Wilson, telegram, March 24, 1906, *Foreign Relations, 1906*, I, 174.

14 Root to Wilson, telegram, March 30, 1906, Instructions: Japan, V. (Paraphrase printed in *Foreign Relations, 1906*, I, 177).

nese were using the period of the military evacuation to further
their own commercial interests, however, was not based on solid
evidence. The United States Consul General at Newchwang,
Thomas Sammons, made a tour of investigation throughout Manchuria, and he concluded that the Japanese military administration had apparently avoided commercial interference. He found
that some Japanese merchants had been admitted but that they
were largely in the nature of camp followers catering to the army.
Sammons reported to Washington:

> I do not apprehend serious commercial inroads from them in Manchuria
> unless they can cooperate with the Chinese more successfully and satisfac-
> torily than they have been able to do thus far.
> This class of Japanese traders barters mostly in nick-nacks, in mere trifles
> as compared with the extensive traffic in the staples in which Americans, as
> well as other nations, are interested.[15]

Sammons' report probably would have moderated subsequent
notes to Tokyo, but as it turned out no further representations
were necessary. The Japanese government had been deeply impressed by the American and British complaints, and in early
April the government successfully asserted its authority over the
military leaders. Saionji told Wilson on April 5 that the government
had decided to enforce the policy of the open door in Manchuria.
He then gave Wilson assurances that Antung and Tatungkau would
be open to foreigners from May 1 and that Mukden would be open
from June 1. Furthermore, from June 1 Japan would have no objection to the presence of foreigners anywhere in Manchuria except
in certain districts from which they might still be excluded for
military reasons. In the case of Dalny, the commercial port near
Port Arthur, he said that there would be further delay but that the
necessary regulations and arrangements were being hurried.[16] At
Washington the Japanese Chargé, Eki Hioki, assured Root that
nothing was further from the thought of the Imperial government
"than to attempt to monopolize the trade of Manchuria in viola-

15 Sammons to Bacon, March 10, 1906, Consular Letters, Niuchwang, VII, Department of State Records, National Archives, Washington, D.C.
16 Wilson to Root, telegram, April 6, 1906, *Foreign Relations, 1906*, I, 177–178. In a
formal note on April 11 Saionji confirmed these oral assurances. Wilson to Root,
April 12, 1906, *Foreign Relations, 1906*, I, 178–180.

tion of the principles of the open door and equal opportunity for which they have pledged their honor." [17]

In opening Manchuria to foreign trade the Japanese government was responding not only to the representations of foreign powers but also to a growing demand for such a policy within Japan. Ito, Saionji, Kato, and many other Japanese statesmen favored a strict observance of the open door for equal commercial opportunity. The articulate elements of the nation as represented in important newspapers also supported such a policy. The leading independent newspaper of Japan, the *Jiji Shimpo*, gave its powerful support to the open door policy. In an editorial on March 28, 1906, it stated that the opening of Manchuria was a measure demanding the most thorough and energetic attention.[18] In a later editorial the *Jiji Shimpo* argued that it was to Japan's self-interest to have other powers share with it the task of developing Manchuria, for Japan did not have the necessary capital to accomplish the object alone.[19] The *Nichi Nichi Shimbun*, the organ of Takaaki Kato, stated that nothing would be more disadvantageous to Japan than to incur the disfavor of the powers by violating the principle of the open door.[20]

Soon after the announcement that South Manchuria would be opened, Saionji left for the continent to make a month-long personal inspection tour. By the middle of April, the evacuation of Japanese troops was almost completed, but the administrative organization in Manchuria was slow to withdraw. Saionji was determined to get the generals out along with the privates. The army leaders accused the Prime Minister of going beyond his sphere, but Saionji had forestalled any serious opposition to his trip by securing the approval of Yamagata.[21] On May 16 the tour was completed, and the Prime Minister returned to Tokyo. Events followed in rapid succession. On the twentieth he appointed to the Foreign Ministry Viscount Tadasu Hayashi, a known anglophile (he had negotiated the Anglo-Japanese Alliance in 1902) and a firm supporter of the open door policy for Manchuria. Two days later a

17 Memorandum by Hioki, April 12, 1906, *Foreign Relations, 1906*, I, 180–181.
18 *Jiji Shimpo*, March 28, 1906.
19 *Jiji Shimpo*, April 25, 1906.
20 *Nichi Nichi Shimbun*, April 11, 1906.
21 Yasaburo Takekoshi, *Prince Saionji*, trans. by Kozaki Kariaki, Kyoto, 1933, p. 228.

crucial meeting of the Elder Statesmen (Genro) and other government leaders took place at Saionji's residence. The showdown between the civilian and military leaders was at hand.

Marquis Ito came from Seoul to attend the meeting, and he was the dominant figure in the proceedings. He boldly took the military to task. He told of his great apprehension on learning of the protests of the United States and Britain. But even more important than this, he said, was the reaction of China to the actions of Japan in Manchuria. "My opinion is," he informed the assembled leaders, "that Japan's attitude toward China should always be that of a friend and adviser." Judging from the information he had received, said Ito, the military authorities in Manchuria seemed to be laboring under the impression that inasmuch as the time for evacuating troops had been extended to April, 1907, it was perfectly in order for them to take measures that were permissible only under wartime conditions. To remedy this situation Ito proposed the immediate abolishment of the whole system of military government in Manchuria.

The military leaders did their best to postpone any decision. General Masataki Terauchi said that it was too difficult to go into all the details of Ito's proposal, though he agreed with it "on general principles." Ito countered that it would not do merely to agree on general principles. Appropriate steps must be taken to carry out the measure. To this General Gentaro Kodama said that those who had the responsibility could not proceed in so careless a fashion. "The future of South Manchuria is likely to be of varied interest to Japan," he observed. Ito retorted that Kodama and others were laboring under a fundamental misconception regarding Japan's position in Manchuria. Japan's rights there were only those assigned by Russia under the terms of the peace treaty, namely the lease of the Liaotūng peninsula and the railway. Manchuria was not a dependency of Japan's; it was a part of Imperial China. There was no justification, he concluded, for Japan to exercise rights of sovereignty within that area. Saionji came to the support of Ito, and their views prevailed. It was decided to abolish the military administration as soon as possible.[22]

22 Kengi Hamada, *Prince Ito*, Tokyo, 1936, pp. 213–222; Documents relating to the

The decision of the council of May 22 came at an auspicious time in Japanese-American relations. Four days after that meeting, the first American Ambassador to Japan, Luke E. Wright, presented his credentials to the Emperor. At the time of the Portsmouth Peace Conference, Japan had indicated the desire to signal its entrance into the circle of major powers by exchanging ambassadors with the United States, and in the succeeding months the project was carried forward. Japan's Minister at Washington, Takahira, left on leave in December, 1905, hoping to return as his country's first ambassador to the United States. Just before going out of office, however, the Katsura cabinet named to the post Viscount Siuzo Aoki, a distinguished diplomat who had twice served as Foreign Minister under Yamagata. In appointing an ambassador to Tokyo, Roosevelt likewise wished to send a man of high standing. Minister Griscom was regarded by Roosevelt as one of his finest diplomats, but he was a young man with his career ahead of him. Griscom was therefore sent as Ambassador to Brazil, and Roosevelt offered the post to Joseph H. Choate, who had recently returned from his post as Ambassador at London. Choate declined the offer, and the position went to Luke E. Wright of Tennessee, who was then serving as Governor General of the Philippines.

Soon after his arrival in Japan, Wright had several talks with Foreign Minister Hayashi, and he was convinced that Japan would observe the open door for equal commercial opportunity in Manchuria. In a personal letter to Roosevelt, he said that at least all surface indications showed that Japan intended to play fair, although it might be somewhat slow in making good. Hayashi had assured him that the difficulty with the military officers had practically been overcome and that Manchuria would be speedily thrown open to trade. Aside from this assurance, said Wright, the press of Japan was almost unanimous in its support of such a policy and the men who controlled Japan appreciated the necessity of retaining the good will of the powers. The United States need not ap-

conference held at the Prime Minister's residence in 1906 concerning the Manchurian problem (Meiji 39-nen Manshū mondai ni kansi Shushō kantei ni kyōgikai kaisai ikken), MT 1.1.2.42, Japanese Ministry of Foreign Affairs Archives, microfilm collection, Library of Congress, Washington, D.C.

prehend bad faith, Wright concluded, though "gentle pressure" might be necessary from time to time.[23]

Wright's confidence in Japan's good faith did not diminish with the passage of time. In August, 1906, he reported to Root that the policy of equal opportunity for all nations in the commerce of Manchuria was fixed and would be adhered to by Japan. He said that he had sought information from all sources to ascertain whether the Japanese, under the cover of military occupation, were pushing their goods into Manchuria and trying to gain control of the market before turning over that territory to China. He was satisfied that comparatively small quantities of Japanese goods were going into Manchuria. He said he was well aware that American commercial interests were suspicious of Japan but in his judgment "without any sufficient reason therefor." [24]

Rockhill, at Peking, was just as emphatic regarding Japan's observance of the open door. On October 11, 1906, he reported to Root that, while cases of discrimination against American-owned merchandise may have taken place in Manchuria, no specific cases had been brought to the attention of the Consul General at New-chwang. Rockhill reminded the Department of State that conditions had been constantly changing in Manchuria during the last year through the gradual withdrawal of Japanese forces and that trade had been necessarily dislocated. Added to this was the apparent indifference of American commercial interests. He pointed out that much of the American merchandise was handled by foreign or Japanese firms who either imported direct from the United States or procured American products through commission houses at Shanghai. Regarding the American trading interests at Shanghai, Rockhill said that a recent visit of three agents to Manchuria was the first that had been made to a market only eight hundred miles away. This apparent lack of interest, said Rockhill, discriminated more against American trade interests than any other cause, be it Japanese or Chinese.[25]

23 Wright to Roosevelt, June 7, 1906, Roosevelt Papers.
24 Wright to Root, August 11, 1906, *Foreign Relations, 1906*, 217–218.
25 Rockhill to Root, October 11, 1906, State Department File 551/13. (Printed in part in *Foreign Relations, 1906*, I, 225–226). In August, 1906, the Department of State abandoned the archaic filing system wherein documents were filed by country in

The widespread alarm created by the alleged violations of the open door by Japan gradually subsided during the fall of 1906 as normal conditions were restored in Manchuria. During the summer and fall of that year the gradual withdrawal of the military administration had been proceeding, though not as rapidly as had been hoped at the time of the council meeting of May 22. Shortly after that meeting, General Yoshimasa Oshima, the commander of Japanese forces in Manchuria, moved his headquarters from Liaoyang to Port Arthur. Then on June 1, at a banquet given by the Japanese military administration at Mukden, it was formally announced that the evacuation of troops had been completed and that immediate steps would be taken to restore the administration of a large part of South Manchuria to Chinese control.

This objective was not easy to carry out. Rockhill reported on June 29 that the Chinese government was displaying an extraordinary lack of energy, even for it, in taking over the administration of Manchuria.[26] In August the Japanese military administration closed its offices in Mukden, Liaoyang, Tieling, and other smaller places. In the following months the restoration of the remaining territory continued to be complicated by China's seemingly calculated policy of delay. Rockhill noted that the Chinese found this policy advantageous, for the resulting foreign complaints against Japan strengthened China's position with regard to Japan.[27] With the restoration of Newchwang to Chinese control in December, 1906, the Japanese administration was virtually ended, though it was not officially dissolved until April, 1907, when the newly created South Manchuria Railway Company assumed control of the Japanese owned railway lines in South Manchuria.

Thus by the end of 1906 the open door policy for equal commercial opportunity was more firmly established in South Manchuria than it had ever been when Russian influence reigned supreme in the Three Eastern Provinces. This did not mean, how-

volumes marked "Despatches," "Instructions," "Notes to," and "Notes from," and a new subject file system was adopted. This system, designated officially as the Numerical Series, was used until 1910 when the decimal file system was instituted. See Bibliography for a list of important subject files relating to Japanese-American relations during 1906–1910.

26 Rockhill to Root, June 29, 1906, Despatches: China, CXXX.

27 Rockhill to Root, August 15, 1906, S. D. File 551/10–11.

ever, that equality in every respect would prevail in Manchuria. In addition to a commercial interest in South Manchuria, Japan possessed a strategic interest and a capitalistic investment interest, and these interests Tokyo wished to share with no one. By the summer of 1907 the Japanese government had made no claim to *exclusive* investment rights in South Manchuria, but Japan's interests there were so substantial that little doubt existed that Japan would claim a *predominant* role in investment in the area. The Portsmouth treaty did not allot Japan a perfect sphere of influence, as the Germans possessed in Shantung with their exclusive investment rights, but Japan's vast railway enterprises and the naval base at Port Arthur gave her at least a limited sphere of influence.

Japan's position in South Manchuria solidified in the summer of 1907 with the conclusion of important treaties with France and Russia. In June France and Japan signed a treaty recognizing that each possessed a special interest in preserving peace and order in China, "especially in the regions of the Chinese Empire adjoining the territories where they possess rights of sovereignty, protection or occupation." [28] The following month Japan signed a secret treaty with Russia of even greater importance. By its terms a line of demarcation was drawn between the Japanese and Russian spheres of interest in Manchuria, and each engaged not to seek concessions for railways and telegraphs in the other's sphere.[29]

Thus there came into being in Manchuria a situation roughly similar to the one Hay had anticipated when he issued his famous notes in 1899 and 1900. Equality for commercial opportunity existed, but side by side with this were the spheres of influence that entailed preferential investment rights and political influence. Commercial equality was all that Hay had contended for. Though never specifically sanctioning the spheres of influence, he had accepted them as existing facts. In 1907 the facts still existed.

Where Hay's second principle, the integrity of China, fitted in was not yet clear. Certainly the spheres of influence that already existed seriously compromised China's sovereignty, but how far

28 Text in John V. A. MacMurray, *Treaties and Agreements With and Concerning China, 1894–1919*, 2 vols., New York, 1921, I, 640.

29 Text in Ernest B. Price, *The Russo-Japanese Treaties of 1907–1916 Concerning Manchuria and Mongolia*, Baltimore, 1933, pp. 107–111.

would Russia and Japan further compromise that sovereignty? And what stand would the Roosevelt administration take if China's sovereignty were further threatened? Would it beat an ignoble retreat, as it had done during 1901–03, or would it become — albeit reluctantly — the defender of China's sovereignty in Manchuria? Before that question was answered, in the summer and fall of 1908, Tokyo and Washington would be beset with still more difficult problems with the rise of the immigration issue.

CHAPTER EIGHT

The School Segregation Crisis

ON October 21, 1906, Ambassador Luke Wright sent from Tokyo a hurriedly written telegram to the Department:

> All newspapers here publish despatches from the United States giving accounts of agitation in San Francisco for exclusion of Japanese, including alleged hostile utterances of member of Congress Kahn in public speeches; also action of school authorities in segregating Japanese children in public schools. . . .[1]

Thus began the most serious diplomatic crisis that had yet arisen in Japanese-American relations, a crisis that was to leave such ugly memories on both sides of the Pacific that the cordiality that had characterized previous relations could never be fully restored.

Wright's telegram caught Washington by surprise. Root replied to Wright that the trouble was so local that the Department did not know of its existence until the newspapers were checked.[2] The telegram apparently caught Roosevelt off guard, too, but the President was by no means uninformed on the background of the question. Roosevelt had been watching the situation in California for over a year, and by October, 1906, he already had some definite ideas regarding the problem.

The anti-Japanese agitation on the Pacific coast was of comparatively recent origin. In 1880 only about one hundred and fifty Japanese resided in the United States. Beginning in 1891, however, they began to enter in increasing numbers. In 1898 the number of Japanese arriving in the continental United States totaled more than two thousand. With the acquisition of Hawaii in that year, the sixty thousand Japanese in the islands were eligible to enter the

[1] Wright to Root, telegram, October 21, 1906, S. D. File 1797.
[2] Root to Wright, telegram, October 23, 1906, S. D. File 1797.

continental United States without passports. In 1900 over twelve thousand Japanese arrived in Hawaii and the continental United States from Japan. In that year came the first protests against the Japanese, and in August, 1900, the Japanese government announced that no further passports would be issued to laborers desiring to go to the mainland United States.[3] This restriction was not enforced vigorously, and it was ineffective in any case. Japanese laborers could secure a passport for Hawaii and proceed from there to the mainland. Once they reached Hawaii in American territory, immigration authorities had no legal way to prevent their coming to the mainland, regardless of any restriction in their passports. Japanese laborers could likewise enter through Canada and Mexico. In 1902 arrivals in the continental United States totaled over five thousand and in 1904 nearly eight thousand.[4]

In the early months of 1905, when the Japanese were winning great victories in their war with Russia, the anti-Japanese campaign on the Pacific coast of the United States took definite form. On February 23 of that year, the San Francisco *Chronicle* published a nine-column article on the subject of Japanese immigration. Among the numerous arguments advanced in support of its stand, the newspaper devoted particular attention to the expected influx of discharged soldiers at the close of the Russo-Japanese War. On March 1, 1905, less than a week after the *Chronicle* article was printed, a resolution was introduced into the California state legislature which called upon the California delegation in Congress to make representations to the Secretary of State and to the President urging the limitation of Japanese immigration. The resolution, which characterized the Japanese immigrants as "immoral, intemperate, quarrelsome men bound to labor for a pittance," was passed unanimously by both houses of the state legislature.[5] Then

3 Minister A. E. Buck to Hay, August 13, 1900, Despatches: Japan, LXXIV.

4 Statistics are given in Yamato Ichihashi, *Japanese in the United States: A Critical Study of the Problems of the Japanese Immigrants and Their Children*, Stanford, 1932 chs. ii and iv; Jesse Frederick Steiner, *The Japanese Invasion: A Study in the Psychology of Inter-Racial Contacts*, Chicago, 1917, p. 50; and United States, Department of the Treasury, *Annual Report of the United States Superintendent of Immigration*, Washington, 1891–1906.

5 *The Journal of the Assembly during the Thirty-sixth Session of the Legislature of the State of California, 1905*, Sacramento, 1905, p. 1554; *The Journal of the Senate*

on May 7, 1905, a mass meeting was held in San Francisco at which the Japanese and Korean Exclusion League was launched. Late in 1906 the League claimed a membership of 78,500 in California alone, three-fourths of whom were said to live in San Francisco.[6]

While these developments were taking place, President Roosevelt was watching the situation with deep interest. From his friend George Kennan, who was in the Far East covering the Russo-Japanese War, he learned of the Japanese reaction to these events. "It isn't the exclusion of a few emigrants that hurts here . . . ," Kennan wrote to Roosevelt, "it's the putting of Japanese below Hungarians, Italians, Syrians, Polish Jews, and degraded nondescripts from all parts of Europe and western Asia. No proud, high spirited and victorious people will submit to such a classification as that, especially when it is made with insulting reference to personal character and habits."[7] Roosevelt replied that he felt even worse than Kennan about the action of "the idiots of the California Legislature." The legislature had a right to protest against the admission of Japanese laborers, wrote Roosevelt, and he would not have objected to a resolution that was courteous and proper, but he was humiliated by the foolish offensiveness of the resolution that was passed. As for the character of the Japanese, he said he regarded them as a highly civilized people, and he was mortified that any Americans should insult them.[8]

During the summer of 1905 Roosevelt had considerable correspondence with Lodge regarding the Japanese question, and to the Senator he was even more emphatic in expressing his views. On May 15 he wrote:

Meanwhile, I am utterly disgusted at the manifestations which have begun to appear on the Pacific slope in favor of excluding the Japanese exactly as the Chinese are excluded. The California State Legislature and various other bodies have acted in the worst possible taste and in the most offensive

during the Thirty-sixth Session of the Legislature of the State of California, 1905, Sacramento, 1905, pp. 1165–1166.

[6] United States, President, Japanese in the City of San Francisco, California, Message from the President . . . Transmitting the Final Report of Secretary Metcalf on the Situation Affecting the Japanese in the City of San Francisco, California, Senate Documents, 59th Congress, 2nd Session, no. 147, Washington, 1906. Hereafter cited as Metcalf Report.

[7] Kennan to Roosevelt, April 1, 1905, Roosevelt Papers.

[8] Roosevelt to Kennan, May 6, 1906, Morison, Roosevelt Letters, IV, 1168–70.

manner to Japan. Yet the Senators and Congressmen from these very states were lukewarm about the navy last year. It gives me a feeling of contempt and disgust to see them challenge Japanese hostility and justify by their actions any feeling the Japanese might have against us, while at the same time refusing to take steps to defend themselves against the formidable foe whom they are ready with such careless insolence to antagonize. How people can act in this way with the Russo-Japanese war going on before their eyes I cannot understand. I do all I can to counteract the effects, but I cannot accomplish everything.[9]

In June, when recounting to Lodge his efforts to bring Japan and Russia together for peace negotiations, Roosevelt again took up the California question. He said that he had little doubt that the Japanese would have their heads turned to some extent by the victories over Russia, but the Japanese could not behave worse than the state of California. The feeling there, he said, was "as foolish as if conceived by the mind of a Hottentot." In this letter to Lodge, Roosevelt summed up the policy that he was to follow throughout the years of crisis with Japan (1906–07):

I hope that we can persuade our people on the one hand to act in a spirit of generous justice and genuine courtesy toward Japan, and on the other hand to keep the navy respectable in numbers and more than respectable in the efficiency of its units. If we act thus we need not fear the Japanese. But if as Brooks Adams says, we show ourselves "opulent, aggressive and unarmed," the Japanese may sometime work us an injury. In any event we can hold our own in the future, whether against Japan or Germany, whether on the Atlantic or the Pacific, only if we occupy the position of the just man armed — that is, if we do the exact reverse of what the demagogues on the one hand and the mugwumps on the other would like to have us do.[10]

Roosevelt also wrote to Minister Griscom regarding the Pacific coast trouble and asked for detailed information on the status of foreigners in Japan.[11] Griscom responded with a long memorandum on the subject. Summing up his findings, he stated that the only important restriction imposed on foreigners was that they were denied the right to own land in fee simple. Even this restriction was successfully circumvented by various legal devices.[12] "On the

9 Roosevelt to Lodge, May 15, 1906, Morison, *Roosevelt Letters*, V, 1179–1182.
10 Roosevelt to Lodge, June 5, 1905, Morison, *Roosevelt Letters*, IV, 1202–06.
11 Roosevelt to Griscom, May 19, 1905, Roosevelt Papers.
12 From a Japanese subject a foreigner could obtain a conveyance to his heirs and assigns of land for a thousand years under a "superfices" title, the superficiary being

whole," wrote Griscom, "foreigners are very well treated and as far as I am aware there has not been a single case since we gave up extraterritoriality in 1899 where an American has been denied justice in the Japanese courts." [13] If Roosevelt hoped to acquire ammunition to use with the Japanese diplomats, he must have been disappointed, for Griscom's report showed that the Japanese were setting a high mark.

The Pacific coast question did not become a diplomatic issue in the summer of 1905. Roosevelt was sufficiently concerned about the matter, however, to send a personal message to the Japanese government through Griscom stating that the American government and people "have not the slightest sympathy with the outrageous agitation against the Japanese." [14] He made it clear to the Japanese and to his correspondents that his sympathies were with the Japanese in this issue. To Spring Rice he confided his fears for the future and his determination to protect the Japanese:

Some of the people on the Pacific coast under the lead of the San Francisco labor unions apparently think this a good time to insult the Japanese. They will not do one thing against them while I am President — I won't let them — but they may create an ugly feeling of distrust — and of course they are of exactly the type which positively refuses to prepare for the trouble which they are willing to bring about.[15]

After the flare-up in the summer of 1905, the anti-Japanese campaign subsided until April, 1906. In that month came the appalling earthquake and fire in San Francisco, bringing with it a wave of lawlessness and disorder. Between May 6 and November 5, 1906, there occurred two hundred and ninety cases of assault, and many of the victims were Japanese. The most unfortunate of these assaults were those upon Dr. F. Omori and Professor T. Nakamura of the Imperial University at Tokyo. These men, who had been sent to make an investigation of the earthquake, were repeatedly stoned and attacked during the summer of 1906 as they pursued their investigations.[16] Such attacks seemed particularly reprehensi-

---

designated as one who had the right to use another person's land for the purpose of owning thereon structures or trees.

13 Griscom to Roosevelt, June 29, 1905, Roosevelt Papers.

14 Roosevelt to Griscom, July 15, 1905, Roosevelt Papers.

15 Roosevelt to Spring Rice, July 24, 1905, Morison, *Roosevelt Letters*, IV, 1286.

16 *Metcalf Report.*

ble to the Japanese in view of the fact that their government and Red Cross had contributed $246,000 for the relief of San Francisco, more than all other foreign nations combined.

Another manifestation of anti-Japanese sentiment in San Francisco which followed in the wake of the earthquake was the boycotts against Japanese restaurants. Before the earthquake there were only eight of these establishments which served food to Americans, but following the fire about thirty opened for business. In June, 1906, the Exclusion League protested that many union men were patronizing these places, and it began a vigorous campaign against them. A concise statement of the nature of these boycotts was given by Ambassador Aoki to Root on October 25, 1906:

The restaurants which have thus been made victims of boycotts, are ones in which the food served is not cooked in the Japanese style but the cuisine is entirely European or American, although the proprietors and cooks and other employees are exclusively Japanese. Those restaurants are thus patronized no less by Americans than by the Japanese and other foreign residents of San Francisco. The boycotters linger about the restaurants and accost all customers who approach, giving them small match-boxes bearing the words "white men and women patronize your own race." When this is not effective, they frequently stand in front of the doors of the restaurants so as to bar the entrance and prevent customers from going in.[17]

While the attacks and boycotts were taking place in San Francisco, an event in the far north Pacific stirred feeling on both sides of the ocean. On July 16 and 17 the American authorities on St. Paul Island, in repelling a series of raids on the seal rookeries by Japanese poachers, killed five of them, wounded two, and captured twelve. The *Japan Times* stated on August 10 that though it may be found that the men deserved their fate, it would be a false forbearance to try to make it appear that the Japanese nation had received the news of the killings with anything like indifference. The incident also inflamed the people of San Francisco, for reports soon came describing the barbarity of the poaching raid. An official report by the Department of Commerce and Labor revealed that many of the seals were skinned alive and that a number were found half-skinned and still living. The San Franciscans naturally

17 Aoki to Root, October 25, 1906, S. D. File 1797/5.

found in the incident confirmation of their views regarding the character of the Japanese.

Roosevelt's reaction to the incident was in line with his characteristic policy of keeping his powder dry. He wrote to Secretary of the Navy Charles J. Bonaparte that although he did not for a moment anticipate trouble from the Japanese over the issue, he felt that the navy should have possible contingencies clearly in view. He was particularly concerned over the naval ships which were in the Pacific, for the force was too weak to resist attack and too valuable to throw away. He therefore instructed Bonaparte to order the ships out of Asiatic waters as speedily as possible.[18]

By the fall of 1906 events at San Francisco were moving rapidly to a climax. The Exclusion League, which since its inception had advocated segregation of Japanese school children, on August 23 made renewed representations to the San Francisco school board. Then on October 11, 1906, that board passed the fateful resolution which was soon to produce the crisis in Japanese-American relations:

> *Resolved*, that in accordance with Article X, section 1662, of the school law of California, principals are hereby directed to send all Chinese, Japanese, or Korean children to the Oriental Public School, situated on the south

18 Roosevelt to Bonaparte, August 10, 1906, Morison, *Roosevelt Letters*, V, 353. The report of the Department of Commerce and Labor and all the diplomatic records on the issue are found in S. D. File 290. The killing of these Japanese poachers led to a tedious diplomatic exchange extending to May, 1908. Japan pointed out that under the Alaskan Criminal Code seal poaching was not a felony but a misdemeanor and that killing to prevent a misdemeanor was not justified. The Department knew that the Japanese were on sound ground, for James B. Scott, the legal adviser to the Department, had drawn up a memorandum in which he concluded that those who killed the poachers were guilty of murder. Japan demanded that an investigation be made, but the United States refused. The feeling of the Department of State was well expressed by Assistant Solicitor William C. Dennis in a memorandum of September 10, 1907: "The circumstances of a pelagic seal raid in a wild country like Alaska, carried on by armed raiders and accompanied by a brutal and cruel slaughter of the seal herd, put a severe strain on the common-law doctrine defining the rights of misdemeanants. It has not been so long since Kipling could say 'There is never a law of God or man runs north of Fifty-three,' and it may well be that the methods of those heroic days are still sometimes morally justifiable irrespective of the provisions of the penal code." The diplomatic issue was finally closed on May, 1908, when Root presented to Ambassador Takahira the arguments of Attorney General Bonaparte that the poachers were "burglars," that burglary was a felony, and that the killing of a felon to prevent his escape was justified.

side of Clay street, between Powell and Mason streets, on and after October 15, 1906.[19]

The Japanese Consul at San Francisco, S. Uyeno, immediately filed a protest with the board, but he was advised that the board would not reverse its decision.[20]

News of the school board's resolution soon reached Japan, and by October 20 the Japanese people evidenced great concern. The Tokyo correspondent of the New York *Sun* wired that during his nineteen years of residence in Japan he had "never seen the Japanese press so agitated against the Americans." [21] The opposition *Hochi Shimbun* advocated retaliatory measures and castigated the "incapable" Japanese authorities "who sit idly by and look at the affair like disinterested parties." [22] The jingoistic *Mainichi Shimbun* was ready to go to war:

> The whole world knows that the poorly equipped army and navy of the United States are no match for our efficient army and navy. It will be an easy work to awake the United States from her dream of obstinacy when one of our great Admirals appears on the other side of the Pacific. . . . Why do we not insist on sending ships? [23]

Fortunately, the jingo press did not represent the predominant reaction in Japan. The Japanese people undoubtedly were stunned and saddened, but the moderation manifested in the independent and government organs more accurately registered the feelings of the people. The government-subsidized *Japan Times* stated that the anti-Japanese movement was a local phenomenon and, if wisely dealt with, would soon become a thing of the past.[24] The government organ *Kokumin Shimbun* said that the Japanese people would make a serious mistake to consider the voice of the Pacific

19 *Metcalf Report.*
20 Uyeno to the San Francisco School Board, October 12, 1906, and San Francisco School Board to Uyeno, October 22, 1906, Documents Relating to the Limitation and Exclusion of Japanese Immigrants by the United States (Hokubei Gasshūkoku ni oite hompō-jin tōkō seigen oyobi haiseki ikken), MT3.8.2.21, reels 720–727, Japanese Ministry of Foreign Affairs Archives, microfilm collection, Library of Congress, Washington, D.C., reel 721, pp. 2004–05, 2019–20.
21 Washington *Herald*, October 22, 1906.
22 *Hochi Shimbun*, October 20, 1906.
23 *Mainichi Shimbun*, October 22, 1906.
24 *Japan Times*, October 20, 1906.

coast as the voice of the majority of the American nation. It then went on to remind its readers that "the United States has in President Roosevelt a man of distinguished statesmanship and a high order of wisdom, whose ideals are righteousness and humanity." [25] The independent *Jiji Shimpo*, perhaps the most influential newspaper in Japan, was confident that the issue would not cause any serious estrangement in Japanese-American friendship:

> The traditional friendship existing between Japan and the United States can never be wiped out in a single day. The power that binds together the two countries and the two nations comes from a source far more profound than might be imagined, and there is absolutely no fear that any little complication should cut this strong cord of friendship asunder.[26]

Despite the moderation of the more responsible organs of the press, Ambassador Wright was under no illusions concerning the seriousness of the crisis. Other incidents had occurred early in October which also had aroused feeling in Japan: the murder of a Japanese banker in San Francisco; the reported statement of Congressman Julius Kahn of California that he hoped war with Japan would soon be declared; and the reported accusation by John D. Rockefeller that the Japanese were guilty of commercial treachery.[27] Wright realized, however, that these incidents assumed significance largely because of the segregation issue. In his telegram to the Department on October 21 he stated that the exclusion of children from the schools had given "the deepest offense." [28] In a dispatch sent on the following day, Wright elaborated on his views. It was his conviction that the Japanese had a more disinterested regard for Americans than for any other foreigners, even their British allies, and that this sentiment was sincere, genuine, and general. A few more incidents such as those which had occurred, however, might result in a boycott or some other form of retaliation. The segregation of Japanese children provoked the most in-

25 *Kokumin Shimbun*, October 20, 1906.

26 *Jiji Shimpo*, October 17, 1906.

27 The resentment stirred by these incidents was not altogether justified. Robbery was the primary motive in the killing of the Japanese banker. Congressman Kahn's remarks were correctly quoted, but Rockefeller insisted that he had been misquoted. Thomas A. Bailey, *Theodore Roosevelt and the Japanese American Crises*, Stanford, 1934, pp. 54–55.

28 Wright to Root, telegram, October 21, 1906, S. D. File 1797.

dignation, he said, because it was the action of government officials and because it indicated racial hostility. From a remark by Hayashi, he concluded that there was special sensitiveness upon the latter point.[29]

The Department of State was not so quick to perceive the seriousness of the crisis. Adee, the Second Assistant Secretary of State, noted in a memorandum for Root that it appeared that Wright had sent his telegram of October 21 after a disquieting talk with the Tokyo correspondent of the New York *Sun*.[30] When Root telegraphed a reply to Wright, he said that the information he possessed indicated only an ordinary local labor controversy in San Francisco. The trouble about the schools, he said, appeared to have arisen from the fact that the schools which the Japanese had attended were destroyed by the earthquake. Root said, however, that the President had directed the Department of Justice to make a full investigation and that Wright might assure the Japanese government in most positive terms that the United States government would not for a moment entertain the idea of any treatment toward the Japanese people other than that accorded to the people of the most friendly European nation.[31]

The first Japanese representations appeared just a few days after Wright's telegram to Washington. On October 23 Foreign Minister Hayashi telegraphed instructions to Ambassador Aoki telling him to call the serious attention of the Secretary of State to the conditions in San Francisco. The situation there, said Hayashi, was daily growing worse, and already Japanese children were excluded from the ordinary schools, Japanese restaurants were boycotted, and Japanese residents were subject to personal violence. The segregation of the children, he said, carried with it a stigma that would be deeply and justly resented by all Japanese. Hayashi even expressed a veiled hint of possible retaliatory measures by Japan. The Japanese feeling of sorrow, he said, "up to this time is unmixed with any suggestion of retaliation because it is firmly believed that the evil will be speedily removed." Hayashi rested Japan's case on the most-

29 Wright to Root, October 22, 1906, S. D. File 1797/40–46.
30 Memorandum appended to clipping of Tokyo correspondent's report as it appeared in the Washington *Herald* for October 22, 1906, S. D. File 1797.
31 Root to Wright, telegram, October 23, 1906, S. D. File 1797.

favored-nation clause of the Japanese-American treaty of commerce of 1894.[32]

Ambassador Aoki had a long conference with Root on October 25 and left with the Secretary two unsigned memoranda and a paraphrase of his instructions from Tokyo. The memoranda were not formal protests, but they embodied detailed statements of the Japanese grievances concerning the boycotting of Japanese restaurants and assaults on Japanese in San Francisco and concerning the segregation of Japanese school children in San Francisco. In giving Root a paraphrase of his instructions, Aoki toned down Hayashi's statement, omitting any reference to possible retaliation. It was nevertheless made clear that Japan deeply resented the segregation. Aoki's paraphrase said that even though the schools provided for Japanese children were equally as good as those provided for others, the segregation constituted "an act of discrimination carrying with it a stigma and odium which it is impossible to overlook." [33] Aoki felt considerably reassured after his talk with Root. He telegraphed Hayashi that the President was determined to do everything within the power of the government to correct injustice and abuses.[34]

Roosevelt immediately took the matter in hand. On the day following Aoki's representation, he announced that Secretary of Commerce and Labor Victor H. Metcalf was being sent to California, his native state, to investigate the situation. At Roosevelt's suggestion Root prepared a confidential memorandum setting forth the arguments Metcalf would present to the authorities in California.[35] Root stressed the proud and sensitive nature of the Japanese people. One-tenth of the insults the United States had visited upon China would result in war with Japan, said Root, and Japan

---

32 Hayashi to Aoki, October 23, 1906, Telegram Series, LXXXVII, 9087–88.

33 Notes on the Boycotting of Japanese Restaurants and Assaults on Japanese Residents in San Francisco, October 25, 1906; Notes on the Exclusion of Japanese Children from the Public Schools of San Francisco, October 25, 1906; Paraphrase of the Instructions Received from the Imperial Government, October 25, 1906, S. D. File 1797/4–6.

34 Aoki to Hayashi, received October 26, 1906, Telegram Series, LXXXVII, 8297–98. Most of the telegrams from Washington to Tokyo bear only the date they were received at the Foreign Ministry.

35 Loeb to Root, October 26, 1906, Elihu Root Papers, Library of Congress, Washington, D.C.

was ready for war. Furthermore, Japanese hostility would result in enormous injury to American trade in the Orient, and this would have a profound effect upon the trade and prosperity of the Pacific coast. As for the school segregation, Root said that it clearly violated the treaty of 1894 and that the entire power of the federal government "within the limits of the Constitution" would be promptly and vigorously used to enforce the observance of treaties.[36]

Roosevelt's private correspondence during the first days of the crisis reveals that he was deeply concerned. In response to a telegram from Baron Kaneko, he wrote:

The movement in question is giving me the gravest concern. It is so purely local that we never heard of it here in Washington until we got dispatches from Tokyo speaking of the trouble it had caused in Japan. . . . I shall exert all the power I have under the Constitution to protect the rights of the Japanese who are here, and I shall deal with the subject at length in my message to Congress. . . . The action of these people in San Francisco no more represents American sentiment as a whole than the action of the Japanese seal pirates last summer represented Japanese sentiment.[37]

To Senator Lodge he wrote: "Just at present the labor unions of San Francisco bid fair to embroil us with Japan." [38] To his son Kermit he confided:

I am being horribly bothered about the Japanese business. The infernal fools in California, and especially in San Francisco, insult the Japanese recklessly, and in the event of war it will be the Nation as a whole which will pay the consequences. However I hope to keep things straight. I am perfectly willing that this Nation should fight any nation if it has got to, but I would loathe to see it forced into a war in which it was wrong.[39]

Roosevelt did not believe war would come at that moment, but he knew that the crisis was serious and, if not resolved, would become worse.[40] Therefore, while doing everything in his power to

36 Confidential memorandum for Secretary Metcalf, October 27, 1906, S. D. File 1797/13.

37 Roosevelt to Kaneko, October 26, 1906, Morison, *Roosevelt Letters*, V, 473.

38 Roosevelt to Lodge, October 27, 1906, Roosevelt Papers.

39 Roosevelt to Kermit Roosevelt, October 27, 1906, Morison, *Roosevelt Letters*, V, 475–476.

40 Roosevelt to Senator Eugene Hale, October 27, 1906, Morison, *Roosevelt Letters*, V, 473–475.

work out a peaceful solution, he took steps to prepare for war. On October 27 he asked Acting Secretary of the Navy Truman H. Newberry for an exact comparison of Japanese and American naval ships. He also wanted to know if the General Board was studying the plan of operation in the event of hostilities. Three days later Newberry sent to Roosevelt a report by Admiral George Dewey, President of the General Board, stating that the Board had already completed plans which would give the United States sufficient preponderance of force to enable it to command the sea in Eastern waters within ninety days.[41] The comparison of ships which Newberry sent to the President showed that the United States possessed twelve battleships ready for action, four being repaired, and eight building. Japan had only five battleships ready for action, five being repaired, and three building. Counting only those ships that would be available by the summer of 1907, the United States had a preponderance of twenty to twelve.[42] Roosevelt must have felt greatly reassured on seeing these figures.

It is difficult to gauge how genuine was Roosevelt's concern about the possibilities of war with Japan. He doubtless believed that war was a serious possibility in future years, but he also had in view a more immediate object: the building up of the United States navy. He was not reluctant to capitalize upon the crisis with Japan to further the naval construction program. During 1902–05 he had persuaded Congress to authorize ten battleships and, though he announced in December, 1905, that his program would in the future call for only a single battleship a year, the advent of the dreadnought and the beginning of trouble with Japan soon brought the scrapping of this one-ship-a-year program.[43] By the time the school segregation crisis broke out in October, 1906, Roosevelt was already waging a vigorous struggle to secure appropriations for the building of dreadnoughts.

[41] Dewey to Newberry, October 29, 1906, Roosevelt Papers.

[42] In coast defense ships the United States had eight, while Japan had five; in armored cruisers the United States had four ready and four building, while Japan had nine ready and four building; in cruisers the United States had eighteen ready and six building, while Japan had sixteen ready, one being repaired and one building. Newberry to Roosevelt, October 30, 1906, Roosevelt Papers.

[43] Harold and Margaret Sprout, *The Rise of American Naval Power, 1776–1918*, Princeton, 1946, pp. 259–264.

Admiral A. T. Mahan, by now a patriarch among naval experts, and Senator Eugene Hale, Chairman of the Senate Committee on Naval Affairs, were leading the fight against the big ships, while Roosevelt and Lieutenant Commander William S. Sims argued the opposite case.[44] Roosevelt found in the Japanese trouble a legitimate reason for naval expansion, but he seemed inclined to exaggerate the danger of war in order to get support for the construction of dreadnoughts. On October 27, at the height of the Japanese crisis, he wrote a long letter to Hale reviewing the crisis and advocating appropriations for two dreadnoughts:

I do not pretend to have the least idea as to Japan's policy or real feeling, whether towards us or toward anyone else. I do not think that she wishes war as such, and I doubt if she will go to war now; but I am very sure that if sufficiently irritated and humiliated by us she will get to accept us instead of Russia as the national enemy whom she will ultimately have to fight; and under such circumstances her concentration and continuity of purpose, and the exceedingly formidable character of her army and navy, make it necessary to reckon very seriously with her. It seems to me that all of this necessitates our having a definite policy with regard to her; a policy of behaving with absolute good faith, courtesy and justice to her on the one hand, and on the other, of keeping our navy in such shape as to make it a risky thing for Japan to go into war with us.[45]

Hale's reply made it plain that Roosevelt could not rely on him for support. The Senator said he had "not a particle of fear that we shall have war with Japan." As for the dreadnoughts, he was against the "monster ships" which he regarded as experimental, costly, and unwieldy.[46]

The reports emanating from Japan seemed to support Hale's view, so far as the immediate danger of war was concerned. Kaneko wrote to Roosevelt saying that the general tone of the press was now quite moderate and that the government and people fully understood and appreciated the President's attitude and sincerity.[47] Wright reported that the Japanese press was reflecting a quieter tone of confidence in the lasting friendship of the American peo-

44 Eric F. Goldman, *Charles J. Bonaparte, Patrician Reformer: His Earlier Career*, Baltimore, 1943, pp. 105–115.
45 Roosevelt to Hale, October 27, 1906, Morison, *Roosevelt Letters*, V, 473–475.
46 Hale to Roosevelt, October 31, 1906, Roosevelt Papers.
47 Kaneko to Roosevelt, October 31, 1906, Roosevelt Papers.

ple.[48] Wright had released Root's telegram of October 23 to the press and the result had been gratifying.[49] Even the sensational *Yorazu Choho* said that the reply should pacify the feelings of the Japanese people.[50] The opposition *Hochi Shimbun* expressed appreciation for Roosevelt's efforts to settle the issue,[51] while the *Jiji Shimpo* was even more friendly in tone:

> We the people of Japan profoundly regret that such a complication has arisen, and feel as if the private affairs of a harmonious family had been exposed to the general public on account of some little incident. We presume that thoughtful Americans are similarly impressed with the situation, and we hope that the authorities concerned in both countries will deal with the present trouble, as if they were to settle a family matter.[52]

Further reassurance of Japan's peaceful intentions was given on October 30 by the Japanese Ambassador at Paris, Shinichiro Kurino, in an interview in *Le Matin*. Kurino, who as Minister at Washington had signed the treaty of 1894, said that though the treaty had been violated, diplomacy alone would solve the difficulty. "Never has Japan been more desirous of perfect peace," he said.[53] Roosevelt was sufficiently reassured to leave on a scheduled trip to Panama on November 8. Before leaving, however, he authorized Root to use the armed forces, if necessary, to protect the Japanese if menaced by mobs or jeopardized in the rights guaranteed them under the treaty of 1894.[54]

During Roosevelt's absence from Washington, efforts were made in San Francisco to resolve the crisis. Secretary Metcalf arrived there on October 31 and immediately undertook an extensive investigation. He found that despite charges that Japanese children had been overcrowding the schools, only ninety-three Japanese pupils were enrolled in the twenty-three San Francisco schools on October 11, 1906. Other charges against the Japanese pupils were found to be equally specious. It had been alleged that many of the Japanese students were adults and that white girls of tender years

[48] Wright to Root, October 31, 1906, S. D. File 1797/55–58.
[49] Wright to Root, telegram, October 28, 1906, S. D. File 1797/14.
[50] *Yorazu Choho*, October 29, 1906.
[51] *Hochi Shimbun*, October 29, 1906.
[52] *Jiji Shimpo*, October 31, 1906.
[53] Robert S. McCormick to Root, November 2, 1906, S. D. File 1797/33–36.
[54] Roosevelt to Root, October 29, 1906, Morison, *Roosevelt Letters*, V, 484.

had to sit beside these "immoral" and "diseased" Japanese in the classrooms. Metcalf found, however, that though a number of older Japanese attended lower grades, only thirty-three of the ninety-three students were over fifteen years of age and of these the two oldest were twenty. The testimony of the teachers as to the exemplary conduct of the Japanese was overwhelmingly in their favor.[55]

Despite the above facts, Metcalf's efforts to have the segregation resolution rescinded were notably unsuccessful. After a conversation with the President of the Board of Education, he reported to Washington that it was hopeless to look for modification or repeal of the resolution.[56] The Board of Education was willing, however, to submit the case to the Supreme Court of California on an agreed statement of facts. Metcalf conferred with the justices of the Supreme Court and found they would unanimously hold that the action of the board was in violation of the treaty of 1894 if that treaty contained a most-favored-nation clause.[57] But at this point Metcalf encountered an insurmountable obstacle. Metcalf conferred with the United States District Attorney at San Francisco, Robert Devlin, and they both were convinced, after carefully studying the terms of the treaty, that it embodied no general most-favored-nation clause. Article I provided for most-favored-nation treatment in whatever related to rights of residence and travel, and Article II provided for this treatment in matters of commerce and trade. Neither Metcalf nor Devlin, however, thought these clauses could be construed to apply to matters of education, and so they requested clarifying instructions from Washington.[58] Meanwhile, Metcalf conferred with the Japanese Consul, S. Uyeno, and frankly told him that if a court case were instituted, the outcome would likely be unfavorable.[59]

At Washington, Root remained convinced that the treaty had

55 *Metcalf Report.*

56 Metcalf to Roosevelt, November 2, 1906, Roosevelt Papers.

57 Metcalf to Roosevelt, November 2, 1906, Roosevelt Papers; Metcalf to Roosevelt, telegram, November 3, 1906, S. D. File 1797/26.

58 Metcalf to Root, telegram, November 1, 1906, S. D. File 1797/20; Devlin to Attorney General William H. Moody, November 2, 1906, S. D. File 1797/53–54; Metcalf to Roosevelt, November 2, 1906, Roosevelt Papers.

59 Uyeno to Hayashi, received November 2, 3, 4, 1906, Telegram Series, LXXXVII, 9228–29, 9245–46, 9258–59.

been violated. On November 14 Attorney General William H. Moody sent Root's views to Devlin and instructed him to be governed by the Secretary's interpretation of the treaty.[60] Root believed that the rights of residence and travel in Article I were sufficient to guarantee the Japanese equal treatment in matters of education. "The whole purpose and end of the treaty of 1894," wrote Root, "was to do away with and prevent just such exclusions as are now provided by the San Francisco School Board." The resolution, he concluded, "is completely subversive of the purpose and spirit of the treaty, and is, in my judgment, a violation of its terms." [61]

Root may have been on sound ground so far as the spirit of the treaty was concerned, but his legal arguments were weak. Neither Devlin, Metcalf, nor Solicitor James B. Scott, the highest legal officer of the Department, agreed with him. Scott pointed out in a memorandum on November 27 that even if the treaty guaranteed equal treatment in matters of education, "equal" was not necessarily "identical." "What happened to the Fourteenth Amendment may well happen to the Treaty of 1894," said Scott.[62]

Metcalf departed for Washington on November 13, leaving Devlin to work out an agreed case in accordance with Root's views. Roosevelt returned to Washington on November 26, and the following day he conferred with Metcalf. The latter pointed out to the President the difficulties of resolving the crisis through court action, and Roosevelt was inclined to agree with Metcalf's view rather than with that of Root. "If our treaty contains no 'most favored nation' clause," Roosevelt wrote to Metcalf later that day, "then I am inclined to feel as strongly as you do that we had better take no action to upset the action of the Board of Education of the City of San Francisco." [63] A short time later Roosevelt did tell Root to go forward with the suit, but he had little confidence that it would solve the segregation problem. He discerned that the issue could be resolved only by striking at the basic cause of the Pacific coast agitation: the increasing influx of Japanese of the laboring class into the United States.

[60] Moody to Root, November 14, 1906, S. D. File 1797/50.
[61] Root to Moody, November 13, 1906, S. D. File 1797/53–54.
[62] Memorandum by Scott, November 27, 1906, S. D. File 1797/61.
[63] Roosevelt to Metcalf, November 27, 1906, Morison, *Roosevelt Letters*, V, 510.

At Tokyo meanwhile Foreign Minister Hayashi was becoming increasingly impatient. He bombarded Aoki with telegrams urging him to seek speedy action by the Washington government to end the discrimination and abuses. His messages reflected the bitterness in Japan over the racial aspects of the question. At the same time, however, he began to perceive the weakness of Japan's legal case. In one telegram he argued at length that the segregation violated the treaty of 1894, only to end his argument with the statement that it was "inconsistent with the spirit if not the letter of the treaty." [64]

Aoki could only counsel Hayashi to be patient. He pointed out that the crisis had raised a grave constitutional problem and that Roosevelt had to proceed cautiously.[65] Aoki explained, too, that the President was going to discuss the crisis in his annual message to the Congress in early December. As that time approached, Aoki telegraphed Tokyo: "President's message will clarify the situation. It is advisable to wait further development." [66]

[64] Hayashi to Aoki, November 13, 1906, Telegram Series, LXXXIX, 10799–10801.
[65] Aoki to Hayashi, received November 26, 1906, Telegram Series, LXXXVIII, 9852.
[66] Aoki to Hayashi, received December 2, 1906, Telegram Series, LXXXVIII, 10047–48.

CHAPTER NINE

Negotiating
the Gentlemen's Agreement

FROM the outset of the school segregation crisis, Roosevelt realized that it was only one manifestation of the more fundamental problem of Japanese immigration. In the twelve months ending November 30, 1906, over seventeen thousand Japanese entered the mainland United States, some two-thirds coming via Hawaii.[1] If this mass immigration continued, the agitation on the Pacific coast was certain to escalate to even more dangerous proportions. The people on the Pacific coast simply would not accept a large influx of people who could not be easily assimilated. Though Roosevelt himself deplored the manifestations of anti-Japanese sentiment, he was in agreement with the Californians that Japanese immigration should be checked. He felt that the Japanese could not be readily assimilated — not because they were racially *inferior* but because they were racially *different* — and throughout all the trouble with Japan during 1906–07, his one overriding objective was to reduce drastically Japanese immigration.

Roosevelt hoped to check the Japanese tide through an agreement with the Japanese government. The first step therefore was to mollify the Japanese government and people. He chose his message to Congress to achieve this objective. In late November he wrote to Metcalf telling him of a long conversation he had with Ambassador Aoki in which he read to the Ambassador the text of his message and explained the need for restricting Japanese coolie immigration. "Of course the great difficulty in getting the Japanese to take this view," Roosevelt confided to Metcalf, "is the irritation

[1] Oscar S. Straus to Root, December 22, 1906, S. D. File 2542/12–13.

caused by the San Francisco action. I hope that my message will smooth over their feelings so that the Government will quietly stop all immigration of coolies to our country." [2]

In his message to Congress on December 4, 1906, Roosevelt took San Francisco to task in no uncertain terms. He paid tribute to Japan's remarkable development in peace and war, and he noted that the overwhelming majority of Americans treated the Japanese as they deserved. In San Francisco, however, this was not the case. Shutting them out of the schools was a "wicked absurdity," he said, and "a confession of inferiority in our civilization." The President thereupon recommended that Congress pass an act permitting naturalization of the Japanese in the United States and amend the civil and criminal statutes so as to enable the President to enforce the rights of aliens under treaties. In conclusion he stated that he would use all the forces at his command to protect the Japanese.[3]

The reception accorded Roosevelt's message in Japan doubtless exceeded even the expectations of the President. William Sturgis Bigelow, who had suggested the naturalization proposal to Roosevelt, predicted "they will be pleased right into the middle of their souls," [4] and indeed they were. Kaneko wrote to Roosevelt that his message was telegraphed to Japan and published in full in the Japanese press. The editorials, said Kaneko, "showered upon you all the praises they have in store." [5] Wright reported that the naturalization proposal was received with particular enthusiasm and if carried into effect would do more than any other one thing to heal the wounded national pride of Japan.[6]

The good feeling which Roosevelt's message aroused in Japan

[2] Roosevelt to Metcalf, November 27, 1907, Morison, *Roosevelt Letters*, V, 510.

[3] United States, President, *A Compilation of the Messages and Papers of the Presidents*, 20 vols., News York, 1921, XV, 7055. Roosevelt had been interested in the question of naturalization of the Japanese since the flareup of anti-Japanese sentiment in California the previous summer. At that time he requested from Attorney General William H. Moody a statement on the matter. Moody replied that it was clear that Japanese were not eligible for naturalization under the law. It had been the policy of the United States since the beginning, he said, to confine naturalization to persons of white races, and since the Civil War, persons of African descent also. Roosevelt to Moody, July 15, 1905, and Moody to Roosevelt, July 19, 1905, Roosevelt Papers.

[4] Bigelow to Roosevelt, October 30, 1906, Roosevelt Papers.

[5] Kaneko to Roosevelt, December 11, 1906, Roosevelt Papers.

[6] Wright to Root, December 11, 1906, S. D. File 1797/90-91.

was equaled only by the indignation stirred on the Pacific coast. The San Francisco *Chronicle* said, "Our controversy is not with them [the Japanese] but with the President." It went on to observe that the school problem would disappear once the coolies were excluded.[7] The *Examiner* said that the ninety-three Japanese would be forgotten "as soon as President Roosevelt lays aside his pewter sword, sheathes his fire-belching tongue and ceases his tin-soldier yawp about leading the army and navy against our schoolhouses." [8] The San Francisco correspondent of the London *Times* wrote: "The Situation here is certainly graver. . . . Feeling against the Japanese has become so acute . . . that it is feared that nothing that Mr. Roosevelt and the Federal Government can do will have the slightest effect in improving the situation." [9]

San Francisco was not alone in condemning Roosevelt's address. The press throughout the state was almost unanimous in opposing the President's views, and the California congressional delegation at Washington strongly criticized the message. Much criticism was also voiced in other Pacific coast states. Governor Albert E. Mead of Washington vigorously objected to the President's statements, and in Seattle ten thousand signatures were gained for an anti-Japanese petition. Senator John M. Gearin of Oregon, Senator Francis G. Newlands of Nevada, and Senator Thomas M. Patterson of Colorado all pointed out that the people of their states favored the exclusion of Japanese laborers. Many Southern senators also expressed concern over the danger to states' rights implicit in Roosevelt's threat to use the armed forces in a dispute with a local school board.[10]

Two weeks after Roosevelt sent his message to Congress, he inflamed the Californians still more when he submitted to that body the Metcalf report. Enough has been said of the report to indicate that it was an indictment of the San Franciscans. Metcalf, in his efforts to be objective, presented a statement of facts with little interpretation, but the tables and charts were sufficiently damaging in themselves to arouse the San Franciscans to new heights of fury.

[7] San Francisco *Chronicle*, December 5, 1906.
[8] San Francisco *Examiner*, December 21, 1906.
[9] London *Times*, December 20, 1906.
[10] Bailey, *Roosevelt and the Japanese-American Crises*, pp. 102–109.

The correspondent of the London *Times* said the report created more anger than the President's message.[11] The *Chronicle* advised Metcalf that he would do well to stick with the unpatriotic President, for he "could get nothing from the people of his own state." [12]

The indignation stirred by the message to Congress and the Metcalf report was greater than Roosevelt had anticipated and undoubtedly had made immediate prospects for settlement of the school question dim indeed. The public reaction, nevertheless, had confirmed his belief that the basic problem was immigration. The response of the Pacific coast even had a certain educational value for Roosevelt, for he now became convinced that the anti-Japanese feeling was more deep-seated than he had imagined and that genuine racial feeling was involved. On December 18 he wrote to the British Foreign Secretary, Sir Edward Grey, that "most American and Australian workingmen, and I believe Canadian workingmen, will object in the most emphatic way to Japanese laborers coming among them in any number. I think they are right in so objecting." [13] In early January, 1907, Roosevelt wrote to Lyman Abbott: "Whether we like it or not, I think we have to face the fact that the people of the Pacific slope, with the warm approval of the labor men thruout our whole country, will become steadily more and more hostile to the Japanese if their laborers come here. . . ." [14] To his son Kermit he confided:

The San Franciscans are howling and whooping and embarrassing me in every way, and their manners are simply inexcusable. They have no business to have kept the Japanese out of the schools and their whole attitude is very bad. But I have to face facts, and one fact is that, save as between gentlemen of the two nationalities, there is a strong and bitter antipathy to the Japanese on the Pacific slope — the antipathy having been primarily due to labor competition, but complicated by genuine race feeling.[15]

Roosevelt's realization that deep racial feeling was present on the Pacific coast was the most important influence shaping his policy. He was doubtless concerned over his own loss of popularity and

11 London *Times*, December 20, 1906.
12 San Francisco *Chronicle*, December 21, 1906.
13 Roosevelt to Grey, December 18, 1906, Morison, *Roosevelt Letters*, V, 527–529.
14 Roosevelt to Abbott, January 3, 1907, Morison, *Roosevelt Letters*, V, 536–537.
15 Roosevelt to Kermit Roosevelt, February 4, 1907, Roosevelt Papers.

the damage done to the Republican party in the western states by his expressed pro-Japanese sentiments, but such considerations were not decisive in bringing him to champion exclusion of Japanese laborers. What Roosevelt most feared was not the domestic political risks of opposing the Californians but rather the danger of continuous crises with Japan. If the Japanese immigrants continued to arrive in large numbers, it would lead to more mistreatment of those aliens and more flare-ups of indignation in Japan. Roosevelt believed that since the Japanese could not be easily assimilated, racial prejudice against them would be a continuing attitude among Pacific coast residents — an attitude that the government was powerless to combat effectively. The only solution, therefore, was to stop the influx of Japanese and thereby remove the grounds for complaint on the part of Caucasian residents of the Pacific slope.

The solution of the school segregation crisis and the more basic immigration problem could not be achieved by a message to Congress, and Roosevelt did not expect it to be. Neither was it to be solved by the use of federal armed forces against recalcitrant local authorities. Rather, the solution was to be found through bargaining with the Californians and the Japanese government. The complicated bargaining was destined to last over two months (from late December, 1906, to late February, 1907) and was to result in what was later called the Gentlemen's Agreement. The overall settlement which was ultimately to emerge would include three vital components: (1) rescinding of the segregation order by the San Francisco School Board, (2) withholding of passports to the mainland United States by the Japanese government, and (3) the closing of channels of immigration through Hawaii, Canada, and Mexico by federal legislation.

The need for federal legislation to supplement the Gentlemen's Agreement was caused by the Japanese government's unwillingness to restrict emigration to Hawaii, a place where many Japanese were already residing. When the Gentlemen's Agreement of 1900 was arranged, Tokyo had carefully excepted Hawaii from its application, and when the immigration question was taken up in 1906, the Japanese government made clear that it would insist upon a like exception in any future arrangement. Though passports granted Japanese of the laboring class were marked "Hawaii only," there was no American law to prevent an immigrant, once in Hawaii, from proceeding to the mainland.

Since the beginning of the segregation crisis, Japanese immigration via Hawaii had given great concern to the Roosevelt administration, and it was on this aspect of the problem that the first negotiations centered. In late December important talks took place both at Tokyo and at Washington on the Hawaiian question. Since November the Roosevelt administration had been urging Japan to limit emigration to Hawaii, but Hayashi had consented only to a temporary restriction — and this was hedged around with so many qualifications and exceptions that it would be ineffective.[16] In December, Ambassador Wright took up the matter again with Hayashi. The Foreign Minister told Wright that Japan could do no more "without much embarrassment." Wright pointed out that Japanese immigration was the principal cause of the trouble in San Francisco and that Japanese who were given passports to Hawaii were going from there to the mainland in great numbers. To this Hayashi replied that Japan could not be expected to control the Japanese once they were in American territory and that the United States could control their leaving Hawaii.[17]

When Wright telegraphed Hayashi's remarks to Washington on December 26, Root made the reasonable inference that Japan would not object to American legislation restricting the movement of Japanese from Hawaii to the mainland. This belief was reinforced by a talk Root had with Ambassador Aoki two days after the arrival of Wright's report. Aoki posed the question to Root whether the United States could not enforce the limitations on passports issued by the Japanese government marked "Hawaii only" so that the passage of Japanese laborers from Hawaii to the mainland could be stopped. Root told Aoki that this could be done only by additional legislation and that he had hesitated to propose such legislation lest it be misinterpreted by Japan. A suggestion by Japan,

16 Root to Wright, telegram, November 19, 1906, S. D. File 1797/58a; Wright to Root, December 11, 1906, S. D. File 2542/15–16; Wright to Root, telegram, December 15, 1906, S. D. File 1797/76.
17 Wright to Root, telegram, December 26, 1906, S. D. File 1797/88.

however, would not be liable to any such misconstruction, Root
said to Aoki, and he would be very glad to take up the matter
"upon your initiative." Root then suggested that the desired result
could be accomplished by a treaty, which under the United States
Constitution would have the force of law.[18]

Root's hope that Japan would assume the initiative was not to
be realized, but in view of the statements of both Hayashi and
Aoki, Japan could not well object to United States legislation designed to stop the flow of Japanese immigrants from Hawaii to the
mainland. Ambassador Aoki, however, had conceded more than
he was willing to admit to Tokyo. When the United States ultimately passed such legislation as part of the comprehensive settlement, he took the position in his reports to Hayashi that Japan had
valid grounds for objecting to the legislation. Hayashi was under
no such illusion. He learned through Wright of Aoki's statement to
Root, and he remembered his own statement to Wright. He was
fully aware, therefore, that Japan had given a green light to the
United States to go forward with legislation to solve the Hawaiian
problem.

Despite the progress on the Hawaiian question, as the new year
opened the crisis in Japanese-American relations was still far from
being resolved. In the prevailing atmosphere of tension, Japan
decided to cancel the visit of a naval training squadron which had
been scheduled to visit the Pacific coast.[19] As the weeks passed with
little progress being made, Tokyo evidenced renewed impatience.
Hayashi telegraphed Aoki on January 8 inquiring what the United
States government was doing about the school question.[20] The Ambassador's reply was not optimistic. The government of California, he reported, was irrevocably committed to the position taken
in the school question, and the federal government was powerless to accomplish anything except by judicial proceedings. On
the matter of naturalization, Root had informed him that it was

[18] Root to Aoki, December 28, 1906, S. D. File 2542/13a. On January 19, 1907,
Wright gave Hayashi a detailed paraphrase of Root's views as given to Aoki on December 28. Documents Relating to the Limitation and Exclusion of Japanese Immigrants by the United States, MT3.8.2.21, reel 722, pp. 2405–10.
[19] Wright to Root, telegram, January 11, 1907, S. D. File 1797/106.
[20] Hayashi to Aoki, January 8, 1907, Telegram Series, XCI, 1223–24.

doubtful whether a bill as recommended by the President could be introduced during the present session of the Congress.[21]

By mid-January an impasse appeared to have been reached. The San Francisco school board would not retreat, and the Japanese government seemed determined not to tackle the immigration issue until the school problem was out of the way. Aoki even wished to hold out for naturalization rights in addition to the settling of the school problem. He told Hayashi: "I think we have chance of success on naturalization question if we handle negotiation in such way that the settlement of immigration problem would be made to hinge on the satisfactory solution of naturalization and school question." [22] Hayashi, being less sanguine about the naturalization question, did not agree that the immigration question should be tied to that issue. But he was determined to hold back on emigration restriction until the school segregation was ended.

Hayashi's strategy was to offer hope to the Roosevelt administration that emigration would be restricted soon after the school question was resolved. This first became apparent when Wright telegraphed on January 11 a statement by Hayashi: "He again expressed regret that school authorities persisted in discrimination, as with this out of the way there would be no difficulty in restricting coolie emigration." [23] Root considered Hayashi's statement of great importance. He telegraphed Wright that the remarks were "very gratifying" and that he would endeavor to get the school difficulty out of the way.[24] Root interpreted Hayashi's statement to mean that Japan would conclude a formal treaty on immigration, but Wright quickly disabused him of that misinterpretation. Wright reported that Hayashi was merely intimating that when the school question was solved, Japan would issue no more passports to laborers for the mainland and would mark passports for Hawaii "Hawaii only." In substance, Hayashi was offering only a reaffirmation and stricter enforcement of the informal arrangement of 1900.[25] In Hayashi's own account of his remarks, which he sent to

21 Aoki to Hayashi, received January 10, 1907, Telegram Series, XC, 113–114.
22 Aoki to Hayashi, received January 15, 1907, Telegram Series, XC, 210–211.
23 Wright to Root, telegram, January 11, 1907, S. D. File 1797/106.
24 Root to Wright, telegram, January 14, 1907, S. D. File 2542/18a.
25 Wright to Root, January 23, 1907, S. D. File 1797/127–140.

Ambassador Aoki, he gave an even more restricted interpretation: "I only remarked that upon satisfactory adjustment of the school question, the Japanese Government would be able *to consider* the immigration problem."[26]

On January 29 Wright secured a more detailed statement from Hayashi, and this time it was reinforced with full cabinet backing. Hayashi said that the members of the ministry all agreed that when the San Francisco school board could be induced to withdraw its objectionable order, a way might be found to prevent the emigration of Japanese coolie labor to the Pacific coast by entering into "some arrangement" with the United States, provided the agreement should be of such a nature as to prevent the *amour propre* of the Japanese people from being wounded. He explained that Hawaii must be excepted from the arrangement but that Japan would not object to legislation by the United States designed to prevent coolie emigration from Hawaii to the mainland.[27] Wright explained that it would be difficult to get the San Francisco school board to cancel the order unless the Roosevelt administration could certify to California congressmen that a satisfactory agreement could be made. To this Hayashi replied that he had no objection to his views being given to the congressmen so long as his opinion was not exaggerated.[28]

The stage was now set for a comprehensive solution of the entire immigration-segregation crisis. The immediate task was to get the school board to withdraw the segregation order. On January 17 an agreed case had been filed in the Ninth Circuit Court of California, but no one in the administration was optimistic about the prospects of a favorable decision.[29] Now at the end of January, Roosevelt decided to take a dramatic step. On the thirtieth he called the entire California congressional delegation to the White House, where he, Root, and Metcalf conferred with them for two

[26] Italics mine. Hayashi to Aoki, January 19, 1907, Telegram Series, XCI, 1352–53.
[27] Wright to Root, telegram, February 1, 1907, S. D. File 2542/22.
[28] Hayashi to Aoki, January 31, 1907, Telegram Series, XCI, 1457–59. Wright's detailed account of this conversation, which was apparently revised by Hayashi, is in Documents Relating to the Limitation and Exclusion of Japanese Immigrants by the United States, MT3.8.2.21, reel 722, pp. 2423–28.
[29] Roosevelt to Root, December 5, 1906, Morison, *Roosevelt Letters*, V, 521; Root to Attorney General Charles J. Bonaparte, December 24, 1906, S. D. File 1797/85–86.

hours. Following the conference the delegation sent two telegrams to California. One was sent to Governor James N. Gillett asking him to use his influence to defer all legislative action concerning Japanese matters. This request Governor Gillett granted, and his influence was sufficient to achieve the desired objective.[30] The second telegram was addressed to the superintendent of the schools and the president of the Board of Education of San Francisco and invited those men to come to Washington for a conference with the President. In San Francisco a meeting of the board was hastily called, and it sent a telegram to Washington stating that if any decisive action was to be taken, the entire board must come. Thereupon Roosevelt invited the board, and on the following day, at the request of the board, invited Mayor Eugene E. Schmitz as well. Schmitz was at this time at liberty on a $25,000 bail, having been indicted on five counts of extortion. The members of the board, who were personal appointees of Schmitz, were also deeply involved in graft. Thus in the first week of February, 1907, the country witnessed the unique spectacle of an entire Board of Education, accompanied by a city superintendent of schools and a mayor, all members of a corruption-ridden regime, traveling across the continent to confer with the President of the United States on matters of high policy.[31]

While Schmitz and his retinue were journeying to Washington, there occurred the most serious war scare since the initial flareup in October, 1906. Eastern newspapers in the United States spoke of the inevitable outbreak of the long-deferred conflict with Japan. Fortunately the outburst in the United States was not duplicated in Japan. The Tokyo correspondent of the London *Times* noted that there was absolutely no talk of war in Japan and that all the excitement and bellicose rumors emanated from the American side.[32] The war scare nevertheless caused much anxiety in governmental circles in Japan. Hayashi telegraphed Aoki that Japan always trusted the sincerity of the United States government and wanted a peaceful resolution of the San Francisco problem. Aoki was instructed to give to American newspapers assurances of Ja-

30 Senator George C. Perkins to Roosevelt, February 1, 1907, Roosevelt Papers.
31 Bailey, *Roosevelt and the Japanese-American Crises*, pp. 123–133.
32 London *Times*, February 6, 1907.

pan's peaceful intentions and to send the same information to Japanese diplomatic posts in Europe.[33] The Japanese government was so concerned over the war rumors that a second telegram was sent to Aoki asking him to investigate the source of the false report.[34] Aoki replied that he had already denied any intention on the part of Japan to take hostile action against the United States but that in doing so he had to deal with a "delicate situation." It was his belief that the war talk had been started at the White House and that Roosevelt was doing his best "to frighten Californians to submission." [35]

Aoki's suspicion that the war scare emanated from the White House was justified at least in part. It is likely, however, that Roosevelt was motivated primarily by his campaign for increased naval appropriations rather than by the desire to frighten the Californians. Just at this time he was urging Congress to approve funds for battleships and for fortifications at Hawaii and the Philippines, and he was again exaggerating the danger of war with Japan, both in his own mind and in his comments to others. To his son Kermit he wrote regarding the Japanese crisis: "We may have serious trouble ahead. Moreover, Congress has resolutely refused to provide any system of adequate fortification for the Philippines and Hawaii, and has greatly hampered me in building up the navy." [36] A few days later in another letter to Kermit, he said that the Japanese "are pretty cocky and unreasonable and we may have trouble with them any time." [37] Other members of the administration also evidenced the atmosphere of excitement which surrounded the White House. Secretary of War Taft wrote to Major General J. P. Story: "I am anxious to hurry up the fortifications at Hawaii. There are reasons that are imperative why this should be done." [38]

Despite the war scare, by the beginning of February the Roosevelt administration had traveled far along the road to a solution of

[33] Hayashi to Aoki, February 4, 1907, Telegram Series, XCI, 1496–98.
[34] Hayashi to Aoki, February 5, 1907, Telegram Series, XCI, 1516.
[35] Aoki to Hayashi, February 5, 1907, Telegram Series, XC, 693–694, 697.
[36] Roosevelt to Kermit Roosevelt, February 4, 1907, Roosevelt Papers.
[37] Roosevelt to Kermit Roosevelt, February 9, 1907, Roosevelt Papers.
[38] Taft to Story, January 28, 1907, Papers of William Howard Taft, Library of Congress, Washington, D.C.

the crisis. The messages between Tokyo and Washington in January had clearly foreshadowed the informal arrangement on immigration which would soon be concluded. With the school board on its way to Washington, the only serious obstacle could soon be dealt with; and since Japan had already indicated a willingness to cooperate on the immigration problem, Roosevelt had a strong card to play in his negotiations with the school board. Just as events were moving toward a settlement, however, Roosevelt and Root embarked upon a concerted effort to wring an immigration treaty from Japan, a project that was destined to be unsuccessful and that only introduced confusion into an already tedious situation.

The initial move came on January 31 when Root called in Ambassador Aoki and proposed a treaty providing for exclusion of laborers and most-favored-nation treatment in schools. The next day he anxiously telegraphed Ambassador Wright that the situation was worse on the Pacific coast and that there was no practical chance of settling the school question in advance of the immigration question. He told Wright that he had suggested a treaty to Aoki and hoped Japan would take the initiative and formally propose it. "Without some such arrangement," he cautioned, "we can see no escape from increased excitement and conditions growing worse rather than better, to an extent making position of all Japanese on Pacific coast quite intolerable in ways that no Government can control directly." One result, he added, would be the passage of legislation by Congress excluding the Japanese.[39]

Root believed Aoki favored the conclusion of a treaty, but the Ambassador gave no such indication in his report to his government.[40] At Tokyo the reaction to Root's proposal was cool, to say the least. Hayashi deprecated the idea of a treaty giving exclusion of laborers in return for school privileges which the Japanese people believed they already possessed under the treaty of 1894. Previously he had agreed to make "some arrangement" on immigration — presumably an informal, nontreaty arrangement — once the school question was out of the way. He now agreed to make a

39 Root to Wright, telegram, February 1, 1907, S. D. File 2542/22.
40 Aoki to Hayashi, received February 1, 1907, Telegram Series, XC, 615.

treaty but not on the terms Root proposed. In order to get a treaty, the United States must agree that Japanese not within the excluded class entering the United States have the right of naturalization.[41]

In his reports to Washington, Wright betrayed some sympathy for Hayashi's predicament. He told Root that Japanese leaders were anxious to meet the wishes of the United States but feared an outcry against a one-sided treaty. It was his opinion that they did not regard the right of naturalization as intrinsically important but needed a sop to public opinion.[42]

In the succeeding days Root continued to press upon Japan his original proposals for a treaty. On February 5 he telegraphed Tokyo that it was exceedingly doubtful whether the treaty of 1894 had been violated by the establishment of a separate school and that it was at least an even chance that the courts would decide that the school ordinance violated no treaty. It was, he said, "wholly useless to discuss the subject of naturalization at the present time." No statute could be passed or treaty ratified which extended Japanese rights beyond the limits of their contention regarding the schools.[43] When Wright gave these views to Hayashi, the Foreign Minister frankly conceded that it was probably true that under the existing treaty Japan had no right to object to the San Francisco school ordinance. But the Japanese people did not understand this, he said. As far as the cabinet was concerned, it was largely a matter of preserving the *amour propre* of the Japanese. He then suggested that a "private agreement" be made in place of a treaty.[44]

There is no doubt that the Japanese government was eager for a settlement of the crisis, but, like the Roosevelt administration, it faced the problem of public opinion. The opposition in Japan was vigorously attacking the Saionji ministry and particularly Foreign Minister Hayashi. Rumors of a settlement on Root's terms circulated in Japan and brought sharp criticism. Such a treaty, said the opposition *Hochi Shimbun*, would be an absolute surrender on the

    [41] Wright to Root, telegram, February 4, 1907, S. D. File 2542/26. Draft treaties embodying the Japanese position are in Documents Relating to the Limitation and Exclusion of Japanese Immigrants by the United States, MT3.8.2.21, reel 722, pp. 2463–87.
    [42] Wright to Root, telegram, February 6, 1907, S. D. File 2542/27.
    [43] Root to Wright, telegram, February 5, 1907, S. D. File 2542/25a.
    [44] Wright to Root, telegram, February 9, 1907, S. D. File 2542/34.

part of the Japanese government. The reason Americans wanted Japanese laborers excluded, it said, was because of their race. "Our nation," it concluded, "is getting tired of sluggish diplomacy." [45]

Ironically, opposition to the treaty project developed in the United States, too. The outline of Root's proposal leaked out, and opposition developed on two grounds. First, a treaty providing for mutual exclusion of laborers would violate the principle of equality. Aoki reported to Tokyo that some senators maintained that the United States could not conclude an agreement with any nation which deprived any United States citizen of any right to be enjoyed by any other American. A second objection was based upon states' rights. Aoki reported that even senators from states sympathetic with Japan opposed giving Japan most-favored-nation treatment in schools. They felt that the right of a state to control its own school system was one of the fundamental principles of United States institutions "which must be maintained even at the cost of forfeiting friendly relations with Japan." [46]

Japanese leaders were seeking desperately for some concession which the United States could give in return for a Japanese retreat on the immigration question, and on February 13 they presented another possible solution. Henry W. Denison, the American adviser to the Foreign Ministry, called Wright and suggested that the United States consent to a Japan-Korean customs union in return for an immigration treaty. This union would provide for free trade between Japan and Korea and would thus give Japan control of the Korean market. [47] Adee, the Second Assistant Secretary of State, thought this a good way out of the impasse, for, as he noted, "the annexation of Korea by Japan is only a matter of time." [48] Root secured Roosevelt's approval for such a treaty, [49] but the proposal failed to materialize because of opposition to the scheme within the Japanese government. Resident General Ito opposed it, not only on grounds of high policy, but also because it would leave

[45] *Hochi Shimbun*, February 2 and 3, 1907.
[46] Aoki to Hayashi, received February 6, 1907, Telegram Series, XC, 735–36.
[47] Wright to Root, telegram, February 13, 1907, S. D. File 2542/37.
[48] Memorandum by Adee attached to Wright to Root, telegram, February 13, 1907, S. D. File 2542/37.
[49] Root to Wright, telegram, February 14, 1907, S. D. File 2542/37.

the Korean government no customs revenue with which to operate.[50]

While the treaty project was foundering, Roosevelt and Root were seeking a solution in Washington. The delegation from San Francisco arrived on February 8, and on the following day a series of conferences began between the San Franciscans on the one hand and Roosevelt and Root on the other. Roosevelt assured the delegation that he was in entire sympathy with the people of California on the subject of immigration but that he wanted to secure the exclusion of laborers with the least possible offense to Japan. He pointed out emphatically that the school ordinance was the greatest obstacle to the achievement of that objective.[51]

The discussions which followed in the ensuing days were influenced by the conflicting factors of pressure on the delegation from California and the continuing influx of coolies. On February 10 and 11 over four hundred telegrams poured in upon the mayor and the school board urging them to stand firm. The delegation could not help but be impressed, however, by the overriding necessity of clearing the way for a solution to the immigration problem. In January two steamers from Hawaii landed about seven hundred Japanese at San Francisco, and on February 10 two hundred and fifty more were landed.[52] It was touch-and-go during several days of conferences. Roosevelt wrote to Kermit:

Slowly and with infinite difficulty and frequent setbacks, I am getting both the Californians and Japan into an attitude that will permit of a solution of our troubles in that quarter — althou of course the whole business may be upset before I am able to achieve the result I have in mind.[53]

The deadlock was broken on February 15. In return for assurances that coolie immigration would be stopped and that legal proceedings would be abandoned, the school authorities agreed to rescind their order and permit qualified nonadult Japanese to enter the public schools. It was agreed that the prospective pupil must demonstrate a satisfactory familiarity with English, must be sixteen

[50] Wright to Root, March 3, 1907, S. D. File 1166/15–19.
[51] Theodore Roosevelt, *An Autobiography*, New York, 1916, p. 394.
[52] Bailey, *Roosevelt and the Japanese-American Crises*, pp. 140–143.
[53] Roosevelt to Kermit Roosevelt, February 16, 1907, Morison, *Roosevelt Letters*, V, 589.

years of age or under, and must be within the age limits set for a given grade. The restrictions would apply to all alien children alike.[54]

While the agreement with the school board was being worked out, the administration took steps to stop the influx of Japanese of the laboring class via Hawaii and other stepping-stones to the mainland United States. An amendment, authored by Root, was added to a pending immigration bill which was passed on February 18. It provided that:

whenever the President shall be satisfied that passports issued by any foreign government to its citizens to go to any country other than the United States or to any insular possession of the United States or to the Canal Zone are being used for the purpose of enabling holders to come to the continental territory of the United States to the detriment of labor conditions therein, the President may refuse to permit such citizens of the country issuing such passports to enter the continental territory of the United States from such other country or from such insular possessions or from the Canal Zone.[55]

This amendment did not mention the Japanese by name, but it was clearly designed to prevent Japanese laborers from entering the continental United States when they held passports for Canada, Mexico, or Hawaii. With the passage of this legislation, the San Francisco school board publicly announced its determination to revoke the segregation order.

Ambassador Aoki was greatly irritated by the manner in which the immigration legislation was passed. Newspapers reported that the Root amendment had been given to Aoki prior to its passage and that the Japanese government had extended at least its tacit approval. When Root refused to issue a denial of this report, Aoki urged Hayashi to issue one "for the maintaining of the dignity of the Empire."[56] Actually, Aoki had little justification for complaint. Roosevelt and Root undoubtedly told members of Congress that Japan did not object to the amendment, but they had ade-

54 It was agreed that no child of alien birth over the ages of nine, ten, eleven, twelve, thirteen, fourteen, fifteen and sixteen years should be enrolled in any of the first, second, third, fourth, fifth, sixth, seventh and eighth grades respectively. Root to Wright, telegram, February 19, 1907, S. D. File 2542/43a.

55 *Congressional Record*, 59th Congress, 2nd Session, p. 2809.

56 Aoki to Hayashi, February 23 and 24, 1907, Telegram Series, XCI, 1094–95, 1116–17.

quate justification for doing so. Aoki himself had suggested such legislation to Root the previous December, and Hayashi had also provided assurances on several occasions that Japan would raise no objection to the passage of such legislation. Now when Aoki expressed his disgruntlement to Tokyo, Hayashi quickly told him that the Japanese government favored the legislation. Hayashi said that if Japan did not cooperate with the Roosevelt administration along the lines it was proceeding, Japanese immigration would be prohibited not only to the mainland but also to Hawaii. The Foreign Minister even instructed Aoki to ask Roosevelt and Root not to cancel the Root immigration amendment! [57]

Aoki's concern probably had been prompted largely by fear of an adverse reaction to the legislation in Japan. If so, his anxieties were soon dispelled. Generally the settlement was viewed with satisfaction in Japan. The *Nichi Nichi Shimbun* expressed the general tone of the press when it said: "Though we are far from regarding the new restriction as an arrangement favorable to Japan, yet we do not hesitate to accept the settlement reached as the best possible one." [58] In an interview in the *Mainichi Dempo*, Hayashi said that too many Japanese had gone to California and that the United States had a right under the treaty of 1894 to restrict Japanese immigration. The United States had chosen, however, to exercise only part of that right, and Japan should appreciate the profound good will and forbearance of the American government.[59] Two weeks later Wright reported that the powerful *Jiji Shimpo* had swung its support to the settlement.[60]

Though the newspapers in Japan spoke of the immigration legislation of February 18 and the agreement to end the school segregation as "the settlement," the most important part of the settlement, the Gentlemen's Agreement, was yet to be achieved. Roosevelt hoped to secure a treaty rather than an informal arrangement. He wrote to Root on February 15: "Don't you think we ought to communicate with Japan and start that treaty at once? I don't want them to begin to shy off because of this legislation." [61] Four

57 Hayashi to Aoki, February 25, 1907, Telegram Series, XCI, 1694.
58 *Nichi Nichi Shimbun*, February 18, 1907.
59 *Mainichi Dempo*, February 20, 1907.
60 Wright to Root, March 3, 1907, S. D. File 1797/188.
61 Roosevelt to Root, February 15, 1907, Morison, *Roosevelt Letters*, V, 589.

days later Root instructed Wright to inform Hayashi that the United States wished to proceed with the negotiation of a treaty.[62] The treaty project, however, was virtually dead. Aoki still hoped that an acceptable *quid pro quo* could be secured in treaty negotiations, possibly even the right of naturalization,[63] but Hayashi entertained no such illusions. "Naturalization, if obtainable, is of course the best concession we can properly claim," he telegraphed Aoki. "But," he added realistically, "in view of categorical statement of Mr. Root to you and of the American Ambassador to me, I consider naturalization is impossible at this juncture." [64]

In the absence of an acceptable *quid pro quo* for a treaty, Hayashi now favored an informal arrangement which would complete the overall settlement. On February 19 Root had requested that Japan, while the treaty negotiations were proceeding, withhold passports from laborers wishing to go to the mainland United States.[65] Hayashi now sought to make this the definitive settlement. On February 21 he promised Wright that he would write a note containing assurance that the Japanese government would not issue passports to laborers for the mainland but to Hawaii only.[66] Three days later the Foreign Minister sent a note to Wright stating that his government had "no intention of canceling or modifying the order now in force under which no passports are granted to either skilled or unskilled Japanese laborers for the mainland of the United States other than settled agriculturists, farmers owning or having an interest or share in their product or crops." If this did not prove effective, said Hayashi, then the Japanese government would consider the question of a new treaty.[67]

Hayashi later explained the Japanese restrictions in greater detail in a note to Ambassador Thomas James O'Brien in December, 1907. In so doing he indicated that in addition to "settled agriculturists" passports would also be issued to Japanese who had previously resided in the United States and to parents, wives, or chil-

62 Root to Wright, telegram, February 19, 1907, S. D. File 2542/43a.
63 Aoki to Hayashi, received February 19 and 24, 1907, Telegram Series, XCI, 1003–04, 1119–20.
64 Hayashi to Aoki, February 23, 1907, Telegram Series, XCI, 1679.
65 Root to Wright, telegram, February 19, 1907, S. D. File 2542/43a.
66 Wright to Root, telegram, February 21, 1907, S. D. File 2542/46.
67 Wright to Root, telegram, February 24, 1907, S. D. File 2542/48.

dren of Japanese residing in the United States.[68] These notes from Hayashi, together with some subsequent correspondence on the immigration question, constituted what came to be called the Gentlemen's Agreement. It was within the framework of this arrangement that the United States and Japan attempted to resolve the immigration issue in future years.

It remained for the United States to carry out its side of the bargain by rescinding the school board segregation order. In California the reaction to the settlement was so unfavorable that considerable doubt was raised as to whether Schmitz and the school board would be able to carry out the agreement made with Roosevelt. The San Francisco *Argonaut* predicted that the settlement would result in an anti-Japanese campaign that would match the one against the Chinese in former years. It heaped scorn upon Schmitz and the school board, saying, "All the bold talk about demanding reciprocal concessions came to nothing when once this little coterie of cheap men got under the shadow of the big stick." [69] Roosevelt sensed that there was still trouble ahead, for he wrote to Sir Edward Grey on February 28, "We have made good progress toward settlement of the Japanese difficulty; but of course are not quite out of the woods yet." [70]

When the Schmitz party returned to San Francisco, it exhibited no haste in repealing the school order. Before it took action, the entire settlement was endangered by the actions of the California legislature. On February 28 the lower house of that body passed a bill designed to limit the ownership of land by Japanese and Chinese to five years. Then on March 6 the Keane Bill, which was designed to prevent Japanese over ten years of age from attending school with the whites, was reported in the Senate.[71] Roosevelt was alarmed, and he immediately wrote to Root:

I am convinced that it has been a mistake on our part not to take open action before this. . . . If we let things drift, we may get in a very bad situation. Of course we can always refuse to restrain the Japanese immigration;

[68] O'Brien to Root, telegram, January 1, 1908, S. D. File 2542/331–334.
[69] San Francisco *Argonaut*, February 23, 1907.
[70] Roosevelt to Grey, February 28, 1907, Morison, *Roosevelt Letters*, V, 600.
[71] Bailey, *Roosevelt and the Japanese-American Crises*, pp. 168–169.

but while this will treat the San Franciscans just as they deserve, it will not solve the situation but on the contrary will make it worse.[72]

On that same day Roosevelt telegraphed Gillett telling him that the action of the legislature was most unfortunate in its effect on the efforts to secure the exclusion of Japanese laborers and requesting him to secure a suspension of further action.[73] Root telegraphed Schmitz a reminder that the Californians were taking the surest way to defeat their own object.[74]

Roosevelt dispatched two long letters to Governor Gillett. He pointed out that under the recent legislation on immigration he had the power to exclude by executive proclamation those Japanese laborers coming indirectly to the United States but that the exclusion of those coming directly from Japan was dependent upon a voluntary undertaking on the part of the Japanese government. That informal agreement was based upon the understanding that the Japanese in the United States would not be discriminated against. The measures before the California legislature might therefore "just as well be called a proposal to prevent the exclusion of Japanese laborers." Roosevelt then asserted that he would not issue the executive order preventing indirect immigration until the school board rescinded the segregation order, nor would he issue it if other discriminatory steps were taken against the Japanese. Roosevelt even went so far as to hint that if Japan did not have equal school privileges under the treaty of 1894, such privileges might be accorded under a new treaty if the discriminations continued in California.[75]

Before Roosevelt's letters arrived, Gillett and Schmitz were taking steps to save the situation. Upon receiving Roosevelt's telegram of March 10, Gillett used his influence to secure the tabling of the anti-Japanese legislation. Schmitz telegraphed Root that in the face of all odds he would fight for the settlement as agreed upon and would win out.[76] The following day he telegraphed Roosevelt

72 Roosevelt to Root, March 10, 1907, Morison, *Roosevelt Letters*, V, 610.
73 Roosevelt to Gillett, telegram, March 10, 1907, San Francisco *Chronicle*, March 12, 1907.
74 Root to Schmitz, telegram, March 10, 1907, S. D. File 2542/54b.
75 Roosevelt to Gillett, March 9 and 11, 1907, Morison, *Roosevelt Letters*, V, 608–610, 610–614.
76 Schmitz to Root, telegram, March 11, 1907, S. D. File 2542/55.

that the Board of Education would meet on March 13 and would rescind the segregation order.[77] Roosevelt was overjoyed. In sending a copy of the telegram to Root, he said, "Schmitz is a game man and has acted like a trump." [78] On March 13 the board met as scheduled and rescinded the segregation order.[79] The following day Roosevelt issued an executive order putting into effect the passport restrictions, and at the same time he ordered the dismissal of the suit which had been entered in the California court.[80] The school segregation issue was thus finally closed.

By March, 1907, Roosevelt had come a long way in his thinking about the whole question of anti-Japanese sentiment in California and the immigration of Japanese laborers. During 1905 and 1906 he had betrayed little sympathy for the "idiots of the California legislature" and the people of California, but by the time the segregation crisis ended he was professing to be a wholehearted champion of California's interest on the immigration question. When he wrote a congratulatory letter to Governor Gillett on March 14, he promised that if necessary he would himself advocate the passage of an exclusion law.[81] The change in Roosevelt's attitude came gradually as he discerned that genuine race feeling was involved. That realization was revealed in a letter he wrote to George Kennan. The trouble in San Francisco, he said, was at bottom not in the least about the schools. It was "partly labor, and partly a deep-rooted racial antipathy, the extent of which fairly astounds me." [82] Roosevelt himself did not share that racial antipathy, but he was realistic enough to conclude that the federal government was powerless to overcome it.

In characteristic fashion Roosevelt set himself to studying the newly encountered phenomenon. In April, 1907, he told his friend Albert Shaw that he was reading Finot's *Race Prejudice*.[83] Perhaps he foresaw that the trouble in California was not yet at an end.

---

[77] Schmitz to Roosevelt, telegram, March 12, 1907, S. D. File 2542/56–57.
[78] Roosevelt to Root, March 12, 1907, Roosevelt Papers.
[79] Lawrence P. Walsh to Root, telegram, March 13, 1907, S. D. File 2542/58.
[80] Root to Walsh, telegram, March 14, 1907, S. D. File 2542/58.
[81] Roosevelt to Gillett, March 14, 1907, Morison, *Roosevelt Letters*, V, 618–619.
[82] Roosevelt to Kennan, February 9, 1907, Kennan Papers.
[83] Roosevelt to Albert Shaw, April 3, 1907, Morison, *Roosevelt Letters*, V, 637.

CHAPTER TEN

Riot and Discrimination in San Francisco

DURING the two months following the repeal of the school segregation order, relations between the United States and Japan were unusually tranquil. On both sides efforts were made to dispel ill will and to rebuild friendship. Baron Kaneko wrote to Roosevelt saying that he was doing everything he could to explain conditions to the Japanese.[1] Takahira, the former Japanese minister at Washington, wrote reassuringly to Roosevelt that unfortunate as the incident had been, it had added to the admiration of the Japanese people for the President.[2] Japanese Consul Uyeno returned to Japan from San Francisco and assured the public that the restrictions now applied by the school board were not objectionable and did not discriminate against the Japanese children.[3]

On the American side Oscar S. Straus, who replaced Metcalf as Secretary of Commerce and Labor when the latter became Secretary of the Navy, told Aoki that every effort would be made to avoid friction in the enforcement of the new immigration legislation.[4] Roosevelt sent apologetic letters to Kaneko and Takahira explaining that though race prejudice no longer prevailed among the educated classes, "we must be content to wait another generation before we shall have made progress enough to permit the same

[1] Kaneko to Roosevelt, April 15, 1907, Roosevelt Papers.
[2] Takahira to Roosevelt, April 3, 1907, Roosevelt Papers.
[3] Henry S. Miller (Consul General, Yokohama) to Bacon, May 4, 1907, S. D. File 1797/214.
[4] Straus diary, March 16 and 23, 1907, Papers of Oscar S. Straus, Library of Congress, Washington, D.C.

close intimacy between the classes who have had less opportunity for cultivation and whose lives are less easy. . . ." [5]

While making every effort to restore Japanese-American friendship, Roosevelt and Root were keenly aware that the exclusion of Japanese laborers must be resolutely enforced. Roosevelt instructed Straus to make weekly reports on Japanese immigration; [6] Root, fearing that many laborers would enter as "settled agriculturists," continued to press the Japanese government for a treaty providing for the reciprocal exclusion of laborers. [7] Hayashi, however, was not willing to go any further. He told Wright on May 13 that his government would enforce the understanding in such a way as to prevent laborers from slipping through under the guise of farmers, but he stated categorically that Japan could not enter into a treaty on immigration. He feared that to reopen the matter would be like applying a match to powder. Wright agreed with Hayashi regarding the inadvisability of concluding a treaty. An immigration treaty, he believed, would bring the downfall of the Saionji ministry. [8]

Wright had ample justification for his belief that the Saionji ministry was on shaky political ground. Since the fall of the Katsura ministry at the end of 1905, Katsura and his followers had cooperated with the Saionji ministry, but it was well known that they were merely playing a waiting game, watching for a favorable moment to regain power. Katsura's following in the House of Deputies, which was organized into the Daido Club, numbered only sixty-six members, compared with a Seiyukai strength of one hundred and fifty-three; but Katsura had the support of Yamagata, perhaps the most powerful member of the Genro, and in the Japan of 1907 this fact weighed more heavily than any considerations of party strength.

[5] Roosevelt to Takahira, April 28, 1907, and Roosevelt to Kaneko, May 23, 1907, Morison, *Roosevelt Letters*, V, 656–657, 671–672. Quotation is from the letter to Kaneko.

[6] Straus to Loeb, April 4, 1907, S. D. File 2542/67.

[7] Root to Wright, April 17, 1907, S. D. File 2542/76a.

[8] Wright to Root, May 15, 1907, S. D. File 2542/97. On May 26 Hayashi sent to Wright a long memorandum on the subject of "settled agriculturists" in which he stated that less than five hundred in that category had been granted passports in the preceding ten years. Hayashi to Wright, May 26, 1907, Documents Relating to the Limitation and Exclusion of Japanese Immigrants by the United States, MT3.8.2.21, reel 723, pp. 3395–97.

The Saionji ministry was also weakened by the attacks of the open opposition, the Shimpoto party. This party held ninety-four seats in the House of Deputies, and its members conducted an unceasing attack upon the ministry in power. The Shimpoto had long been led by Shigenobu Okuma, one of the first party politicians in Japan. Okuma did not belong to the charmed circle of the Genro, and only once — and then for but a short time — had he held the premiership. Apart from Okuma's short ministry in 1898, the premiership had passed back and forth among the Elder Statesmen from the Satsuma and Choshu clans and their loyal favorites with monotonous regularity ever since the Imperial restoration in 1868. During these years, Okuma and his followers had poured out a stream of abusive criticism against the oligarchs in power.[9] This opposition drew its strength from a deep-laid discontent among the lower classes of Japan, and in giving voice to the common people, they succeeded in producing an unofficial nationalism so intense that it outshone the official nationalism so carefully cultivated by the ruling oligarchy.[10]

Thus in 1907 the Saionji ministry found itself under fire from a virulent opposition which claimed a patriotism superior to that of the Genro and which was bitter from years of having no voice in the government. The realization that even if they succeeded in toppling the Saionji ministry it would merely pave the way for another oligarch, Katsura, seemed to make the opposition only more bitter. During the school segregation crisis, the Shimpoto had attacked the ministry both in the Diet and through its newspaper, the *Hochi Shimbun*, charging it with lack of vigor in safeguarding the interests of Japanese abroad. In January, 1907, the aged Okuma stepped down from the leadership of the party, but the party remained militant in its attacks on Saionji and Hayashi. With the ending of school segregation in March, 1907, the Shimpoto no longer was able to capitalize on the discrimination issue to any great extent, but if the Saionji ministry signed an exclusion treaty or if trouble broke out again in California, the Shimpoto was sure to seize upon either of these issues with renewed vigor.

9 Robert Karl Reischauer, *Japan: Government — Politics*, New York, 1939, pp. 107–124.
10 Hilary Conroy, "Japanese Nationalism and Expansionism," *American Historical Review*, LX (1955), 822–826.

During the early part of May, 1907, it appeared that the ill feeling on both sides of the Pacific was rapidly evaporating. A Japanese delegation, headed by General Itei Kuroki and Vice Admiral Goro Ijuin, visited the Jamestown Exposition, and these distinguished guests were treated with warm cordiality throughout the United States.[11] The delegation dined with Roosevelt on May 11, and he was much impressed with the Japanese group. "They are a formidable outfit," he wrote to Kermit. "I want to try to keep on the best possible terms with Japan and never do her any wrong; but I want still more to see our navy maintained at the highest of efficiency, for it is the real keeper of the peace."[12]

The festivities surrounding the Kuroki visit were just drawing to a happy close when the San Francisco mob broke out of control, and all that had been accomplished toward restoring friendship with Japan was suddenly swept away. On the evening of May 20 a mob of about fifty San Franciscans attacked a Japanese restaurant rendering it unfit for business. The mob then crossed the street and stoned a bath house which was also operated by Japanese. For more than a week following the attack, mobs menaced other Japanese restaurants, though by this time the authorities were sufficiently forewarned to prevent further damage.

The Acting Japanese Consul in San Francisco, Kazuo Matsubara, investigated the attacks and concluded that they were simply the result of race hatred. He further charged that the police had been purposely negligent and had ignored his warnings of impending disturbances.[13] The San Francisco authorities claimed, on the other hand, that the riots were merely the outgrowth of labor difficulties from which the city had been suffering for some months.[14] There was some truth in the contentions of both sides. No members of the mob were ever apprehended, but both white and Japanese witnesses testified that the trouble began when some union men approached several white customers who were eating in a non-

11 Oscar S. Straus, *Under Four Administrations: from Cleveland to Taft*, New York, 1922, p. 219.

12 Roosevelt to Kermit Roosevelt, May 13, 1907, Roosevelt Papers.

13 Matsubara to District Attorney Robert Devlin, May 28, 1907, Matsubara to Chief of Police J. F. Dinan, May 28, 1907, enclosed in Aoki to Bacon, June 4, 1907, S. D. File 1797/225–232.

14 Gillett to Root, May 28, 1907, S. D. File 1797/215–224.

union Japanese restaurant. The whites claimed that the riot started when a Japanese cook threw a knife into the crowd. The Japanese denied this charge, however, and alleged that the fight was instigated merely to provide an excuse for demolishing the restaurant. The facts that the bath house was also attacked and that other Japanese restaurants were threatened indicate that racial hostility was involved. The contention that the police were negligent was also true, but whether they were purposely so was questionable. A streetcar strike was taking place in San Francisco, and the cars were operating under police protection. The strike drew so many policemen from their regular assignments that only six could be spared for the neighborhood where the riot occurred, an area that was usually patroled by forty.[15]

News of the riot reached Tokyo before it reached Washington. On May 23 Hayashi telegraphed Aoki to take up the matter with the United States government and ask that protection be given to Japanese in the United States.[16] Before Aoki appeared at the State Department, a telegram arrived from Ambassador Wright reporting that Japanese newspapers were publishing sensational accounts of attacks on Japanese stores in San Francisco.[17] Root replied that he had heard nothing of any attacks but would investigate immediately.[18] He then asked Attorney General Charles J. Bonaparte to request a telegraphic report from District Attorney Robert Devlin.[19] Later on the same day, Aoki came to make representations on the matter and to give Root copies of reports arriving from the Japanese Consulate in San Francisco. Aoki also pointed out the state of affairs to Roosevelt when he called on him that day.[20]

Roosevelt was greatly concerned about the renewal of trouble in San Francisco. He had Root send a telegram to Governor Gillett detailing the developments and urging prompt and effective en-

15 Evidence is given in Devlin to Attorney General Charles J. Bonaparte, telegram, May 27, 1907, S. D. File 1797/209, Gillett to Root, May 28, 1907, S. D. File 1797/215–224, Bonaparte to Root, June 11, 1907, S. D. File 1797/238–239.

16 Hayashi to Aoki, May 23, 1907, Telegram Series, XCVI, 6397.

17 Wright to Root, telegram, May 25, 1907, S. D. File 1797/204.

18 Root to Wright, telegram, May 25, 1907, S. D. File 1797/204.

19 Root to Bonaparte, May 25, 1907, S. D. File 1797/204.

20 Aoki to Hayashi, received May 26, 1907, Telegram Series, XCV, 4937.

forcement of the law.[21] Gillett immediately telegraphed assurance that he would request the police to use every effort to protect the Japanese.[22] Gillett also sent a letter explaining the disturbed conditions prevailing in San Francisco during the strike and giving further assurance that everything possible would be done to restrain the lawless element.[23] In San Francisco Mayor Schmitz told Acting Consul Matsubara that he would not tolerate the abuse of individuals, no matter what nationality, creed, or color they might be.[24]

Fortunately for the Roosevelt administration, the new outbreak in San Francisco could probably be settled through court action. The Japanese had been on shaky legal ground during the school segregation crisis, but in this new instance they were in a strong position to secure redress through local remedies. Under the political code of California, every municipality was responsible for injuries caused by mobs or riots, a fact Matsubara was quick to discern. Ambassador Aoki was reluctant to seek a solution through a suit against San Francisco, fearing that an attitude of hostility toward the San Francisco authorities might make matters still worse,[25] but Foreign Minister Hayashi favored pressing the suit. Hayashi even gave secret financial aid to the Japanese claimants for legal expenses.[26]

Roosevelt and Root worked in close cooperation with Aoki in resolving the crisis. Copies of all the correspondence and reports on the subject were sent to the Ambassador, and District Attorney Devlin was instructed to render all possible assistance to the Japanese in pressing the suit for damages against the city.[27] Root also sent a note to Aoki stating that the United States "shares in the expression of regret of the authorities of San Francisco." [28] In his desire to placate the Japanese, Root overreached himself on this occasion. San Francisco had not expressed any regrets — and it

[21] Root to Gillett, telegram, May 25, 1907, S. D. File 1797/206–207.
[22] Gillett to Root, telegram, May 27, 1907, S. D. File 1797/208.
[23] Gillett to Root, May 28, 1907, S. D. File 1797/215–224.
[24] Schmitz to Matsubara, May 23, 1907, Documents Relating to the Limitation and Exclusion of Japanese Immigrants by the United States, MT3.8.2.21, reel 723, p. 3594.
[25] Aoki to Hayashi, received June 6, 1907, Telegram Series, XCV, 5310–12.
[26] Hayashi to Aoki, June 6, 1907, Telegram Series, XCVII, 6609.
[27] Bonaparte to Devlin, June 7, 1907, S. D. File 1797/236–237.
[28] Root to Aoki, June 5, 1907, S. D. File 1797/215–224.

was unlikely that it could be induced to do so. Aoki was apparently also eager to appease Tokyo, for when Hayashi questioned him regarding San Francisco's expression of regret, he responded with a rather labored explanation to the effect that it was his understanding that San Francisco had expressed regret "in document not transmitted to me." [29]

Relations between Aoki and Root were so cordial that Root could write to Roosevelt on June 7, 1907, that "so far as the two governments go this San Francisco affair is getting on all right as an ordinary diplomatic affair about which there is no occasion to get excited. All the trouble is being made by the leprous vampires who are eager to involve their country in war in order to sell a few more newspapers." [30] Roosevelt was nevertheless alarmed. To Henry White he confided that he saw no prospect of the Japanese-California situation growing better. In the wake of the financial panic which swept the country in March, 1907, many men were being put out of work and this factor made conditions in San Francisco still worse. In the light of these circumstances, Roosevelt feared a recurrence of trouble at any time. "Between ourselves," he wrote to White, "I have arranged to have plenty of troops in the neighborhood." [31]

The riot of May, 1907, never became a formal diplomatic question, for local remedies proved effective. In July a suit was filed against the city of San Francisco and was scheduled for trial in March, 1908. Before the trial could take place, District Attorney Devlin suggested an out-of-court settlement. He pointed out to the city authorities that this would have the effect of removing in a friendly way the grievance of the Japanese and would avoid the bitterness and ill feeling resulting from a conflict in court. [32] Both sides accepted Devlin's suggestion, and the issue was closed in March, 1908, when the city of San Francisco paid four hundred and fifty dollars to the injured parties. [33]

29 Hayashi to Aoki, June 7, 1907, Telegram Series, XCVII, 6618; Aoki to Hayashi, received June 8, 1907, Telegram Series, XCV, 5384–86.

30 Root to Roosevelt, June 7, 1907, Roosevelt Papers.

31 Roosevelt to White, June 15, 1907, Roosevelt Papers.

32 Consul Chozo Koike to Hayashi, received February 28, 1908, Telegram Series, CIV, 976–77.

33 Devlin to Bonaparte, March 11, 1908, S. D. File 1797/452–453.

Though the riot did not become a diplomatic issue, its impact on Japanese-American relations can scarcely be overestimated. Soon after the outbreak of the trouble, the "leprous vampires" of the journalist fraternity on both sides of the Pacific were transforming it into an issue that was to snowball into a serious war scare. When reports first reached Japan, Wright reported that they did not stir much excitement,[34] but by June 6 the Japanese press had so thoroughly aroused the Japanese people that an Associated Press dispatch from Tokyo stated that popular indignation had reached a height never before witnessed in the history of Japan's relations with the United States.[35] On June 12 Wright reported that the agitation had continued to grow until, of all the newspapers in the capital, only the *Jiji Shimpo* had retained an attitude of moderation. All the other leading papers had expressed surprise, dissatisfaction, annoyance or apprehension, while journals of the second and lower ranks had gone to absurd extremes. Wright gave the following analysis of the Japanese reaction:

There are certain things, however, that must be considered in connection with this apparently unreasonable display of public temper. The first is that the recent incidents have been regarded as a continuation of the school question in spite of all official assurances to the contrary. The people of Japan as a whole are undoubtedly dissatisfied with the solution of that question, involving as it did new restrictions upon Japanese immigration to the United States. Some are influenced by considerations of national pride, others by pecuniary interests and still others by political motives, but all unite to add strength to the present agitation.[36]

The excitement in Japan soared to such a peak that the political parties took occasion to express their views in formal manifestoes. The Seiyukai resolution was moderately worded and reflected the views of the government, but the Shimpoto statement was a strong arraignment of the Japanese and American governments. Katsura's Daido Club expressed regret that the Japanese government, on account of its "negligence and temporizing methods," had failed to take appropriate measures. The agitation also took definite form in a resolution adopted at a joint meeting of the chambers of com-

[34] Wright to Root, May 28, 1907, S. D. File 1797/432.
[35] Associated Press dispatch, June 6, 1907, Roosevelt Papers.
[36] Wright to Root, June 12, 1907, S. D. File 1797/247.

merce of Japan held on June 22, 1907. Though the resolution was carefully worded, it hinted at the possibility of a boycott.[37] A week later the presidents of the principal chambers of commerce of Japan addressed letters to Roosevelt and to the chambers of commerce of the United States stating that if the hostile demonstrations against the Japanese continued, the commerce between the two countries might be "retarded." Wright reported that he had definite information that the subject of a boycott had been discussed at the meeting of the chambers of commerce.[38]

Ambassador Aoki was appalled at the jingoistic outburst in Japan and its effect upon American public opinion. In his reports to Tokyo, he singled out in particular certain inflammatory statements attributed to Okuma. "Anti-American agitation in Japan for which . . . Okuma and his press organ are responsible primarily," he anxiously telegraphed, "is making unfavorable impression on the general sentiment in this country." [39] Aoki also reported that wide publicity had been accorded a report from Japan that he would be replaced and that the change would mark the beginning of a more aggressive policy on the part of Japan toward the United States. He pleaded with Hayashi for an official denial if the report was "not founded upon fact." [40] Much to the relief of Aoki and American officials, Hayashi immediately issued a statement saying that all rumors regarding an ambassadorial change were absolutely unfounded.[41]

Much of the feeling aroused in Japan was doubtless genuine, but it was soon evident to Wright and to the Japanese themselves that most of the agitation was attributable to considerations of party politics. The *Hochi Shimbun*, the recognized organ of the opposition Shimpoto party, took the lead in attacking both the United States for its persecutions of the Japanese and the Saionji cabinet for its inaction. Wright reported that an attempt was being made to discredit Hayashi and Aoki as part of a larger scheme to unseat the cabinet. Hayashi himself told Wright that about seventy

37 Wright to Root, June 27, 1907, S. D. File 1797/270–290.
38 Wright to Root, July 10, 1907, S. D. File 1797/298–308.
39 Aoki to Hayashi, received June 9, 1907, Telegram Series, XCV, 5398–99.
40 Aoki to Hayashi, received June 19, 1907, Telegram Series, XCV, 5680–81.
41 Hayashi to Aoki, June 21, 1907, Telegram Series, XCVII, 6840.

per cent of the feeling displayed in the newspapers was for political effect and that the remainder was probably genuine resentment over the San Francisco situation. Wright reported that Count Okuma himself had privately admitted that his utterances on the question were for political effect.[42] The *Japan Times* sensed the nature of the agitation and stated:

> the irrepressible loquacity and freelance habits of Count Okuma have recently betrayed him into indulging in premature utterances. The fearless old peer is no longer the leader of any political party and he spoke only as an individual who had succumbed to the temptations of an American yellow journal. The rancorous voice of an ambitious man in disappointment must not be taken for that of the nation.[43]

The agitation was so obviously inspired in large part by politics that by the end of June a reaction had taken place. Wright reported on June 27 that practically all the responsible newspapers were counseling moderation.[44]

The agitation was rapidly declining when suddenly a new issue arose to stir more feeling in Japan. On June 27 the Board of Police Commissioners of San Francisco refused to license six Japanese to conduct employment offices. Four of the applications were for renewals and two were new. Roosevelt's exasperation was evident in a letter to Root: "I see that a new San Francisco fool has cropped up to add to our difficulties with the Japanese. What will be the outcome, I do not know. I have called upon Bonaparte to investigate the matter." [45] The Attorney General telegraphed Devlin to make an immediate investigation, and on July 8 the latter sent in a report. Devlin reported that the Charter of the City and County of San Francisco empowered the chief of police to supervise and control such businesses as pawnbrokers, peddlers, and employment agencies, and that the Board of Police Commissioners was now carrying out a policy of awarding preference to United States citizens.[46] Roosevelt forwarded this report to Root, who was at his

[42] Wright to Root, June 12, 1907, S. D. File 1797/247.
[43] *Japan Times*, June 13, 1907.
[44] Wright to Root, June 27, 1907, S. D. File 1797/270–290.
[45] Roosevelt to Root, July 2, 1907, Morison, *Roosevelt Letters*, V, 699–700.
[46] Devlin to Bonaparte, July 8, 1907, Roosevelt Papers.

home in Clinton, New York, mending his health. Root was equally disgusted:

What I feel and think about it is not fit to write. Apparently nothing will disturb the smug satisfaction with which San Francisco officials pursue a policy of insult and irritation sure to land us in war, except some explicit official statement pointing out the inevitable result of their conduct. Probably that would not and I do not yet see that it is admissible for us officially to impute warlike intentions to Japan.[47]

During subsequent weeks Roosevelt and Root took no action, but their concern persisted. "As for the San Francisco business," Roosevelt wrote to Root on July 23, "I am quite prepared to issue the most solemn possible warning to our people as to the effect of such a fatuous policy of insult and injury." [48] He wrote Root again a few days later, saying that everything must be done to remedy the wrongs inflicted on the Japanese:

I am only waiting to hear from you to take any further action on the subject of the last discrimination about the Japanese employment agencies. Shall I direct a suit to be brought so that it may be tested in court? As you know, we now have plenty of troops in the neighborhood of San Francisco, so that in the event of riot we can interfere effectively should the State and municipal authorities be unable or unwilling to afford the protection which we are bound to give the Japanese.[49]

In Japan the news of the discrimination aroused ill feeling, but in comparison to the recent agitation over the riot of May 20 the reaction was mild. One of the reasons was that the Japanese were preoccupied with developments concerning Korea. The Korean Emperor had dispatched a delegation to the Hague Conference to appeal for aid against Japan, and the question of his abdication was hanging in the balance. Another factor was Secretary of the Navy Metcalf's announcement on July 4 that the United States fleet was going to the Pacific. This important development will be considered subsequently, but suffice it to say here that this had a sobering effect upon the Japanese press. The moderate reaction in Japan was also owing to Japan's weak legal position in this issue. As

47 Root to Roosevelt, July 21, 1907, Roosevelt Papers.
48 Roosevelt to Root, July 23, 1907, Morison, *Roosevelt Letters*, V, 724–725.
49 Roosevelt to Root, July 26, 1907, Morison, *Roosevelt Letters*, V, 729–730.

the *Japan Times* pointed out, it was doubtful whether the most-favored-nation clause in the treaty of 1894 guaranteed to Japanese the right to engage in business in all respects equally with the nationals of other countries.[50]

In the controversy over the refusal of licenses, the Japanese government assumed a stiffer position than the legalities warranted and — it might be added — a stiffer position than its own ambassador favored. When the dispute first arose, Hayashi sought telegraphic advice from the Foreign Ministry adviser, Henry W. Denison, who was at the Hague Conference.[51] Denison replied with a somewhat strained interpretation of the treaty of 1894. He conceded that the treaty did not specifically give to Japanese the right to reside in the United States except for purposes of trade, but he went on to say that residence rights included by implication the right to ordinary means of livelihood. He also advised that where the refusal of licenses was based on national or racial grounds the Japanese government should make representations directly to the United States government.[52]

Hayashi accepted Denison's advice *in toto* and sent strongly worded instructions to Aoki directing him to object to the peremptory action which was "in utter disregard of indisputable rights of Japanese residents." He was to tell Root to take steps at once to have the decisions of the San Francisco authorities immediately withdrawn.[53] The Ambassador was dumbfounded by Hayashi's telegram. He waited almost a week without doing anything, and then instead of carrying out the instructions, he dispatched a long telegram to Tokyo pleading for a change in his government's position. He reminded Hayashi of how powerless the federal government had been over local authorities in the school segregation crisis, and he recommended that a judicial solution be sought. There was absolutely no way in which the government could compel municipal authorities to abstain from certain acts. The injured parties should file suit, he said, and the Japanese government should await

50 *Japan Times*, July 4, 1907.
51 Hayashi to Denison, July 3, 1907, Telegram Series, XCIX, 8719–20.
52 Denison to Hayashi, July 7, 1907, Telegram Series, XCVII, 7206–09.
53 Hayashi to Aoki, July 13, 1907, Telegram Series, XCIX, 8857–59.

the result of this action before making the matter a diplomatic question.[54]

Hayashi relented only slightly. He insisted to Aoki that Japan had to force the United States government to stop the action of the San Francisco authorities, but he agreed to a softening of the note that was to be presented at Washington.[55] When Aoki made the representation to Acting Secretary Adee on July 31, he softened it even further by saying that he was "very sorry" to bring up the matter and that he wished to give his representation "an altogether informal character." [56] He left a *promemoria* at the Department embodying Hayashi's sweeping statement that the treaty right to reside implied the right to labor for a living.[57]

Adee sent the Japanese *promemoria* to Root at Clinton, pointing out in a covering letter that licenses for employment agencies were generally within the domain of police power.[58] Roosevelt, who was at Oyster Bay, was also informed, and he immediately wrote to Root saying he was anxious to go over the matter with him before a reply was made.[59] Before drafting a reply to Aoki's representation, Root asked Bonaparte to have Devlin investigate further. The result was not encouraging. Devlin telegraphed on August 7 that the licenses clearly were being denied on grounds of nationality and that no change in policy could be expected so long as the present Board of Police Commissioners was in power. The board had been appointed by Mayor Schmitz, who was now convicted of felony and in jail, but as the right to office of the new mayor, E. R. Taylor, was being disputed, a new board might not be appointed for some time.[60] When this report was received, Adee advised Root to tell Aoki frankly that racial discrimination was at the bottom of the matter and that a present remedy was beyond the reach of the federal government.[61]

54 Aoki to Hayashi, received July 21, 1907, Telegram Series, XCVIII, 7599–7601.
55 Hayashi to Aoki, July 27, 1907, Telegram Series, XCIX, 9027.
56 Adee to Root, July 31, 1907, S. D. File 1797/323.
57 *Promemoria* handed to Adee by Aoki, July 31, 1907, S. D. File 1797/323.
58 Adee to Root, July 31, 1907, S. D. File 1797/323.
59 Roosevelt to Root, August 2, 1907, Roosevelt Papers.
60 Devlin to Bonaparte, August 7, 1907, enclosed in Acting Attorney General Charles W. Russell to Root, August 7, 1907, S. D. File 1797/311.
61 Memorandum by Adee, enclosed in Bacon to Root, August 7, 1907, S. D. File 1797/311.

Root made no immediate reply to Aoki, and before he returned to Washington in September, events in San Francisco took a turn for the better. In August the new mayor appointed a new police board. Kikujiro Ishii, a roving Japanese diplomat, visited San Francisco in late August, and he concluded that by allowing due time to the new board the license matter would be solved.[62] "Due time," it soon became apparent, would be after the local elections in November. Acting Consul Matsubara recommended to Tokyo that that date be patiently awaited, for to embarrass the board before the election would only benefit the anti-Japanese labor union ticket.[63]

In the interim before the election, the federal government tactfully exerted its influence upon the police board. Root had District Attorney Devlin explain to the board the importance of the issue "as bearing upon the peaceful relations between Japan and the United States" and to point out that this matter of comparatively trifling importance was hindering the "vastly more important matter of labor exclusion."[64] Root confided to Aoki that the federal government was using its influence but cautioned that if news of such federal intervention should leak out the administration would be subject to strong adverse criticism on constitutional grounds.[65]

In late November, the elections now out of the way, the president of the Board of Police Commissioners suggested to Matsubara that the license applications be renewed,[66] and in December the long-pending issue was resolved. On December 11 the new Japanese Consul at San Francisco, Chozo Koike, informed Devlin that the licenses had been granted.[67] He added that he presumed the news would be gratifying to the Department of State — and indeed it was.

62 Ishii to Hayashi, received August 23, 1907, Telegram Series, XCIX, 8441.
63 Matsubara to Hayashi, October 3 and 4, 1907, Telegram Series, CI, 10341, 10368–69.
64 Root to Bonaparte, September 23, 1907, S. D. File 1797/325a.
65 Aoki to Hayashi, September 27, 1907, Telegram Series, C, 10119.
66 Matsubara to Hayashi, received November 22, 1907, Telegram Series, CIII, 12133.
67 Devlin to Bonaparte, December 11, 1907, S. D. File 1797/424–425.

CHAPTER ELEVEN

The War Scare of 1907

THE riot of May 20 and the license discrimination of June 27 would not have been serious matters had they not come in the wake of the school segregation crisis and at a time when the Shimpoto party in Japan was seeking an issue with which to harass the Saionji ministry. Coming in that context, however, they set in motion forces that were to bring the most serious war scare that had ever occurred in Japanese-American relations. The warlike utterances in Japan aroused not only the Japanese people but also many Americans, who — not knowing that such statements were politically inspired — feared that a Japanese attack on the United States was imminent. The journalists made the most of the situation, and with each passing day the predictions of war became increasingly vivid. By the end of June, 1907, the agitation was dying down in Japan, but by that time the more excitable journals in the United States were waxing sensational in their interpretation of events. Then came a development which raised excitement to new heights: the announcement that the United States battleship fleet would be sent to the Pacific.

Ever since the beginning of the trouble with Japan, there had been some agitation in the United States in favor of moving part of the fleet to the Pacific. Roosevelt was convinced that to send only part of the fleet would be an "act of utter folly." When Mahan wrote to him in alarm in January, 1907, concerning reports that some but not all battleships were to be sent to the Pacific, Roosevelt replied: "I have no more thought of sending four battleships to the Pacific while there is the least possible friction with Japan than I have of going thither in a rowboat myself." [1]

[1] Mahan to Roosevelt, January 10, 1907, Roosevelt Papers; Roosevelt to Mahan, January 12, 1907, Morison, *Roosevelt Letters*, V, 550–551.

Late in June, 1907, following the agitation in Japan over the riot of May 20, Roosevelt decided to order the entire battleship fleet to the Pacific. On June 14 he requested a report from the Joint Army and Navy Board regarding plans in case of war with Japan, and three days later, as a result of this request, the Board decided that not less than sixteen battleships should be assembled in the Pacific as soon as possible. At a meeting at Oyster Bay on June 27, at which Secretary of the Navy Metcalf and Postmaster General George von Lengerke Meyer were present, Roosevelt accepted the Joint Board's recommendation. He stated, however, that the voyage of the battleships should assume the character of a practice cruise, for he had no serious apprehensions regarding war with Japan.[2] On July 4 Metcalf publicly announced that the fleet would go to San Francisco.[3]

Roosevelt's decision to send the fleet to the Pacific was prompted by several considerations. In his autobiography he said that his primary purpose was to impress the American public and arouse popular support for a more ambitious battleship program.[4] He had encountered strong opposition to his naval program, and the sending of the fleet on a long voyage would stir the pride and interest of the American people. The news was not publicly released until February, 1908, that the fleet would continue around the world, but from the beginning Roosevelt conceived of the movement in terms of a world cruise. In writing to Lodge just six days after Metcalf's announcement, Roosevelt referred to a "world cruise."[5] Building up the navy was, of course, not unrelated to the Japanese question, for Roosevelt's interest in a big navy increased tremendously as the friction with Japan developed.

Roosevelt's decision was also motivated by a desire to give the

[2] Braisted, *United States Navy in the Pacific*, pp. 204–207; Howe, *Meyer*, pp. 362–363.

[3] The first news of the fleet transfer was given on July 1 in the Boston *Evening Transcript*. Assistant Secretary of the Navy Truman H. Newberry and Roosevelt's secretary, William Loeb, both issued denials on the following day, but Metcalf, who was then on a visit to California, announced on July 4 that the fleet was going to San Francisco. It was not until August 1 that the announcement was confirmed in Washington by Loeb. Bailey, *Roosevelt and the Japanese-American Crises*, pp. 211–215.

[4] Theodore Roosevelt, *Theodore Roosevelt; an Autobiography*, New York, 1929, pp. 549–550.

[5] Roosevelt to Lodge, July 10, 1907, Morison, *Roosevelt Letters*, V, 709–710.

navy a much needed practice voyage, which would prepare it for possible hostilities with Japan. Soon after he resolved to send the fleet to the Pacific, he confided to Lodge his reason for the "practice cruise":

It became evident to me, from talking with the naval authorities, that in the event of war they would have a good deal to find out in the way of sending the fleet to the Pacific. Now, the one thing that I won't run the risk of is to experiment for the first time in a matter of vital importance in time of war. Accordingly I concluded that it was imperative that we should send the fleet on what would practically be a practice voyage.[6]

There was still another reason for Roosevelt's decision to send the fleet to the Pacific, a reason that was quickly discerned by both Americans and Japanese: the desire to impress Japan with the strength of the United States and thereby silence the Japanese extremists. Roosevelt's correspondence reveals that he was greatly disturbed over the chauvinistic utterances in Japan. On July 1 he wrote to Spring Rice: "The San Francisco mob bids fair, if not to embroil us with Japan, at any rate to arouse in Japan a feeling of rankling anger toward us that may at any time bear evil result; and the Japanese Jingoes are in their turn about as bad as ours."[7] He wrote to Henry White that "the utterances of the extremists in Japan have begun to make an unpleasant feeling in this country."[8] On July 13 he wrote to Root: "I am more concerned over this Japanese situation than almost any other. Thank Heaven we have the navy in good shape. It is high time, however, that it should go on a cruise around the world. In the first place I think it will have a pacific effect to show that it can be done. . . ."[9] To British Ambassador James Bryce he stated that his principal reason for sending the fleet to the Pacific was to "impress Japan with the seriousness of the situation."[10] Four years later Roosevelt wrote even more positively:

6 Roosevelt to Lodge, July 10, 1907, Morison, *Roosevelt Letters*, V, 709–710. See also Roosevelt to Root, July 13, 1907, Morison, *Roosevelt Letters*, V, 717–719.

7 Roosevelt to Spring Rice, July 1, 1907, Morison, *Roosevelt Letters*, V, 698–699.

8 Roosevelt to White, June 15, 1907, Allen Nevins, *Henry White: Thirty Years of American Diplomacy*, New York, 1930, p. 292.

9 Roosevelt to Root, July 13, 1907, Morison, *Roosevelt Letters*, V, 717–719.

10 Sir Claude M. MacDonald to Sir Edward Grey, March 17, 1908, *British Documents*, VIII, 457–458.

I had been doing my best to be polite to the Japanese, and had finally become uncomfortably conscious of a very, very slight undertone of veiled
truculence in their communications in connection with things that happened on the Pacific Slope; and I finally made up my mind that they thought
I was afraid of them. . . . I found that the Japanese war party firmly believed that they could beat us, and, unlike the Elder Statesmen, thought I
also believed this. . . . I definitely came to the conclusion that . . . it
was time for a show down.[11]

Roosevelt's memory did not serve him well when he referred to
"veiled truculence" in the communications of the Japanese government. There were few communications received from Japan on the
California trouble, and those which were received were certainly
not truculent. Doubtless the utterances of the opposition party in
Japan, rather than the communications of the Japanese government, had prompted the sending of the fleet. In a letter written in
1916, Roosevelt came closer to the truth. Writing to Hugo Müns-
terberg, he said: "You, of course, know that the voyage of the battle
fleet around the world was really an answer to the very ugly war
talk that had begun to spring up in Japan; and it was the best
example that I know of, 'of speaking softly and carrying a big
stick.' " [12]

The Japanese reaction to the announcement of the fleet movement was outwardly calm. The Japanese Ambassador gave assurances that the dispatch of ships from one American port to another
would not be regarded as an unfriendly act, even if the fleet were
to be sent on to the Philippines.[13] The *Japan Times* assured its
readers that the cruise had no warlike significance.[14] The Tokyo
Asahi viewed the movement as a normal incident in American expansion and the newspaper extended assurances to America —
prophetic assurances, it turned out — that if the fleet visited Japan
it would receive a warm welcome.[15] Such expressions, however, represented only the outward reaction of the Japanese. Wright re-

[11] Roosevelt to George Otto Trevelyan, October 1, 1911, Morison, *Roosevelt Letters*,
VII, 393–394.
[12] Roosevelt to Munsterberg, February 8, 1916, Morison, *Roosevelt Letters*, VIII,
1018.
[13] New York *Times*, July 3, 1907.
[14] *Japan Times*, July 7, 1907.
[15] Tokyo *Asahi* quoted in *Japan Daily Mail*, July 9, 1907.

ported that though the Japanese press had received the news calmly, he believed the movement of the fleet at this time would have
an unfavorable effect upon the mind of the average Japanese.[16]
Wright was probably correct. Certainly Japanese leaders were deeply concerned about the new turn of events. Even Aoki, who was
generally friendly to the United States, was greatly irritated. He
reported to Tokyo that Roosevelt was motivated by domestic politics and was "playing a dangerous game." Ever since he alienated
the Californians by over-praising the Japanese in his message to
Congress, Aoki said, he had been anxious to undo the effects of
the message. It was Aoki's opinion that Roosevelt was showing a
strong attitude toward Japan to strengthen his party in the coming presidential election.[17]

The extremists in Japan were visibly shaken by the announcement of the fleet movement. It put them squarely on the spot. They
were now painfully aware that they had violated the old American
frontier maxim so dear to Roosevelt, "Never draw unless you
mean to shoot." To save face the Japanese now had to either attack the fleet, make a counter demonstration, or proclaim their
satisfaction with the President's decision as though it had no meaning for Japan. They chose the latter alternative. Okuma, spokes-
man of the chauvinistic opposition, announced that with regard
to the "little cloud" hovering over Japanese-American relations,
Japan was the complainant and the United States was the defendant. Surely, he told the Japanese people, the movement of the fleet
could have no relation to this matter, for a defendant would not
logically make an armed demonstration against the complainant.
That would be much as a man putting his hat on his feet and his
socks on his head! "It cannot be supposed for a moment that the
United States Government contemplates such a reversal of the
proper order of things." [18] Okuma also expressed the happy thought
that the fleet could get to Japan at just the right time for the officers to participate in the chrysanthemum festivals! [19]

In the weeks that followed, there was a noticeable quieting of the

16 Wright to Root, July 10, 1907, S. D. File 1797/298–308.
17 Aoki to Hayashi, received July 9, 1907, Telegram Series, XCVII, 7244–45.
18 *Japan Daily Mail*, July 10, 1907.
19 *Japan Daily Mail*, July 9, 1907.

Japanese press. Roosevelt could write to Albert Shaw on September 3, 1907:

You know far too much of foreign events and of the needs of the navy for it to be necessary for me to explain to you how important it is that we should now see by actual experiment just how our battle fleet can go to the Pacific, and you perhaps know how useful the mere statement that it was going there has already been in preventing clamor for hostilities against us by the Japanese yellow press.[20]

The dispatching of the fleet to the Pacific continued to have a quieting effect upon the Japanese in subsequent months. Roosevelt's recollection was largely correct when he wrote many years later that "every particle of trouble with the Japanese Government and the Japanese press stopped like magic as soon as they found that our fleet had actually sailed and was obviously in good trim." [21]

Despite the quieting of the extremist agitation in Japan, the rumors of war which were circulating in Europe and the United States continued to increase. One of the underlying reasons for concern among Western observers was the Japanese armaments program which had been proceeding apace since the close of the Russo-Japanese War. The budget for 1907 caused particular concern, for the amount designated for armaments was more than double that alloted in the previous budget. It provided for an increase of two divisions in the army and a change in the period of military service from three to two years, thus giving more men an opportunity for training. The *Hochi Shimbun* estimated that these changes would enable Japan to put a million men in the field in time of war.[22] The enormous military outlay caused misgivings even in Japan. Oishi Masami, a member of the Budget Committee, inquired of the ministry as to what enemy the government was preparing to meet.[23]

In the American press the war rumors spiraled upward in in-

20 Roosevelt to Shaw, September 3, 1907, Roosevelt Papers.

21 Roosevelt to Trevelyan, October 1, 1911, Morison, *Roosevelt Letters*, VII, 393–394.

22 Wright to Root, January 19, 1907, S. D. File 4080; Wright to Root, April 4, 1907, S. D. File 6273/1.

23 Walter W. McLaren, *A Political History of Japan During the Meiji Era, 1867–1912*, London, 1916, pp. 309–310.

tensity when it was announced that the fleet would go to the Pacific. As the newspapers beat the tom-toms of war, Roosevelt's concern mounted. He wrote to Lodge on July 10:

I shall continue to do everything I can by politeness and consideration to the Japs to offset the worse than criminal stupidity of the San Francisco mob, the San Francisco press, and such papers as the New York *Herald*. I do not believe we shall have war; but it is no fault of the yellow press if we do not have it.[24]

Three days later he wrote to Root: "A goodly number of our papers spend their time in insulting the Japanese and in writing articles which, when they are repeated, as they are sure to be, in Japan, cause the greatest irritation against us."[25]

Both sides took steps to counteract the war rumors. Hayashi telegraphed Joseph Pulitzer of the New York *World* stating that it was fully understood that the cruise of the United States fleet implied no indication of a disquieting nature in the relations between the United States and Japan. The whole nation of Japan, he asserted, had unshaken confidence in the policy of justice and peace that characterized the American government.[26] At Washington, Roosevelt told Aoki that he hoped Japan would not regard the cruise of the fleet as intended in any way to be a hostile demonstration, and he added that so long as he was President, war between the United States and Japan was an impossibility.[27] But despite these assurances passing between the United States and Japan, the war rumors continued to increase.

If the newspapers had known of the disquieting reports coming in to Roosevelt at this time, the panic would have been even greater. The German Ambassador, Speck von Sternberg, sent to Oyster Bay alarming information about the influx of disguised Japanese troops into Mexico. The German representative in Mexico City had reported that two Japanese merchant ships had landed about four thousand reserve troops, some of them wearing uniforms and badges.[28] Secretary of War Taft learned through an officer return-

24 Roosevelt to Lodge, July 10, 1907, Morison, *Roosevelt Letters*, V, 709–710.
25 Roosevelt to Root, July 13, 1907, Morison, *Roosevelt Letters*, V, 717–719.
26 Hayashi to Pulitzer, July 17, 1907, Telegram Series, XCIX, 8893.
27 Aoki to Hayashi, received July 18, 1907, Telegram Series, XCVIII, 7502–03.
28 Sternberg to Roosevelt, July 14, 1907, Roosevelt Papers.

ing from Hawaii that the people there were greatly perturbed, believing that from five to ten thousand of the seventy thousand Japanese in the islands were recently discharged soldiers and that they had a definite military organization.[29]

On July 21 Secretary of State Root forwarded to Roosevelt a report from Consul General Charles Denby, who was then in Europe, and this report was so alarming and so strikingly similar to a letter from Ambassador Tower at Berlin that it upset even the usually imperturbable Root. In transmitting the report Root said that he did not yet see that it was admissable to impute warlike intentions to Japan but that there was food for thought in Denby's letter.[30] It was generally believed in France and Germany, Denby reported, that Japan had definitely decided on war with the United States. The outcome of such a war, he said, had received technical consideration in military circles in Germany and Britain, and the estimate was five to four in favor of a Japanese victory.[31] Tower, in a personal letter to Root, confirmed Denby's information. He reported that it was the consensus of opinion throughout Europe that the United States would have trouble with Japan in spite of itself. Both the German General Staff and the British Admiralty had ventured estimates on the outcome of the war, he said, and though the calculations had been made separately, the conclusion was the same: the odds favored Japan five to four.[32]

Roosevelt had already received information from Europe identical to that which came to Root. Melville E. Stone of the Associated Press had forwarded to him a letter from Elmer Roberts telling of a conversation with the British Military Attaché at Berlin, Captain Philip Dumas. Dumas, who had just returned from London where he had conferred with high government officials, predicted that war would come within thirty months and that the issue would be mastery of the Pacific. The British Admiralty and the German Naval General Staff, he told Roberts, believed that Japan's chances of winning would be about five to four.[33]

[29] Clarence R. Edwards to Taft, July 15, 1907, Taft Papers.
[30] Root to Roosevelt, July 21, 1907, Roosevelt Papers.
[31] Denby to Root, July 2, 1907, S. D. File 1797/347.
[32] Tower to Root, July 10, 1907, S. D. File 1797/348–349.
[33] Roberts to Stone, July 10, 1907, Roosevelt Papers.

On July 27 a disturbing report arrived in Washington from Colombia. The United States Chargé at Bogota, William Heimké, reported rumors that an alliance had been concluded between Colombia and Japan by which Colombia ceded to Japan coaling stations on the Pacific and on the Caribbean. These rumors, which later proved to be unfounded, caused such uneasiness at the Department of State that Robert Bacon, the First Assistant Secretary of State, sent a copy to Root at Clinton. The Secretary, knowing the strategic location of Colombia and the disgruntlement of its government over the loss of Panama, was greatly concerned. He sent a copy of the report to Roosevelt with the reminder, "Colombia as an enemy is a source of vital danger if we have *any other enemy*." [34]

Throughout July, 1907, as sensational reports came into Washington and Oyster Bay, Roosevelt refused to succumb to the hysteria which was overtaking many Americans. He was, of course, concerned about the bad effect of the war rumors, but he did not believe that the Japanese intended to go to war in the near future, and he held to that belief throughout the crisis. In a letter to General Leonard Wood over a year before, he had expressed the basis of his reasoning:

Moreover, I entirely agree with you that we can retain the Philippines only so long as we have a first-class fighting navy, superior to the navy of any possible opponent. I do not for a moment agree, however, that Japan has any immediate intention of moving against us in the Philippines. Her eyes for some time to come will be directed toward Korea and southern Manchuria. . . . No man can prophesy about the future, but I see not the slightest chance of Japan attacking us in the Philippines for a decade or two, or until the present conditions of international politics change.[35]

At the time of the school segregation crisis, Roosevelt's views regarding the intentions of Japan were substantiated by a letter coming from Durham Stevens, the American adviser to the Residency General in Korea. In a letter to Clarence R. Edwards, extracts of which were forwarded to Root, Stevens said:

34 William Heimké to Root, June 20, 1907; attached note from Root to Roosevelt, n.d., S. D. File 7804/1.
35 Roosevelt to Wood, January 22, 1906, Morison, *Roosevelt Letters*, V, 135–136.

What's the matter with our newspapers anyway — especially the N. Y. Herald? Just plain common garden variety foolishness, or what? The idea of a war between the United States and Japan is more than foolish, it is criminal. . . . Japan is thinking of other things than war. She has problems to solve nearer home, and needs a long, a very long period of recuperation before anything save a war in defense of what she has already gained can be even remotely possible. The acquisition of the Philippines has never figured in her plans.[36]

Root considered Stevens' letter "full of sound sense,"[37] and he doubtless communicated Stevens' views to the President.

An American military observer, Major Samuel Reber, who had been sent to Japan to make a special investigation regarding Japan's intentions, agreed that Japan was not planning war against the United States. In a report which was forwarded to Roosevelt by Taft on July 2, Reber said that the Japanese were making no immediate preparations for war. Indeed, he continued, "I do not believe that anything is farther from their thoughts at the present time." The whole future of the empire, he said, depended upon the success of its commercial expansion, and hostilities with the United States would absolutely stop this. From a strictly military point of view, Japan was ready for war at any time but could not afford it for financial and commercial reasons.[38] Taft wrote to Roosevelt saying that the report merely confirmed his own view of the situation,[39] and Roosevelt agreed that it stated "exactly the facts."[40]

Other reassuring information came to Roosevelt. John Callan O'Laughlin informed him that he had talked with Aoki, and the Japanese Ambassador had told him frankly that Japan did not want war with the United States. O'Laughlin had a friend who had very close relations with the Japanese embassy, and this person confirmed the truth of the Ambassador's statement.[41] Roosevelt doubtless believed that this report was correct. An incident which occurred at this time clearly indicates that he did not believe Japan

36 Edwards to Root, March 11, 1907, Root Papers.
37 Root to Edwards, March 12, 1907, Root Papers.
38 Reber to Taft, May 23, 1907, Roosevelt Papers.
39 Taft to Roosevelt, July 2, 1907, Roosevelt Papers.
40 Roosevelt to Taft, July 4, 1907, Morison, *Roosevelt Letters*, V, 705.
41 O'Laughlin to Roosevelt, July 7, 1907, Roosevelt Papers.

was contemplating an attack. Major Eben Swift, who was in the Far East surveying the situation, had Rockhill telegraph the following message through the Department of State to the General Staff on July 12:

Shall I report by cable Japanese war vessels now ready, the time when additional Japanese war vessels will be ready, numbers of army, progress of the new armament, recent movements of naval reserves, arms smuggled into the Philippine Islands, character Hawaiian immigration? [42]

Roosevelt was consulted and he immediately instructed Adee, "there is no need for cabling." [43]

Despite Roosevelt's belief that Japan was not planning to attack, his confidence was not complete. His correspondence during July evidenced continuing anxiety. In a letter to Speck von Sternberg on July 16 he said that he did not believe there would be trouble and he was taking all steps possible both to prevent it and to prevent its being disastrous if it should come. "But of course the situation gives me some concern," he confided, "for the Japanese are a formidable military power and have unknown possibilities both as regards their power and as regards their motives and purposes." [44] A week later he wrote to Root:

In France, England, and Germany the best information is that we shall have war with Japan and that we shall be beaten. My own judgment is that the only thing that will prevent war is the Japanese feeling that we shall not be beaten, and this feeling we can only excite by keeping and making our navy efficient in the highest degree. It was evidently high time that we should get our whole battle fleet on a practice voyage to the Pacific. [45]

Roosevelt's concern reached a high point on July 26. Altogether he wrote five letters on that day concerning the Japanese question. To Root he stated:

. . . nothing that has been done affords the slightest justification or excuse for the Japanese thinking of war. . . . If the Japanese attack us now, as the German, English and French authorities evidently think they will, it will be nakedly because they wish the Philippines and Hawaii — or, as their

42 Rockhill to Root, telegram, July 12, 1907, S. D. File 1797/252–254.
43 Rudolph Forster, Assistant Secretary to the President, to Adee, July 13, 1907, S. D. File 1797/252–254.
44 Roosevelt to Sternberg, July 16, 1907, Morison, *Roosevelt Letters*, V, 720–721.
45 Roosevelt to Root, July 23, 1907, Morison, *Roosevelt Letters*, V, 724–725.

heads seem to be swollen to a marvelous degree, it is possible they may wish Alaska. I do not think they will attack us. I think these foreign observers are in error. But there is enough uncertainty to make it evident that we should be very much on our guard and should be ready for anything that comes.[46]

One of the other letters written on July 26 went to Rear Admiral Willard Brownson asking, "Is there any way in which we can hurry up the building of our big battleships?" [47]

Secretary of War Taft was even more certain than Roosevelt that Japan did not contemplate war, and he did not betray any anxiety whatsoever. After reading the reports from Europe, he wrote the President: "Personally I never have been able to believe that Japan is serious about a war with us the next three or four years." It was true, he said, that Japan had a jingo party whose views were regarded as worthy of consideration by the Elder Statesmen, but, he continued, "I cannot think that in their present financial condition they desire to measure swords with us." Taft was willing, however, to capitalize upon the troubles with Japan, just as Roosevelt at times was inclined to do. He told Roosevelt that it might be well to publish some of the alarming reports that had come in, for this would enable the administration to obtain more money from Congress for Philippine fortifications.[48]

In the meantime the war rumors continued to appear in the newspapers. On July 27 the *Literary Digest* printed excerpts from the French press which predicted a clash between Japan and the United States.[49] In Japan, too, there was a brief revival of jingo agitation. Roosevelt was much disconcerted by a copy of the Tokyo *Puck* which came into his hands at this time. The *Puck* had devoted a whole issue to vicious anti-American agitation. "Our own yellow press," Roosevelt wrote to Root, "is now surpassed by the Japanese yellow press in the effort to do mischief and stir up

[46] Roosevelt to Root, July 26, 1907, Morison, *Roosevelt Letters*, V, 729–730.

[47] Roosevelt to Brownson, July 26, 1907, Morison, *Roosevelt Letters*, V, 730. See also Roosevelt to Reid, July 26, 1907, Roosevelt Papers; Roosevelt to Bigelow, July 26, 1907, Roosevelt Papers; and Roosevelt to Stone, July 26, 1907, Morison, *Roosevelt Letters*, V, 727–728.

[48] Taft to Roosevelt, July 26, 1907, Roosevelt Papers.

[49] *Literary Digest*, July 27, 1907.

war." [50] Writing to Henry White, who was now Ambassador at Paris, the President was even more explicit:

I am sorry to say that the Japanese yellow press is showing itself to be quite as obnoxious as our yellow press at its worst, and I think it is high time for our fleet to visit the Pacific. I am exceedingly anxious to impress upon the Japanese that I have nothing but the friendliest possible intentions toward them, but I am none the less anxious that they should realize that I am not afraid of them and that the United States will no more submit to bullying than it will bully.[51]

Despite Roosevelt's disquietude at this time, the worst of the war scare was now over. Wright reported that the agitation in Japan was waning. Admiral Gombei Yamamoto had visited the United States in mid-July, and the accounts of his friendly reception by the President at Oyster Bay had been received in Japan and had closed the discussion of the "American affair" for the present.[52] By the first of August the agitation in Europe and the United States was also quieting down, and by August 8 Root was feeling better about the situation. "On the whole," he wrote to Roosevelt, "I am convinced that our European friends are overexcited. I think the tendency is towards war, not now but in a few years. But much can be done to check or divert the tendency." [53]

In the meantime Sternberg had forwarded to Roosevelt a reassuring report from the German Military Attaché at Tokyo, Major von Etzel. This report embodied a comprehensive analysis of Japan's present position and intentions for the future. The armaments program, he wrote, was simply the result of the situation created by the Russo-Japanese War. Japanese leaders were convinced that Russia would postpone but never abandon the idea of Eastern expansion, and the Japanese army expected another war with Russia in five or ten years. Japan's intentions toward Russia, however, were not aggressive, for Japan could gain little by a second round with that country. Japan likewise had no aggressive intentions toward the United States. Japanese leaders knew

50 Roosevelt to Root, July 29, 1907, Roosevelt Papers.
51 Roosevelt to White, July 30, 1907, quoted in Nevins, *Henry White*, pp. 292–293.
52 Wright to Root, July 26, 1907, S. D. File 1797/314–319.
53 Root to Roosevelt, August 8, 1907, Roosevelt Papers.

that they could gain far more by consolidating what they had already won. Furthermore, Japan did not have the money for another war. "There is not a warlike feeling against the United States, neither in the army of Japan or among her people," he said. It would be a mistake, of course, to think that the national pride of a sensitive people had not been hurt by the California troubles, but, he queried, "has not Japan received deeper humiliation in Australia, and look at the attitude of British Columbia towards Japanese immigration!" In conclusion, he stated that though Japan intended eventually to establish her leadership in Asia, war between the United States and Japan in the near future was "absolutely out of the question." [54]

Sternberg regarded Etzel's report as the most convincing estimate he had read, and Roosevelt likewise considered it showed "sound judgment." [55] There is little doubt that the opinions expressed in it were well founded. The war scare was simply a product of press sensationalism which had seized upon the agitation of the opposition party in Japan. By the time Roosevelt read the report, the war scare had played out. Unfortunately, however, the war scare of July, 1907, was merely the first of a series of scares that were to punctuate Japanese-American relations for the next year. The journalists were to repeat their performance again and again, while the genuine uneasiness created by the first scare was to linger. The later scares were no more justified than the first one. There is no evidence to indicate that Prime Minister Katsura was not stating the truth when he told O'Laughlin in October, 1908, that Japan never had the "slightest intention of making war upon the United States." [56]

No discussion of the war scare would be complete without mention of one of its most intriguing results: the change in Roosevelt's thinking regarding the Philippine Islands. Roosevelt had been one of the staunchest imperialists at the turn of the century, but now the realities of responsibility and the danger of war with Japan gave him quite a different view. "I am bound to say," he wrote Taft on August 21, "that in the physical sense I don't see

54 Sternberg to Roosevelt, July 29, 1907, Roosevelt Papers.
55 Roosevelt to Sternberg, August 3, 1907, Roosevelt Papers.
56 O'Laughlin to Roosevelt, October 20, 1908, Roosevelt Papers.

where they are of any value to us or where they are likely to be of any value." The Islands, he now thought, should be given their independence as soon as possible:

The Philippines form our heel of Achilles. They are all that makes the present situation with Japan dangerous. I think that in some way and with some phraseology that you think wise you should state to them that if they handle themselves wisely in their legislative assembly we shall at the earliest possible moment give them a nearly complete independence.[57]

With these words American imperialism passed a milestone.

[57] Roosevelt to Taft, August 21, 1907, Morison, *Roosevelt Letters*, V, 761–762.

CHAPTER TWELVE

The Quest
for an Immigration Treaty

THE subsidence of the war scare permitted Roosevelt to turn his attention to the plans for the dispatch of the fleet to the Pacific. In early August he took up the matter with the officials concerned, and after much discussion he decided that the fleet would proceed through the Straits of Magellan to the Pacific coast and thence around the world by the Suez route. On August 23, following a conference of high naval officials with Roosevelt at Oyster Bay, it was officially announced that a fleet of sixteen battleships would leave for San Francisco in December.[1]

When easterners, including Senator Hale, expressed opposition to the movement of the fleet, Roosevelt was undeterred.[2] He told Sternberg that he would "pay not the slightest heed to the yell of physical cowards like Hale against our sending this fleet to the Pacific." [3] Writing to Taft on September 5, he attributed much of the opposition to the "wealthy malefactor class." "At the moment the attack of the high financiers on me takes the shape of objection to the fleet going to the Pacific. But *I* am commander in chief." [4] When Hale asserted that Congress would not appropriate the

1 New York *Times*, August 24, 1907.

2 On July 27 Hale wrote to Assistant Secretary of the Navy Truman Newberry the first of many letters expressing his opposition to the sending of the fleet to the Pacific. Hale to Newberry, July 27, 1907, Roosevelt Papers. To Lodge, Roosevelt wrote: "Hale has been writing Newberry a series of bullying letters to which I have told Newberry to pay not the slightest heed." Roosevelt to Lodge, September 2, 1907, Morison, *Roosevelt Letters*, V, 779.

3 Roosevelt to Sternberg, July 16, 1907, Morison, *Roosevelt Letters*, V, 720–721.

4 Roosevelt to Taft, September 5, 1907, Morison, *Roosevelt Letters*, V, 784. See also Roosevelt to Shaw, September 3, 1907, and Roosevelt to Congressman E. A. Hayes, September 19, 1907, Roosevelt Papers.

money to send the fleet to the Pacific, Roosevelt replied that he had enough money on hand to send it, and if Congress refused to vote the funds to bring it back, the fleet could remain there! [5] When December came, the fleet departed as scheduled.

The ordering of the fleet to the Pacific was a bold and resourceful stroke. It helped to silence the extremists in Japan, and this brought an over-all improvement in Japanese-American relations. But the dispatch of the fleet was not a panacea. The most crucial issue between the two countries, the immigration question, was as yet unresolved. Despite the Gentlemen's Agreement, this problem was no nearer solution than it had been the previous March. During the months April through July, three thousand Japanese had arrived in the mainland United States, including 416 "farm laborers" and 244 other laborers. Many who came as students and petty merchants also joined the laboring class once in the United States. In the month of June alone, 1,134 Japanese had been admitted, the highest number for any month, with the exception of January, 1907, when 1,359 had been admitted. All the immigrants had passports entitling them to enter the mainland United States, except for a few non-laborers who came through Canada.[6] These statistics made it clear to Roosevelt and Root that the Japanese government was not effectively implementing the Gentlemen's Agreement.

Throughout the agitation over the riot of May 20 and the war scare, the Roosevelt administration clung to the chimerical hope that an immigration treaty might be concluded with Japan whereby Japanese laborers would be excluded. In May and June soundings were made through Henry W. Denison, the American adviser to the Japanese Foreign Ministry, which at first gave hope for a treaty, but eventually it became clear that Japan would insist upon the right of naturalization as a *quid pro quo*.[7] In the Roosevelt cabinet the Secretary of Commerce and Labor, Oscar S. Straus, became the champion of Japanese naturalization, but he received lit-

[5] Roosevelt, *Autobiography*, pp. 552–553.

[6] Sargent to Loeb, August 27 and October 5, 1907, Roosevelt Papers.

[7] F. M. Huntington Wilson to Root, June 6, 1907, S. D. File 2542/105–108; Wilson to Denison, June 18, 1907, S. D. File 2542/428a; Denison to Wilson, July 7, 1907, S. D. Confidential File.

tle encouragement even from Roosevelt.[8] He finally convinced the cabinet that naturalization rights should be offered to Japan in order to secure an immigration treaty, but the whole scheme had an aura of unreality. It was unlikely that the Senate would approve a treaty granting such rights even in exchange for exclusion of Japanese laborers.

By mid-July no progress had been made on the immigration question. Roosevelt was at this time concerned about the war scare, but it is probable that he was even more disturbed about the immigration question. When Aoki and Admiral Yamamoto lunched with him at Oyster Bay on July 12, he tried to explain to them the position of the United States. He made little progress with the Admiral, for as Roosevelt wrote to Root: "He kept insisting that the Japanese must not be kept out save as we kept out Europeans." [9]

Meanwhile the President had received the disquieting statistics on Japanese arrivals in the continental United States for the fiscal year just ended. He wrote to Root in alarm: "I believe we shall have to urge most strongly upon the Japanese Government the need of restricting the total number of passports if we are not to have trouble." Without a falling off in the number of Japanese arrivals, he warned, the administration could count on a very dangerous agitation in Congress next year for their total exclusion.[10] On the same day this letter was written, Roosevelt communicated with Acting Secretary of Commerce and Labor Lawrence O. Murray instructing him to obtain full particulars on Japanese immigrants. "There is no one matter where we want to be armed with so full a statement of facts," he wrote. "I am more concerned over this Japanese question in all its bearings than over any other, including that of the trusts." [11]

The administration delayed taking any important steps on the immigration question, for a new ambassador was shortly to be sent to Tokyo. Wright had submitted his resignation the previous March, pleading pressing affairs at home, and Roosevelt had ac-

8 Straus diary, June 7, 1907, Straus Papers; Straus, *Under Four Administrations*, pp. 220–221.

9 Roosevelt to Root, July 13, 1907, Morison, *Roosevelt Letters*, V, 717–719.

10 Roosevelt to Root, July 13, 1907, Morison, *Roosevelt Letters*, V, 717–719.

11 Roosevelt to Murray, July 13, 1907, Morison, *Roosevelt Letters*, V, 719.

cepted it.[12] The resignation was not to take effect until September 1, and before that date Roosevelt selected Thomas James O'Brien of Michigan for the Tokyo post. O'Brien was an extremely capable career diplomat, who at the time was serving as minister at Copen-hagen. His appointment to Tokyo was fortunate. In 1907 there was perhaps no assignment in the United States foreign service more difficult than that of ambassador to Japan, and O'Brien's personality combined a firmness and patience that particularly fitted him for the Tokyo post.

Action on the immigration issue was delayed also because Taft was planning a trip to Japan. The Secretary of War was *persona grata* with Japanese leaders, having visited Japan on several occa-sions, and his visit could be used to sound the Japanese again on the immigration question. Taft was going to the Philippines for the inauguration of the Philippine Assembly, and since his politi-cal aspirations were by this time well advanced, he decided to make the trip into a newsworthy, globe-circling tour. When his plans were completed, they included travel through Japan, the Philip-pines, Shanghai, Manchuria, Russia (via the Trans-Siberian Rail-way), and Europe. Meanwhile, O'Brien returned from Copenhag-en, and arrangements were made for him and Taft to take the same steamship to Japan.

Before Taft and O'Brien embarked for Japan, two developments changed the tenor of the immigration question. The first came in the latter part of August when Japanese authorities expelled sev-eral hundred Chinese coolies from Japan. News of this was printed in the New York *Evening Sun* on September 3, and Roosevelt im-mediately instructed Adee to telegraph Tokyo for verification.[13] H. Percival Dodge, who had taken charge of the Tokyo embassy when Wright left in August, confirmed the fact that under an Imperial Ordinance issued in 1899 the Japanese government had recently deported several hundred Chinese coolies on the grounds of labor competition.[14] Dodge was not slow to take up the question

12 Wright to Roosevelt, March 3, 1907, and Roosevelt to Wright, March 23, 1907, Roosevelt Papers.
13 Loeb to Adee, September 4, 1907, S. D. File 7423/5; Adee to Dodge, telegram, September 4, 1907, S. D. File 7423/5.
14 Dodge to Root, August 21, 1907, S. D. File 7423/8–13; Dodge to Root, telegram,

with Hayashi. The Foreign Minister said that the matter was of "no interest" and that he thought the ordinance would soon be abrogated.[15] Hayashi and other Japanese leaders were doubtless much embarrassed by the incident. The *Japan Daily Mail* noted: "While Japan is girding against the exclusion of her own labourers from the United States and elsewhere, fate with its usual irony has contrived that she herself should be confronted by a precisely analogous problem in the matter of Chinese labour." [16]

A second incident fraught with great significance for the immigration issue occurred in early September. On the evening of September 7 a mob in Vancouver, British Columbia, estimated at one thousand men, attacked Japanese, Chinese, and Hindus, wrecking over fifty Oriental stores. The Japanese fought back with vigor, and both sides sustained numerous wounds. The reasons for the riot were the same as those in California: labor competition and racial prejudice, made acute by the influx of Orientals in large numbers. The number of Japanese coming into Canada had increased from 354 in the fiscal year of 1904–05 to 8,124 in the first ten months of 1907. Many of these held passports for the United States and continued on to that destination, but more than half of those admitted remained in Canada. When an exclusion measure was vetoed by the lieutenant governor, the people of Vancouver decided to take measures into their own hands. The result was a riot more serious than any that had occurred in the United States.[17]

The sense of relief which swept over official Washington when news of the Vancouver riot arrived can scarcely be exaggerated. It was expressed well by Lodge in a letter to Roosevelt:

September 7, 1907, S. D. File 7423/6; Dodge to Root, September 12, 1907, United States, Department of State, *Papers Relating to the Foreign Relations of the United States, 1907*, 2 parts, Washington, 1910, II, 766–769.

15 Dodge to Root, September 12, 1907, *Foreign Relations, 1907*, II, 766–769.

16 *Japan Daily Mail*, August 16, 1907.

17 For information on Oriental immigration into Canada see: Canada, Department of Labour, *Report by W. L. MacKenzie King . . . of the Royal Commission Appointed to Enquire Into the Methods by Which Oriental Labourous Have Been Induced to Come to Canada*, Ottawa, 1908; and Canada, Department of Labour, *Report by W. L. MacKenzie King . . . Appointed to Investigate Into the Losses Sustained By the Japanese Population of Vancouver, B. C. on the Occasion of the Riots in that City in September, 1907 . . .* , Ottawa, 1908.

I do not wish ill to my neighbors but I cannot help feeling a certain gentle interest in the performances now going on in Vancouver in regard to the Japanese and other Asiatics. It is a demonstration of the fact that the white peoples will not suffer Asiatic competition in their own country and I think it will perhaps make England a little less inclined to preach in a patronizing way at us about San Francisco.[18]

Roosevelt replied that he had precisely the same feeling. The incident, he thought, would do good in two ways:

In the first place it will bring sharply home to the British public the fact that the British commonwealth along the Pacific will take precisely the same attitude as the American States along the Pacific; and in the next place, it will bring Japan toward a realization of the fact that in this matter she will have to face the same feeling in the British Empire which she does in the American Republic.[19]

Ambassador Whitelaw Reid at London noted that the English point of view underwent the "most amusing revolution." Before the Vancouver riot the British viewed America's troubles with Japan with a certain condescension. "This morning," Reid wrote to Mrs. Roosevelt on September 10, "they are rubbing their eyes in a dazed sort of way, and discovering that they are themselves a good deal deeper in the mire than we are." [20] "I fancy the point that really disturbs them as much as anything else," Reid wrote to Root, "is that, whereas our mobs did what they set out to do, their mob got beaten, and the pugnacious little Japs not only chased their assailants, but afterwards fortified themselves and defied them." [21]

In Japan the newspapers and government officials attempted to play down the incident. The comments in the press, even those of the opposition *Hochi Shimbun*, had a moderate tone. In speaking of the riot to Dodge, Hayashi minimized the seriousness of the matter.[22] The Japanese reaction revealed only too clearly that Japan, like her ally Britain, was deeply embarrassed. The effect on

18 Lodge to Roosevelt, September 10, 1907, Roosevelt Papers.
19 Roosevelt to Lodge, September 11, 1907, Morison, *Roosevelt Letters*, V, 790.
20 Reid to Mrs. Roosevelt, September 10, 1907, Papers of Whitelaw Reid, Library of Congress, Washington, D.C.
21 Reid to Root, September 10, 1907, Reid Papers.
22 Dodge to Root, September 17, 1907, S. D. File 8599/3–9.

Japanese-American relations was profound. Root summed it up in a letter to Roosevelt on September 25:

> I think Loeb [Roosevelt's secretary] must have sent someone there to make the demonstration and relieve our Japanese situation. It is not logical but it is certain that the strain is off. I had a talk with Aoki the other day and without a word being said the atmosphere was different.[23]

Just five days after the Vancouver riot, Taft and O'Brien embarked at Seattle for Japan, and on the morning of September 28 they arrived at Yokohama. The few days that Taft was in Japan were filled with conversations with Japanese officials.[24] Immigration was the most important topic discussed, and Taft canvassed this issue in a long talk with Hayashi. Taft had been authorized by Roosevelt to propose an immigration treaty providing for naturalization rights for Japanese in the United States and reciprocal exclusion of laborers. When Taft proposed it, Hayashi indicated that Japan was now even more averse to a treaty than previously. The Foreign Minister said that while Japan would welcome the right of naturalization as a friendly concession, this could not be accepted in exchange for reciprocal exclusion. Only an immigration treaty applying equally to immigrants from all countries could be accepted. Hayashi's rejection of the treaty proposal was probably due in part to his belief — which was well founded — that the United States Senate would in any case not approve a treaty granting naturalization.[25]

Having rebuffed Taft's proposal, Hayashi went on to discuss the immigration question quite frankly. He said that only a small number of Japanese were interested in immigration as such but that syndicates which were financially interested had successfully aroused the Japanese people. The excitement over the question, he said, was not owing to the desire among people to emigrate but was caused by the "patriotic self conceit" of the Japanese people.

[23] Root to Roosevelt, September 25, 1907, Roosevelt Papers.

[24] The account of Taft's conversations is taken from Taft to Captain Frank McIntyre (for transmission to Root and Roosevelt), telegram, October 18, 1907, Roosevelt Papers; Sutemi Chinda to Taft, October 1, 1907, Roosevelt Papers; Taft to Roosevelt, October 7, 1907, Roosevelt Papers; and Hayashi to Aoki, October 3, 1907, Telegram Series, CII, 11416–18.

[25] Hayashi to Aoki, September 9, 1907, Telegram Series, CI, 11158–60.

It was apparent that Japan wished to solve the immigration question through the Gentlemen's Agreement rather than by a treaty. Hayashi, though not admitting that measures adopted thus far were ineffective, promised to take additional administrative steps. The Foreign Minister also made one very important concession. He told Taft that passports to Hawaii were now restricted to five hundred per month and would shortly be cut to three hundred. Since the Gentlemen's Agreement of February, 1907, had not applied at all to Hawaii, this represented a major step toward incorporating Hawaii into that arrangement.

The Philippines were second in importance only to the immigration issue in Taft's conversations in Japan. Ambassador Aoki had reported rumors that the United States contemplated selling the Islands, and this report caused concern in Tokyo. Hayashi had informed Aoki that Japan had no intention, at least for the present, to acquire the Philippines but that it would be a matter of concern to Japan if some other nation attached them.[26] In their first talk Hayashi questioned Taft about the matter. He said he could give the same assurance Katsura had conveyed two years previously that Japan had no designs upon the Philippines but that Japan would feel some concern if the Islands were sold to a European power. Taft replied that the rumors had no foundation, that on the contary the United States had an obligation to retain the Philippines and lead them to self government. This statement doubtless satisfied the Japanese. When Taft later met with Saionji, the Prime Minister said that he, too, could offer the same assurance that Katsura had given on Taft's previous visit.

In addition to the conversations Taft had with Japanese officials, his visit was noteworthy because of a much-publicized speech he delivered at a dinner given by the Tokyo Municipality and Chamber of Commerce. Taft discussed frankly the circulating war rumors and assured his audience that he did not believe Japan intended to go to war. He likewise gave assurances that the United States had no such intention. Taft's speech was well received by the Japanese people, who expressed particular admiration for the frankness of his statements. Ransford Miller, the Japanese Secretary of the

26 Aoki to Hayashi, received September 20, 1907, Telegram Series, C, 9915; Hayashi to Aoki, September 25, 1907, Telegram Series, CII, 11326.

embassy, felt that the effect of the speech had been excellent. "We are all," he wrote Taft's secretary, 'breathing in a much clearer atmosphere." [27]

The Taft party left Japan on October 3, and on the following day Taft drew up a long report which was subsequently telegraphed to Washington at a cost of fifteen hundred dollars. He told Roosevelt and Root that it would be impossible to secure a treaty of reciprocal exclusion and that he doubted the wisdom of making any further attempt. It would be wiser, he thought, to maintain the status quo and to secure a solution through administrative action by the Japanese government. He said that the Japanese government was "most anxious to avoid war." It was his belief that Japan had enlarged her army not to fight the United States but because of China. "They are determined," he stated, "to secure a predominance in China affairs." [28]

While Taft was visiting Japan, the press in the United States gave forth with another jingo outburst. The New York *Times*, previously very conservative in its expressions, accused the Japanese government of a "hectoring policy" which necessitated the dispatch of the battle fleet. The New York *Sun* taunted the Japanese with their silence as soon as they learned of the fleet movement and stated that war between the United States and Japan was inevitable. These articles caused much perplexity in Japan, though Taft's speech did much to counteract their effect.[29] Disquietude in Japan was caused also by reports that the United States and Germany had entered into a naval combination whereby Germany would protect the Atlantic coast while the American fleet was in the Pacific.[30] These reports, though without foundation, were published in Europe, the United States, and Japan.[31]

27 Miller to Fred W. Carpenter, October 3, 1907, Taft Papers. A fuller account of Taft's speech is given in Ralph E. Minger, "Taft's Missions to Japan: A Study in Personal Diplomacy," *Pacific Historical Review*, XXX (1961), 279–294.

28 Taft to McIntyre (for transmission to Root and Roosevelt), telegram, October 18, 1907, Roosevelt Papers.

29 Dodge to Root, October 11, 1907, S. D. File 1797/355–379.

30 O'Brien to Root, October 21, 1907, S. D. File 1797/394–409.

31 Sternberg reported early in November that Roosevelt threw out a veiled invitation to a naval alliance between the United States and Germany. Sternberg to Bülow, November 8, 1907, *Die Grosse Politik*, XXV, 79. It is highly doubtful, however, that Roosevelt seriously proposed any such arrangement. Roosevelt was inclined to talk quite freely with his old friend Specky, and in the course of those conversations he

In answer to such stories, the Japanese press reiterated Japan's peaceful intentions.

Despite the renewal of the war scare, both Ambassador O'Brien and Roosevelt were convinced that Japan did not plan war against the United States. "As near as I can judge," O'Brien reported to Root, "the Japanese Government would be found very reluctant to have difficulties with the United States, and the tone of the press seems to bear out this view." [32] When in November Roose velt received a prediction of war through Ambassador Tower — this time from a high-ranking German naval official — Roosevelt replied: "I hardly believe that Japan is intending to strike us, but I am taking and have taken every step to be ready." [33] When his son Theodore wrote for permission to volunteer in the event of war with Japan, the President told him: "I do not think there is any chance of war with Japan at this time or in the immediate future; so the Brothers will have to possess their souls in peace." [34]

The Japanese Ambassador at Washington viewed the renewal of the war scare with great concern, and he concluded that some positive step should be taken to counteract the trend of public sentiment. This was the origin of the abortive Aoki proposal of October 25, 1907, an initiative that is significant both because of the insight it affords into Aoki's views and because it foreshadowed the famous Root-Takahira exchange of notes of November 30, 1908. Aoki was not only a good diplomat but was generally friendly toward the United States. Throughout the trouble over the school segregation crisis, the riot of May, 1907, and the war scare of July, 1907, he viewed the difficulties of the Roosevelt administration with at least a measure of sympathetic understanding. Now he came forward with a proposal for a Japanese-American entente which was as well intentioned in conception as it was temporarily ill-fated in culmination.

---

made many speculations. When Sternberg suggested the possibility of using German troops in the event of a Japanese attack on the United States, Roosevelt interposed objections to the scheme.

32 O'Brien to Root, October 25, 1907, S. D. File 1797/410.

33 Tower to Roosevelt, November 2, 1907, Roosevelt Papers; Roosevelt to Tower, November 19, 1907, Morison, *Roosevelt Letters*, V, 853.

34 Roosevelt to Theodore Roosevelt, Jr., October 29, 1907, Morison, *Roosevelt Letters*, V, 824.

Aoki's first suggestion of an entente came in a conversation he had with Roosevelt's friend John Callan O'Laughlin, who was at this time in the Washington bureau of the Chicago *Tribune*. O'Laughlin in turn mentioned the Ambassador's suggestion to Roosevelt, and the President indicated that he looked with favor upon the proposition.[35] Then on October 25 Aoki lunched with Roosevelt and discussed his proposal in detail. He stated his belief that some positive declaration of the friendly intentions of the two nations by an exchange of notes would inspire public confidence and dispel the war rumors. He explained that he had no authority from his government to propose such an arrangement and that his views must therefore be taken as purely personal. Regarding the substance of the exchange, Aoki suggested:

1. Recognition of the Pacific Ocean as an international highway of commerce.
2. Respect for the territorial rights of each and maintenance of the existing order of things on the Pacific.
3. Support of the territorial integrity and open door in China.

Roosevelt told Aoki that he thought his suggestion was an "excellent idea." He urged him to telegraph his government immediately so that the exchange of notes could take place before Congress convened. The President hoped thereby to head off any congressional legislation on Japanese immigration.[36]

When Aoki reported his proposal to Tokyo, Hayashi's reaction was quick and decisive. This was one of the few occasions when the Foreign Minister betrayed an ability to act with dispatch. He told O'Brien on October 31 that he considered the proposal "wholly uncalled for and ill-advised." Two days later he handed to O'Brien, for transmission to Washington, a copy of his telegram to Aoki disavowing the Japanese Ambassador's action. Hayashi said that the Japanese government was in complete accord with the topics suggested but that it feared the proposed agreement would admit by implication the existence of a situation of a grave nature and would therefore aggravate rather than mollify the public senti-

[35] O'Laughlin to Roosevelt, October 25, 1907, Roosevelt Papers.
[36] Aoki to Hayashi, received October 28, 1907, Telegram Series, CI, 11017–18, 11023–24.

ment. While every effort should be made to disabuse the public mind of imaginary ill conditions, this could be safely left to the natural tendency of time for rectification. Hayashi said that the real source of all the trouble was the immigration question, and he felt that any compact that appeared to gloss over this fact would be regarded as white-washing and would prove disappointing rather than reassuring. At the same, he said, any settlement of the question in the form of a further agreement was "out of the question." He promised, however, to restrict stringently the emigration of Japanese laborers to the United States.[37]

The Aoki proposal was thus stillborn. The embarrassed Ambassador gave to Roosevelt a copy of Hayashi's telegram.[38] He then composed three long telegrams to Tokyo pleading for a change in policy. He said that the belief was gaining ground that Japan, fresh from her victories, was pushing herself forward in disregard of the interests of other countries. In this situation, unless something were done to assure the public of Japan's friendship for the United States, Congress might pass exclusion legislation in spite of the good will and best efforts of the President. Aoki believed that if the agreement were concluded, Roosevelt would recommend naturalization rights for the Japanese to the Congress. He also pointed out that the cruise of the fleet was viewed as a demonstration toward Japan but if a declaration of friendly relations were made, the cruise would lose all demonstrative character. The conclusion of an amicable declaration would make it appropriate for Japan to extend an invitation to the fleet and its visit to Japan would become a political stroke, a celebration of the *entente cordiale*. Aoki even argued that the declaration would help establish the claim of Japan and the United States to a "preponderating position" in the Pacific. There is no evidence that this consideration had anything to do with Aoki's initiative for an agreement, but now that the

37 *Promemoria* of statement by Hayashi to O'Brien, November 2, 1907, Documents Relating to the Limitation and Exclusion of Japanese Immigrants by the United States, MT3.8.2.21, reel 726, pp. 6390–94; Hayashi to Aoki, n.d., enclosed in O'Brien to Root, November 4, 1907, S. D. File 2542/210–214; O'Brien to Root, telegram, November 3, 1907, S. D. File 1797/353; Hayashi to Aoki, November 2, 1907, Telegram Series, CIII, 12907–09.

38 Loeb to Root, November 5, 1907, S. D. File 1797/388–389.

project was in peril he wished to throw everything into the scales.[39]

Hayashi was not convinced. He told Aoki that the Japanese government could not adopt his opinion and instructed him to keep off the subject.[40] The Ambassador was crestfallen and dumfounded. "It is difficult for me to understand the causes underlying the action of Viscount Hayashi," he confided to O'Laughlin. The position of his government, he said, was, to say the least, open to suspicion and seemed to vindicate the President's policy of concentrating the United States naval strength in the Pacific. Aoki felt that as ambassador he had the right to initiate diplomatic negotiations, and in view of this rebuke, he thought that he should telegraph his resignation to Tokyo. O'Laughlin, however, urged him not to resign, for it was of the highest importance that a man of his sympathetic understanding be at the Washington post.[41]

Aoki was not given long to ponder his resignation. Within a few weeks he was notified that he would be replaced. Hayashi took the position that modern telegraphic facilities had invalidated the ancient ambassadorial right to initiate negotiations, and he desired a man at Washington who was willing to accept that fact. Personal factors and politics were also involved in Aoki's dismissal. The Ambassador's membership in the Yamagata-Katsura faction did not endear him to the Foreign Minister; and for more than a decade there had been a personal coolness between them. When Aoki negotiated the Japanese-British treaty of 1894, Hayashi, then Vice Minister of Foreign Affairs, had disapproved of some of the provisions of the treaty, and this difference led to an estrangement between the two men.[42] Hayashi now welcomed the opportunity to be rid of his old foe.

The Roosevelt administration did as much as it could properly do to save Aoki. Root telegraphed Tokyo that he would be very sorry to see the Ambassador called home, for the public probably would regard this as a consequence of Aoki's friendliness to the

39 Aoki to Hayashi, received November 7, 1907, Telegram Series, CII, 11822–23, 11824–25, 11826–28.

40 Hayashi to Aoki, November 26, 1907, Telegram Series, CIII, 12970–73.

41 O'Laughlin to Roosevelt, November 4, 1907, Roosevelt Papers.

42 Hayashi, Memoirs, p. 10.

United States.[43] Hayashi, however, was adamant, and Aoki left for Japan in December. As Root had predicted, this development precipitated rumors in the press that Japan was about to adopt a stronger policy toward the United States. Hayashi gave assurances that these rumors had no valid foundation, and when it was learned that Takahira would be returned to Washington, Roosevelt and Root were reconciled to Aoki's recall.[44] Takahira had been on cordial terms with Roosevelt while minister at Washington during the Russo-Japanese War, and his return to the United States substantiated that Japan had not determined upon any change of policy.

Thus the autumn of 1907 passed with still no solution to the fundamental problem of Japanese immigration. The quest for an immigration treaty was over. That search had not been pursued with great vigor, but even had this been the case, the outcome would doubtless have been the same. The United States had nothing to offer that could induce Japan to sign a treaty excluding her laborers from the United States. As Hayashi pointed out, the real question at issue, so far as the Japanese were concerned, was not immigration but discrimination. No sugar coating could make that discrimination palatable to the Japanese. Some solution had to be found to stop the influx of Japanese laborers into the United States and at the same time preserve the *amour propre* of the Japanese. This a treaty could not do.

43 Root to O'Brien, telegram, November 16, 1907, S. D. File 6429/7.

44 O'Brien to Root, telegram, December 4, 1907, S. D. File 6429/8; O'Brien to Root, December 5, 1907, S. D. File 2542/259.

CHAPTER THIRTEEN

Implementing
the Gentlemen's Agreement

THE summer and fall of 1907 had witnessed dramatic developments in Japanese-American relations — the war scare, the ordering of the fleet to the Pacific, the Taft visit, the Aoki proposal —
and through it all persisted the undercurrent of anxiety over the
yet unsolved immigration question. As the months passed, Roosevelt and Root became increasingly worried over this issue. Despite
the repeated assurances of Hayashi that no passports would be issued to laborers desiring to go to the mainland, Japanese laborers
were still landing in the United States with passports issued to them
by the Japanese authorities. Over 1,800 Japanese laborers were admitted in the six months ending September 30, 1907.[1]

Roosevelt personally took the immigration question in hand in
late October. During the conference with Aoki on October 25 concerning the proposed friendly declaration, Roosevelt had discussed
the immigration issue at great length. He told Aoki that he was
greatly concerned at the steady increase in the immigration of Japanese laborers and that if this condition continued he feared Congress would act. He assured Aoki that he was not only a friend but
also an admirer of Japan and that he would use his influence to
avert Congressional action; but he reminded Aoki of the Vancouver
incident and that not even an alliance could prevent grave trouble
over labor competition.[2]

On the day following the Roosevelt-Aoki talk, Root met with the
Ambassador and spoke in even stronger terms. Unless the Japa-

[1] Wilson to Root, November 6, 1907, S. D. File 2542/160–161.
[2] Aoki to Hayashi, received October 28 and November 7, 1907, Telegram Series, CI,
11019–20, and CII, 11826–28.

nese government could exercise more stringent control over emigration, he said, Congress would take legislative measures which
would seriously embarrass the situation. When Aoki protested that
the Japanese government was endeavoring to prevent emigration,
Root replied that a more direct action would have to be taken by
Japan to implement the Gentlemen's Agreement. After the conference with Root, Aoki telegraphed anxiously to Tokyo that there
were strong misgivings that Japan was not giving *bona fide* cooperation on preventing labor emigration, and he recommended that
effective steps be taken to prevent such emigration.[3]

Even before the Roosevelt administration knew that Aoki was
to be recalled, it had decided to make the principal effort on immigration at Tokyo rather than through the Ambassador at Washington. At a meeting of the cabinet on November 8 the issue was
discussed at length, and on the following day Root instructed
O'Brien to make vigorous representations.[4] Meanwhile at Washington specific recommendations for Japanese administrative measures
were drafted for presentation to the Tokyo government.

O'Brien made representations to Hayashi on November 14.[5] A
few days later Root telegraphed to Tokyo the suggestions for administrative measures which he hoped Japan would adopt. Among
them were proposals for limiting passports to Hawaii to one thousand per year, forfeiture of passport rights by nonlaborers who
came to the United States and engaged in manual labor, and a
system of registration for Japanese laborers already in the United
States.[6] Root did not expect Japan to adopt all the measures but
hoped the suggestions would stir the Japanese to present adequate
counter proposals.[7] O'Brien presented the recommendations on
November 27, and though the note accompanying them stated

3 Aoki to Hayashi, received October 30, 1907, Telegram Series, CI, 11069–70,
11071–72.

4 Straus diary, November 8, 1907, Straus Papers; Root to O'Brien, telegram, November 9, 1907, S. D. File 2542/161a.

5 O'Brien to Root, telegram, November 14, 1907, S. D. File 2542/162. Two days
later O'Brien, at Hayashi's request, presented Root's views in writing. O'Brien to
Hayashi, November 16, 1907, Documents Relating to the Limitation and Exclusion of
Japanese Immigrants by the United States, MT3.8.2.21, reel 726, pp. 6408–18.

6 Root to O'Brien, telegram, November 18, 1907, S.D. File 2542/164a.

7 Straus to Root, November 13, 1907, S. D. File 2542/163–164; Straus diary, January
4 and 7, 1908, Straus Papers.

bluntly that the arrangement of February, 1907, had been a complete failure, Hayashi evidenced no irritation. "The best feeling apparently prevails in all circles," O'Brien reported to Washington.[8]

Over a month passed before Hayashi replied to the *démarche*. In the interim the pressure was kept up, both by the administration and the Congress. On December 2 Representative E. A. Hayes of California introduced an exclusion bill in the Congress. On the same day Secretary Straus ordered immigration officials not to admit Japanese to the mainland who had passports issued by the Japanese Consul General in Hawaii. This action was taken when it was learned that the Consul General was issuing passports to Japanese laborers. When Counsellor Miyaoka of the Japanese embassy complained about this action to Straus, he was told that the United States had ample evidence to show that not only the Consul General at Hawaii but the Japanese government at Tokyo was issuing to laborers passports for the continental United States.[9] Later in the month the United States revoked the exequatur of the Japanese Consular Agent at Portland, who was allegedly issuing passports to Japanese laborers who had illegally entered the United States.[10]

While the pressure from the United States continued, Hayashi's position was alleviated somewhat by developments in Japan. On November 20 Count Okuma, the bitterest critic of the Saionji ministry, issued a statement to the press in which he urged the ministry to cooperate with the United States in resolving the immigration question. The Japanese government, he said, should take steps promptly to assist the United States at this time when passion or prejudice, coupled with the existing economic and political conditions, could render the emigration of Japanese to the United

[8] O'Brien to Root, telegram, November 27, 1907, S. D. File 2542/204; O'Brien to Hayashi, November 26, 1907, Documents Relating to the Limitation and Exclusion of Japanese Immigrants by the United States, MT3.8.2.21, Reel 726, pp. 6420–24.

[9] Aoki to Hayashi, received December 14 and 19, 1907, Telegram Series, CIII, 12558, 12648–49. See also Koike to Hayashi, received December 20, 1907, Telegram Series, CIII, 12662–63; Hayashi to Aoki, December 17 and 20, 1907, Telegram Series, CIII, 13141, 13164–65.

[10] Miyaoka to Hayashi, received January 1, 1907, Telegram Series, CIV, 9–10.

States inexpedient.[11] This statement represented a major change in Okuma's position, for since the beginning of the immigration trouble he had used the issue to badger the ministry in power. There is little doubt that this change of front was caused, not by a new insight into the immigration question on the part of the aged statesman, but rather by the dispatch of the fleet to the Pacific and the threat of exclusion legislation by the United States Congress.

While the Department of State was pressing Japan to implement the Gentlemen's Agreement, Roosevelt took the occasion of his message to Congress on December 3, 1907, to further Japanese-American friendship. In early November Aoki had transmitted to Root the invitation to the United States to participate in an exposition to be held in Tokyo in 1912.[12] Roosevelt saw the chance to assure Japan of the good will of the United States, and he did everything possible to further the success of the planned exposition. In his message to Congress, he enthusiastically recommended an appropriation for American participation.[13] In Japan the reaction to Roosevelt's message was excellent. Baron Kaneko, who had been named Director General of the exposition, reported to Roosevelt: "Now, the whole Empire is resounding with the keen appreciation for your message, and with the highest praise for your enthusiasm."[14]

In the succeeding weeks Roosevelt and Root urged Congress to make a generous appropriation for the exposition. The connection between the administration's policy in this matter and the immigration question was obvious. As O'Brien wrote to Root: "Japan will have to yield on the immigration question. By way of slight compensation we could improve the situation by being generous in this."[15] This aspect of the question, as well as the commercial opportunities involved, became increasingly apparent to congres-

[11] Telegram sent to the Associated Press by its representative to Tokyo, November 20, 1907, enclosed in O'Brien to Root, November 26, 1907, S. D. File 2542/223–232.
[12] Aoki to Root, November 7, 1907, United States, Department of State, *Papers Relating to the Foreign Relations of the United States, 1908*, Washington, 1912, p. 515.
[13] *Messages and Papers of the Presidents*, XV, 7070–7125.
[14] Kaneko to Roosevelt, December 5 and 6, 1907, Roosevelt Papers.
[15] O'Brien to Root, February 3, 1908, S. D. File 6292.

sional leaders. Root first suggested that $350,000 be appropriated; Roosevelt was soon urging that the amount be raised to $500,000; and when in May, 1908, Congress finally acted, the appropriation was for $1,500,000, a figure even greater than that appropriated for the Paris Exposition of 1900.[16]

The good will in Japan resulting from Roosevelt's message was still in evidence when late in December the European press flew into another frenzy of war predictions. The scare was precipitated by the departure from Hampton Roads on December 16 of the United States fleet. The official destination of the fleet was still San Francisco, but it was generally believed that the force of sixteen battleships would be sent into Far Eastern waters on a cruise around the world. The sailing of the fleet caused apprehension in administration and diplomatic circles as well. Roosevelt himself was apparently not entirely free from anxiety, for in his final instructions to Admiral Bob Evans, the commander of the fleet, he told him to guard his ships as though he were at war.[17]

Rumors in Europe of an impending Japanese-American war were still circulating freely when on December 23 the United States Ambassador at Paris, Henry White, telegraphed Root regarding an alleged plot to damage the fleet during its voyage around South America. A report had come to the United States Naval Attaché that explosives had been shipped from Bremen to Rio de Janeiro and that eight men at Rio, whom the informant named, were conspiring to lay mines in the path of the fleet.[18] Roosevelt was doubtless relieved when the United States Ambassador at Rio, Irving B. Dudley, reported early in January that the Brazilian police had taken into custody many of the alleged conspirators and that the investigation discredited the existence of the plot.[19] When the fleet arrived in Rio in mid-January, it met not Japanese-purchased explosives but a hearty welcome by the Brazilian people. Later in

[16] Root to Senator Shelby M. Cullom, January 28, 1908, S. D. File 6292; Roosevelt to Kaneko, March 2 and 7, 1908, Roosevelt Papers; Root to O'Brien, May 21, 1908, *Foreign Relations, 1908*, pp. 515–516.

[17] John R. Leary, Jr., *Talks with T. R.*, New York, 1920, pp. 11–12. Leary records that Roosevelt considered the chances of war about one chance in ten.

[18] White to Root, telegram, December 23, 1907, S. D. File 10799/1; White to Roosevelt, December 20, 1907, Papers of Henry White, Library of Congress, Washington, D. C.; White to Root, December 20, 1907, White Papers.

[19] Dudley to Root, January 7, 1908, S. D. File 10799/10.

the same month White reported that when the Paris police investigated the informant, he turned out to be a "pretty shady character" who needed money.[20]

The rumors in Europe at this time attributing hostile intentions to Japan had no more valid foundation than those of the previous summer. White reported that the information received by the French and Italian government from their representatives in Japan all bore out the truth of this fact. Even more significant, White had a conversation with Sir Edward Grey in which the Foreign Secretary assured him that neither Hayashi nor the Japanese Ambassador at London had ever intimated that the situation was serious between the United States and Japan, "much less that they have any fear of war."[21] The Japanese Ambassador at Paris, Shinichiro Kurino, told White that he was at a loss to understand why there was a general feeling in Paris that his nation contemplated war against the United States.[22]

Reports coming from Japan similarly confirmed Japan's peaceful intentions. O'Brien wrote to Reid: "One thing is quite certain, there is not a shadow of warlike spirit in the country. . . ."[23] O'Brien's impressions were substantiated by Durham Stevens, the long-time adviser to the Japanese Foreign Ministry who was at this time adviser to Resident General Ito in Korea. In a letter to Willard H. Brownson, which was forwarded to the Department of State, Stevens stated that the rumors of war were repeated in Japan with "incredulity and amazement," for the people of Japan had a friendship for America that was "a deeper and a more genuine feeling than that customarily expressed in the honeyed phrases of diplomatic intercourse." Not even the passage of an exclusion act, he said, would bring war, though the influence of the United States in Japan would lessen to the disappearing point.[24]

Throughout December, 1907, neither the departure of the fleet nor the resulting war rumors distracted the Department of State from the immigration question. Hayashi's reply to the American

20 White to Root, January 17, 1908, White Papers.
21 White to Roosevelt, December 20, 1907, White Papers.
22 White to Root, January 3, 1908, White Papers; White to Roosevelt, January 3, 1908, Roosevelt Papers.
23 O'Brien to Reid, December 31, 1907, Reid Papers.
24 Stevens to Willard H. Brownson, December 24, 1907, S. D. File 12611/4.

démarche was anxiously awaited, and as each week passed, the impatience of Roosevelt and Root became more pronounced. On December 21 Root telegraphed O'Brien to hasten the reply,[25] and a week later he drafted a stiff note which O'Brien was instructed to read verbatim to the Foreign Minister. "I regret to say," the note said emphatically, "that unless there is a very speedy change in the course of immigration it will be impossible to prevent the passage of exclusion legislation by Congress and the Executive Department of this Government will not feel justified in continuing a hopeless opposition to such legislation." [26]

Root's telegram reached Tokyo just as O'Brien was receiving Hayashi's long-awaited reply. The Foreign Minister now promised rigorous enforcement of the Gentlemen's Agreement to withhold passports from laborers who wished to go to the mainland United States. He also agreed to take measures regarding emigration of Japanese laborers to territory adjacent to the United States which would remove all cause for complaint. Since prefectural governors in Japan had the authority to issue passports, Hayashi proposed to issue orders instructing them to make a thorough investigation of passport applicants claiming to be students, tourists, and merchants in order to determine whether they were likely to become laborers after reaching the United States. He also agreed to prohibit emigration of laborers to Hawaii, except for those who had previously resided there or the parents, wives or children of residents there. These excepted categories were the same as applied to the mainland United States. Though Hayashi refused to put Hawaii officially within the bounds of the Gentlemen's Agreement, Hayashi's assurance made it a part of it *de facto*. He said that if it should appear desirable to depart from that prohibition relating to Hawaii, it would be done only "after ascertaining through an American official source the labor conditions prevailing in the islands and the need thereof." [27]

O'Brien was pleased with the Japanese reply, though he hoped to secure still other concessions. "It seems certain," he reported,

[25] Root to O'Brien, telegram, December 21, 1907, S. D. File 2542/239.
[26] Root to O'Brien, telegram, December 31, 1907, S. D. File 2542/256a.
[27] Hayashi to O'Brien, December 30 and 31, 1907, S. D. File 2542/331–334.

"that what the Japanese Government promises, and what they will still further undertake, will be sufficient to put an end to the controversy, leaving nothing but resolute activity in carrying them out." O'Brien told Root that Hayashi admitted that methods had been too lax but that he believed the Foreign Minister was sincere in his intention to remedy the difficulty. "Count Hayashi is especially sensitive as to his personal motives being impugned," O'Brien reported, "and once or twice has expressed a good deal of feeling at what has come from you and what I have been obliged to say to him." [28]

Roosevelt and Root were also pleased with the Japanese reply. On January 7 it was discussed at a cabinet meeting and all agreed that Japanese objections to some of the American proposals were reasonable.[29] Three days later the Department of State issued a long statement to the press revealing the nature of the negotiations and the fact that they were proceeding satisfactorily. Root also indicated to the Japanese government the feelings of the administration. When the Saionji ministry failed to get a vote of confidence on an issue in the Diet, Root expressed satisfaction when he learned from Chargé d'Affaires Miyaoka that this would not necessarily bring the fall of the ministry. Miyaoki reported to Tokyo that Root spoke in "very appreciative terms" of the pleasant relations maintained with the Saionji ministry "owing to its kind and conciliatory attitude." [30]

Though the Roosevelt administration was happy about Hayashi's initial reply on the immigration question, in the subsequent weeks Root pressed for still more administrative measures. On January 23, 1908, he instructed O'Brien to urge again the establishment of a registration system in the United States, though this time he suggested only a Japanese-administered system rather than a jointly administered setup as previously proposed. He urged, too, that the Japanese government adopt the American definition of "laborer," which included skilled as well as unskilled laborers. He

28 O'Brien to Root, telegram, January 1, 1908, S. D. File 2542/258; O'Brien to Root, January 2, 1908, S. D. File 2542/331–334.

29 Straus diary, January 7, 1907, Straus Papers.

30 Miyaoki to Hayashi, received January 12 and 24, 1908, Telegram Series, CIV, 151–153, 361.

also stressed the need for a more careful examination of applications by "settled agriculturists."[31]

Root's note was presented to Hayashi on January 25, and on February 18 Hayashi met almost all of the requests. He said that his government would soon establish a system of registration similar to that used by the United States government, though it would not construe absence of registration as constituting forfeiture of residential rights. Regarding settled agriculturists, Hayashi said that persons in that category must invest capital in the enterprise, and all applications for such passports must go directly to the Foreign Ministry. In reporting this note to Washington, O'Brien stated that he had already received information that the American definition of "laborer" had been adopted by the Japanese government.[32]

O'Brien discerned that the Japanese government was giving ground rapidly, and in another note to the Foreign Ministry on February 21 he immediately pressed his advantage. Hayashi now agreed to enlarge the clerical staff of the Foreign Ministry so that all cases of passport applications involving questions of doubt could be referred directly to that office rather than being decided by local governors. When Hayashi gave these assurances, O'Brien was completely satisfied. He believed the Japanese concessions to be "as full and responsive as could be expected." The Foreign Minister, he told Root, had shown a "constant desire to yield to our suggestions."[33]

Roosevelt and Root were well satisfied. At a meeting of the cabinet on February 28, Root and Straus discussed the immigration question at length and it was agreed that it would be better to depend upon the good faith of the Japanese government rather than to insist upon further details of how the restrictions would be effected.[34] Root was ready to telegraph the appreciation of the United States government to Tokyo, but Huntington Wilson cautioned

[31] Root to O'Brien, telegram, January 23, 1908, S. D. File 2542/258.

[32] Hayashi to O'Brien, February 18, 1908, enclosed in O'Brien to Root, February 19, 1908, S. D. File 2542/453–455.

[33] O'Brien to Hayashi, February 21, 1908, enclosed in O'Brien to Root, February 25, 1908, S. D. File 2542/471–474; Hayashi to O'Brien, February 23, 1908, enclosed in O'Brien to Root, telegram, February 26, 1908, S. D. File 2542/438.

[34] Loeb to Root, February 26, 1908, S. D. File 2542/443; Straus diary, February 28, 1908, Straus Papers.

that "we ought not to seem too pleased." To reply instantaneously, he advised Root, "gives the impression that we have got more than we expected." [35] Root nevertheless did not wait long to send a message of appreciation to Tokyo. On March 9 he instructed O'Brien to thank Hayashi for the kind and considerate way in which the Japanese government had treated the American suggestions.[36]

The implementation of the Gentlemen's Agreement was due in large measure to the capable diplomacy of Ambassador O'Brien. Though the representations had been drafted almost entirely in Washington, O'Brien had handled his role with great skill. He possessed a keenness of intellect and a dignity of bearing which greatly impressed the Japanese. The Austrian diplomat Otto Franz, who was in Tokyo at this time, told Huntington Wilson that O'Brien was "the best ambassador he ever saw."

His manner with the Japanese [said Franz] is perfection, i.e., he has perfect self-control and never shows temper except purposely. He states his point simply and quietly, lets his interlocutor set forth elaborate remarks, objections, and alternatives; then he comes back unruffled with the same calm little statement of his original position.[37]

It would take some time before O'Brien's efforts would be fully reflected in United States immigration statistics, but by the end of February, 1908, a noticeable improvement had already occurred. Total Japanese arrivals had fallen from 1,170 in November, 1907, to 468 in February, 1908.[38] If O'Brien had a feeling of self-satisfaction, it was indeed well deserved.

While implementing the Gentlemen's Agreement through negotiations with Japan, the Roosevelt administration made parallel efforts to undergird that agreement with British diplomatic support. Ever since the beginning of the Pacific coast problem in 1905, Roosevelt had energetically courted Britain, hoping to gain the support of Japan's ally on the immigration question. During the

35 Wilson to Root, February 27, 1908, S. D. File 2542/438.

36 Root to O'Brien, telegram, March 9, 1908, S. D. File 2542/456; O'Brien to Hayashi, March 12, 1908, Documents Relating to the Limitation and Exclusion of Japanese Immigrants by the United States, MT3.8.2.21, reel 726, pp. 6560–62.

37 Memorandum of a private and confidential conversation between Otto Franz and Huntington Wilson, March 1, 1908, S. D. File 12611.

38 Sargent to Roosevelt, April 23, 1908, S. D. File 2542/543–548.

Algeciras Conference in 1906, which was called to settle the Moroccan crisis, he consistently pursued a pro-entente policy. At the same time he wrote many letters to his British friends — Spring Rice, Arthur Lee, John St. Loe Strachey, and even Sir Edward Grey — assuring them of his pro-British sympathies and attempting to dispel the belief that he was under the Kaiser's influence.

Roosevelt's efforts to win British support on the immigration question met little success until after the Vancouver riot, and even after that event the British evidenced great reluctance to fall in step with the United States. Root timed the immigration *démarche* of November, 1907, to coincide with Japanese-Canadian negotiations,[39] but when O'Brien sounded Sir Claude MacDonald, the British Ambassador, on the possibilities of the two embassies working together, he was rebuffed.[40] Sir Claude confided to O'Brien on one occasion, however, that he was surprised at the "considerable interest" in the subject taken by his government in the way of sympathy for the Canadian people in their objection to further Japanese immigration.[41]

The Canadian government was more willing to work in cooperation with the United States than was the British government. Though the Canadians were successful in negotiating an informal agreement whereby Japan would limit the number of passports to Canada, they were greatly worried over the long-term aspects of the immigration problem. In late January, 1908, events turned decisively in favor of Roosevelt's plans for Anglo-American cooperation. Through a mutual friend, Roosevelt invited to Washington W. L. Mackenzie King, the Canadian Deputy Commissioner of Labour.[42] Mackenzie King had headed the Royal Commission appointed to investigate the Vancouver riot and had also been commissioned to investigate the methods by which Orientals had been encouraged to come to Canada.[43]

---

[39] Root to Roosevelt, November 19, 1907, Roosevelt Papers.
[40] MacDonald to Grey, March 17, 1908, *British Documents*, VIII, 457–458.
[41] O'Brien to Root, November 19, 1907, S. D. File 2542/217–219.
[42] John J. McCook to Roosevelt, January 12, 1908, Roosevelt Papers.
[43] Canada, Department of Labour, *Report by W. L. Mackenzie King . . . Commissioner Appointed to Investigate into the Losses Sustained by the Japanese Population of Vancouver, B. C., on the Occasion of the Riots in that City in September, 1907 . . .* , Ottawa, 1908; Canada, Department of Labour, *Report of the Royal Commission*

On January 25 Mackenzie King lunched at the White House, and Roosevelt told him of his great anxiety concerning Japan's failure to restrict effectively the emigration of coolies to the United States. He said further that the interests of the British Empire and the United States were one on the matter.[44] Mackenzie King was in full agreement with these views. He told the President that the western portions of Canada were prepared to make the exclusion of the Japanese their cardinal political tenet, and if the central government of Canada or the empire should object, they would secede from Canada. He stated further that he wished that the London government and the people in the eastern parts of Canada and the United States could be awakened to the feeling. He also thanked Roosevelt for sending the fleet to the Pacific.[45]

Mackenzie King returned to Ottawa after the conference with Roosevelt on January 25, but within a few days he was back in Washington. During the course of the talk on the twenty-fifth a project for a visit to London by Mackenzie King to explain the immigration problem to British leaders had emerged. Which side first broached the idea of such a trip is uncertain. Mackenzie King recorded in his diary that Roosevelt suggested the project, but Roosevelt told his British friend Arthur Lee and Ambassador Reid that the initiative was on the Canadian side.[46] It is likely that in the talk with Mackenzie King on January 25 Roosevelt hinted

Appointed to Inquire Into the Methods by which Oriental Labourers have been Induced to Come to Canada, W. L. Mackenzie King, *C. M. G. Commissioner,* Ottawa, 1908.

[44] Diary of W. L. Mackenzie King, January 25, 1908, quoted in R. MacGregor Dawson, *William Lyon Mackenzie King: A Political Biography,* Toronto, 1958, p. 152.

[45] Roosevelt to Lee, February 2, 1908, Morison, *Roosevelt Letters,* VI, 919–921. The Roosevelt-Mackenzie King talks can not be recounted with precision because many contradictions exist in the accounts recorded by the two participants. Somewhat more credence can be given to the Roosevelt version because Mackenzie King attributes statements to Roosevelt and Root which they could not have made. He interpreted their remarks to mean that the United States must have what it demanded of Japan or war — as though the United States was about to attack Japan! Mackenzie King diary, January 25, 1908, quoted in Dawson, *Mackenzie King,* p. 154. Mackenzie King also attributes to Roosevelt the view that the Western states of the United States might secede — an idea Roosevelt rightly ridiculed in a letter to Arthur Lee. Dawson, *Mackenzie King,* p. 153; Roosevelt to Lee, February 2, 1908, Morison, *Roosevelt Letters,* VI, 919–921.

[46] Roosevelt to Lee, February 2, 1908, Morison, *Roosevelt Letters,* VI, 919–921; Roosevelt to Reid, March 30, 1908, Morison, *Roosevelt Letters,* VI, 985.

that such a trip might be helpful, but that the first definite proposal for the project came from the Canadian side after Mackenzie King's return to Ottawa. In any case, upon his return to Washington for his second meeting with Roosevelt, Mackenzie King told the President that the Prime Minister, Sir Wilfrid Laurier, wished him to go to London in order to explain the immigration problem to government leaders there. Roosevelt was, of course, enthusiastic over the project. It was his feeling, as he wrote to Arthur Lee, that,

the mere fact that there was cordial understanding and agreement between the two nations as to what was to be done, always provided that there was a real purpose to prevent any humiliation to Japan, would be of immense importance from every standpoint, and would be a guarantee of peace.[47]

While in Washington, Mackenzie King conferred with Root and was shown the American diplomatic documents on the immigration question.[48] Then on February 1, shortly before returning to Ottawa, he lunched with the President, and they canvassed the whole matter together. British Ambassador James Bryce, who was invited to the luncheon, expressed his approval of the project and agreed to telegraph Sir Edward Grey concerning the mission.[49] Roosevelt also did what he could to pave the way for the mission. After Mackenzie King's departure, he sent a long account of the conference to Arthur Lee and asked him to show the letter to Grey, Balfour, and Strachey.[50] He also sent a personal letter to Edward VII expressing his belief that the interests of the United States and Britain were one, alike in the Atlantic and Pacific, and that wage-workers of an alien race must be kept out of English-speaking countries.[51]

At the luncheon with Mackenzie King and Bryce, Roosevelt had asked Bryce to sound London on the possibility of England addressing Japan in a friendly manner about the attitude of the American government on the immigration question. It was soon apparent that Roosevelt should have awaited the outcome of Mackenzie King's visit to Britain before pressing the British on the

47 Roosevelt to Lee, February 2, 1908, Morison, *Roosevelt Letters*, VI, 919–921.
48 Roosevelt to Laurier, February 1, 1908, Morison, *Roosevelt Letters*, VI, 917–918.
49 Roosevelt to Lee, February 2, 1908, Morison, *Roosevelt Letters*, VI, 919–921.
50 Roosevelt to Lee, February 2, 1908, Morison, *Roosevelt Letters*, VI, 919–921.
51 Roosevelt to Edward VII, February 12, 1908, Morison, *Roosevelt Letters*, VI, 940.

question. Grey was cool toward Roosevelt's suggestion, replying that as Japan had never mentioned her difficulties with the United States to the Foreign Office, to initiate the matter would produce suspicion.[52] The British Ambassador at Tokyo likewise opposed the move. "I am of opinion," he telegraphed Grey, "that anything like joint action between ourselves and the United States in this matter would have a bad effect with the Japanese." [53]

Roosevelt soon realized that he had overplayed his hand, and when he next talked with Bryce he explained that what he really wanted was a complete understanding between the two countries and the adoption of a similar attitude on the question of Asiatic immigration. He agreed that harm might come from a British statement to Japan at this time, but he thought it desirable, in the event of a critical crisis arising over the immigration question, that England and the United States speak in the same sense and with equal decision.[54]

Meanwhile Mackenzie King was making preparations for the trip to England. Before his departure the project almost foundered due to confusion among Canadian leaders regarding the nature of the mission. After the luncheon with Mackenzie King on February 1, Roosevelt had written to Prime Minister Laurier expressing his delight at *Laurier's proposal* to send Mackenzie King to London,[55] and the Prime Minister took offense at Roosevelt's letter. He believed the responsibility for the mission was Roosevelt's, and he thought the President was engaging in "a smart Yankee trick" in shifting the responsibility for the mission to the Canadian side. He even remarked to Mackenzie King that he feared he was being drawn into a "deep-laid plot." [56] At the same time, however, Laurier could not accept the logic of his own position. If the mission was really Roosevelt's rather than Canada's, then Laurier was in the ridiculous position of merely providing an errand boy for the United States government. Laurier could hardly defend such a position before his ministerial colleagues.

52 Grey to Bryce, telegram, February 5, 1908, *British Documents*, VIII, 455.
53 MacDonald to Grey, March 17, 1908, *British Documents*, VIII, 457–458.
54 Bryce to Grey, February 14, 1908, *British Documents*, VIII, 455–456.
55 Roosevelt to Laurier, February 1, 1908, Morison, *Roosevelt Letters*, VI, 917–918.
56 Dawson, *Mackenzie King*, pp. 158–159; Donald C. Gordon, "Roosevelt's 'Smart Yankee Trick,'" *Pacific Historical Review*, XXX (1961), 351–358.

Laurier's qualms and confusion were entirely unnecessary. The mission to London, as Roosevelt certainly realized, had no meaning except on the premise that Canada and the United States had common interests on the immigration question. If Mackenzie King went to London as just a messenger for Roosevelt the project could not achieve success. He would be able to influence leaders in London only to the extent that Ottawa and Washington had interests that coincided. That they possessed common interests could hardly be ignored. Even Laurier, amidst his confusion, recognized this.[57] The mission to London was by its very nature, therefore, a joint undertaking in which Canada had as great an interest as the United States.

A week before Mackenzie King left for England, Canada's own interest in the subject of Oriental immigration was underlined. Ottawa received word that a ship had left India for Canada carrying immigrants. Previously Indians had been kept out by an order-in-council requiring Asiatic immigrants to come to Canada by direct voyage, and since no ships sailed directly from India to Canada the restriction had proved effective. But now a ship was bringing passengers direct from India, and the Canadian government feared that rioting would result if the ship attempted to land the Indians. Laurier therefore instructed Mackenzie King to inform the London government that this immigration must be stopped.[58]

In March, Mackenzie King left for London. Before his arrival there, the Empire's interest in the immigration issue was further pointed up by the announcement that the United States fleet would visit Australia. On March 12 the fleet arrived at Magdelena Bay, having completed a triumphant voyage around South America; and on the following day Secretary Metcalf announced that the fleet would cruise around the world via Australia, the Philippines, and Suez.[59] The decision to send the fleet to Australia was an obvious attempt on Roosevelt's part to cement close relations with a section of the British Empire which saw eye-to-eye with the United States on the Japanese question. ". . . for reasons which Secretary Root

[57] Dawson, *Mackenzie King,* p. 154.
[58] Dawson, *Mackenzie King,* p. 160.
[59] New York *Times,* March 14, 1908.

will explain to you," Roosevelt wrote to Metcalf, "I particularly desire the fleet to visit Australia." [60] Prime Minister Alfred Deakin's invitation which had reached the United States in December, 1907, had been motivated by the same consideration. He wrote to a friend in London saying that the white races which faced the common immigration problem should form some kind of *entente cordiale*.[61]

On the day following Metcalf's announcement that the fleet would go to Australia, Mackenzie King arrived in London. He thereupon began a series of interviews with British leaders which were to last for an entire month. He found immediately that the task of winning the home government to the American-Canadian-Australian view was not going to be an easy one.[62] The Foreign Office was at first inclined to dismiss him as merely a messenger from Roosevelt. Ambassador Reid had an interview with Grey immediately after Mackenzie King's first conference at the Foreign Office, and Grey opened the conversation with Reid by saying he had just been having an interview with a gentleman whom he supposed he ought to call another American ambassador — he "also comes from your President." Reid asserted emphatically that such was not the case, that the mission was undertaken on the initiative of the Canadians and was entirely "off their own bat." [63]

Despite the difficulties encountered, by the end of March Mackenzie King had made considerable headway in bringing the British leaders around to his view. Grey wrote to Bryce on the thirty-first that the Japanese immigration question was "very critical," not because war was imminent, but because of the political ramifications of the problem. The Pacific slope, he wrote, was in a high state of fever, and he feared that a suspicion might arise among the people there that when the pinch came the home government would not support them in resisting Japanese immigration. "Should such a suspicion get hold of them," he continued, "there would be no limit to the untoward political consequences which might

60 Roosevelt to Metcalf, February 21, 1908, Morison, *Roosevelt Letters*, VI, 952.
61 Gordon, "Roosevelt's 'Smart Yankee Trick' " p. 355.
62 Reid to Roosevelt, March 20, 1908, Roosevelt Papers.
63 Reid to Roosevelt, March 18, 1908, Roosevelt Papers.

ensue." Grey then informed Bryce that he had given explicit assurances to Mackenzie King that there was no reason for such a
suspicion.[64]

On the same day that Grey wrote this letter, Arthur Lee sent a
report to Roosevelt which further confirmed the success of Mackenzie King's work. Lee said that the Canadian commissioner had
made an "excellent impression" and that practically every responsible person agreed that a complete halt should be called to the immigration of Japanese laborers into the British Empire and America and that, if necessary, the English-speaking countries should
cooperate to make the exclusion effective. Should the subject come
up in Parliament, wrote Lee, the Japanese would not be able to
"detect any real joint in our armour." Furthermore, Grey himself had confided to Lee that he was "most anxious" to cooperate
with the President.[65]

When Mackenzie King left England on April 17, he ended a mission that had been successful from every standpoint. Not only had
he won the Colonial and Foreign offices to his view, but he had
also made a remarkably good impression upon British leaders.[66]
Ambassador Reid even thought that the attempt of the Foreign
Office to regard Mackenzie King at first as only an agent of the
President had redounded to the benefit of the United States, for
Grey had had to beat a hasty retreat on the issue. "I am sure," Reid
reported to Roosevelt, "they have had a distinct object lesson on
the subject, and are not likely to give us any further example of that
'certain condescension' on the part of foreigners about our em-
barrassments on this subject, which we used to fancy that we de-
tected." [67]

Roosevelt was elated at the outcome of the mission. "The visit
has achieved just what I hoped," he wrote to Lee. It did not result
in any concrete plan for joint Anglo-American action, but this
was no longer desired by the President. The immigration ques-

[64] Grey to Bryce, March 30, 1908, quoted in George M. Trevelyan, *Grey of Fallodon:
The Life and Letters of Sir Edward Grey, afterwards Viscount Grey of Fallodon,*
Boston, 1937, p. 230.

[65] Lee to Roosevelt, March 31, 1908, Roosevelt Papers.

[66] John R. Carter to Roosevelt, April 13, 1908, Reid to Roosevelt, April 14, 1908,
Roosevelt Papers.

[67] Reid to Roosevelt, April 14, 1908, Roosevelt Papers.

tion, if not yet completely resolved, was well on the road to solution. Roosevelt's objective was to gain a common understanding with England on the issue so that if the situation became acute at some time in the future, the two countries could work in cooperation. He was never sure, as he wrote to Lee, when the "bricks may begin to fly." [68] The understanding with England which had now been achieved, however, was more than an insurance policy for future crises. Its most important aspect was that it would help prevent the development of a future crisis. The objectives and outcome of Mackenzie King's mission were doubtless known in Tokyo and appreciated at full value. Japan's leaders were thus made even more aware of the necessity for strict implementation of the informal arrangements on immigration with the United States and Canada.

In the months following Mackenzie King's mission to London, American immigration statistics continued to show improvement. The Roosevelt administration, confident of British support, now sought to attain something approaching perfection in the operation of the Gentlemen's Agreement. When the statistics for April, 1908, were given to Roosevelt in mid-June showing that some six hundred Japanese had entered the United States in that month, he was very disturbed. "I think that the Japanese Government should be notified in the plainest manner," he wrote to Root, "that they have nothing to expect but a Japanese exclusion law unless the figures soon begin to show a totally different complexion." [69]

When O'Brien took up the matter in Tokyo, he found that the Foreign Ministry had just recently taken into its own hands the granting of all passports to the United States and Hawaii. On the very day that O'Brien appeared at the Foreign Ministry, Hayashi had telegraphed this news to Washington accompanied by renewed assurances that unsparing efforts would be made to enforce the Gentlemen's Agreement.[70] Even after the receipt of this assurance, however, O'Brien kept the steady pressure upon the Foreign Ministry. When he departed on leave to the United States in June, he left at the Foreign Ministry a memorandum contain-

[68] Roosevelt to Lee, April 8, 1908, Morison, *Roosevelt Letters*, VI, 995–996.
[69] Roosevelt to Root, June 18, 1908, Roosevelt Papers.
[70] Takahira to Root, June 19, 1908, S. D. File 2542/643–644.

ing his own views. They were even more candid than those that had emanated from Washington. He told Hayashi that when his government accepted the plan for the solution of the immigration problem, it assumed that the result "would not be very different from what might be expected if a law of exclusion was in force." [71]

Despite Roosevelt's concern over the number of Japanese arrivals, the immigration statistics in the succeeding months gave increasing evidence that Japan was effectively implementing the agreement. In June, 1907, 2,208 Japanese had entered the United States and Hawaii, while in June, 1908, the number had dropped to 702. By August of 1908 the number of Japanese leaving the continental United States exceeded those entering. When the statistics for the year 1908 were later compiled, it was found that 4,477 had been admitted to the mainland, while 5,035 had departed. When Roosevelt went out of office in March, 1909, the departures still were in excess of arrivals.[72]

[71] O'Brien to Hayashi, June 28, 1908, Documents Relating to the Limitation and Exclusion of Japanese Immigrants by the United States, MT3.8.2.21, reel 726, pp. 6603–06.

[72] Charles Nagel to Philander C. Knox, March 19, 1909, S. D. File 2542/843–852.

CHAPTER FOURTEEN

Straight's Crusade in Manchuria

DURING the years 1907–08, when Roosevelt and Root were gravely concerned over Japanese immigration and their letters were filled with a discussion of that question, it is surprising that their voluminous correspondence contained hardly a mention of the Manchurian question. Yet, during those years developments were occurring in the Three Eastern Provinces which were fraught with great significance for Japanese-American relations. The most important of these developments was the program of commercial and capital penetration being formulated by Willard Straight, the young United States Consul General at Mukden.

When Straight left Korea in December, 1905, his career in the Far East had by no means ended. In the summer of 1906 he was appointed Consul General at Mukden,[1] and in October of that year he arrived at his post. He was obliged to establish the Consulate General in a forlorn Chinese hotel until March of 1907, but in that month he secured a former viceroy's memorial temple, which consisted of a series of buildings grouped around a spacious court. For a Consulate General on the frontier of civilization, it was indeed a sumptuous residence. There Straight raised a tall white flagstaff

[1] Some mystery surrounds the reasons for Straight's appointment to the Mukden post. Edwin Morgan believed that E. H. Harriman had a hand in it, but Straight's biographer, Herbert Croly, stated that Roosevelt "discovered" him when he visited the President at Oyster Bay in the summer of 1906. Croly, *Willard Straight*, pp. 197–202. Roosevelt's correspondence reveals that Richard Harding Davis was among those recommending Straight's appointment. Roosevelt to Davis, May 12, 1906, Roosevelt Papers. Charles Lyon Chandler, who was acting consul at Dairen in 1907 and a close acquaintance of Straight's believed the appointment was due to the influence of Lady Susan Townley, who, as the wife of the secretary of the British legation at Peking, had known Straight in China. At the time of Straight's appointment, the Townleys were at the British embassy at Washington. Chandler to the author, July 1, 1955.

— believed to be the highest in North China! — and unfurled the Stars and Stripes above the Manchurian plains.[2]

During his first year at Mukden, Straight was occupied principally with the task of promoting American commerce. Though he greatly disliked the Japanese, he could find little to complain about insofar as opportunity for ordinary commerce was concerned. Once normal conditions were re-established in Manchuria in the summer of 1907, the open door for commerce, as distinguished from capital investment, prevailed. On many occasions Japanese leaders proclaimed adherence to that policy, and almost all American officials accepted these statements as representing an existing condition.[3] Charles Lyon Chandler, who was Vice Consul in charge at Dairen (Dalny) during 1907, expressed the prevailing view in a letter to Ambassador O'Brien:

While it is undoubtedly true that the Japanese have enjoyed especial privileges in their own leased territory — privileges which most nations, including our own, accord their nationals in their dependencies — I have not as yet been able to substantiate an instance in those parts of Manchuria said to be under the "sphere of influence" of Japan of discrimination against American citizens or American trade. . . . The oversuspicion and incessant distrust of a people who have shown far more tolerance and far more of the "open door" spirit in their leased territory of Liaotung than their predecessors there are not supported by facts.[4]

The chief obstacle to Straight's attempts to further American trade was not the lack of equal opportunity but rather the apathy of American commercial interests. "When all is said and done," Straight wrote to William Phillips at the end of 1907, "it's a rather thankless task, this endeavor to increase the American export trade." The American merchants, he found, were not prepared to expend either time or trouble to introduce their wares in Manchuria. The merchants, he told Phillips,

seem to feel that the benighted Chinese should consider himself highly honored if allowed to glance through an illustrated booklet printed in a lan-

2 Croly, *Willard Straight*, pp. 202–222.

3 Wright to Root, August 11, 1906, S. D. File 551/9; Wright to Rockhill, August 15, 1906, Post Records: Wright to Miscellaneous, I; Rockhill to Root, October 11, 1906, S. D. File 551/13; Roger S. Greene to Bacon, January 29, 1908, S. D. File 551/90–91.

4 Chandler to O'Brien, November 23, 1907, Post Records: O'Brien, from Miscellaneous, II.

guage which he does not understand, but which represents the highest development of "American inventive genius," whether it be in corset making
or in the manufacture of electric curling irons.[5]

Straight would never have admitted it, but it seems clear that during the time he was at Mukden and in the subsequent years, American commercial interests were accorded a fair opportunity to exploit the South Manchurian market; and, according to Straight's
own assessment, that trade would have been of much greater volume had it been energetically pushed.

The international rivalry in Manchuria was not to revolve
around the question of commercial interests. The bone of contention was, rather, the question of capital investment. In the months
that followed the rejection of the Katsura-Harriman scheme for
joint Japanese-American exploitation of Manchuria, Japanese leaders had gradually come to the decision that Japan should reserve
to herself the field of capital investment in South Manchuria. Many
Americans, including Straight, were inclined to look upon Japan's
developing sphere of influence and pre-eminence in capital investment in South Manchuria as a violation of John Hay's open door
principle, but there was no justification for this view. In his notes
of September 6, 1899, Hay requested only equal commercial opportunity and he tacitly accepted the spheres of influence as existing facts. When Japan pledged her adherence to the open door
policy, she was, of course, pledging adherence to equal commercial
opportunity. Any other interpretation of that pledge would mean
that she was pledging not to erect a sphere of influence in South
Manchuria. It would take a good measure of naiveté to believe
that Japan had intended to make any such pledge. But in the
years that followed the Russo-Japanese War, Japan's critics were
inclined to interpret loosely the term "open door" and, indeed, it
was not long before American policy makers themselves were doing
likewise. Thus, a new open door policy was emerging which was
all-inclusive in its demands and which bore little relation to the
realities of Far Eastern power politics.

It was against the background of Japan's emerging sphere of influence that Straight embarked upon an ambitious but hopeless

[5] Straight to William Phillips, December 18, 1907, Straight Papers.

crusade to inject American capital into South Manchuria and thereby to check and destroy that sphere of influence. The odds were stacked heavily against him, but Straight relished the role of the underdog. As Straight's biographer has noted:

The young American Consul-General at Mukden prepared almost single-handed to make the fight. . . . Mounted though he appeared to be on a crazy little pony and armed with a lath for a sword and a reed for a lance, he was not afraid to enter the lists against the dragon of Japanese imperialism. He became for some years a man with a mission.[6]

Straight was not, however, entirely without allies. In April, 1907, the Chinese administration in Manchuria was reorganized and the new officials, who arrived the following June, were eager to cooperate with the United States Consul General. Hsu Shih-chang, the newly appointed Viceroy of Manchuria, and Tang Shao-yi, the new Governor of Fengtien, were particularly desirous of blocking Japan's advance. Since Mukden was the capital of Fengtien, as well as of Manchuria, Straight was able to work closely with these officials.

Straight found another ally in the person of George Marvin, who came to fill the position of Deputy Consul General. Marvin was a brilliant young man who had been an instructor of English at Harvard and was at this time on leave from his position as master at Groton. He was as adventurous as Straight, and he plunged enthusiastically into the struggle against the Japanese.

Straight needed all the allies he could get, for he had a formidable foe, the United States Minister at Peking, W. W. Rockhill. Rockhill took a dim view of Straight's activities, and personal antipathy soon developed between them. "Even were I a Mr. Pepys with a cipher of my own," Straight noted in his diary, "I would not write here what I think of His Eccentricity." [7] Rockhill and Straight were at opposite poles in their approach to the Manchurian question. Rockhill, who along with A. E. Hippisley had drafted Hay's open door notes of September 6, 1899, had a more realistic understanding of the limitations of that policy, while Straight was the foremost proponent of a militant, all-embracing open door policy. And

[6] Croly, *Willard Straight*, p. 212.
[7] Straight diary, January 11, 1907, Straight Papers.

Straight was a man with a cause and was quite willing to proceed without the blessing of Rockhill. "This game in Manchuria must be well played," he wrote to Consul Fred Fisher at Harbin, "and if Peking cannot see the importance of doing it along the lines which to us on the ground seem best, we will take it up with Washington." [8]

Straight's first project took the form of an American financed Manchurian Bank. After many conferences with Tang Shao-yi, the Governor of Fengtien, he drew up a scheme for an American loan of twenty million dollars to capitalize a bank which would be the financial agent of the Manchurian administration. Its services would be used for railway construction, industrial enterprises, and the stabilization of the Manchurian currency. Straight hoped to interest his friend E. H. Harriman in the project, and on August 7, 1907, he dispatched a draft agreement to him. Straight's diary contains the following entry for that day: "Tang approves draft. Letter mailed. Fraught with tremendous possibilities. If adopted it means we play principal part in the development of Manchuria. Our influence in China tremendously enhanced." [9] But despite Straight's great expectations, the project collapsed. The financial panic of 1907 in the United States caused Harriman to turn down the proposal.[10]

While Straight was promoting the ill-fated Manchuria Bank scheme, some of his British acquaintances, J. O. P. Bland and Lord ffrench, were concocting a project which was as bold and as fraught with international complications as any conceived by the resourceful Straight: the Hsinmintun-Fakumen railway project. How much Straight himself had to do with the initiation of this project can only be conjectured. He was certainly in close touch with all the men involved, and it fitted in perfectly with his anti-Japanese crusade. To understand the nature of this amazing scheme, it is necessary to examine in detail the circumstances surrounding its inception.

J. O. P. Bland represented at Peking the British and Chinese

8 Straight to Fisher, January 21, 1908, Straight Papers.
9 Croly, *Willard Straight*, pp. 241–242; Straight diary, August 7, 1907, Straight Papers.
10 Harriman to Straight, October 5, 1907, Straight Papers.

Corporation, the syndicate that had financed the construction of the Shanhaikwan-Newchwang-Hsinmintun railway, the Chinese-owned line stretching from China proper into South Manchuria. In May of 1907 Bland went to London to try to convince the London *Times* that it was mistaken in its pro-Japanese policy. In August, 1907, Bland returned to the East, bringing with him Lord ffrench of Pauling and Company. They came to Mukden to see Tang Shao-yi and while there they lodged with Straight. They stayed only a few days, but ten days after their departure Lord ffrench returned again with an engineer, who immediately carried out a flying survey of the land from Hsinmintun (the northern terminus of the Chinese railway line) to Tsitsihar in northern Manchuria. Then in early November, Lord ffrench returned to Mukden again and signed a contract with Tang for the construction by Pauling and Company of a railway from Hsinmintun to Fakumen, a city fifty miles north of Hsinmintun. Bland returned on November 20 and signed an agreement with Tang by which the British and Chinese Corporation agreed to loan to China the funds required for the project.[11]

This project appeared on the surface to be only a short extension of the North China Railway northward from Hsinmintun, but in actuality it was far more. It was the first step in a carefully laid scheme to run a line from Hsinmintun to Tsitsihar in northern Manchuria which would parallel and compete with the Japanese-controlled South Manchuria Railway. Lord ffrench confided to Straight and Marvin that though the preliminary contract only covered the fifty mile extension to Fakumen, a secret agreement had been signed with Tang for the construction of the rest of the line to Tsitsihar.[12] Neither Straight, Marvin, Bland, Lord ffrench, nor Tang was under any illusion as to the implications of the project. In a letter to Huntington Wilson, Straight was quite frank about the nature of the scheme:

The Hsinmintun-Fakumen line will surely be extended to Tsitsihar, will very seriously compete with the South Manchurian railway, will not only tap a rich and rapidly developing country, part of the produce of which is

[11] Straight to Wilson, January 31, 1908, Straight Papers.
[12] Straight diary, November 5, 1907, and Marvin diary, November 6, 1907, Straight Papers.

now carried over the Japanese road, but will almost certainly attract all the through European traffic as well as secure all the mails. More than that even, it will threaten the Japanese strategic position and place a splendid line of communication along the Japanese flank and within easy reach of the Russians whose activities in Mongolia have already aroused the apprehensions of their late, and possible future enemies.[13]

Straight wrote an equally revealing description of the signing of the contract to a friend: "The contract was signed by ffrench who was staying with me at the time and that night, the 9th of November we broke a large bot on the deal that we knew would set the whole crowd by the ears. Then we sat by and watched for the explosion which sure came." [14]

Before the explosion came, Straight had still another project underway. He undertook to win over to his views the Secretary of War and likely next President of the United States — Taft. Just at this time Taft was journeying home from the Far East by way of Vladivostok and the Trans-Siberian Railway. Straight tried to get Taft to visit Mukden, but he had to settle for conferences with the Secretary at Vladivostok and on the train from that point to Harbin.[15] Even before arriving at Vladivostok, Taft had been partially won over to the anti-Japanese campaign. Thomas F. Millard, Far Eastern correspondent of the New York *Herald*, an avowedly anti-Japanese writer, had sent a long memorandum to Taft pointing out the danger of dismemberment hanging over China and urging him to allay the fears of Americans in China who believed that the United States would sit idly by and watch such an eventuality take place.[16] Taft was apparently very impressed with Millard's views, for in his speech at Shanghai he said that it would be difficult to predict how far the United States government would go in support of its open door policy — the implication being that it would go farther than many believed.[17] After leaving Shanghai, Taft wrote to Root: "It is quite possible that you will have to assert

13 Straight to Wilson, January 31, 1908, Straight Papers.

14 Straight to Henry Schoelkopf, March 22, 1908, Straight Papers.

15 Straight to Taft, September 15, 1907, and Taft to Straight, October 10, 1907, Taft Papers.

16 Millard to Taft, September 26, 1907, Taft Papers.

17 Taft sent a copy of his speech to Roosevelt. Taft to Roosevelt, October 10, 1907, Roosevelt Papers.

with considerable stiffness the determination of America to insist on the Open Door policy and not to allow it to be set aside by underhand methods." [18]

When Taft and Straight met at Vladivostok on November 18, the Secretary inclined a receptive ear to Straight's entreaties. Straight recorded in his diary concerning the first conversation:

He had been much impressed by his reception at Shanghai and felt strongly that China was turning to us as the one disinterested friend. He hoped that we might do something. I assured him that we could — that now is the time — and that the fruit is ripe and it is ours to pluck. With this he seemed to agree.[19]

Straight had a concrete plan to present to Taft for carrying out such a policy. On June 15, 1907, Root had informed the Chinese minister at Washington that Roosevelt would recommend remission of that portion of the Boxer indemnity in excess of the actual expenses incurred by the Boxer expedition (approximately one-half of the twenty-four million dollar indemnity).[20] Tang and Straight hit upon the idea of using the remitted funds, which would be refunded as each payment came due, for the service of a loan to be floated in the United States for the development of Manchuria. This scheme he now proposed to the Secretary of War, and according to Straight's diary, "Taft rather took to Tang's scheme of applying the indemnity for an American loan." [21] After his return to Mukden, Straight wrote hopefully to a friend:

I think that the President and the Secretary of State will be inclined, if they accept the advice which I think Mr. Taft will give, to regard Manchuria as a fair field and not as one that must be approached either with the acquiescense, or with special regard for the sensibilities, of the Japanese.[22]

Straight followed up the conference with a long memorandum to Taft on Manchurian affairs. He stated frankly that the Chinese wished to secure funds either in the United States or England "in

18 Taft to Root, October 10, 1907, Taft Papers.

19 Croly, *Willard Straight*, pp. 249–251; Straight diary, November 18, 1907, Straight Papers.

20 Root to Chentung Liang Cheng, June 15, 1907, *Foreign Relations, 1907*, I, 174.

21 Croly, *Willard Straight*, pp. 250–251; Straight diary, November 19, 1907, Straight Papers.

22 Straight to G. Casenave, December 4, 1907, Straight Papers.

order to shield themselves behind the political support which would be accorded such capital." When Taft forwarded this memorandum to the Department of State, Root marked this suspicious passage with his thick blue pencil.[23] The records do not reveal that Taft vigorously urged Straight's views upon the Department. When Straight sent a report to Washington recommending his indemnity remission scheme,[24] he received no encouragement from that quarter. Rockhill had recommended that the refund be devoted to the education of Chinese students in the United States, and his views prevailed. While on leave in the United States in January, 1908, Rockhill talked with Root about the matter, and as he recorded in his diary, "We practically agreed on method." [25] Shortly after this meeting, Straight was pointedly told not to meddle in the affair:

The Department trusts . . . that you have not failed to bear in mind the fact that this is a delicate matter of diplomacy with which the Consulate General at Mukden has no direct concern. . . . If the Congress shall authorize some remission of the indemnity all arrangements will be exclusively in the hands of the Minister at Peking.[26]

When late in November, 1907, Straight returned from his conference with Taft, the storm over the Hsinmintun-Fakumen railway project was rapidly gathering. Before it broke, the Consul General had launched still another measure to check the Japanese. Straight believed that China suffered badly from the lack of an effective news outlet. It was now decided that Marvin should resign his position of Deputy Consul General and establish an anti-Japanese propaganda bureau. His resignation was accepted by Root on December 28; and on January 1, 1908, the bureau was formally opened, having been provided with a carte-blanche expense account by Tang. For a time Marvin continued to reside in the Consulate General, and from there he sent out "publicity" to the China coast papers and foreign correspondents. When Japanese irritation became pronounced, he thought it expedient to

23 Straight to Taft, December 2, 1907 (forwarded to Root, January 31, 1908), S. D. File 2413/97–99.
24 Straight to Bacon, December 9, 1907, S. D. File 2413/92–93.
25 Rockhill diary, January 25, 1908, Rockhill Papers.
26 Wilbur J. Carr, Chief Clerk, to Straight, February 10, 1908, S. D. File 2413/92–94.

move out of the Consulate General, and so he leased the compound next door! Sometimes Marvin's work carried him far from Mukden, but, he later wrote, "I remained in spirit throughout my absence closely linked to the originator of the plan, who was chiefly interested in its development and success." [27]

A few days after the news bureau was set up the storm over the Hsinmintun-Fakumen project broke. Japan made it known that China had agreed by the "secret protocols" of December 22, 1905, which had been signed by Tang himself, not to construct any main line in the neighborhood of and parallel to the South Manchuria Railway or any branch line which might be prejudicial to the interest of that railway, and the Tokyo government stood firmly on that position. Japan had lodged a protest at Peking while the line was being surveyed — that is, even before Tang signed the contract. When two more protests were ineffective, Japan made public the "secret protocols."

Straight hoped at first that the project could be carried through over the opposition of the Japanese. Bland was not so sanguine. He wrote to Straight:

Tang agreed (unless the documentary evidence in the hands of the Japanese is all a fake) to subsidiary conditions in the Manchurian Convention which make the open door policy (as far as the China Govt. is concerned) impossible. Then, without telling us of any of these things, he gets us to contract to build the railway, and it looks very much as if his sole object was to embroil us with the Japanese in a case where his own action cuts the ground from under our feet. . . .

I feel rather sore about this business because Tang had the Japanese protest in his possession when we signed our contract and he never said a word about there being any possible difficulty, but led us to believe that the business was all fair and square, and only needed the sanction of the Throne. Now, it appears that it requires *our* political intervention to recover the rights which China has given away.

Bland said that he had learned from Marvin that Tang said that he never agreed to the supplementary conditions to the Komura treaty, but, Bland wrote to Straight, "this is denied even by the Chinese who are familiar with the facts." [28] Is England or the

27 Croly, *Willard Straight*, pp. 252–256.
28 Bland to Straight, January 23, 1908, Straight Papers.

United States, he asked Straight, "going to fight to protect China against her own foolishness. Are we going to bolster up the Sick Man against his will?" [29]

In conversations with Straight, Tang at first tried to deny the existence of the "secret protocols." [30] Then he admitted that the minutes of the negotiations with Komura had been signed and that he and Komura had agreed to something vague about leaving the matter of competing or parallel lines to "international usage." But, Tang now explained, this was not an issue in the case, for the Hsinmintun-Fakumen line would not parallel or compete with the Japanese line." [31] Straight was by now somewhat disillusioned himself. If the "secret protocols" did exist, he wrote to Bland, "Tang is only one thing, and his diplomacy has decidedly the smack of Korea about it." As for Tang's new defence, Straight said: ". . . if the Chinese can only excuse themselves by saying that the new road would not compete, they had better chuck it as a rotten bad case." [32]

In the subsequent weeks the Chinese did not deny the validity of the "secret protocols." The Associated Press representative at Peking, Frederick McCormick, wrote to Straight in late February: "Nobody in the Wai-wu-pu here denied the binding force nor the actuality of those minutes forbidding China to build a competing line." Furthermore, he said, "There is a sad uniformity of conviction in Peking that China hasn't done much to deserve sympathy." McCormick perceived that all now depended upon what position Britain would take, and he had a feeling that Britain would not contradict Japan's claim to supremacy in that sphere.[33]

It was not long before Britain's policy was made clear. On March 3, Sir Edward Grey told the House of Commons that the existence of the "secret protocols" was not disputed by China and that it was open to the contractors (Pauling and Company) to prove to the satisfaction of Japan that the proposed line would not preju-

29 Bland to Straight, February 1, 1908, Straight Papers.
30 Straight to Henry P. Fletcher, January 19, 1908, Papers of Henry P. Fletcher, Library of Congress, Washington, D. C.
31 Straight to Bacon, January 4, 1908, S. D. File 6625/40; Straight to Bacon, February 12, 1908, S. D. File 6625/41–45; Bland to Straight, February 1, 1908, Straight Papers.
32 Straight to Bland, February 6, 1908, Straight Papers.
33 McCormick to Straight, February 21, 1908, Straight Papers.

dice the South Manchuria Railway.[34] This statement virtually ended the Hsinmintun-Fakumen controversy as a serious international issue. Negotiations continued between China and Japan for over a year, and finally on September 4, 1909, a convention was signed whereby China agreed to arrange the matter previously with Japan if she undertook the construction of the line.[35]

Straight was discouraged over the failure of the Hsinmintun-Fakumen scheme, but had he known what was occurring at the Department of State at this very time he would have been much encouraged. In the same month that the railway project was rejected by Sir Edward Grey, the newly created Far Eastern Division at the Department took steps to support Straight's crusade. This new division, which was set up at the suggestion and under the supervision of Huntington Wilson, was created in March, 1908. Wilson, who as Third Assistant Secretary of State had handled Far Eastern matters since his arrival at the Department in the summer of 1906, selected William Phillips, Second Secretary at Peking, as chief of the new division.[36] The division was no sooner created than Wilson and Phillips took steps to reconstitute Hay's open door policy. The first move was a long memorandum by Wilson to Root accusing Japan of violating the open door and the integrity of China.[37] Root showed no enthusiasm for taking any vigorous action to support China, but he did authorize Wilson and Phillips to draw up an Information Series circular on the open door policy which would be sent to the principal United States embassies and legations. While compiling the documents for this publication, Wilson continued to urge Root to take strong action to support the open door and the integrity of China. He even suggested that Root confer with the Chinese Minister and elicit from him a request for American support! [38]

During March and early April, Wilson and Phillips were busily

---

[34] Great Britain, *The Parliamentary Debates, Fourth Series*, 199 vols., London, 1892–1908, CLXXXV, 527. The Japanese Ambassador at London had already been told the same. Komura to Hayashi, received February 28, 1908, Telegram Series, CIV, 967–968.

[35] *Manchuria: Treaties and Agreements*, p. 129.

[36] F. M. Huntington Wilson, *Memoirs of an Ex-Diplomat*, Boston, 1945, pp. 161–165.

[37] Wilson to Root, March 6, 1908, S. D. File 551/92.

[38] Wilson to Root, March 9, 1908, S. D. File 551/102.

engaged in gathering the documents for the Information Series circular. Wilson also drew up an analysis of the open door policy which was to accompany the documents. This paper revealed clearly that Wilson had only the vaguest knowledge of the history of the open door policy. Regarding Hay's open door note of September 6, 1899, he stated that the powers had given their assent to the policy enunciated. Had Wilson studied the replies which Hay received from the powers, he could hardly have reached such a conclusion. Wilson even brought to the support of the record the Anglo-German Agreement of October 16, 1900, though Bülow had specifically excepted Manchuria from the open door in his interpretation of this agreement.

The key part of Wilson's analysis was his discussion of the present situation in Manchuria. It was a severe indictment of Japan. That country was accused of violating the open door and the integrity of China by the opposition to the Hsinmintun-Fakumen project, the operation of telegraph and postal stations outside the railway area, the designation of Japanese Consuls in Manchuria as secretaries to the Governor General of the Kwantung leasehold, and the granting of preferential treatment to Japanese goods on the South Manchuria Railway. These charges, with but one exception, were either without foundation or were not in any way related to the policy enunciated by Hay. The blocking of the Hsinmintun-Fakumen project was no more a violation of the open door than many other railway agreements signed by China. The agreement between China and the American-China Development Company signed on July 13, 1900, for the construction of the Hankow-Canton line, and the agreement between China and the British and Chinese Corporation signed on July 9, 1903, for the construction of the Shanghai-Nanking line, both contained clauses protecting the lines from parallel or competing lines.[39] The designation of Japanese Consuls as secretaries to the Governor General related only to police matters and was merely intended to resolve a conflict in authority between the Foreign Ministry and the Governor General regarding consuls in the railway zone. When the Department asked

[39] Texts in Percy H. Kent, *Railway Enterprise in China: An Account of Its Origin and Development*, London, 1907, Appendix.

O'Brien for a full report on the matter, he saw in it no violation
of China's integrity.[40] The charge that the South Manchuria Railway granted preferential rates was never substantiated. Only the
charge concerning the operation by Japan of telegraph and postal
offices outside the railway zone had any validity, and this was undoubtedly a violation of China's sovereignty. This was soon to be
disposed of, however, by the sale of such facilities to China.

Root realized that Wilson was on weak ground, and though he
did not believe that Japan should go completely unrestrained in
Manchuria, he agreed with a report coming at this time from Consul Roger S. Greene at Dairen stating that sweeping and unjust
charges against Japan created a spirit of antagonism and might do
immense harm.[41] When Wilson submitted the galley proof of the
Information Series publication for approval, Root took his blue
pencil and struck out the long indictment of Japan.[42] And so, when
Information Series No. 3, Section A, was sent out on April 10,
1908, it included everything except the diatribe against Japan.

The significance of this attempt by Wilson and Phillips to rein-
terpret the policy of the open door and the integrity of China can
hardly be overestimated. The move made little headway while
Roosevelt and Root were in office, but the cause was to meet success in later years. Wilson went on to become Assistant Secretary of
State during the Taft administration, and his views found fruition
in the Dollar Diplomacy of that era. During the Roosevelt administration, Wilson and Phillips, along with Straight in Manchuria,
were taking the first steps toward Dollar Diplomacy with its cham-
pionship of the "new" open door and the integrity of China. These
men were in essence doing more than reinvigorating an old policy.
They were creating a new policy, an all-embracing open door policy which bore little relation to the policy of Rockhill and Hay.
Unbeknown to themselves they were resolving the inherent con-
tradiction in Hay's position — which recognized the spheres of
influence and at the same time declared support for China's in-

[40] Root to O'Brien, April 16, 1908, S. D. File 560/29–31; O'Brien to Root, May 26,
1908, S. D. File 560/41–42.
[41] Greene to Bacon, January 29, 1908, S. D. File 551/90–91.
[42] The galley proof is in S. D. File 551.

tegrity — and they were resolving it in favor of China's integrity. They were thus creating a new open door policy which Japan could not accept.[43]

While Wilson and Phillips were coming to Straight's support in Washington, the young Consul General was still pushing his campaign in Manchuria. In March, 1908, the Viceroy called a conference of the governors of the three Manchurian provinces and the assembly endorsed Tang's scheme for the flotation of a Manchurian loan in the United States. Tang then went to Peking and obtained the endorsement of the Empress Dowager for the plan. It was subsequently decided that Tang himself should go to the United States to express China's appreciation for the Boxer indemnity remission and to promote the loan project.[44] Tang and Straight still hoped that they might use the remission funds to service the loan, and Straight asked permission to proceed to Peking to discuss the matter with Rockhill.[45] His counsel, however, was not desired at the Peking legation. "Peking I never hear from," he lamented. "The superior diplomatic intelligence does not deem it advisable I presume to take mere consular worms into the Olympian realms." [46]

Straight was in the midst of his anti-Japanese campaign when in early April the crusade was abruptly halted by the "Mukden incident." On the morning of April 3 a Japanese postman and some of his compatriots got into a scuffle with some of Straight's Chinese servants on the grounds of the consulate general. Straight stopped the row and took the offending Japanese to their consul, Motoshiro Kato. Straight thought that Kato was a bit impertinent to him, and two days later he sent a semi-humorous account of the incident to Marvin, who was then at Peking.[47] Marvin, unconscious of what the effect would be, published in a Tientsin newspaper a lively account of the affair, including quotations from the cor-

[43] This change in the open door policy has been summarized in Raymond A. Esthus, "The Changing Concept of the Open Door, 1899–1910," *The Mississippi Valley Historical Review*, XLVI (1959–60), 435–454.

[44] Croly, *Willard Straight*, p. 255.

[45] Straight to Fletcher, March 11, 1908, Straight Papers.

[46] Straight to Charles J. Arnell, March 15, 1908, Straight Papers.

[47] Straight to Marvin, April 5, 1908, Straight Papers.

respondence that passed between Kato and Straight. The incident was taken up by American journalists who soon telegraphed Straight for particulars. Straight was alarmed, for his close connection with Marvin's anti-Japanese propaganda bureau was now clearly revealed. He did his best to suppress the story, but it was too late.[48] He wrote remorsefully to Marvin:

> Now I know, of course, that when you wrote your article, if you did do it, you were probably in a hurry, and probably unaware of the danger that you were playing with. . . . You make me look like a swash-buckler, with my revolver, the state of riot, heroic Consul protecting helpless Chinese, etc. It's damned funny, really, but I tell you that I am about as sick an individual as ever walked. . . . Take Tang's advice and go slow.[49]

Straight feared repercussion from Washington, and his fear was well founded. The Department of State telegraphed Marvin suggesting that he resign from his publicity work. Marvin regretfully complied.[50] The Department then sent Straight on an exploring expedition into northern Manchuria. Straight had been asking for permission for such a journey for some months, but he knew that he was now being sent for reasons other than the Department's "anxiety to learn of the trade of Petuna."[51] "I am afraid W. W. [Rockhill] has been toppling things," he confided to Marvin. "Personally I am loathe to go north on the trip."[52] But go north he did on May 24. When in July he was nearing the end of his explorations, he received a telegram from the Department ordering him home. The crusade in Manchuria was over — at least for a time.

Straight's recall to Washington, though coming in the wake of the Mukden incident, was not due to Washington's apprehension over his anti-Japanese program. It resulted rather from the Department's desire to get the latest information on Manchuria. Roosevelt and Root apparently took little note of Straight's activities in Manchuria. There is little doubt that if either the President

[48] Straight to Fletcher, telegram, April 14, 1908, Straight Papers.
[49] Straight to Marvin, April 14, 1908, Straight Papers.
[50] Bacon to Rockhill, telegram, April 14, 1908, and April 16, 1908, Straight Papers.
[51] Straight to Marvin, May 7, 1908, Straight Papers.
[52] Straight to Marvin, May 5, 1908, Straight Papers.

or the Secretary of State had fully appreciated the nature of Straight's crusade, his stay in Manchuria would have been much shorter than it was. Nor would he have been given a responsible position in the Department upon his return. As it turned out, however, the young crusader was soon made Acting Chief of the Far Eastern Division at the Department, a position from which he continued to push his anti-Japanese program.

CHAPTER FIFTEEN

The Beginning of the Japanese-American Rapprochement

THE spring and summer of 1908 witnessed the first moves toward the Japanese-American rapprochement which was to culminate in the famous Root-Takahira exchange of notes on November 30, 1908. After months of strained relations and rumors of war, the pendulum at last began to swing in the other direction. An important step came on March 18, 1908, when Ambassador Takahira delivered an invitation for the United States fleet to visit Japan.[1] After some anxious consultation in the Roosevelt cabinet concerning whether the sailors were sufficiently well disciplined for such a mission, it was decided that the fleet would go to Japan.[2] "The Japanese have asked our fleet to come to Japan," Roosevelt confided to Whitelaw Reid, "and I suppose they will have to go. I had hoped they would not be asked, because there is always the chance of some desperado doing something that will have very bad effects."[3] Despite the President's concern, the news that the fleet would visit Japan was received with great satisfaction both in that country and the United States and did much to silence further rumors of war.[4]

The fleet invitation, together with the favorable outcome of the

[1] Hayashi to Takahira, March 18, 1908, Telegram Series, CV, 2443; Takahira to Root, March 18, 1908, Roosevelt Papers.

[2] Takahira to Hayashi, received March 22, 1908, Telegram Series, CV, 2022.

[3] Roosevelt to Reid, March 20, 1908, Roosevelt Papers.

[4] Bailey, *Roosevelt and the Japanese-American Crises*, pp. 275–276.

immigration *démarche*, should have been sufficient indication to Roosevelt that relations with Japan were improving. Yet at this very time the President betrayed great concern over the possibilities of war. His apprehension was precipitated partly by several memoranda sent to him on April 14 by German Ambassador Sternberg which embodied the views of the German Military Attaché at Tokyo and a German consular official in Japan. These officials agreed that Japan was making no war preparations and could not go to war because of Japan's weak financial condition, but they went on to point out that many Japanese military officers considered America's immigration policy an insult to Japan which could not remain forever unavenged.[5] One view in the reports which particularly irritated Roosevelt was that the Japanese military party accepted as a matter of course that in the event of war they would win naval supremacy and land an army on the Pacific coast. Roosevelt immediately sent these papers to Root with the comment: "I think that the probabilities are that that war will not take place; but there is a sufficient likelihood to make it inexcusable for us not to take such measures as will surely prevent it. If we have adequate coast defenses and a really large navy, the war cannot take place."[6]

Two days later Roosevelt expressed more concern in a letter to Kermit discussing his efforts to get appropriations for naval construction: "I cannot give in public my reasons for being apprehensive about Japan, for of course to do so might bring on grave trouble; but I said enough to put Congress thoroly on guard, if it cared to be on its guard." He went on to confide that he knew the Japanese military party was "inclined for war with us" and confident that they could land an expeditionary force in California.[7] On the same day that this letter was written, Roosevelt sent an excited note to Secretary of the Treasury George B. Cortelyou:

I do not at all like having so much gold in San Francisco. Have you yet shipped much of it to Denver? If not please take steps to get at least the bulk of it there during the next six months. San Francisco is on every ac-

5 Sternberg to Roosevelt, April 14, 1908, Roosevelt Papers.
6 Roosevelt to Root, April 17, 1908, Morison, *Roosevelt Letters*, VI, 1010.
7 Roosevelt to Kermit Roosevelt, April 19, 1908, Morison, *Roosevelt Letters*, VI, 1012–1013.

count an undesirable place in which to leave it; a fatal place should there ever be a war.[8]

Thus at the very time that most signs pointed to peace, Roosevelt succumbed to the war hysteria. The primary reason is not to be found in any development in Japanese-American relations, nor in the reports relayed through Sternberg, but rather in the debates then taking place in Congress. Earlier in the year Roosevelt had recommended increased naval construction and the building of fortifications at Pearl Harbor in the Hawaiian Islands.[9] During the heated debate in the Senate, Roosevelt's supporters made the most of the Japanese threat in stressing the need for naval construction, and Roosevelt himself, as he told Kermit, played up the Japanese threat in conferences with congressional leaders. While doing so he exaggerated in his own mind the danger of war. His tactics with Congress while in an excited state of mind produced at least one unfortunate repercussion. Richmond P. Hobson, one of the chief supporters of Roosevelt's naval program in the House, told the Democratic convention in July that Roosevelt said that war with Japan was "probable." Roosevelt issued a prompt denial that he made such a statement, but it is likely that Hobson was not greatly exaggerating what Roosevelt had said.[10]

Though Roosevelt overestimated the immediate danger of war with Japan, his naval program was not a product of this miscalculation. The naval construction program was rather a result of long-term considerations. The crises with Japan in 1906–07 were the principal determining factor, for they pointed up that friction and possible trouble with Japan would be a continuing feature of American foreign relations. In a letter to Senator Joseph G. Can-

[8] Roosevelt to Cortelyou, April 19, 1908, Morison, *Roosevelt Letters*, VI, 1013.

[9] Roosevelt to Speaker Joseph G. Cannon, February 29, 1908, Morison, *Roosevelt Letters*, VI, 956; Roosevelt to Senator Francis Emory Warren, January 17, 1908, Morison, *Roosevelt Letters*, VI, 912–913. Military and naval experts had concluded that it was impossible to build Subig Bay in the Philippines into a defensible bastion. See Braisted, *United States Navy in the Pacific*, pp. 216–223.

[10] Roosevelt made both a public and a private denial, the latter in a letter to Hobson on July 9. Hobson refused to back down, and when Roosevelt persisted in his denial in a blustering letter on July 24, Hobson replied in an equally frank letter in which he called the President a liar. Roosevelt to Hobson, July 9, 1908, Morison, *Roosevelt Letters*, VI, 1116; Hobson to Roosevelt, July 21, 1908, Roosevelt Papers; Roosevelt to Hobson, July 24, 1908, Morison, *Roosevelt Letters*, VI, 1142; Hobson to Roosevelt, August 1, 1908, Roosevelt Papers.

non urging the fortification of Pearl Harbor, he said: "I am not acting with a view to an emergency of the next year or two. I am acting with a view to the emergencies that there is a reasonable chance may arise within the next decade or two." [11] The future emergency he had in mind, of course, was a crisis with Japan. In letters to Secretary of Navy Metcalf he revealed his preoccupation with the future Japanese threat. "In the present Japanese fleet," he noted with evident concern, "there are four battleships superior to any four of ours. . . . Now it seems to me we should be taking steps to keep in advance of other nations rather than behind them in matters of construction." [12]

The General Board of the Navy, which had been created in 1900 to advise on war plans, naval bases, and building programs, had been urging the construction of two battleships a year, but until 1908 the President had refused to recommend such a program to Congress. Now in the spring of 1908 Roosevelt and his congressional supporters sought approval for, not two, but four new dreadnoughts. On April 14 Roosevelt sent a strong message to Congress urging the authorization of four battleships, and though he did not get all four ships in the vote that ended a spectacular debate, he did secure the adoption of a two-ships-a-year program. As he wrote to Henry White:

Congress will not stand for the four battleships. To be frank, I did not suppose that they would; but I knew I would not get thru two and have those two hurried up unless I made a violent fight for four. Moreover they have now, as a result of the fight, announced as a steady policy that of building two ships a year — a great gain. [13]

Fortunately the struggle over the naval bill caused no repercussions in Japan, and the Japanese-American rapprochement continued to develop. In May, 1908, the United States and Japan signed a treaty of arbitration and treaties for the protection of trade-marks in China and Korea. The arbitration treaty provided for the arbitration by the Permanent Court of Arbitration of all differences, not settled by diplomacy, which were of a legal nature

11 Roosevelt to Cannon, February 29, 1908, Morison, *Roosevelt Letters*, VI, 956.
12 Roosevelt to Metcalf, March 9, 1908, Morison, *Roosevelt Letters*, VI, 967–968. See also Roosevelt to Metcalf, March 14, 1908, Morison, *Roosevelt Letters*, VI, 970–971.
13 Roosevelt to White, April 27, 1908, Morison, *Roosevelt Letters*, VI, 1017–1018.

or relating to the interpretation of treaties, but it excepted questions affecting the vital interests, the honor, the independence of either party, or the interests of third powers. At the Senate's insistence a provision was included requiring Senate consent to any *compromis* arranging arbitration of a particular dispute. This provision robbed the treaty of most of its substance, but Roosevelt and Root nevertheless thought the conclusion of the treaty would have a good effect upon public opinion in both countries and would help silence the war rumors. In the last stages of the negotiations, Takahira reported to Hayashi that Root's only desire in urging Japan to sign the treaty was to allay the anxiety of an ill-informed public as soon as possible.[14]

Just two weeks after the signing of the arbitration convention on May 5, the United States and Japan signed the trade-mark treaties relating to China and Korea. During the two years of negotiations which preceded the conclusion of the treaties, the United States had insisted that copyrights, patents, and designs be included in addition to trade-marks. Though Japan was reluctant to agree to such broad conventions, the Tokyo government finally consented. The treaties were signed on May 19, 1908, just in time to be approved by the United States Senate before adjournment. Ambassador O'Brien, who handled most of the negotiations, was elated at the outcome. "These Conventions," he wrote to Rockhill, "embody practically all we have been asking for the past three years — the Japanese Government yielding one thing after another of our demands. . . ."[15]

The conclusion of the arbitration treaty and the trade-mark treaties in May, 1908, was followed in June with the settlement of the contentious Kapsan mining case. During the first days of the Russo-Japanese War, two American investors, Henry Collbran and Harry Bostwick, had secured a valuable mining concession from the Korean Emperor. After the war, when they attempted to implement the concession, Japanese opposition prevented confirmation of the concession. The Korean government, which was largely un-

<hr>

[14] Takahira to Hayashi, received April 28, 1908, Telegram Series, CVI, 3417–19; text in United States, Department of State, *Papers Relating to the Foreign Relations of the United States, 1908*, Washington, 1912, pp. 503–505.

[15] O'Brien to Rockhill, May 28, 1908, Post Records: O'Brien to Miscellaneous, II.

der Japanese control, and the Japanese government, which was handling all Korea's foreign relations, raised many technical objections to the grant. The real reason for Japan's opposition, however, was the belief that the Korean Emperor had granted the concession in hopes of getting United States support against the Japanese. Tedious negotiations took place between Washington and Tokyo, and finally on June 17, 1908, an agreement was made confirming the grant with some modifications. There were still some issues pending between the American investors and the Japanese, but these were resolved in the following year by the sale of the American utilities holdings in Seoul to a Japanese syndicate. This was welcomed by Collbran and Bostwick, for they wished to concentrate on their mining enterprises. Though there had been much bitterness between the Japanese and the investors, when all the questions had finally been settled, Collbran and Bostwick believed they had been well treated by the Japanese. The United States Consul General at Seoul, Thomas Sammons, reported that Collbran "flatly repudiates the assertions of those writers on Far Eastern topics (as well as his former personal views) who have persistently denied that ordinary justice or fair dealing could be had at the hands of the Japanese." [16]

Thus the summer of 1908 saw the solution of every important diplomatic issue in Japanese-American relations. The further development of the rapprochement was left to a new Japanese ministry, for in July the Saionji ministry fell from power and Katsura formed a new cabinet. The fall of the Saionji cabinet came as a surprise, for in the elections of the previous May his Seiyukai party won 185 of the 379 seats in the lower house, while the opposition Shimpoto won 75 and Katsura's Daido Club only 29.[17] The reason for Saionji's resignation was to be found in the precarious status of Japan's finances. The ambitious armaments program, along with other expenses, had dangerously overextended the government finances. Rather than face the consequences, Saionji preferred to step aside and let Katsura assume the unhappy burden of

[16] Sammons to Chargé Peter Augustus Jay (Tokyo), August 2, 1909, S. D. File 4151/103–106. All the records of the Kapsan case are found in S. D. File 4151.
[17] O'Brien to Root, April 19, 1908, S. D. File 4592/70.

carrying out a policy of retrenchment. In reporting the change of ministry, Chargé Peter Augustus Jay observed:

> The change in the Cabinet does not indicate any such difference in policy as might be inferred from the substitution of a military Premier for a civil one. The issue is clearly a financial one and it is expected that the cardinal plank in the policy of the new Cabinet will be the reduction of military and naval expenditures and all unproductive enterprises.[18]

One of the first steps taken by the Katsura ministry was to give assurances to the United States on the immigration issue. On July 20 Takahira sent Roosevelt a copy of a telegram from Prime Minister Katsura stating that not only would the new cabinet strictly enforce the limitation on emigration, but it would also endeavor to promote still more friendly relations between the two countries.[19] Root's evaluation of this message, contained in a letter to Roosevelt, affords a deep insight into his views on the immigration question:

> Takahira's letter that you sent me was as satisfactory as any mere verbal assurance can be. Of course, performance is the only real test of sincerity. I think, however, that we must not be too extreme in our expectations of perfection in the working of a new system of repression on the part of the Japanese — a system in which, however good the faith of the Government may be, they cannot, in the nature of things, have the really hearty cooperation and sympathy of the great body of Japanese officials. . . . Time and patience and persistency will doubtless be necessary, but I am sure that the subject is being dealt with in the right spirit and in the right way. . . .[20]

To this the President replied, "I entirely agree with what you say in the Japanese matter."[21]

Further reassurance came from the new Foreign Minister, Jutaro Komura, and from Henry W. Denison. Before leaving London, where he was serving as ambassador, Komura asked Ambassador Reid to tell Root that he had no stronger desire in entering upon his new duties than to maintain and improve the excellent relations between the United States and Japan.[22] Denison wrote to

18 Jay to Root, July 15, 1908, S. D. File 4592/84–87.
19 Takahira to Roosevelt, July 20, 1908, S. D. File 2542/691–692.
20 Root to Roosevelt, August 1, 1908, Roosevelt Papers.
21 Roosevelt to Root, August 3, 1908, Morison, *Roosevelt Letters*, VI, 1150.
22 Reid to Roosevelt, August 1, 1908, Reid Papers.

O'Brien, who was in the United States on leave, and told him that Katsura would deal with the immigration question in "a wise and conciliatory manner." Denison cautioned, however, that what he feared most was hostile legislation in the United States, "not that an exclusion law would cause war between the countries — that is utter nonsense and moon shine — but it would hurt the sensibilities of the Japanese very greatly." Such a development, he felt, would bring about an estrangement which would "defy the statesmanship and diplomacy of even Mr. Root for many years." [23]

The financial crisis which brought the downfall of the Saionji ministry pointed up a fact which many observers had noted throughout the months of crises in Japanese-American relations: Japan was in no condition to go to war. The correctness of this estimate was made emphatically clear to Roosevelt when on August 19 Takahira sent to the President a statement explaining that in view of the great expense involved, the Japanese government felt that it would be best to postpone the Tokyo Exposition from 1912 to 1917. "The counter wave of policy which accompanied the downfall of the Saionji ministry," noted Root, "must be pretty deep and strong to urge them to the point of such a change before the world." [24]

The manner in which the postponement was finally decided upon and publicly announced gave further evidence of Japan's friendly and peaceful policy. Before making a final decision, the Japanese government — in view of the "cordial and sympathetic encouragement" which the President had given the exposition — asked Roosevelt's advice.[25] Roosevelt not only concurred in the wisdom of such a decision but asked Takahira: "Now, my dear Mr. Ambassador, is there any way in which I can help to put this matter before our countrymen, or before the world, in the proper light?" [26] To Whitelaw Reid the President confided:

23 Denison to O'Brien, July 12, 1908, enclosed in O'Brien to Root, August 17, 1908, S. D. File 2542/717–720.
24 Root to Roosevelt, August 23, 1908, Roosevelt Papers.
25 Takahira to Roosevelt, August 19, 1908, quoted in Roosevelt to Reid, August 20, 1908, Morison, *Roosevelt Letters*, VI, 1188–90.
26 Roosevelt to Takahira, August 20, 1908, quoted in Roosevelt to Reid, August 20, 1908, Morison, *Roosevelt Letters*, VI, 1188–90.

I thought it rather touching of the Japanese to write me in this way, and of course I want in any way I can to help them and to make their position more easy; for much tho I admire their common sense in not going into the exposition when it will evidently be such a drain on an already straightened treasury, I can understand that they may feel sensitive at having to make the public avowal that they are not in shape to carry thru the matter as they had hoped, and if I can help them put a good face on it I am delighted to do so.[27]

In the succeeding days it was arranged that Roosevelt would write a letter to Root explaining the reasons for the postponement and that this would be given to the press at the same time that the Japanese government published its own announcement on September 1. This was done as scheduled, and Roosevelt's letter did much to present the matter in the best light. He noted that a great deal of time was necessary to make the exposition what it should be and that the year 1917 would possess a peculiar fitness for the occasion, it marking the closing of a half-century of the reign of the Japanese Emperor.[28] A few days after the announcement, Takahira expressed to Root the appreciation of his government for the "habitual friendliness" shown by the United States government in regard to the postponement.[29]

On the same day Takahira sent the above message to Root, the Secretary of State sent to Whitelaw Reid a letter which not only provided a deep insight into Root's views but also gave ample evidence that by September, 1908, the Japanese-American rapprochement was far advanced:

I have always felt confident that the Japanese Government wishes to keep on friendly terms with the United States. . . . I am sure that they have not been trying to pick a quarrel with us and that no person of intelligence would do many of the things that they have done if he wanted to quarrel. I did think a year and a half ago that there were forces at work here which might bring the two nations into conflict at some time in the future. I think those forces have been very materially checked, but they may become active again. In the meantime, however, I think both Governments and most leaders of opinion in both countries are sincerely desirous of peace for a variety of reasons. Both Governments are certainly doing everything they can to make the conditions favorable for peace. Takahira has just been here

27 Roosevelt to Reid, August 20, 1908, *Roosevelt Letters*, VI, 1188–90.
28 Roosevelt to Root, September 1, 1908, Roosevelt Papers.
29 Takahira to Root, September 3, 1908, Root Papers.

to arrange about the announcement of the postponement of the exposition, and that whole subject has been arranged as if we were their main reliance, guide, philosopher and friend.[30]

The developing Japanese-American rapprochement — soon to be publicly declared by an exchange of notes — was of great importance, not only in the relations between the two countries but also in the general and broader area of international politics. The international aspects of the rapprochement must now be considered against the background of a counter movement emanating from Berlin. For more than a year Kaiser William had been working to prevent just such a development as was now taking place in Japanese-American relations. The German ruler had his heart set on a German-American-Chinese entente which could counter the Japanese-British-French-Russian combination. In vain the Kaiser had sought to break the ententes and alliances progressively encircling Germany. His courtship of Tsar Nicholas at Björkö in 1905 had ended in a fiasco, and the challenge flung at France in Morocco that same year had only cemented the Anglo-French entente. 1907 brought the further development of the entente structure by Franco-Japanese, Russo-Japanese, and Anglo-Russian treaties. These agreements were of tremendous significance for the Far Eastern balance of power, for they tied together an almost irresistible combination and left Germany virtually isolated.

It was Russia that took the initiative for the entente with Japan in 1907. The Russian Foreign Minister, Alexander Iswolsky, was greatly interested in reasserting Russian power in Europe, and he wished to gain a really durable accord with Japan in order to free Russia from anxiety in the East. Japan was receptive, especially because many Japanese leaders, including Ambassador Motono at St. Petersburg, were convinced that Japan would eventually have to annex Korea. In the negotiations that followed in the first half of 1907 the thoughts of Japan's leaders were fixed primarily upon Korea, as they had been during the Russo-Japanese War. Japan now wished to win from Russia advanced approval for the "further development" of Japan's relations with the Hermit Kingdom. At the same time, however, both Japan and Russia thought it would

[30] Root to Reid, September 3, 1908, Root Papers.

be beneficial to demark a boundary line between their spheres of influence in Manchuria in order to avoid friction there. Since the arrangement on Manchuria would be an even trade, Russia insisted that Mongolia be injected into the negotiations so Russia could get something to balance the concession to Japan regarding Korea.[31]

The Russo-Japanese negotiations culminated in the summer of 1907 just after the conclusion of a Franco-Japanese entente. While bargaining with St. Petersburg, Tokyo carried on parallel negotiations with Paris. France had no sizeable interests in Korea, and so the coming-to-terms could be easier and more general than was the case with Russia. In June the Franco-Japanese treaty was signed. Each recognized that they possessed a special interest in preserving peace and order in China, "especially in the regions of the Chinese Empire adjoining the territories where they possess rights of sovereignty, protection or occupation." [32] The following month came the more important entente between Japan and Russia. On July 30 those powers subscribed in a public convention to support the independence and territorial integrity of China and the maintenance of the status quo. By a secret treaty on the same day Russia agreed to place no obstacle in the way of the "further development" of the "relations of political solidarity" between Japan and Korea. Japan in return recognized Russia's special interests in Outer Mongolia. The secret treaty also drew a line of demarcation between the Japanese and Russian spheres in Manchuria, and each power agreed not to seek concessions for railroads and telegraphs in the sphere of the other.[33]

The United States was informed of the Franco-Japanese agreement as soon as it was concluded. Ambassador Aoki stressed the provisions it contained in support of China's integrity and the open door, and Root assured him that the agreement was "entirely satisfactory" to the United States.[34] The Japanese also communicated to

31 Motono to Hayashi, February 21, 22, March 12, May 11, June 1 (two telegrams), 1907, Telegram Series, XCI, 1073–77, 1080–82, XCII, 2026–28, XCIV, 4469–72, 4473–76, XCV, 5159–62, 5163–66.

32 Text in MacMurray, Treaties and Agreements With and Concerning China, I, 640.

33 Text in Price, Russo-Japanese Treaties of 1907–1916, pp. 107–111.

34 Aoki to Hayashi, June 14, 1907, Telegram Series, XCV, 5538.

the Department of State the text of the public treaty with Russia, but of course the secret treaty was withheld. Its provisions were made known, however, to Aoki. Within a few weeks the American embassy at Tokyo reported rumors among the diplomatic corps concerning the existence of the secret treaty, and the speculation as to its provisions was fairly accurate.[35]

When Root mentioned the public treaty in a conversation with Aoki in September, 1907, he added significantly that he believed the public treaty was not the whole understanding arrived at between Japan and Russia. In one of the rare occasions when Aoki was not completely frank and open with Root, the Ambassador said that as far as he knew there was nothing beyond the public convention.[36] By the end of 1907 Root was certain the secret treaty existed. Montgomery Schuyler at the American embassy at St. Petersburg reported to Root that when he called the Russian Foreign Ministry to inquire about the Russo-Japanese treaty the official who answered the telephone asked whether he was referring to the published or the secret treaty! [37]

Japan's ententes with France and Russia tied her closely to the Franco-Russian alliance group. Meanwhile Britain had undertaken to reach an entente with Russia to supplement her entente cordiale of 1904 with France. Since the conclusion of the entente with France, Anglo-German relations had continued to deteriorate as Germany persisted in building a navy that would threaten Britain's naval supremacy in the North Sea. Britain therefore sought to maintain continued close relations with Japan, a naval power of some consequence, and simultaneously draw closer to Russia. The St. Petersburg government was receptive and after months of difficult negotiations the Anglo-Russian entente, composing conflicting interests in Persia, Afghanistan, and Tibet, was concluded in August, 1907.[38]

The consolidation of the entente structure by the treaties of 1907 alarmed the German government and threw the Kaiser into an attempt to contruct a counter entente. Beginning in Septem-

35 Dodge to Root, August 22 and September 14, 1907, S. D. File 3919/13–21; 3919/34.
36 Aoki to Hayashi, September 27, 1907, Telegram Series, C, 101124.
37 Schuyler to Root, December 7, 1907, S. D. File 3919/42.
38 *British Documents*, IV, 618–620.

ber, 1907 he sent repeated instructions to Ambassador Sternberg telling him to sound Roosevelt regarding a German-American-Chinese entente. Roosevelt betrayed no enthusiasm whatever for the project. His replies to his friend Specky were polite and vague but should have left Berlin under no illusions.[39] The Kaiser, however, was not easily discouraged. He urged China to take the initiative and formally propose an alliance or entente to Washington.[40] Peking was almost as unenthusiastic as Washington. The Chinese government was always eager for diplomatic support from any quarter, but the risks of openly pitting itself against the Anglo-Japanese-French-Russian entente were too obvious to ignore. Month after month Peking hesitated, while the Kaiser kept informing Roosevelt that China was going to propose a German-American-Chinese understanding.[41] In August, 1908, the German Minister at Peking reported that Tang Shao-yi was going to the United States to express appreciation for the remission of the Boxer indemnity and to pave the way for the entente,[42] but it was by no means certain that Tang would broach the subject of an entente or alliance.

At this juncture an incident occurred which gives an insight into Roosevelt's views on the German project, the extraordinary "Hale interview." In July the Kaiser gave an interview to William B. Hale, a correspondent of the New York *Times*. For nearly two hours the German ruler railed against England, saying that Germany would shortly have to go to war with her. He characterized England as a traitor to the white race for allying with Japan and declared that he had arranged with the United States to back up China against Japan and that a Chinese statesman, Tang Shao-yi, was on the way to Washington to arrange the details.[43]

[39] Heinrich von Tschirschky to Sternberg, September 15, 1907, Bülow to Sternberg, telegram, October 17, 1907, Sternberg to Bülow, telegram, November 8, 1907, and Sternberg to the Foreign Minister, December 5, 1907, *Die Grosse Politik*, XXV, pt. 1, pp. 71, 74–75, 78–79, 80.

[40] Bülow to Artur von Rex, telegram, January 3, 1908, *Die Grosse Politik*, XXV, pt. 1, pp. 89–90. (Translated in Dugdale, *German Diplomatic Documents*, III, 265–266). A full account from the German side is given in Luella J. Hall, "The Abortive German-American-Chinese Entente of 1907–08," *Journal of Modern History*, I (1929), 219–235.

[41] Tower to Roosevelt, March 16, 1908, Roosevelt Papers.

[42] Rex to the Foreign Minister, telegram, August 5, 1908, *Die Grosse Politik*, XXV, pt. 1, p. 96.

[43] Hale to William C. Reick, July 19 and 24, 1908, quoted in Oscar King Davis, *Released for Publication: Some Inside Political History of Theodore Roosevelt and*

Hale sent an account of the interview to the home office of the New York *Times*, and there it was immediately recognized that publication of the interview would cause international repercussions. Oscar King Davis was thereupon dispatched to Oyster Bay to lay the matter before the President. Roosevelt urged strongly that it not be published, and the *Times* agreed to suppress it.[44] Davis made notes of what Roosevelt said on this occasion, and his account, which was published many years later, is as follows:

This is the funniest thing I have ever known. That Jack of an Emperor talks just as if what he happens to want is already an accomplished fact. He has been at me for over a year to make this kind of an agreement about China, but every time I have replied, "That means a treaty, to which the Senate must consent." . . . This is the first time I have ever heard the name Tang-Shao-yi. For at least nine months he — that Jack — has been telling me that a distinguished Chinese official was "on his way" to this country and Germany to settle affairs, but he has never come. I do not know whether this is the man or not. But the policy [the open door and the integrity of China], as I have always told the Emperor, is ours. It has been our policy for seven or eight years, ever since Hay first enunciated it.[45]

Roosevelt's reaction to the Hale interview indicates that he had no intention of abandoning his pro-Entente policy in favor of a German-American-Chinese entente directed against Japan and the other Entente powers.

In the meantime Tang Shao-yi was preparing to go to the United States. What his objectives were is not altogether clear. It is possible that Tang was seeking an alliance or entente, but he was probably more interested in wangling an American loan for a Manchurian bank which would be secured by the remission funds.

His Times, 1898–1918, Boston, 1925, pp. 81–84. An account is also given in Roosevelt to Root, August 8, 1908, Morison, *Roosevelt Letters*, VI, 1163–64; Roosevelt to Arthur Lee, October 17, 1908, Morison, *Roosevelt Letters*, VI, 1292–94; Roosevelt to Theodore Roosevelt, Jr., November 20, 1908, Morison, *Roosevelt Letters*, VI, 1370–74; and Roosevelt to Reid, January 6, 1909, Morison, *Roosevelt Letters*, VI, 1465–67. The full text of the interview is in the records of the Japanese Foreign Ministry, Telegram Series, CXII, 11029–38.

[44] Part of the interview was arranged for publication in the *Century*, but the German government succeeded in having it suppressed. Whitelaw Reid reported to Roosevelt that King Edward knew the contents of the *Century* article, for several copies were circulating in London. Reid to Roosevelt, January 22, 1909, Roosevelt Papers.

[45] In a conversation with Davis in 1917, Roosevelt confirmed these notes. Davis, *Released for Publication*, pp. 87–88.

Washington — at Rockhill's urging — had already decided that the remission should be used for the education of Chinese students in the United States, and China had given assurance that the funds would be used for that purpose. Thus, when Tang left for Washington in September, his chance of getting the remission funds for use in Manchuria was exceedingly small.

Before Tang's arrival in the United States, his chief promoters, Marvin and Straight, were already in Washington pushing the Manchurian bank project. When Straight left Manchuria in August, he took with him a memorandum outlining a loan agreement. Straight's friend E. H. Harriman was now showing some interest in the project, and indeed may have been in part responsible for Straight's transfer to Washington. The reason for Straight's recall, Phillips wrote to Rockhill, was that "Wall Street" was feeling confident again and wanted the latest advice on investment possibilities in Manchuria.[46] If Phillips' information was correct, Root, by calling Straight to Washington, was unwittingly aiding the revival of the anti-Japanese crusade in Manchuria. It is a safe assumption that though Root was willing that American capital flow into Manchuria if it could be done in such a way that did not threaten Japan's established interests, he would not have knowingly supported Straight's aggressive crusade.

Root attempted to keep the Department of State scrupulously aloof from the negotiations that ensued between Straight and Harriman's bankers, Kuhn, Loeb and Company,[47] but it became increasingly difficult to do so. Straight was soon serving a dual role, for when Phillips went on a trip to South America in November, Straight became acting chief of the Far Eastern Division.[48]

Marvin, who had come to Washington with Straight to make preparations for Tang's arrival, received no encouragement from

[46] Phillips to Rockhill, July 16, 1908, Rockhill Papers. The evidence is by no means conclusive, for Phillips wrote to Straight: "Neither Mr. Bacon nor I *know* precisely why the Secretary instructed you to return, but we both *believe* it was for the purpose of having you at hand to give whatever information you could regarding commercial affairs in Manchuria to those wanting knowledge of the subject." Phillips to Straight, October 9, 1908, Straight Papers. (Italics mine.)

[47] Croly, *Willard Straight*, pp. 270–272.

[48] Straight's appointment to this position was probably due to Huntington Wilson's influence. Wilson had known Straight in the Far East, and their mutual anti-Japanese sympathies doubtless drew them close together.

administration leaders concerning the approaching visit. He found
Roosevelt, Root, and Bacon "a little chary of the Embassy undertaking." [49] Neither Roosevelt nor Root desired to embark upon an
anti-Japanese campaign in Manchuria. At last, after months of
crisis, the friendly relations between the two nations were being
rebuilt, and this weighed more heavily in the balance than any
possible advantages to be gained in Manchuria.

The Japanese government was fully informed regarding the
Kaiser's scheme for an anti-Japanese alliance, and it gave close attention to the Tang Shao-yi mission to Washington. In August
Takahira telegraphed to Tokyo a detailed account of the Hale
interview which had come into his possession. The Kaiser's rant-
ings about the "yellow peril" were long familiar to the Japanese,
but Tokyo doubtless carefully analyzed that part of the interview
dealing with the projected alliance. Takahira's report, however,
did not cause alarm in Tokyo, for in the same telegram the Ambassador told of Oscar King Davis' interview with Roosevelt. Takahira had no detailed knowledge of this interview, but he did know
that Roosevelt had stated that he could not agree to the Kaiser's
scheme for a German-American-Chinese combination. [50]

In early September, shortly after sending to Tokyo the account
of the Hale interview, Takahira met with Roosevelt and obtained
reassurance regarding the President's position. Roosevelt told him
that China should be friendly to *all* powers and that the possible
scheme of the Tang Shao-yi mission could not be realized. [51] A
month later in early October, the Chinese Minister at Washington
told Takahira he did not believe a United States-China pact possible and that China should have friendly relations with Japan for
a long time. [52] When Takahira had a conference with Root later in
October, he gained still more reassurance. The Secretary spoke emphatically regarding the projected German-American-Chinese pact:
"It will be absolutely impossible." [53]

[49] Charles Vevier, *The United States and China, 1906–1913*, New Brunswick, New
Jersey, 1955, pp. 74–75.
[50] Takahira to Komura, August 29, 1908, Telegram Series, CIX, 6843–53. Text of
Hale interview in Telegram Series, CXII, 11029–38.
[51] Takahira to Komura, September 6, 1908, Telegram Series, CX, 7699–7704.
[52] Takahira to Komura, October 6, 1908, Telegram Series, CX, 8207–09.
[53] Takahira to Komura, October 27, 1908, Telegram Series, CX, 8734–37.

Though the reports reaching Tokyo were sufficiently reassuring to allay any great anxiety, the Kaiser's scheme and the approaching visit of Tang Shao-yi to Washington reinforced Tokyo's desire for more friendly relations with the United States. By mid-October the Japanese-American rapprochement was far advanced, and now the visit of the United States fleet provided the Japanese with a perfectly timed opportunity to further the movement. The fleet, after a visit at San Francisco and Puget Sound, had steamed for the Far East on July 7, 1908, under the command of Admiral Charles Sperry. After a week at Hawaii, the fleet went to Auckland, New Zealand, reaching there on August 9. The reception in New Zealand was more enthusiastic than any encountered on the western coast of the United States. At Sydney, Melbourne, and Albany, which were visited in turn, the welcome was even more unrestrained.[54]

The warmth of the reception by the New Zealanders and Australians was due both to their desire to express friendship for their American cousins and to their wish to serve notice on the British home government that they stood shoulder to shoulder with the United States on the question of Japanese immigration. This latter consideration, of course, was the same that had prompted Roosevelt to send the fleet there.[55] This factor was so apparent that some uneasiness was expressed in Japan over the hysterical greeting in Australia and New Zealand.[56] "I cannot but feel," Sperry wrote to Roosevelt, "that the visit of the fleet to Australia, while there has not been a trace of an attempt to construe it as promising armed alliance, has awakened a very strong feeling of a community of material interests in the Pacific which is the necessary basis for any friendship." [57]

The Japanese were soon given an opportunity to outdo the Australians and New Zealanders. After surviving a heavy gale north of

[54] London *Times*, August 10 and 21, 1908.

[55] When Roosevelt discussed the Hale interview with Oscar King Davis, he stated: "It is true the invitation to the fleet to go to New Zealand and Australia was to show England — I cannot say a 'renegade mother country' — that those colonies are white men's country — and that is why the fleet was sent there." Davis, *Released for Publication*, pp. 87–88.

[56] O'Brien to Root, October 25, 1908, S. D. File 8258.

[57] Sperry to Roosevelt, September 12, 1908, Papers of Admiral Charles S. Sperry, Library of Congress, Washington, D. C.

the Philippines, the fleet arrived at Yokohama on October 18. It received a welcome that surpassed anything that had been encountered on the entire voyage — indeed a welcome that exceeded the reception accorded Admiral Togo when he returned from his victory over the Russian fleet.[58] The sailors were greeted by tens of thousands of Japanese school children singing American national songs. A thousand English-speaking Japanese college students were on hand to act as volunteer guides.[59] Sperry wrote to his son Charles describing the diversions which had been arranged for the naval personnel:

In Yokohama and Tokyo there were countless entertainments for them; usually a sort of garden party in a park with exhibitions of juggling, dancing, wrestling, theaters, etc., and booths where they could get light beer, very good beer, and luncheon. There were thousands of chairs about the grounds for those who would sit. The city of Tokyo gave one party of this kind for 2500 men at once and sent them up and back in three special trains. I sent them up and back in charge of officers. There was literally nothing in the way of comfort or convenience that was not provided.[60]

The festivities continued for an entire week, during which time the flag officers were the guests of the Emperor at Shiba Palace. Receptions and dinners were given for the high naval officers by Komura, Navy Minister Ninoru Saito, Admiral Togo, the Mayor of Tokyo, and the Chamber of Commerce. Sperry was given an audience at the Imperial Palace and on that occasion felicitious messages were exchanged between the President and the Emperor.[61]

The success of the visit was in large measure attributable to

[58] Franklin Matthews, *Back to Hampton Roads*, New York, 1909, p. 183; O'Brien to Root, October 25, 1908, S. D. File 8258.

[59] Sperry to Roosevelt, October 28, 1908, Sperry Papers; Komura to Takahira, October 19, 1908, Telegram Series, CXI, 9281.

[60] Sperry to Charles Sperry, October 30, 1908, Sperry Papers.

[61] Sperry to Roosevelt, October 28, 1908, Sperry Papers; Sperry to General Horace Porter, November 30, 1908, Sperry Papers; Metcalf to Sperry, telegram, October 18, 1908, Sperry Papers; Sperry to Metcalf, October 20, 1908, Sperry Papers; Komura to Takahira, October 21 and 23, 1908, Telegram Series, CXI, 9309, 9332. At the same time that the fleet visit took place, a committee of Pacific coast merchants visited Japan as guests of the Chambers of Commerce of Tokyo, Osaka, Kyoto, Yokohama, and Kobe. After the committee returned to the United States, it made a report which concluded: "It would be absurd and wrong, after the manifestations of affection which were accorded us by the Japanese people, to question the sincerity of their friendship." F. W. Dohrmann to Post Wheeler, November 14, 1908, Post Records: O'Brien to Miscellaneous, III.

Sperry's capable handling of his command. Before he left the United States, Roosevelt had instructed him to guard his ships carefully against possible attack by fanatics and to make sure that he gave shore leave only to those men upon whom he could absolutely depend.[62] But despite the President's warning and despite some anxiety among his own staff,[63] Sperry was confident that there would be no trouble, and he decided to give shore leave to almost all officers and men.[64] To facilitate this, he had contacted Henry W. Denison, whom he had met at the Hague Conference, and through their correspondence detailed preparations were made in advance for the landing of the men and their entertainment ashore.[65] Though there was some nervousness on both sides in the initial stages of the visit, everything went off smoothly. Sperry wrote to his wife noting how the President must have gasped when he heard that three thousand men had been put ashore at one time. "I am of the opinion," he concluded, "that the president has suffered from bad advice from the General Board. . . ."[66]

When the fleet departed from Japan on October 25, the last vestiges of war rumors had been swept away. O'Brien reported that the good effects of the visit would be far-reaching.[67] The British Ambassador was equally enthusiastic. "The visit of the American fleet," he wrote Grey, "has been an unqualified success and has produced a marked and favourable impression on both officers and men of the fleet — in fact it has had the effect our Allies wanted it to and has put an end to all nonsensical war talk."[68]

[62] Roosevelt to Sperry, March 21, 1908, Morison, *Roosevelt Letters*, VI, 979–980.

[63] Sperry to Charles Sperry, January 6, 1909, Sperry Papers.

[64] Sperry to Roosevelt, April 7, 1908, and Sperry to Denison, June 19, 1908, Sperry Papers.

[65] Sperry to Denison, April 10 and June 19, 1908, and Sperry to Roosevelt, October 28, 1908, Sperry Papers.

[66] Sperry to Edith Sperry, November 1, 1908, Sperry Papers.

[67] O'Brien to Root, October 25, 1908, S. D. File 8258.

[68] Sir Claude also added the following amusing note: "Speaking to the Prime Minister who is also for the moment Finance Minister I said, to entertain 14,000 men for seven days must have cost a lot of money — not so much he replied with a twinkle in his eye as they have left behind them. As the men were not allowed ashore at Manila on account of the cholera they had lots of back pay to dispose of and I understand Tokyo and Yokohama are now full of Uncle Sam's gold. The Japanese have therefore got what they wanted, and are not out of pocket in the getting." MacDonald to Grey, October 26, 1908, *British Documents*, VIII, 459–460.

Roosevelt was elated. "Am greatly impressed by your reception," he telegraphed Sperry, "and do not know whether to be most pleased at behavior of our men or at cordiality of Japanese reception." [69] Some weeks later he wrote to Sperry: "I anticipated good in every way from the voyage of the Fleet; but it has far more than come up to my anticipations." [70]

[69] Roosevelt to Sperry, October 24, 1908, Roosevelt Papers.

[70] Roosevelt to Sperry, December 5, 1908, Morison, *Roosevelt Letters*, VI, 1411–12. Further details on the fleet visit are given in Robert A. Hart, *The Great White Fleet: Its Voyage Around the World, 1907–1909*, Boston, 1965, pp. 204–236. This work must be read with caution, however, for the discussion of the diplomatic aspects of the visit is inaccurate.

CHAPTER SIXTEEN

The Root-Takahira Exchange of Notes

EVEN before the visit of the fleet to Japan, the Tokyo government had decided to propose to the United States an exchange of notes which would provide an impressive consummation to the developing rapprochement. On October 14 John Callan O'Laughlin, who was in Tokyo as secretary of the United States commission for the exposition, telegraphed Roosevelt that the Katsura ministry wished to revive the Aoki proposal of October, 1907.[1] In a letter to Roosevelt which later arrived in Washington, O'Laughlin explained that the change had been effected by the representations of Aoki. The proposal now had the backing of Katsura and Yamagata, and the Prime Minister particularly was "anxious to give some striking indication of the friendly relations between the United States and Japan." O'Laughlin said further that Komura had told him that "the emigration of Japanese to the United States would be completely shut off or he would know the reason why."[2]

Katsura and Komura were apparently aware that O'Laughlin was a confidante of Roosevelt's, for in the subsequent weeks they gave interviews to him in which they expressed ideas obviously intended for the ear of the President. On October 20 O'Laughlin sent Roosevelt an account of another conversation with Katsura. The Prime Minister said that he had always felt that the President was the strong friend of Japan and that he desired the President to know that he appreciated his friendship from the bottom of his

[1] O'Laughlin to Roosevelt, telegram, October 14, 1908, Roosevelt Papers.
[2] O'Laughlin to Roosevelt, October 11, 1908, Roosevelt Papers.

heart. As for China, Katsura agreed with O'Laughlin that it was to Japan's interest to support the open door and the integrity of China. The conversation then passed to a discussion of the recent years of crises in Japanese-American relations. "I want to assure you," said Katsura, "that so far as Japan is concerned, there has never been the slightest intention of making war upon the United States." Though he had been out of office during these years, he had, as one of the Elder Statesmen, been privy to all important policy-making conferences. "I can state on my honor," he said emphatically, "that in those councils, which direct the affairs of the Empire, no reference whatever was made to the advisability of making military preparations for a war with the United States." [3]

On October 25, the day that the fleet departed from Japan, Foreign Minister Komura instructed Takahira to revive the Aoki proposal. Some weeks before, Takahira had been informed of the cabinet's decision to seek an agreement with the United States, and now he was told that the time was right for the project. The President and other American officials knew of the cordial welcome given to the fleet, and this provided the "biggest chance" to start successful negotiations. Komura explained that the Japanese government wanted three principal items in the agreement: (1) recognition of the Pacific Ocean as an avenue of trade in order to counter the idea of rivalry over "control" of the Pacific, (2) respect for the insular possessions of one another in the Pacific area, and (3) support for equal opportunity in China.

These provisions were identical with those of the Aoki proposal of the year before, except for one noticeable omission. There was no provision supporting China's integrity. Komura confided to Takahira that the cabinet had discussed this point thoroughly but had decided to omit it. The only reasons given to Takahira were that the present conditions in China did not necessitate such a statement and that China's sensibilities might be offended if other powers made decisions about its territory. Komura pointed out that China had strongly protested such a provision in the Franco-Japanese entente of June, 1907.[4] Japan's reluctance to include a pro-

3 O'Laughlin to Roosevelt, October 20, 1908, Roosevelt Papers.
4 Komura to Takahira, October 25, 1908, Telegram Series, CXI, 9342–46.

vision on China's integrity in the proposed agreement doubtless also was based upon another consideration, a consideration unmentioned in Komura's instruction to Takahira but known to both. During 1908 serious questions had arisen concerning the rights of Japan and Russia in Manchuria and the relation between those rights and China's sovereignty. Japan feared that the inclusion of a provision on China's integrity would tie her hands in this dispute which was then going on with China.

The controversy over China's sovereignty in Manchuria is so intertwined with the Root-Takahira negotiations — and so vital to an interpretation of the Root-Takahira exchange of notes — that it is necessary to review it in some detail.

Early in 1908 Russia began to put regulations into effect at Harbin in northern Manchuria enforcing a claim to an exclusive Russian right of administration in this city in the railway zone. The question was first presented officially to Washington when the Russian Ambassador called on Root to protest the support given to China by the American Consul at Harbin, Fred Fisher. Root, with his usual keen discernment, knew the issue was of unusual significance for both the Russian and Japanese spheres in Manchuria. On the occasion of the Ambassador's call, he took a piece of paper and drawing two lines across it said: "If there is to be a broad belt of sovereignty drawn through the center of Manchuria, Russian at the one end and Japanese at the other, like our Canal Zone across the Isthmus of Panama, it may be very serious." [5] Root's private observation, written several weeks before the Russian protest, was even more explicit: "We cannot recognize this attempt to exclude Chinese sovereignty." [6]

Root was well aware that there was more at stake in the Harbin question than the status of the municipal administration at that city, a place where American commercial interests were practically nonexistent. The larger question was the effect it might have in encouraging similar action by Japan in South Manchuria where the United States had sizable commercial interests. Chargé d'Affaires Henry P. Fletcher at Peking already had reminded Root that if the

[5] Memorandum by Root, March 26, 1908, S. D. File 4002/2.
[6] Note by Root, March 10, 1908, S. D. File 4002/24-26.

right of municipal administration were conceded to the Russians in their railway zone, the Japanese, having succeeded to the rights of the Chinese Eastern Railway Company in southern Manchuria, would claim the same privilege there.[7] William Phillips, head of the newly created Far Eastern Division, also warned Root of the same danger:

Japan is undoubtedly waiting for the moment to attempt to enforce a similar proposition in Southern Manchuria. The result of a recognition now by the United States Government of an absolute Russian administration of Harbin would be our formal acquiescence in the principle of the erection by Russia and Japan of large foreign and commercial cities within Manchuria wholly independent of China, and maintained on the supposition that they are appurtenances to railway property. The integrity of China would be at an end.[8]

In the succeeding months Root made determined efforts to prevent Russia from perfecting her claim at Harbin. He also put pressure upon Sir Edward Grey to get him to restrain the Japanese from making a similar demand. "We do not wish to have any controversy on the subject," Root wrote to Ambassador Reid at London, "but all the treaty powers would seem to be equally interested in having the municipal government to be established at Harbin and at other points along the line of the railroad, both in Russian and Japanese control, based upon an extraterritorial right under the treaties rather than upon an erroneous construction of the railroad grant." [9] In June, 1908, Reid telegraphed that Sir Edward had seen the Japanese Ambassador and had told him that he hoped that Japan would be very cautious about committing herself to a claim of such consequence to the open door and to the territorial integrity of China.[10] Root also sought and obtained German support on the matter.[11]

During the spring and summer of 1908, Root had several talks with Takahira seeking to dissuade the Japanese from supporting

7 Fletcher to Root, February 14, 1908, S. D. File 4002/36–42.

8 Memorandum by Phillips, March 6, 1908, S. D. File 4002/26.

9 Root to Reid, April 11, 1908, Reid Papers. Root continued to urge the matter in instructions and personal letters to Reid: Root to Reid, May 20, 1908, S. D. File 4002/80; Root to Reid, May 22, 1908, Reid Papers.

10 Reid to Root, telegram, June 18, 1908, S. D. File 4002/112.

11 Ambassador David J. Hill to Root, telegram, July 1, 1908, S. D. File 4002/119.

the Russian contention or from asserting similar rights in their railway zone in Manchuria. In a conversation in April, Takahira conceded that China theoretically had supreme sovereignty in Manchuria, but he added that in handling Manchurian controversies it was important to consider China's actual ability in governing the territory. Almost all the troubles which had emerged from Manchuria, he told Root, had been caused by China's "imperfect maintenance and suicidal disregard of her own sovereignty." [12]

Later in April the Japanese government sent long instructions to Takahira detailing Japan's position on the question and instructing him to explain the matter to Root. The instructions revealed that Japan supported Russia in part but that Japan did not make such sweeping claims to jurisdiction as were being made by Russia. Japan claimed "police powers" in the railway zone but did not claim legal jurisdiction over foreigners, as Russia was doing. Manchuria (including the railway zone) belonged to China and the right of justice must be given to the consuls of the various powers having extraterritorial rights through their treaties with China. The instructions even reminded Takahira that by Article III of the Portsmouth Treaty, Russia had declared that she had no concessions in Manchuria impairing the sovereignty of China.[13]

When Takahira explained Japan's position to Root, the latter was no doubt somewhat encouraged to learn that Japan was not backing Russia's most extreme contentions. His apprehensions were not entirely allayed, however, for the whole issue was fraught with vagueness. Where the dividing line lay between Japan's "police power" and China's sovereignty was not clear. Furthermore, the change of ministry which came in Japan in July, 1908, returned to power the Katsura-Yamagata faction which was more inclined toward furthering Japan's position on the continent that was the Saionji-Ito faction. This was clearly indicated in a conversation which O'Laughlin had with Foreign Minister Komura on October 21, 1908. Komura said that South Manchuria constituted Japan's outer line of defense and that Japan no longer considered the prin-

12 Takahira to Hayashi, received April 6, 1908, Telegram Series, CVI, 3012–14.
13 Hayashi to Takahira, April 17, 1908, Telegram Series, CVI, 2759–66.

ciple of China's integrity to include Manchuria.[14] Root did not learn of the O'Laughlin-Komura conversation until November 30, but in the meantime he remained wary of Japan's position on the Harbin dispute.

Throughout the summer and fall of 1908 Root continued to oppose the threat to China's sovereignty in Manchuria, reluctant though he was to become involved in a vexatious controversy over the Harbin issue. "We do not want to get into the position of being a protagonist in a controversy in China with Russia and Japan or with either of them," he wrote to Ambassador Reid in July. "At the same time we feel that the position taken by the Russian Railroad Company is quite without foundation." [15] In September, 1908, just two months before the Root-Takahira exchange of notes, William Phillips, in a letter to Rockhill, accurately summed up Root's attitude. "I do not think," he said, "that the Department intends to have trouble in Manchuria, either with Russia or Japan. The Secretary is especially anxious not to become embroiled in little incidents with either of those two powers; but when Russia makes a demand that we relinquish our extraterritorial rights in Harbin and on all railway property, in favor of Russia, we can not very well agree to her proposal without hitting China pretty hard." [16]

By the time Takahira received the instructions to revive the Aoki proposal on October 25, he was well aware that Root had been struggling for many months to defend China's sovereignty in Manchuria. Three days before receiving the instructions, he had gained further clarification of Root's position. Anticipating the instructions to revive the Aoki proposal, he had conferred with Root on October 22, sounding him on including the Manchurian question in the coming negotiations. Three obvious possibilities were open: (1) the Manchurian issue might be included and result in a provision supporting Root's position and detaching Japan altogether from the support of Russia, (2) the Manchurian issue might

14 O'Laughlin to Root, November 18, 1908, S. D. File 12611/23–24; O'Laughlin to Roosevelt, November 20, 1908, Roosevelt Papers.
15 Root to Reid, July 31, 1908, Root Papers.
16 Phillips to Rockhill, September 19, 1908, Rockhill Papers.

be included and result in a provision supporting Japan's claims there, or (3) the Manchurian issue might be omitted from the negotiations, thus leaving the dispute over rights in the railway zone in the same undecided state it was then in. Since in the projected entente the United States was offering Japan nothing substantial — other than friendship — Root had no hope of achieving the first alternative, and he did not press this upon Takahira. The Japanese Ambassador, however, hoped that the second alternative could be adopted. He had talked with Roosevelt in September and had gained the impression that the President was willing to treat Manchuria differently from other Chinese territory.[17] Takahira doubted, though, that Root agreed with Roosevelt, and this conversation with Root on October 22 confirmed his doubts. Root made it clear that he would not agree to the second alternative. If a provision were included on Manchuria, he warned Takahira, it would have to be one that restricted Japan's freedom of action. Root and Takahira therefore agreed to adopt the third alternative. The Manchurian issue (which was centered on the question of rights in the railway zone) would be omitted from the entente negotiations, thus leaving Washington and Tokyo free to argue that issue in the future if necessary.[18]

The decision to omit the Manchurian question from the entente negotiations would not be easy to carry out. If a statement on China's integrity were omitted from the projected exchange of notes, it would tend to support Takahira's position. On the other hand, if a statement on China's integrity were included, it would tend to support Root's position. How to steer the middle course and do no serious damage to either side became the principal problem of the Root-Takahira negotiations.

Soon after Root's talk with Takahira, the Secretary left Washington for New York, where he was then a candidate for the United States Senate. During his absence, Takahira took up the project directly with Roosevelt. On October 25 he gave the President a copy of Komura's formal proposal. By its provisions the two nations would declare that they wished to encourage the free and

17 Takahira to Komura, September 6, 1908, Telegram Series, CX, 7699–7704.
18 Takahira to Komura, October 25, 1908, Telegram Series, CX, 8687–95.

peaceful development of the commerce of the two nations on the Pacific Ocean; that the policy of both governments, uninfluenced by any aggressive tendencies, was directed to the maintenance of the existing status quo; that they were resolved to preserve intact their territorial possessions in the Pacific Ocean area and to respect reciprocally the possessions belonging to each other in that area; and that they were resolved to support and defend by all pacific means at their disposal the principle of equal opportunity for the commerce and industry of all nations in China. Should any event occur threatening the status quo or the principle of equal opportunity, the parties would communicate to arrive at an understanding as to what measures they may consider it useful to take.[19]

Roosevelt, after reading the memorandum, told Takahira that he knew of the Ambassador's meeting with Root three days before and he understood the necessity for such an agreement. The proposal, he said, was "very admirable!" Takahira was told, however, that since Root was out of town a decision would have to await his return.[20]

Root returned to Washington two weeks later, and Takahira conferred with him at once. Two problems were discussed: what form the agreement should take, and whether a statement supporting China's integrity should be included. In his previous talk with Takahira on October 22, Root had stated that he wished the declaration of common policy to be in the form of an exchange of notes rather than in treaty form which would have to go before the Senate. Takahira now told Root that a signed treaty would have more impact on other countries, and he indicated that Japan preferred that form. Root nevertheless continued to insist upon an exchange of notes. He obviously preferred a declaration of common policy which would achieve the basic purpose of silencing all war rumors but one which would not entangle the United States in binding obligations. Before the conversation ended, Takahira said that if Root insisted upon an exchange of notes rather than a

19 Memorandum handed to the President by the Japanese Ambassador, October 26, 1908, S. D. File 16533/1.
20 Takahira to Komura, October 27, 1908, Telegram Series, CX, 8734-37.

signed pact, he would be forced to agree.[21] On the question of including or omitting a provision in support of China's integrity,
there was no meeting of minds. Takahira did his best to explain to
Root Japan's reasons for wishing to omit such a clause, but he
apparently was not entirely convincing. Takahira reported to Komura that Root seemed to agree with him but that the Secretary's
response was obscure.[22]

There were good grounds for Takahira's apprehension that Root
was not entirely persuaded regarding the omission of China's integrity from the proposed declaration of policy. When Takahira
sent Root a revised draft on November 9 which put the substance
in proper form for an exchange of notes,[23] Root immediately set
his advisers to work drafting a provision supporting China's integrity.[24] Willard Straight, acting chief of the Far Eastern Division,
strongly advised that such a provision be included. Subscription to
a declaration which did not confirm the previously stated policy
of the United States concerning the integrity of China, said Straight,
"would be a severe blow to American prestige in the Orient."
Straight even went on to voice opposition to the whole project for
an entente with Japan. "In case we signed such a joint declaration," he advised Root, "even though the words 'territorial integrity' were included therein, we would offend, by even more completely isolating, Germany, and by placing that power and China
alone outside the network of ententes, conventions, and under-
standings regarding the Far East, create a situation which might
well be used to our detriment." China particularly, he said, would
view with deep concern a declaration that arrayed the United
States morally on the side of Japan.[25]

Straight's opposition was unavailing. Root did, however, propose

21 Komura had reluctantly agreed to such a form in an instruction to Takahira on
October 29. Telegram Series, CXI, 9402–03.

22 Takahira to Komura, November 8, 1908, Telegram Series, CXI, 9558–60.

23 Takahira to Root, November 9, 1908, S. D. File 16533/4–5.

24 Notes by Adee and Huntington Wilson attached to Takahira's draft of November
9, 1908, S. D. File 16533/4–5.

25 Straight to Root, November 11, 1908, S. D. File 16533/6. In a second memorandum
written on the same day, Straight said that the declaration would "set the seal of our
approval of Japanese action since the war and might well afford encouragement to the
continuation of her insidious efforts to undermine Chinese sovereignty." Straight to
Bacon, November 11, 1908, S. D. File 16533/8.

to Takahira on November 11 that a clause be inserted declaring that the parties would "exercise their influence to maintain the territorial integrity and administrative entity of China, in accordance with the policy frequently declared by both of them." The inclusion of the term "administrative entity" made it apparent that the clause was following the phraseology of Hay's famous circular to the powers of July 3, 1900. Root also proposed modification of the clause that asserted the resolve of the parties to "preserve intact" their possessions in the Pacific. This statement, Root explained, might lead to some misunderstanding among the American people, for many of them were desirous that at some time in the future the Philippines be given "more or less complete autonomy." He therefore proposed that the clause simply state the resolve of both powers to respect the territorial possessions belonging to the other.[26]

When Takahira reported Root's suggestions to Tokyo, Komura readily accepted the deletion of the resolve to "preserve intact" their possessions. The proposal on China's integrity and administrative entity, however, was scrutinized closely. The term "territorial integrity" was capable of a wide range of interpretation, but "administrative entity" gave Komura particular concern. Komura telegraphed Takahira that the inclusion of this latter term might lead to misunderstandings in the future regarding Japan's administrative rights in the leased territory and the railway zone. Japan could not agree to the proposal, therefore, unless "administrative entity" were deleted. Furthermore, wrote Komura, the conditions in China that had prompted the enunciation of the policy supporting China's integrity were now greatly changed, and such a declaration was not only no longer necessary but might wound the pride of the Chinese people. The Japanese government would therefore prefer that the clause be altogether omitted. If the United States insisted on the inclusion of such a clause, however, Japan desired that it be worded as follows: "to exercise their influence to maintain the independence and territorial integrity of China." [27]

26 Root to Takahira, November 11, 1908, S. D. File 16533/4-5; Takahira to Komura, November 12, 1908, Telegram Series, CXI, 9664-65.
27 Komura to Takahira, November 12, 1908, Telegram Series, CXII, 10845-48.

Takahira sent a note to Root on November 14 setting forth Komura's modification of the clause on the integrity of China. The communication did not explain the reason for Japan's desire to delete "administrative entity," but merely stated that Japan wished to put the declaration into the form used in Japan's agreements with other powers. It did state that Japan would prefer to leave out altogether any reference to China's integrity, as to include such a statement might affect the susceptibilities of the Chinese people.[28] Root accepted the phraseology proposed.[29]

There is no evidence in the Japanese or American records that Takahira confided to Root the real objection to the use of the phrase "administrative entity." If Root discerned the reason for the change in wording, he did not press the Japanese on the matter. To have done so would have compelled the Japanese to commit themselves categorically on the Harbin issue, and Root, at least at this stage, was content to leave that issue out of the negotiations. The inclusion of any phrase on China's integrity would tend to support the position of the United States, and he was willing to settle for this limited gain.

In the subsequent days the provision on China's integrity went through several changes in phraseology, but these revisions possessed no great significance. Root suggested a rephrasing, modeled on the Anglo-Japanese Alliance, stating the determination "to preserve through all pacific means at their disposal the common interests of all Powers in China by assuring the independence and integrity of the Chinese Empire." [30] Root's new version was somewhat stronger than the previous wording, but he omitted the word "territorial." Some historians have seen in this omission a major concession to the Japanese,[31] but the evidence lends no support to this conjecture. The deletion was not made at the request of Japan, and, indeed, the matter was not even specifically discussed in the negotiations. The Japanese had previously used the terms "integrity" and "territorial integrity" indiscriminately. The Anglo-Japa-

28 Takahira to Root, November 14, 1908, S. D. File 16533/7.
29 Takahira to Komura, November 15 and 16, Telegram Series, CXI, 9737–38, 9767–68.
30 Takahira to Komura, November 17, 1908, Telegram Series, CXI, 9796–99.
31 Griswold, *Far Eastern Policy*, pp. 129–130; Harley Farnsworth MacNair and Donald F. Lach, *Modern Far Eastern International Relations*, New York, 1950, p. 163.

nese Alliance and the Franco-Japanese Entente used the term "integrity" of China, while the Russo-Japanese Entente used the term "territorial integrity" of China.

When Takahira reported Root's new phraseology to Tokyo, Komura thought it smacked of a military commitment to defend China's integrity, and he insisted upon further changes. The word "assuring" was replaced by "supporting," and the phrase "by all pacific means" was shifted closer to the term "integrity of China." [32] Even Takahira was unable to discern the importance of these changes suggested by Komura.[33]

Root accepted the revisions, thus making the final draft: "They are also determined to preserve the common interests of all Powers in China, by supporting by all pacific means at their disposal, the independence and integrity of China and the principle of equal opportunity for the commerce and industry of all nations in that Empire." [34]

While the final wording of the exchange of notes was being decided, the entire project was thrown into temporary disarray by a last-minute attempt to bring the Harbin dispute into the arrangement. Root and other high officials at the Department of State seriously considered issuing a separate public declaration outlining the Far Eastern policy of the United States. They also considered making the American reply in the exchange of notes not identical

32 Komura to Takahira, November 18 and 19, 1908, Telegram Series, CXII 10952, 10959.

33 Takahira to Komura, received November 19, 1908, Telegram Series, CXI, 9869.

34 The use of the term "commerce *and industry*" raises the question whether it was intended that investment enterprises be included in the open door principle along with ordinary commerce. It is unlikely, however, that Root and Takahira had this specifically in mind. The same phraseology had been used in the Russo-Japanese public treaty of 1907. When Aoki proposed an entente in October, 1907, he took the term directly from the Russo-Japanese treaty. Then when Takahira revived the entente proposal in October, 1908, he accepted Aoki's wording without change. So far as the records reveal, the inclusion of "and industry" was not specifically discussed in the Root-Takahira negotiations. It is likely that on each occasion the term was used perfunctorily with little or no thought as to what it might mean. The powers holding spheres of influence were almost exclusively concerned with mining and railroad enterprises, and they had no great concern about preferential or exclusive rights in building textile mills and similar industry. It is certain, however, that the powers would not interpret equality in "industry" to include equality in mining and railroad enterprises, for that would mean the end of the spheres of influence. The secret treaty which accompanied the public Russo-Japanese treaty of 1907 would rule out any intention to soften the spheres of influence.

with the Japanese note. Still another idea was that of sending an accompanying letter with the American reply asking Japan to support American rights in the railway zone in Manchuria.[35]

Tokyo was alarmed when it learned of this turn of events. Komura telegraphed Takahira anxiously: "You will express to the Secretary of State earnest hope of the Japanese Government that he . . . will find it possible to limit the American Note to an unconditional confirmation of such understanding in the words of the Japanese Note." Takahira was also instructed to discourage the idea of any separate announcement of policy by the United States.[36] When Takahira conferred with Root on November 19, he questioned the Secretary closely about the matter. If it was intended to add any detailed statement which must affect the interest of some other power, said Takahira, this would tend to cause misunderstanding in some quarters. Root then asked if Japan "meant to avoid any statement which may interfere in the interest of railways." Takahira replied that if the statement was of such tenor as to require Japan to withdraw from her position in South Manchuria, the balance of power would be shaken and serious trouble would arise.[37]

It was apparent to Root that the entire negotiations would collapse if he insisted on forcing Japan's hand regarding her disputed rights in the railway zone in South Manchuria. He therefore returned to his original position, that of leaving the Harbin dispute out of the negotiations. There was thus no meeting of minds on the Manchurian issue. Though some historians have speculated that in the exchange of notes Japan was given a "free hand" in Manchuria in return for a guarantee of the Philippines,[38] there is no evidence for this in the records of the negotiations. The exchange of notes did not recognize, by implication or otherwise, Japan's disputed claims in South Manchuria. Rather, it left those

[35] Takahira to Komura, November 15 and 17, Telegram Series, CXI, 9737–38, 9796–99; Straight to Bacon, November 19, 1908, S. D. File 16533/9.

[36] Komura to Takahira, November 16, 1908, Telegram Series, CXII, 10901–02.

[37] Takahira to Komura, received November 20, 1908, Telegram Series, CXI, 9897–98.

[38] Griswold, *Far Eastern Policy*, pp. 129–130; MacNair and Lach, *Modern Far Eastern International Relations*, pp. 161–163; Claude A. Buss, *The Far East: A History of Recent and Contemporary International Relations in East Asia*, New York, 1955, 378–379.

claims in the same indeterminate state they were before the negotiations began. Moreover, Root had made it abundantly clear
throughout the negotiations that he gave neither moral nor legal
backing to any claims, Japanese or Russian, which seriously damaged China's sovereignty in Manchuria. The provision in the exchange of notes supporting the status quo did recognize Japan's
legally established rights there, but this represented no new departure in United States policy. In 1905 Japan had secured those
rights at Portsmouth with the full blessing of the United States.
What was new was that Japan had now been clearly informed
that the United States would resist any interpretation or extension
of those rights which further infringed China's sovereignty.

One final question must be considered regarding the negotiations: were Root and Takahira drafting a binding treaty or merely
a public declaration of policy which created no legal contractual
obligations? The answer to this question is not easy to discern,
for the negotiators never came to grips with this matter. At times
they spoke as though they were negotiating a treaty, at other times
they talked as though they were merely drafting a publicity statement. It has sometimes been asserted that the exchange of notes
was an executive agreement binding only the Roosevelt administration, but United States law and international law knows of no such
distinction. If it was binding at all, it bound both parties until
abrogated by mutual assent. If a single document had been signed
by both sides, it could be concluded that a contractual obligation
was created, but the use of an exchange of notes throws the whole
question into a hazy area. An exchange of notes may or may not
create a binding obligation, depending upon the *intent* of the negotiators. But this very question of intent is difficult to assess. The
Japanese seemed inclined to regard the negotiations as creating a
contractual instrument; the Americans, on the other hand, tended
to regard the whole affair as an enunciation of common policy
which created no legal obligations.

The intent of the negotiators was thus not clear and the question of whether a legally binding agreement resulted remains de-
batable. In viewing the whole tenor of the negotiations, the evi-

dence that no contractual obligation was created seems stronger than the evidence to the contrary. Later events also support this interpretation. During all the changes that Japan made in the status quo in the subsequent years, the United States invoked the Root-Takahira exchange of notes on only one occasion. In 1940 Cordell Hull reminded Japan of the exchange of notes when the Netherlands East Indies appeared to be threatened. Hull doubtless made no study of whether the notes were binding; he merely wished to throw everything he could lay hold of into the battle of words with Japan. J. V. A. MacMurray, when chargé at Peking in 1914, made what was probably a more valid interpretation than did Secretary Hull. He reported a conversation with Wellington Koo as follows: ". . . I furthermore reminded him that the Root-Takahira exchange of notes, although frequently referred to for convenience as an agreement, was in fact simply a joint declaration of policy rather than a convention establishing a legal status which either party might invoke against the other." [39] Acting Secretary of State Robert Lansing, the highest legal officer at the Department, instructed Minister Paul Reinsch on that occasion that MacMurray interpreted the exchange of notes "very correctly." [40]

The Root-Takahira negotiations were completed by November 20, and on November 21 and 22 the text was telegraphed to the United States representatives in Britain, France, Russia, China, and Germany, and they were instructed to communicate it confidentially to those governments.[41] The text was also sent to the United States embassy at Tokyo, and Root stated to O'Brien that the purpose of the declaration was to put an end to "absurd rumors of ill will between America and Japan." [42] When Komura sent the text to London, he gave a similar interpretation. The reason for the understanding, he said, was that the "very slight differences between the two Governments, never acute, but always greatly ex-

[39] MacMurray to Secretary of State William Jennings Bryan, September 10, 1914, United States, Department of State, *Papers Relating to the Foreign Relations of the United States, 1914, Supplement*, Washington, 1928, p. 187.

[40] Lansing to Reinsch, November 4, 1914, *Foreign Relations, 1914, Supplement*, p. 190.

[41] S. D. File 16533/8b.

[42] Root to O'Brien, telegram, November 21, 1908, S. D. File 16533/8a.

aggerated by the press, seem to make it highly desirable in the interest of repose, that an entente should be established." [43]

Two days after sending the text to London, Komura telegraphed Washington his official acceptance of the final draft. Takahira gave this notification on November 27 and asked that an early date be set for the exchange of notes. Since Tang Shao-yi was expected to arrive in Washington within a few days, Root accepted the suggestion of Huntington Wilson that the exchange of notes be delayed until after Tang's arrival.[44]

The stage was thus set for the final scene of the drama. At this juncture there arrived in Washington O'Laughlin's letters to Roosevelt and Root telling of his conversation with Foreign Minister Komura on October 21.[45] A memorandum of the conversation was included which clearly detailed Komura's statement that South Manchuria was Japan's outer line of defense and that Japan did not regard the principle of China's integrity as including Manchuria. When Roosevelt and Root read these words is uncertain. The letters arrived in Washington either on November 28, 29, or 30. Root's copy bears his official stamp of November 30, but it is not known whether he read it before or after the exchange of notes which took place at 4 P.M. on that day. If Roosevelt or Root read O'Laughlin's letter before the exchange, they may have considered abandoning the whole project — Root doubtless would have been more inclined to do so than Roosevelt. To have done so at that late date, however, would have plunged Japanese-American relations into a deep crisis. News of the impending exchange of notes had already leaked to the press and the text of the notes had been communicated to the powers. Moreover, Japan would be publicly committed by the exchange of notes to uphold China's integrity with no qualification excluding Manchuria. Japan was well aware that the principle enunciated in the notes was understood to include Manchuria. Indeed, the Japanese had obtained the

43 Komura to Yamaza, November 25, 1908, Telegram Series, CXII, 11052.
44 Wilson to Root, November 28, 1908, S. D. File 16533/24.
45 O'Laughlin to Root, November 18, 1908, S. D. File 12611/22–23; O'Laughlin to Roosevelt, November 20, 1908, Roosevelt Papers. O'Laughlin was at sea on his way to the United States when he wrote the letters.

deletion of "administrative entity" so that Manchuria could be accommodated within the concept. Thus if Roosevelt and Root learned of Komura's statement before the exchange of notes, there were considerations which dictated proceeding with the exchange.

Tang arrived at noon on November 30. He was allowed to see the drafts of the Japanese-American declaration, and at four o'clock that afternoon the exchange of notes took place. By the notes the two governments declared their policy as follows:

1. It is the wish of the two Governments to encourage the free and peaceful development of their commerce on the Pacific Ocean.
2. The policy of both Governments, uninfluenced by any aggressive tendencies, is directed to the maintenance of the existing status quo in the region above mentioned and to the defense of the principle of equal opportunity for commerce and industry in China.
3. They are accordingly firmly resolved reciprocally to respect the territorial possessions belonging to each other in said region.
4. They are also determined to preserve the common interest of all powers in China by supporting by all pacific means at their disposal the independence and integrity of China and the principle of equal opportunity for commerce and industry of all nations in that Empire.
5. Should any event occur threatening the status quo as above described or the principle of equal opportunity as above defined, it remains for the two Governments to communicate with each other in order to arrive at an understanding as to what measures they may consider useful to take.[46]

This joint declaration of policy was almost universally praised. Roosevelt was greatly pleased with Root's handiwork. He wrote a warm letter to Aoki thanking the former Ambassador for his part in bringing about the entente.[47] To Bishop M. C. Harris he wrote: "Few things have given me more pleasure than this agreement with Japan." [48] The public reaction in the United States was almost equally enthusiastic. News of the diplomatic exchange was also well received in Japan, though a few discordant notes were sounded. Some disappointment regarding the omission of any reference to the immigration issue was expressed, and a few former members of the Saionji ministry, including Hayashi, characterized

[46] Foreign Relations, 1908, pp. 510–512.
[47] Roosevelt to Aoki, December 19, 1908, Roosevelt Papers.
[48] Roosevelt to Harris, December 2, 1908, Roosevelt Papers.

the exchange of notes as "unnecessary." [49] The *Kokumin Shimbun* was nevertheless close to the truth when it noted: "The conclusion of the entente cordiale between Japan and America is universally welcomed in Tokyo." [50]

In Europe the Entente powers applauded the development. Foreign Secretary Grey told Ambassador Reid that if British leaders had been asked to name what news would be most welcome from the Far East, "he could scarcely have thought of anything better than this agreement." [51] In Paris the President, the Prime Minister, and the Foreign Minister all expressed their delight to Ambassador Henry White.[52] In Berlin the Kaiser was doubtless greatly disappointed by the Japanese-American entente, but the German government attempted to put the best face on the matter. The Foreign Minister assured Ambassador David J. Hill that the terms were in accord with Germany's policy in the Far East; and Chancellor Bülow, in a speech to the Reichstag, denied that Germany had been unfavorably affected by the agreement.[53] At Peking China's leading statesman Yuan Shih-k'ai at first evidenced disappointment and irritation, but after some deliberation he assured Rockhill that his government realized the beneficial effect such a declaration would have for China.[54]

While most world leaders and diplomats praised the Root-Takahira exchange of notes, two voices did not join in the acclaim, those of Huntington Wilson and Willard Straight. Straight probably expressed the views of both himself and Wilson when he wrote in his diary: "This, like the Korean withdrawal, was a terrible diplomatic blunder to be laid to the door of T. R." [55] To Straight and Wilson it appeared that the Japanese had effected a clever coup whereby a Chinese-American agreement had been forestalled. Whether Tang did have bigger objectives than loans can only be conjectured. Yuan Shih-k'ai told Rockhill that Tang had no

49 *Asahi Shimbun*, December 1, 1908; *Jiji Shimpo*, December 3, 1908; *Japan Daily Mail*, December 3 and 5, 1908.
50 *Kokumin Shimbun*, December 1, 1908.
51 Reid to Root, November 30, 1908, S. D. File 16533/19.
52 White to Reid, January 8, 1909, Root Papers.
53 Hill to Root, December 4, 9, and 11, 1908, S. D. File 16533/39–45.
54 Rockhill to Root, December 3, 1908, S. D. File 16533/46.
55 Croly, *Willard Straight*, p. 276.

instructions to negotiate an agreement, though he had been told
that he might be empowered to negotiate if he found conditions
favorable.[56]

Factors other than the Root-Takahira exchange, however, assured the failure of such an endeavor. From the beginning Tang's
position was weak. Shortly before Tang's arrival in the United
States, the Empress Dowager and the Emperor Kuang Hsu died
suddenly, and this brought to the regency Prince Chun, an enemy
of Yuan. Tang, who was of Yuan's party, could depend upon no
firm backing at Peking. As it turned out, Yuan was dismissed from
office in January, 1909, and Tang's mission was abruptly ended.
Roosevelt's views also assured the failure of any scheme for a German-American-Chinese combination, whether or not a Root-Takahira exchange of notes had taken place. Renewed evidence of this
came on December 31 when Roosevelt talked with Count Johann
Heinrich von Bernstorff, the new German Ambassador who had
been appointed to Washington following the death of Sternberg
in August, 1908. Bernstorff's report of Roosevelt's views was as
follows:

My predecessor has often discussed with him the idea of a joint guarantee
of China's integrity by Germany and America in conjunction with China.
He had been unable to go into it, because it might have driven China into a
policy hostile to Japan. A Chino-Japanese conflict would have found China
totally unarmed, in which case neither Germany nor America were prepared
to defend her against Japan. . . . If there had to be an American-Japanese
war, it could only be for purely American interests. The American people
would then willingly put forward its strength and also be certain of victory.
He had explained this idea quite frankly to the Chinese Ambassador, Tang
Shao Yi as far as it concerned America, for complete frankness was the right
policy.[57]

The principal importance of the Root-Takahira exchange of
notes lay not in its effect upon the Tang mission. Nor did it lie in
the specific terms of that policy declaration. The provisions were
sufficiently general that the text represented no genuine coming-

[56] Rockhill to Root, December 3, 1908, S. D. File 16533/46. On December 30, 1908,
Root told Takahira that Tang never discussed the subject of an alliance with him.
Takahira to Komura, January 1, 1909, Telegram Series, CXIII, 11–13.

[57] Bernstorff to the Foreign Minister, January 2, 1909, *Die Grosse Politik*, XXV, 97.
(Translated in Dugdale, *German Diplomatic Documents*, III, 267).

to-terms. If a real meeting of minds was to take place between Tokyo and Washington, the Harbin issue, with all its ramifications, could scarcely have been omitted, as it deliberately was. The significance of the exchange of notes was rather in its effect upon public opinion. Throughout the negotiations both governments had been motivated primarily by the desire to signalize the Japanese-American rapprochement with a publicity statement which would smooth over the friction of the preceding two years and silence the war rumors. Root was likely telling the whole truth when he told Ambassador O'Brien that the purpose of the agreement was to put an end to "absurd rumors of ill will between America and Japan." [58] Perhaps the most accurate characterization of the affair was that made by British Ambassador Bryce. He reported to London that the importance of the agreement "lies not so much in its terms as in the fact of its conclusion, which latter marks a period in the Pacific policy of this country, and silences the last echoes of the war cries of last year." [59]

Thus the historical accounts which have pictured the Root-Takahira episode as a moment of great decision in America's Far Eastern policy have greatly over-dramatized the affair. There was no great confrontation of China and Japan in the arena of American policy making. In the minds of Roosevelt and Root in 1908 there was no momentous question to decide, whether to be more friendly to China or to Japan. Indeed, never during the seven years he was in office did Roosevelt even entertain the idea of seeking closer relations with China than with Japan. Characteristic of this attitude was a statement by Root to Ambassador Takahira in May, 1908. The sending of the entire battleship fleet to visit Japan while sending only part of the fleet to China, he said, was intended to show that the United States was more in sympathy with Japan.[60] But in 1908 the Roosevelt administration did not forsake its equipoise amid its marked inclination toward Japan. A pro-Japanese policy did not mean that all Japan's actions or intentions were unopposed or approved. As during the Russo-Japanese War friendship for Japan was combined with the wish to see the Japanese armies

58 Root to O'Brien, telegram, November 21, 1908, S. D. File 16533/8a.
59 Bryce to Grey, December 1, 1908, British Documents, VIII, 464.
60 Takahira to Hayashi, received May 29, 1908, Telegram Series, CVII, 4067–68.

move no farther north than Mukden, so in 1908 that friendship was coupled with the desire to see no further infringement of China's sovereignty in Manchuria. Unlike Hay's neutrality note of 1904 which specified no "metes and bounds," the pro-Japanese policy of the Roosevelt administration had very definite boundary lines. Root had made this crystal clear in the negotiations over the Harbin dispute both before and during the Root-Takahira negotiations of November, 1908. It was a fact which Japanese leaders could not have failed to perceive. Amid the intoxication and rejoicing over the entente with the United States, they had one sobering thought — they did not have a "free hand" in Manchuria.

CHAPTER SEVENTEEN

The Renewal of Anti-Japanese Agitation in California

THE Japanese-American rapprochement, which culminated in the Root-Takahira exchange of notes on November 30, 1908, effected a clearing of the atmosphere that was welcomed on both sides of the Pacific. The inherent limitations of that rapprochement, however, soon were manifest. On the Pacific slope of the United States anti-Japanese sentiment was still strong, a factor which made impossible the re-establishment of the former cordial relations. Early in 1909 the agitation flared up again with the introduction of a series of anti-Japanese bills in the California legislature.

The issue came to a head when on January 15, 1909, the Assembly judiciary committee reported favorably on an alien land bill. This measure provided that an alien acquiring title to land within the state must become a citizen within five years or dispose of his holding. The bill did not mention the Japanese by name, but their ineligibility to citizenship made it clear that the measure was directed against them.[1] On the same day O'Brien telegraphed that Komura had expressed concern regarding the measures before the California legislature. The Foreign Minister said that he did not believe the bills would pass, but if they did the Japanese government would consider it "very embarrassing." [2]

O'Brien's report prompted Roosevelt to write a long letter to Governor Gillett on January 16. He then telegraphed the Governor asking that the measures be held up until his letter arrived. "My

[1] Franklin Hichborn, *Story of the Session of the California Legislature of 1909*, San Francisco, 1909, p. 203.
[2] O'Brien to Root, January 15, 1909, S. D. File 2543/796.

knowledge of the international situation, particularly with reference to emigration of Japanese laborers from United States," he wired, "satisfies me that passage of proposed legislation would be of incalculable damage to State of California." [3] In his letter Roosevelt pointed out that at last the United States had gotten "in first-class working order" an arrangement with Japan excluding Japanese laborers and that this was now being endangered by the proposed anti-Japanese legislation. He went on to state that during the six months ending October 31, 1908, only 2,074 Japanese had been admitted to the continental United States, while 3,181 had departed. "There is, therefore," he said, "no shadow of excuse for action which will simply produce great irritation and may result in upsetting the present agreement and throwing open the whole situation again." [4]

As soon as Gillett received Roosevelt's telegram, he dispatched a letter assuring the President that he was anxious that no legislation should pass which would affect the friendly relations now existing between the United States and Japan. He enclosed copies of bills which had been introduced and requested the administration's view concerning them. Included were two alien land bills and a bill segregating the Japanese school children. [5] Senator Frank P. Flint of California was in telegraphic communication with Governor Gillett, and Roosevelt learned through Flint that the Governor's letter was on the way to Washington. [6] While awaiting its arrival, Roosevelt took steps to marshal public opinion. On January 19 he released to the press copies of his telegram and letter to Gillett. Secretary of Commerce and Labor Straus also held several interviews at which he gave reporters statistics showing that more Japanese were leaving the United States than were arriving. [7]

As Roosevelt waited impatiently for the arrival of Gillett's letter, his worry mounted. "I wish I could get California to call a halt in its proposed Japanese action," he wrote to William Kent. "The

[3] Roosevelt to Gillett, telegram, January 16, 1909, Morison, *Roosevelt Letters*, VI, 1477.

[4] Roosevelt to Gillett, January 16, 1908, Morison, *Roosevelt Letters*, VI, 1477–78.

[5] Gillett to Roosevelt, January 18, 1909, Roosevelt Papers.

[6] Flint to Roosevelt, January 18, 1909, S. D. File 12611/28–29.

[7] Straus diary, January 23, 1909, Straus Papers; Straus, *Under Four Administrations*, pp. 228–229.

whole business has been most unfortunate, and I am more concerned over it than over any of the other rather stormy incidents during my career as President." [8] To his son Kermit he wrote:

I am having hard work in connection with the California matters in the effort to keep things so that Japan will not be outraged. I think I shall succeed but it has been rather ticklish and as usual I had to refuse to accept the strict and limited constitutional, or President Buchanan view. If I had not gone outside of my duty and appealed to the Californians we should have had trouble.[9]

Roosevelt's great concern was more than justified by the serious friction in Japanese American relations which had grown out of the previous agitation in California. Fortunately, however, the reports coming from Japan seemed to indicate that the new flare-up would not produce anything like the war scare of 1907. The comments of the Japanese press were almost without exception moderate in tone. "California is not without fair-minded people," said the *Mainichi Shimbun*, "nor has the American Government ceased to be Japan's good friend." [10] "The fraternal feelings existing between Japan and America," said the *Asahi Shimbun*, "are such that either through the efforts of the American authorities or through the force of public sentiment the work of those who disturb the peaceful relations between the two countries may be frustrated." [11] Japanese leaders were equally restrained in their statements. Komura told O'Brien that the Japanese government understood that the people of the United States were friendly and that even in the state of California the proposed laws would not have the support of a majority of the people.[12] When questioned by a representative of the *Japan Times* regarding a rumor that Takahira had been instructed to lodge a protest, Vice Minister of Foreign Affairs Ishii replied that the idea was "preposterous." [13]

Roosevelt was so eager for Gillett's letter that he alerted the Post Office Department to watch for it. On Sunday, January 24, the

8 Roosevelt to Kent, January 22, 1909, Morison, *Roosevelt Letters*, VI, 1478–79.

9 Roosevelt to Kermit Roosevelt, January 23, 1909, Morison, *Roosevelt Letters*, VI, 1480–81.

10 *Mainichi Shimbun*, January 13, 1909.

11 *Asahi Shimbun*, January 12, 1909.

12 O'Brien to Root, January 15, 1909, S. D. File 12611/50–60.

13 *Japan Times*, January 23, 1909.

letter arrived. Roosevelt sent it to Root with the note, "It seems to me that the alien land law is all right." [14] Root, having been elected senator from New York, was just preparing to turn over his duties to Robert Bacon, who was to fill out the remainder of Roosevelt's term as Secretary of State. Root gave Gillett's letter and the accompanying bills only a hurried appraisal. He, like Roosevelt, apparently missed the point that the land bill was directed against the Japanese. He told Roosevelt that he saw no objection to the measure so long as it applied to aliens generally.

Technically Roosevelt and Root were correct in their assessment that the bill applied to all aliens alike. But in practice it was otherwise. The Japanese and other Orientals did not have the option that white aliens possessed, that of becoming citizens and thus escaping the prohibitions of the law. If Root perceived this, he chose not to register an objection. He did object most emphatically, however, to the school segregation measure. "If this bill were to be passed," he advised Roosevelt, "that arrangement with the Japanese Government [on immigration] would necessarily come to an immediate end." In conclusion, he wrote:

Viewing in a larger aspect the relations of California to the rest of the Union, it is difficult to find words strong enough to characterize the violation of patriotic duty which would be involved in a causeless and objectless enactment constituting a serious affront to a friendly nation and certain to plunge the entire Union into the doubtful conditions of enmity to a great and hitherto most friendly power which is our neighbor upon the Pacific.[15]

Root's views, which Roosevelt accepted without change, were sent to Gillett by letter on January 26.[16] Before that date — and long before these views arrived in California — Gillett learned that Roosevelt and Root did not object to an alien land law. James D. Phelan, a former mayor of San Francisco, talked with Roosevelt even before Gillett's letter arrived, and he secured a statement from the President that the administration would not oppose a land bill which treated all aliens alike.[17] Phelan telegraphed this informa-

14 Roosevelt to Root, January 24, 1908, Root Papers.
15 Root to Roosevelt, January 25, 1909, Morison, *Roosevelt Letters*, VI, 1483–85.
16 Roosevelt to Gillett, January 26, 1909, Morison, *Roosevelt Letters*, VI, 1483–85.
17 Straight to Root, January 25, 1909, S. D. File 12611/31.

tion to California on January 23,[18] and Gillett immediately telegraphed Roosevelt and Root for confirmation.[19] On January 25
both the President and the Secretary of State telegraphed Gillett
that they had no objection to a land law which treated all aliens
alike.[20]

On the same day that Gillett learned that Washington would
not object to the land bill, the Governor sent a special message to
the legislature urging that nothing be done to disrupt the cordial
relations between the United States and Japan. He pleaded against
the enactment of the various anti-Japanese bills, though he did
hint that an alien land law might be passed which would not embarrass the federal government. In the days immediately following
his message, Gillett became convinced that even the land bill should
not be passed. He first secured the substitution of a milder measure
which would have no retroactive provisions. The substitute bill,
which was similar to an Oklahoma law, would allow aliens who
already owned land to retain it. This bill was introduced on February 1, and before it came to a vote two days later, the state authorities decided to oppose this measure also. The Governor and Speaker
Philip A. Stanton employed their influence against it, and the bill
was defeated by a vote of 28 to 48.[21]

Thus by February 3 it appeared that events were moving toward
the defeat of the various anti-Japanese measures. An attack on a
Japanese in Berkeley by some town rowdies on January 30 injected
a discordant note, but this incident was smoothed over quietly.[22]
Reports from Japan were encouraging. O'Brien telegraphed on
February 2 that Komura had made a most friendly speech before
the lower house of the Diet.[23] In a dispatch which reached the Department later, O'Brien noted that neither Komura nor any other
Japanese official had betrayed the least excitement concerning the

18 Takahashi to Komura, received January 25, 1909, Telegram Series, CXIII, 499.

19 Gillett to Roosevelt, telegram, January 23, 1909, Roosevelt Papers; Gillett to Root,
telegram, January 23, 1909, S. D. File 12611/31.

20 Roosevelt to Gillett, telegram, January 25, 1909, Roosevelt Papers; Root to
Gillett, telegram, January 25, 1909, S. D. File 12611/33b.

21 Hichborn, California Legislature of 1909, pp. 203–206.

22 Bailey, Roosevelt and the Japanese-American Crises, pp. 308–309.

23 O'Brien to Bacon, telegram, February 2, 1909, S. D. File 12611/40.

California affair.[24] Furthermore, the editorials in the Japanese press continued to be moderate and friendly.[25]

On the day following the defeat of the alien land law, two other anti-Japanese measures were defeated in the Assembly (lower house) of the California legislature. Assembly Bill 15, denying aliens the right to serve as directors in California corporations, and the Municipal Segregation Bill, which provided for segregating into separate areas of cities "persons whose practices are dangerous to public morals and health and peace," were both voted down. Grove L. Johnson, who introduced these measures, told the Assembly sarcastically that he expected someone to introduce a bill, the first section of which would read: "Before any legislation is enacted it shall bear the approval of James N. Gillett and President Roosevelt and if it is denied, the bill shall be withdrawn." Johnson then made an impassioned speech in support of his school segregation bill, pointing out how the "pure maids of California" were being compelled to sit side by side in the school rooms with "matured Japs, with their base minds, their lascivious thoughts." Thereupon the lower house passed the segregation bill by a vote of 45 to 29.[26]

Until this time Roosevelt and Gillett had remained confident that in the end none of the anti-Japanese bills would pass, but now with the passage of the school segregation bill by a lopsided vote in the lower house, the atmosphere of crisis thickened. Roosevelt was thoroughly aroused. "This is the most offensive bill of all and in my judgment is clearly unconstitutional and we should at once have to test it in the court," he telegraphed Gillett. "Can it not be stopt in the legislature or by veto?"[27] News from Nevada also stirred the President's anger. The Nevada Assembly had passed a resolution addressed to the California legislature in support of the anti-Japanese measures. To his military aide, Archie Butt, Roosevelt exclaimed: "It has only been three years since Nevada was calling

---

[24] O'Brien to Bacon, February 1, 1909, S. D. File 12611/74.

[25] O'Brien to Bacon, February 2, 1909, S. D. File 12611/75–87.

[26] Hichborn, *California Legislature of 1909*, pp. 206–208.

[27] Roosevelt to Gillett, telegram, February 4, 1909, Morison, *Roosevelt Letters*, VI, 1502.

upon me to police the state with the United States Army because it could not control a few striking miners, and now she sits a sovereign state in the Union, with sixty thousand inhabitants, and thinks herself capable of settling international affairs."[28] Fortunately, Roosevelt was able to have the offensive resolution tabled in the Nevada Senate through the intercession of the Nevada senators in Washington, but his anger towards the Nevadans was slow to subside. He doubtless classified Nevada with California, which, he told his cabinet, "was too small to become a nation, and too large to put into a lunatic asylum."[29]

In the succeeding days the school segregation issue was fought out in the lower house of the California legislature. On February 5 Gillett sent a message to the legislature enclosing Roosevelt's telegram. "A telegram so forcible as this, from the President of the United States," he said, "is entitled to full consideration, and demands that no hasty or ill-considered action be taken by this State which may involve the whole country." From the hour the bill had passed, the Governor had been in consultation with his lieutenants in the Assembly hoping to get the bill reconsidered and voted down. Speaker Stanton canvassed the situation but made little headway against the bill. Delaying tactics were then employed. A motion was made to postpone reconsideration of the bill, and an amendment was thereupon proposed to refer it again to the judiciary committee. "I know what you want," declared Johnson, "and you know it. You want to bury this bill." Had the measure been reconsidered at this time it probably would have passed. To prevent this, Speaker Stanton left his desk and took the floor to plead for delay. He did not say much, but there was in his voice a suggestion of thundering guns and marching armies:

It was not my intention to take the floor unless we were confronted by some grave crisis. Such a crisis is, in my opinion, upon us. I not only believe it, but I know it. But my lips are sealed. I would that I could tell you what I know, but I cannot for the present. But I can tell you that we are treading upon dangerous ground. I can feel it slipping from under my feet.

[28] Archie Butt, *The Letters of Archie Butt, Personal Aide to President Roosevelt*, edited by Lawrence F. Abbott, New York, 1924, p. 325.
[29] Howe, *Meyer*, pp. 415–416.

Actually, Stanton had no secret information, but his impressive warning turned the tide. Johnson agreed to a delay, and the Assembly voted to postpone reconsideration until February 10.[30]

At Washington Roosevelt made concerted efforts to bring about the defeat of the school segregation bill. He conferred with Senator Frank P. Flint of California and obtained his support.[31] Senator George C. Perkins, the other senator from that state, was reluctant to side with the President, but before the bill was reconsidered, he telegraphed his friends in the Assembly advising them to heed the advice of Governor Gillett.[32] Roosevelt himself sent two telegrams to Speaker Stanton expressing his appreciation for the service the Speaker was rendering and explaining the administration's position.[33] At Roosevelt's suggestion these telegrams were released to the press in California.[34] The second of the two telegrams was a detailed statement and was — in Roosevelt's words — "just as much a message to Japan as it was to California." [35] It announced that in accordance with the wishes of California, the exclusion of Japanese laborers had been accomplished through an arrangement with Japan and that the Japanese government was "loyally and in good faith" abiding by that agreement. Such a measure as the school bill, however, accomplished nothing toward achieving exclusion, he said, but "gives just and grave cause for irritation." If in the next year or two the figures of immigration prove that the arrangement with Japan is no longer working, then, he said, there would be ground for the reversal by the United States government of its present policy.[36]

In his private correspondence Roosevelt continued to express great concern. In a letter to Theodore Roosevelt, Jr., on February 6

---

[30] Hichborn, *California Legislature of 1909*, pp. 210–211.

[31] Roosevelt to Gillett, February 6, 1909, Morison, *Roosevelt Letters*, VI, 1505.

[32] Washington *Post*, February 7, 11, 1909.

[33] Roosevelt to Stanton, telegrams, February 6 and 8, 1909, Morison, *Roosevelt Letters*, VI, 1505–06, 1509–10.

[34] Roosevelt to Gillett, telegram, February 7, 1909, Roosevelt Papers.

[35] Roosevelt to Chester H. Rowell, February 11, 1909, Roosevelt Papers. The Japanese government received the message. Takahira telegraphed Tokyo: "It is said that the telegram is meant as a veiled warning to Japan that if she fails to perform her agreement, there will be an exclusion law." Takahira to Komura; received February 10, 1909, Telegram Series, CXIII, 892–893.

[36] Roosevelt to Stanton, telegram, February 8, 1909, Morison, *Roosevelt Letters*, VI, 1509–10.

he stated: "I have spent my usual week; but the troubles I have with Congress don't count at all when compared with the troubles I am having with California over Japan. I have been vigorously holding the lid down for the last three weeks, with varying success. I think I shall succeed but I cannot be sure." [37] The renewal of the California trouble made even more clear to Roosevelt that the Japanese laborers had to be kept out of the United States. "The thing that gives me serious uneasiness," he wrote to Arthur Lee, "is the friction with Japan. I have been reluctantly forced to the conclusion that it is indispensable for the Japanese to be kept from coming in any numbers as settlers to the United States. . . ." [38]

The popular sentiment in Japan exhibited a perceptible change with the passage of the segregation bill by the lower house of the California legislature and the outbreak of anti-Japanese agitation in Nevada. Various legislative leaders in California had assured the Japanese Consul General at San Francisco that the measures inimical to the Japanese would not pass. [39] In Japan newspapers and governmental leaders had been assuring the Japanese people in turn that the agitation was of a local nature and that the measures would not pass. These optimistic estimates now seemed to have gone awry. The Tokyo *Mainichi Shimbun* editorialized on February 5:

In a diplomatic sense we naturally appreciate the goodwill of the American Government and people. It is when we go deeper that we discover a dark current which gives us concern. How does the public account for the crazy agitation in Nevada? There are only some 2,000 Japanese in that State and very few of them own land. It is nothing but an expression of hostile feeling toward the Japanese. The anti-Japanese movement in America is no longer a local affair confined to San Francisco and its vicinity. [40]

Even the usually moderate *Jiji Shimpo* expressed resentment: "The denial of equal treatment is so serious a matter that it demands a permanent settlement by diplomatic means; it is not a wise policy

37 Roosevelt to Theodore Roosevelt, Jr., February 6, 1909, Morison, *Roosevelt Letters*, VI, 1506.
38 Roosevelt to Lee, February 7, 1909, Morison, *Roosevelt Letters*, VI, 1507–08.
39 Takahashi to Komura, received January 17, 21, and 23, 1909, Telegram Series, CXIII, 361–362, 422, 476.
40 *Mainichi Shimbun*, February 5, 1909.

merely to rely upon the sense of justice and friendly disposition of the other party concerned." [41]

Meanwhile the issue was approaching a climax in the California legislature. When the question of reconsideration of the school segregation bill came up in the lower house on February 10, a bitter debate took place. Gillett and Stanton marshaled their forces and were able to carry the day. Enough members of the San Francisco delegation were won over to secure reconsideration, and in the final vote on the bill it was defeated by the narrow margin of 37 to 41.[42] Roosevelt was overjoyed. He immediately sent messages of appreciation to Gillett, Stanton, and Senator Flint.[43] A week later Gillett wrote to the President reporting that the Japanese question was now very quiet and that the people of California were delighted with the way in which it was terminated.[44]

Thus passed another phase of the anti-Japanese agitation on the Pacific slope. Roosevelt could now leave office with the question at least temporarily resolved. His intervention in California politics had succeeded in 1909 as it had in 1907. Roosevelt was well aware, however, that the issue would arise again. Indeed, his firm policy in January and February of 1909 was motivated in large measure by his desire to establish a fixed policy for the future.

On February 8 he wrote a long letter on the Japanese question to Philander C. Knox, who, it was now known, would take over the Secretaryship of State in the Taft administration. "The events of the last three years," he wrote, "have forced me to the clear understanding that our people will not permit the Japanese to come in large numbers among them; will not accept them as citizens; will not tolerate their presence as large bodies of permanent settlers." Roosevelt said that he had reluctantly come to feel that the opposition to the presence of the Japanese was "entirely warranted, and not only must be, but ought to be heeded. . . ." To permit them to come would cause a race problem. It was equally necessary, however, that the United States should both show all possible cour-

---

[41] *Jiji Shimpo*, February 4, 1909.

[42] Hichborn, *California Legislature of 1909*, pp. 212–214.

[43] Roosevelt to Gillett, telegram, February 10, 1909, Morison, *Roosevelt Letters*, VI, 1517; Roosevelt to Stanton, telegram, February 10, 1909, Roosevelt Papers; Roosevelt to Flint, February 11, 1909, Roosevelt Papers.

[44] Gillett to Roosevelt, February 17, 1909, Roosevelt Papers.

tesy and consideration in carrying out this policy of exclusion and be thoroughly armed. The policy of the American government must be shaped, he said, not to meet the exigencies of this year or the next, but to meet what might occur in the next few decades. Japan was poor and therefore reluctant to go to war. Moreover, Japan was vitally interested in China and would on that account be very anxious to avoid war with the United States. "But with so proud and sensitive a people," he cautioned, "neither lack of money nor possible future complications will prevent a war if once they get sufficiently hurt and angry." In conclusion, he wrote:

There is no more important continuing feature of our foreign policy then this in reference to our dealing with Japan; the whole question of our dealings with the Orient is certain to grow in importance. I do not believe that there will be war, but there is always the chance that war will come, and if it did come, the calamity would be very great, and while I believe we would win, there is at least a chance of disaster. We should therefore do everything in our power to guard against the possibility of war by preventing the occurrence of conditions which would invite war and by keeping our navy so strong that war may not come or that we may be successful if it does come.[45]

[45] Roosevelt to Knox, February 8, 1909, Morison, *Roosevelt Letters*, VI, 1510–14.

CHAPTER EIGHTEEN

Conclusions

THE period of the Roosevelt administration was a time of difficult readjustment in Japanese-American relations. The new issues which arose in the wake of the Russo-Japanese War brought a fundamental change in those relations. These problems were new and strange to the leaders of both countries, and it is a favorable commentary on the abilities of those leaders that they resolved those perplexing questions so well that by the autumn of 1908 a rapprochement had been achieved and the war rumors had been silenced.

That Japan and the United States came through this agonizing period without serious mishap was attributable largely to the friendliness and frankness which characterized the relations between the two governments. In its communications with Washington, the Japanese government displayed forbearance and courtesy, despite the fact that it was the aggrieved party. As T. A. Bailey has observed, "It is difficult to see how the Japanese Foreign Office could have conducted itself with a greater regard for the historic friendship which had long existed between the two powers." [1]

At Washington the Japanese representatives found Roosevelt, Hay, and Root to be friendly and candid counselors. At Tokyo, though the contacts between American officials and the Foreign Ministry were not so intimate as was the case at Washington, they were courteous and at times characterized by a surprising frankness. Henry W. Denison and Durham W. Stevens (before his assassination by a Korean in 1908) doubtless exerted a strong influence within the Japanese government in the direction of friendly relations. In addition, many Japanese leaders had a genuine admiration

[1] Bailey, *Roosevelt and the Japanese-American Crises*, p. 322.

for Roosevelt. An incident recounted by an American missionary in Korea illustrates how great this admiration was:

As you enter Prince Ito's Drawing Room in the Residency General at Seoul Korea, to the right of the entrance high on the wall is a portrait of H. M. the Emperor of Japan. On the opposite wall further in is an autograph photo of President Roosevelt. One day during a call on the Prince I called attention to it, and expressed my pleasure that he should give the portrait of our President this prominence. In reply he said, "President Roosevelt is a man I admire for he is an honest man. He always means just what he says. He is frank and straight forward and never leaves you in doubt. He gives every man a square deal." [2]

Most of the Japanese people shared Ito's admiration for Roosevelt. There was, of course, a militant segment among the populace which exhibited hatred for the United States as a result of the discriminations against the Japanese in California. It is true, too, that all Japanese were deeply hurt by the stigma of racial inferiority — a factor which the United States government and people were to underestimate greatly throughout the era from Portsmouth to Pearl Harbor. Nevertheless, during the years 1905–08, most Japanese continued to look upon the United States as their historic friend. Carl J. Arnell, who took charge of the Mukden Consulate General upon Straight's departure in 1908, notes this in a letter he sent to Straight after observing the visit of the fleet to Japan:

There has probably never been so spontaneous and cordial an exchange of feelings between Japanese and foreigners before. The Japanese undeniably crave our friendship. . . . While they resent our interference in Manchuria and are grieved at our treatment of their immigrants, down deep in their hearts they cherish our friendship. They appreciate that the maintenance of this friendship is beset with racial and political obstacles, and many of them sorrowfully apprehend that this friendship will some day be broken off by inevitable causes. The word "American" has not yet lost all of its original charm to the Japanese ear, for every introduction to a Japanese brings an unmistakable smile of pleasure at the mention of my nationality.[3]

It was fortunate that in meeting the new problems in Japanese-American relations the leaders of both countries could draw upon this reservoir of good will. It was equally fortunate that capable

[2] George H. Jones to Dr. Thompson, June 1, 1908, Roosevelt Papers.
[3] Arnell to Straight, January 28, 1909, Straight Papers.

leadership existed both at Washington and Tokyo. In Roosevelt the United States possessed a President who was not reluctant to lead when leadership was needed. Despite Roosevelt's well-known impulsive and bumptious approach to foreign relations, he displayed caution and finesse when the chips were down in a Japanese-American crisis. Root's handling of Japanese matters was likewise capable, and indeed at times his perception of the difficulties faced by Japanese leaders was keener than Roosevelt's. The two men worked as a harmonious team, Roosevelt taking the lead in matters relating to discrimination against the Japanese in California and the resulting war scares, Root handling largely by himself all the other issues in Japanese-American relations. So far as the records reveal, there was never a serious disagreement between them concerning policy toward Japan. Each had affection for and confidence in the other. As Richard Leopold has observed in his excellent portrait of Root: "Between Roosevelt and Root there was no question of one dominating the other. Both men were too independent and strong-willed to play a subordinate role; each loved and admired his associate." [4]

On the Japanese side the leadership was likewise able. During Roosevelt's presidency, Japanese leadership resided in the Genro. Though Saionji and Katsura occupied alternately the official position of leadership, the major policy decisions were made by the Genro, composed of — in addition to Saionji and Katsura — Ito, Yamagata, Kaoru Inouye, Iwao Oyama, and Masayoshi Matsukata. Japan's emergence as a modern and powerful nation was traceable largely to the capable leadership of these men; and during Roosevelt's period in office, they continued to provide Japan with a leadership whose objective was to make their nation respected and admired by other nations. The role played by the Elder Statesmen was clearly indicated in a report from Chargé Jay describing the formation of the Katsura ministry in July, 1908:

An interesting feature of the negotiations which have resulted in the Emperor's decision to call upon Marquis Katsura to form a cabinet has been the extraordinary degree of importance attached to the opinion of the "Gen-

[4] Richard W. Leopold, *Elihu Root and the Conservative Tradition*, Boston, 1954, p. 51.

ro" or Elder Statesmen. The Emperor not only sent one of the highest officers of his household, Prince Iwakura, to consult with and obtain the views of Prince Yamagata, Marquis Matsukata and Marquis Inouye, who are out of town, but an Imperial messenger was also sent post-haste to Seoul to obtain the full opinion and wishes of Prince Ito.[5]

It was fortunate indeed that during the crucial years of the Russo-Japanese War and the Japanese-American crises which followed, Japan possessed leaders of high caliber — and tragic that in later years no leaders of comparable stature appeared to fill the places left vacant by their deaths.

The two most important issues with which the Japanese and American leaders had to grapple were the immigration question and the complications arising from Japan's new position on the continent of Asia. The immigration trouble took many forms — school segregation, riots against Japanese restaurants, anti-Japanese bills in the California legislature — but at the crux of the matter was racial prejudice. At first Roosevelt underestimated the strength of the anti-Japanese sentiment on the Pacific coast, but he quickly changed his position to adjust to realities once he was confronted by the unpleasant facts. No matter how much he deplored the manifestations of race feeling, he came to believe that the sentiment was too formidable to oppose, that it would be a mistake to attempt to intermingle the two races. He became convinced that the white races and the Oriental races could not be mixed without the emergence of serious economic and social problems. The effective exclusion of Japanese laborers from the United States became a cardinal feature of his foreign policy.

The exclusion of Japanese laborers was satisfactorily achieved by the Gentlemen's Agreement. From 1909 to 1924, when the agreement was superseded by exclusion legislation, 120,317 Japanese entered the continental United States and 111,636 departed.[6] The net gain of 8,681 Japanese of all classes over a period of sixteen years was not unnatural in view of the growing trade relations between the two countries.

Roosevelt's handling of the Japanese immigration problem has

5 Jay to Root, July 15, 1908, S. D. File 4592/84–87.
6 Ichihashi, *Japanese in the United States*, p. 406.

led a recent writer to characterize Roosevelt as a "racist." [7] This judgment seems unnecessarily harsh, particularly in view of the connotations the word "racist" possesses in the United States of the 1960's. Certainly Roosevelt did not believe that all races were equal, but he did not classify the Japanese among the inferior races. He did believe that the Japanese were sufficiently *different* in race that they could not be easily assimilated among the whites. He also believed that an attempt to mix the races would produce race prejudice. This he accepted as an unpleasant reality. When Americans of two generations later look back upon the Roosevelt era, they can perhaps afford a measure of equanimity. Under Roosevelt's Gentlemen's Agreement an average of over five hundred Japanese entered the United States each year. In the enlightened United States of the early 1960's the "nondiscriminatory" quota system allowed admission of one hundred and five Japanese per year.

Though Roosevelt was determined to stop the influx of Japanese laborers, he was equally resolute in his determination that those who were already in the United States, as well as those of other classes who continued to come, should be treated with courtesy and justice. To achieve this objective he was compelled to intervene in California politics in order to bridge the gap in federal authority. Much criticism was directed at the President for allegedly exceeding the limits of his constitutional authority, but his critics came forth with no proposals to resolve the trouble in California. It is difficult to discern how the discriminations could have been ended without Roosevelt's intervention. Administration leaders recognized that court action could not resolve the school segregation issue in a manner favorable to the Japanese, and Roosevelt did not decide to intervene until this became apparent. There was always the alternative of letting matters run their course in California, of allowing the Japanese only those rights and protections they could secure through legal remedies. Had this course been followed, it is unlikely that war would have resulted — almost certainly it would not have resulted — but the Japanese people would have been even more deeply offended. Such a course in any case ran counter to

[7] Roger Daniels, *The Politics of Prejudice: The Anti-Japanese Movement in California and the Struggle for Japanese Exclusion*, Berkeley and Los Angeles, 1962, p. 36.

Roosevelt's own sense of justice and his respect for the most powerful nation in the western Pacific.

Though the immigration question brought serious crises in Japanese-American relations, the questions growing out of Japan's new position on the continent caused no serious friction during the Roosevelt administration. Roosevelt himself set the pattern for American policy on this issue during and immediately following the Russo-Japanese War. He wished a balance of power established in the Far East, and since the Portsmouth settlement was just that, he bestowed on it his full blessing. By his policy in the Korean question in 1905, he made it plain to Japan and to the world that he approved of Japan's new position on the continent.

In the succeeding years Root was to wrestle with the more complex questions of the open door and the integrity of China in relation to Japan's position. Root shared Roosevelt's view that Japan's legitimate rights in Korea and Manchuria ought not to be threatened. This did not mean, however, that he believed Japan should be allowed a free hand on the continent. Root believed that there was a middle course between giving Japan a free hand and attacking Japan's legitimate interests, as Straight attempted to do. Root followed this middle road as best he could. The course was not always easy to navigate, for the question of precisely what constituted Japan's legitimate rights was still an issue in Sino-Japanese relations. Root's policy in the Harbin question indicates, however, that he was not willing to interpret Japanese and Russian rights to the serious infringement of China's sovereignty. China, in granting the Liaotung leasehold and the railway rights in Manchuria, had already compromised her sovereignty, and this Root did not propose to upset. But he did resist, in as tactful and friendly a manner as possible, further infringement of China's sovereignty. This was the case despite Root's reluctance to become a protagonist for China against Japan or Russia.

William Phillips accurately summed up Root's attitude when he wrote to Rockhill in September, 1908:

I do not think that the Department intends to have trouble in Manchuria, either with Russia or Japan. The Secretary is especially anxious not to become embroiled in little incidents with either of those two powers; but when

Russia makes a demand that we relinquish our extraterritorial rights in Harbin and on all railway property, in favor of Russia, we can not very well agree to her proposal without hitting China pretty hard.[8]

Root was no crusader of the Straight variety, but he did not propose to let Russia or Japan go unrestrained in Manchuria. The Harbin issue outlasted Root's service as Secretary of State, but his policy was to meet with some measure of success. In May, 1909, a Russian-Chinese preliminary agreement was signed which recognized the sovereignty of China in the railway zone as a fundamental principle.[9]

Root's firm yet friendly attitude concerning Japanese rights in Manchuria brought no friction in Japanese-American relations. The same can not be said of Straight's program in that area. The activities of the American Consul General and those of his friends and associates were greatly resented by the Japanese. Such schemes as the Hsinmintun-Fakumen railway project, which avowedly threatened Japan's strategic position in Manchuria, touched the Japanese in a sensitive spot. Rightly or wrongly, during the years 1906–08 Japan came to consider her position on the continent as absolutely necessary for her defense. However much Straight appreciated Japan's economic interests on the continent, he greatly underestimated her strategic interests there.

This misjudgment Straight carried into the succeeding Taft administration when he became the agent of the American banking group. Together with his old associates Lord ffrench and J. O. P. Bland, he concocted still another plan to parallel the Japanese-owned railway in Manchuria, the Chinchow-Aigun railway project. Secretary of State Philander C. Knox, who had as his First Assistant Secretary Huntington Wilson, even proposed putting all Manchurian railways under international control. The Chinchow-Aigun scheme and the Knox neutralization proposal were destined to founder on the rock of the Anglo-Japanese Alliance — just as the Hsinmintun-Fakumen project had done — but despite this ignominious failure of Straight's crusade, his expanded open door

8 Phillips to Rockhill, September 19, 1908, Rockhill Papers.
9 Rockhill to Secretary of State Philander C. Knox, telegram, May 14, 1909, S. D. File 4002/186.

policy lived on. Indeed, the expanded concept of the open door, demanding equal investment as well as commercial rights, became the basis of future American policy. Thus the gap between what was sought and what was attainable was dangerously widened.

While the expanded concept of the open door lived on, Straight's own faith in his crusade did not. Both Straight and Marvin ultimately came to appreciate more fully both the Japanese point of view and the difficulties of helping China. Straight's disillusionment with his crusade began as early as 1912 when he made a trip through Korea and Manchuria. He wrote to his old comrade Bland:

Bland, our hats are off to the Japanese! It may be all advertisement, but it's a damned effective one, for they are efficient, and you can't get away from what they are doing, or do ought but admire it. In Korea I was tremendously interested to hear that the natives were better off than ever before, and it was not a Japanese who told me, either. They are beginning to wake up from the lethargy of centuries of oppression and are producing and making money, and saving, and gaining some self-respect, which in the old days was denied them. Perish the thought, but one could not help thinking that we might all be better off if these people had charge of China's destiny, after all.[10]

Straight also came to view as chimerical the project for a Chinese railroad which would threaten the supremacy of the Japanese owned South Manchuria Railway. Writing to Bland in 1914 concerning the Chinchow-Aigun railway project, he said:

With the Ulster situation so near at Home, I can't for the life of me understand why you do not there find an outlet for your belligerent instinct, instead of trying to set our Russian and Japanese friends by the ears by stirring up the Chinchou-Aigun once more. . . .

Blando, it can't be did. There is nothing to it.

I still claim a certain parental interest in this Changeling Child, but ffrench has been nursing the baby and if it won't thrive at his breast, I doubt very much if any of our bottled wisdom will be of much avail.[11]

Writing to Bland two years later regarding the possibilities of Britain's recognition of Japan's domination in China, he indicated that his disillusionment was virtually complete:

[10] Straight to Bland, February 24, 1912, Straight Papers.
[11] Straight to Bland, March 24, 1914, Straight Papers.

Take it all in all, I am not sure that it is a bad thing. We love our China, but our Chinese friends seem to be so persistently inapt and so incorrigibly foolish, that I don't believe they can ever work out their own salvation, nor do I believe they will ever let their friends do it for them.[12]

Marvin came to share Straight's disillusionment. Looking back on those exciting times in Manchuria, he wrote many years later: "From this distance in time and geography a series of events which appeared to us then so important and dramatic, events which tended toward tragedy, appear now rather as the materials of an amusing comedy greatly exaggerated in character." [13]

Roosevelt, unlike his Consul General at Mukden, fully appreciated Japan's strategic interest on the continent, and there was a close connection between this factor and his policy on immigration. Both Roosevelt and Root were particularly anxious not to become involved in disputes with Japan in Manchuria because of the friction already resulting from the immigration question. Roosevelt was more inclined than Root, however, to give Japan a wide berth in Manchuria in compensation for the sins of the Californians. Had Japan pushed its program in Manchuria with greater vigor and with less regard for China's sovereignty and foreign treaty rights, Roosevelt probably would have been willing to concede Tokyo almost anything it wanted. He would have done so not only to counterbalance discrimination against the Japanese in the United States, but also because he had a high regard for Japan's strategic interests in Manchuria. This is clearly shown in his correspondence with Taft in 1910.

When his chosen successor embarked upon the program of Dollar Diplomacy in Manchuria which threatened Japan's strategic position, Roosevelt was sorely troubled. What made the offensive against the Japanese particularly illogical to Roosevelt was that it was pushed in the face of renewed outbreaks of anti-Japanese sentiment on the Pacific slope. ". . . it is almost impossible to accomplish much by a single isolated action," Roosevelt confided to his son Theodore. "This poor Taft cannot understand. He does not realize that to get good results from any policy toward Japan, for instance, it is necessary to have a coherent plan for treating affairs

12 Straight to Bland, November 13, 1916, Straight Papers.
13 Marvin's memoir, Straight Papers.

in Manchuria, affairs in China, affairs about immigration to the Pacific Slope, etc., etc." [14] Roosevelt dispatched two letters to President Taft pointing out the need for an integrated policy. In the first he attempted to make clear the strategic importance of Manchuria to Japan:

Japan is not rich, her main interests are on the Continent of Asia, and especially in Manchuria and Korea; and she is obliged steadily to keep in mind that Russia is a great military power, with rankling memories of injury, with which power Japan is and must remain face to face. On the other hand, the Japanese are very sensitive both as regards their vital interests in Manchuria (where powers, interests and intentions must, if we are sensible, be judged on the actual facts of the case, and not by mere study of treaties), and as to the Pacific Slope. I have reluctantly come to the conclusion that Japanese immigration must be kept out; but the way in which this shall be done is not only all-important in itself, but must be considered in connection with our entire Japanese policy.[15]

Roosevelt's second letter was an even clearer statement of his views:

Our vital interest is to keep the Japanese out of our country and at the same time to preserve the good will of Japan. The vital interest of the Japanese, on the other hand, is in Manchuria and Korea. It is therefore peculiarly our interest not to take any steps as regards Manchuria which will give the Japanese cause to feel, with or without reason, that we are hostile to them, or a menace — in however slight a degree — to their interests. . . . How vital Manchuria is to Japan, and how impossible that she should submit to much outside interference therein, may be gathered from the fact — which I learned from Kitchener in England last year — that she is laying down triple lines of track from her coast bases to Mukden, as an answer to the double tracking of the Siberian Railway by the Russians. However friendly the superficial relations of Russia and Japan may at any given time become, both nations are accustomed to measure their foreign policy in sections of centuries; and Japan knows perfectly well that sometime in the future, if a good occasion offers, Russia will wish to play a game of bowls for the prize she lost in their last contest.[16]

[14] Roosevelt to Theodore Roosevelt, Jr., December 5, 1910, Morison, *Roosevelt Letters*, VII, 178.

[15] Roosevelt to Taft, December 8, 1910, Morison, *Roosevelt Letters*, VII, 180–181.

[16] Roosevelt to Taft, December 22, 1910, Morison, *Roosevelt Letters*, VII, 189–190. Howard K. Beale concludes that Roosevelt's balance of power in the Far East was already dissolved by the Russo-Japanese treaty of 1907, and he thereby implies that Japan's strategic interest in Manchuria was not as vital as Roosevelt believed. Beale, *Theodore Roosevelt and the Rise of America to World Power*, Baltimore, 1956, pp. 332–334. Roosevelt's assessment, however, seems to be the more realistic, for despite the Russo-Japanese treaties of 1907, 1910, 1912, and 1916, the basic power conflict

These letters reveal that Roosevelt was willing to sacrifice the open door and the integrity of China in favor of the strategic and economic interests of Japan in Manchuria in order to compensate Japan for discrimination in the United States against Japanese and the exclusion of Japanese laborers. Later writers have concluded that Roosevelt was not only willing but actually did make such concessions. It was Root, however, who was the key architect of United States policy on the Manchurian question during the years 1906–08, and though he, like Roosevelt, was sympathetic toward Japan's position on the continent and fully appreciative of the need for an integrated policy, he nevertheless made no significant concession to Japan at the expense of China's integrity and the open door. Had Japan pressed for such concessions, a conflict of opinions might have developed between the President and his Secretary of State. Happily, the issue was not pressed. Roosevelt and Root, working together, were able to lead the nation through the years of crises with Japan without making any concessions to Japan in Manchuria other than those implicit in their resolve not to take the offensive against her position there.

The rapprochement which came in Japanese-American relations in 1908 brought to fruition the Roosevelt administration's policy of friendliness toward Japan. The limitations of that rapprochement, however, were sensed both in Tokyo and Washington. The immigration question and the Manchurian question were almost certain to reappear to complicate their relations in the future. But even though the intimate relations of former years could not be fully restored, Roosevelt could at least leave office with the assurance that he and Root had resolved the difficulties with Japan as well as was possible under the limitations reality imposed upon them. Moreover, while meeting the problems of each day, Roosevelt always kept an eye to the future, hoping that his policy would set a pattern for the handling of these difficult issues in the coming years. But this hope was to remain largely unfulfilled.

---

continued. The balance of power was not substantially disrupted until the collapse of Russian power in World War I.

Bibliography

UNPUBLISHED MATERIALS

I. Private Papers

Charles J. Bonaparte Papers, Library of Congress.
Henry Prather Fletcher Papers, Library of Congress.
Lloyd C. Griscom Papers, Library of Congress.
John Hay Papers, Library of Congress.
George Kennan Papers, Library of Congress.
George von Lengerke Meyer Papers, Library of Congress.
Whitelaw Reid Papers, Library of Congress.
William Woodville Rockhill Papers, Houghton Library, Harvard University.
Theodore Roosevelt Papers, Library of Congress.
Elihu Root Papers, Library of Congress.
Charles S. Sperry Papers, Library of Congress.
Willard D. Straight Papers, Albert R. Mann Library, Cornell University.
Oscar S. Straus Papers, Library of Congress.
William H. Taft Papers, Library of Congress.
Henry White Papers, Library of Congress.

II. Official Records

Post Records of the United States Embassy at Tokyo, National Archives.
Records of the Department of State, National Archives:
    Instructions, Despatches, Notes to, Notes from, 1901–1906, for Japan,
    Korea, Russia, Great Britain, France, Germany, and China.
    Numerical Series, 1906–1910:
        221   South Manchuria Railway
        290   Raid by Japanese on Seal (Fur) Fisheries
        406   Trade-Marks Conventions
        551   Open Door in Manchuria
        560   Japanese Administration of Kwantung
        1166   Korea
        1797   Treatment of the Japanese in California
        2321   Conditions in Manchuria
        2413   Remission of Boxer Indemnity

2542   Japanese Immigration
3275   Mukden Consulate
3919   Treaty Negotiations between Russia and Japan
4002   Railroad Administration at Harbin
4085   Visit of Japanese Squadron
4151   Kapsan Claim
4592   Political Affairs in Japan
6292   Domestic Exposition at Tokyo
6351   Treaty Negotiations between France and Japan
6429   Recall of Aoki
6625   Manchurian Railways
7423   Exclusion of Chinese Laborers from Japan
7614   Japanese Seal (Fur) Fisheries Poachers
7804   Treaty between Japan and Colombia
7818   Visit of K. Ishii to the United States
8258   Battleship Cruise
8422   Visit of Taft to Japan, China, and Russia
8599   Japanese Immigration into Canada
10799   Precautions for Safety of the Fleet
11991   Convention on Arbitration with Japan
12611   Relations between the United States and Japan
15636   Visit to Japan of the Chambers of Commerce
16533   Agreement between the United States and Japan

Records of the Japanese Ministry of Foreign Affairs, microfilm collection,
Library of Congress:

Telegram Series, 1902–1909, reels 32–115.

MT 1.1.2.42 Documents relating to the conference held at the Prime
    Minister's residence in 1906 concerning the Manchurian problem (Meiji
    39-nen Manshū mondai ni kanshi Shushō kantei ni kyōgikai kaisai ikken),
    reel 14.

MT 1.1.3.3 Miscellaneous documents relating to diplomatic relations be-
    tween Japan and various countries: U. S.–Japanese relations (Teikoku
    sho-gaikoku gaikō kankei zassan; Nichi-Bei kan), section 1, reel 26.

MT 1.2.2.1 Miscellaneous documents relating to the foreign policies of
    various countries: The U. S. (Kakkoku taigai seisaku kankei zassan: Beiko-
    ku no bu), volume 1, reel 45.

MT 3.8.2.21 Documents relating to the limitation and exclusion of Japa-
    nese immigrants by the U. S. (Hokubei Gasshūkoku ni oite himpō-jin tōkō
    seigen oyobi haiseki ikken), reels 720–727.

MT 5.2.18.33 Documents relating to the despatch of Barons Suematsu
    and Kaneko to Europe and the United States for the purpose of enlighten-
    ing public opinion in various countries regarding the Russo-Japanese
    War (Nichi-Ro Sen'eki kankei kakkoku yoron keihatsu no tame Suemat-
    su, Kaneko ryō-Danshaku ōbei e haken ikken), reel 804.

PVM 9–55   Collection of Cabinet Decisions (Kakugi kettei-sho shūroku), reels P14–P15.

Published Materials

I. Official Documents

Canada, Department of Labour. *Report by W. L. MacKenzie King . . . Commissioner Appointed to Investigate into the Losses Sustained by the Japanese Population of Vancouver, B. C. on the Occasion of the Riots in that City in September, 1907 . . .* , Ottawa, 1908.

————. *Report by W. L. MacKenzie King . . . on Mission to Confer with the British Authorities on the Subject of Immigration to Canada from the Orient and Immigration from India in Particular,* Ottawa, 1908.

————. *Report of the Royal Commission Appointed to Inquire into the Methods by which Oriental Labourers have been Induced to Come to Canada, W. L. MacKenzie King, C. M. G. Commissioner,* Ottawa, 1908.

Carnegie Endowment for International Peace. *Korea: Treaties and Agreements,* Washington, 1921.

————. *Manchuria: Treaties and Agreements,* Washington, 1921.

Germany, Auswärtiges Amt. *Die Grosse Politik der Europäischen Kabinette, 1871–1914,* 40 vols., Berlin, 1922–27, XIX, XXV.

Gooch, G. P., and Harold Temperley, *British Documents on the Origins of the War, 1898–1914,* 11 vols., London, 1926–38.

Japan. *Correspondence Regarding the Negotiations between Japan and Russia, 1903–1904,* Tokyo, London, and Washington, 1904.

Japan, Gaimusho. *Komura Gaikoshi,* 2 vols., Tokyo, 1953.

MacMurray, John V. A. *Treaties and Agreements With and Concerning China, 1894–1919,* 2 vols., New York, 1921.

Russia, Ministerstvo inostrannykh del. *Sbornik diplomaticheskikh dokumentov, kasaiushchikhsia peregovorov mezhdu Rossiei i Iaponiei o zakliuchenii mirnogo dogovora, 24 maia-3 oktiabria, 1905,* St. Petersburg, 1906.

Russia (USSR), Tsentral'nyi Arkhiv. "Portsmouth Correspondence of S. Y. Witte and Others," *Krasnyi Arkhiv,* 73, vols., Moscow, 1922–41, VI, 3–47.

United States, Department of Commerce. *Monthly Consular and Trade Reports,* 1906–1909, Washington, 1906–09.

United States, Department of State. *Occupation of Korea,* Message of the President of the United States transmitting in response to a Senate resolution of February 21, 1916, a report from the Secretary of State submitting copies of certain correspondence had between the official representatives of the United States and the representatives of Korea relative to the occupation of Korea, 64th Congress, 1st Session, Senate Document No. 342.

————. *Papers Relating to the Foreign Relations of the United States, 1902,* Washington, 1903.

————. *Papers Relating to the Foreign Relations of the United States, 1903,* Washington, 1904.

――――. *Papers Relating to the Foreign Relations of the United States, 1904*, Washington, 1905.

――――. *Papers Relating to the Foreign Relations of the United States, 1905*, Washington, 1906.

――――. *Papers Relating to the Foreign Relations of the United States, 1906*, 2 pts., Washington, 1909.

――――. *Papers Relating to the Foreign Relations of the United States, 1907*, 2 pts., Washington, 1910.

――――. *Papers Relating to the Foreign Relations of the United States, 1908*, Washington, 1912.

――――. *Papers Relating to the Foreign Relations of the United States, 1909*, Washington, 1914.

――――. *Papers Relating to the Foreign Relations of the United States, 1914, Supplement*, Washington, 1928.

United States, President. *A Compilation of the Messages and Papers of the Presidents*, 20 vols., New York, 1921.

――――. Japanese in the City of San Francisco, California, *Message from the President . . . Transmitting the Final Report of Secretary Metcalf on the Situation Affecting the Japanese in the City of San Francisco, California*, 59th Congress, 2nd Session, Senate Document No. 147.

II. Correspondence

Abbott, Lawrence F., ed. *The Letters of Archie Butt, Personal Aide to President Roosevelt*, New York, 1924.

Gwynn, Stephen Lucius, ed. *The Letters and Friendships of Sir Cecil Spring Rice*, 2 vols., New York, 1929.

Lodge, Henry Cabot. *Selections from the Correspondence of Theodore Roosevelt and Henry Cabot Lodge, 1884–1918*, 2 vols., New York, 1925.

Morison, Elting E., ed. *The Letters of Theodore Roosevelt*, 8 vols., Cambridge, 1951–54.

III. Memoirs and Autobiographies

Bülow, Prince Bernhard von. *Memoirs of Prince von Bülow*, trans. by F. A. Voigt, 4 vols., Boston, 1931.

Davis, Oscar King. *Released for Publication: Some Inside Political History of Theodore Roosevelt and His Times, 1898–1918*, Boston, 1925.

Griscom, Lloyd C. *Diplomatically Speaking*, Boston, 1940.

Hayashi, Count Tadasu. *The Secret Memoirs of Count Tadasu Hayashi*, ed. by A. M. Pooley, New York, 1915.

Hiratsuka, Atsushi, ed. *Ito Hakubun Hiroku*, 2 vols., Tokyo, 1929–30.

Ishii, Viscount Kikujiro. *Diplomatic Commentaries*, ed. and trans. by William R. Langdon, Baltimore, 1936.

――――. *Gaiko Yoroku*, Tokyo, 1931.

Jusserand, Jean Adrien Antoine Jules. *What Me Befell: The Reminiscences of J. J. Jusserand*, Boston, 1933.

Kokovtsov, Count V. N. *Out of My Past: The Memoirs of Count Kokovtsov, Russian Minister of Finance, 1904–1914, Chairman of the Council of Ministers, 1911–1914*, ed. by H. H. Fisher, trans. by L. Matveev, Stanford, 1935.

Korostovetz, J. J. *Pre-War Diplomacy: The Russo-Japanese Problem, Treaty Signed at Portsmouth, U. S. A., 1905, Diary of J. J. Korostovetz*, London, 1920.

Paléologue, Maurice. *Three Critical Years (1904–05–06)*, New York, 1957.

Phillips, William. *Ventures in Diplomacy*, Boston, 1952.

Roosevelt, Theodore. *Theodore Roosevelt: An Autobiography*, New York, 1929.

Rosen, Baron Roman Romanovich. *Forty Years Diplomacy*, 2 vols., New York, 1922.

Stone, Melville. *Fifty Years a Journalist*, New York, 1922.

Straus, Oscar S. *Under Four Administrations, from Cleveland to Taft*, New York, 1922.

Wilson, F. M. Huntington. *Memoirs of An Ex-Diplomat*, Boston, 1945.

Witte, Sergius. *The Memoirs of Count Witte*, trans. and ed. by Abraham Yarmolinsky, New York, 1921.

IV. Biographies

Bishop, Joseph B. *Theodore Roosevelt and His Time*, 2 vols., New York, 1920.

Cortissoz, Royal. *The Life of Whitelaw Reid*, 2 vols., New York, 1921.

Croly, Herbert. *Willard Straight*, New York, 1924.

Dawson, R. MacGregor. *William Lyon Mackenzie King: A Political Biography*, Toronto, 1958.

Dennett, Tyler. *John Hay: From Poetry to Politics*, New York, 1933.

Goldman, Eric F. *Charles J. Bonaparte, Patrician Reformer: His Earlier Career*, Baltimore, 1943.

Hamada, Kengi. *Prince Ito*, Tokyo, 1936.

Harrington, Fred Harvey. *God, Mammon, and the Japanese: Dr. Horace N. Allen and Korean-American Relations, 1884–1905*, Madison, 1944.

Howe, M. A. De Wolfe. *George von Lengerke Meyer, His Life and Public Services*, New York, 1920.

Jessup, Philip C. *Elihu Root*, 2 vols., New York, 1938.

Kennan, George. *E. H. Harriman: A Biography*, 2 vols., New York, 1922.

Leopold, Richard W. *Elihu Root and the Conservative Tradition*, Boston, 1954.

Nevins, Allan. *Henry White: Thirty Years of American Diplomacy*, New York, 1930.

Newton, Lord. *Lord Lansdowne, A Biography*, London, 1929.

Pringle, Henry F. *Theodore Roosevelt*, New York, 1931.

———. *The Life and Times of William Howard Taft*, 2 vols., New York, 1939.

Sykes, Sir Percey M. *The Right Honourable Sir Mortimer Durand*, London, 1926.

Takekoshi, Yasaburo. *Prince Saionji*, trans. by Kozaki Nariaki, Kyoto, 1933.

Thayer, William Roscoe. *Theodore Roosevelt: An Intimate Biography*, New York, 1919.

————. *The Life and Letters of John Hay*, 2 vols., New York, 1916.

Varg, Paul A. *Open Door Diplomat — The Life of W. W. Rockhill*, Urbana, 1952.

V. Special Studies

Asakawa, Kanichi. *The Russo-Japanese Conflict: Its Causes and Issues*, Boston and New York, 1904.

Bailey, Thomas A. *Theodore Roosevelt and the Japanese-American Crises*, Stanford, 1934.

Beale, Howard K. *Theodore Roosevelt and the Rise of America to World Power*, Baltimore, 1956.

Bland, J. O. P. *Recent Events and Present Policies in China*, London, 1912.

Braisted, William R. *The United States Navy in the Pacific, 1897–1909*, Austin, 1958.

Clyde, Paul H. *International Rivalries in Manchuria, 1689–1922*, 2nd ed., Columbus, 1928.

Conroy, Hilary. *The Japanese Seizure of Korea, 1868–1910: A Study of Realism and Idealism in International Relations*, Philadelphia, 1960.

Daniels, Roger. *The Politics of Prejudice: The Anti-Japanese Movement in California and the Struggle for Japanese Exclusion*, Berkeley and Los Angeles, 1962.

Dennett, Tyler. *Roosevelt and the Russo-Japanese War*, New York, 1925.

Dennis, Alfred L. P. *Adventures in American Diplomacy, 1896–1906*, New York, 1928.

————. *The Anglo-Japanese Alliance*, Berkeley, 1923.

Dillon, Emile Joseph. *The Eclipse of Russia*, New York, 1918.

Griswold, A. Whitney. *The Far Eastern Policy of the United States*, New York, 1938.

Hart, Robert A. *The Great White Fleet: Its Voyage Around the World, 1907–1909*, Boston, 1965.

Hichborn, Franklin. *Story of the Session of the California Legislature of 1909*, San Francisco, 1909.

Hulbert, Homer B. *The Passing of Korea*, New York, 1906.

Ichihashi, Yamato. *Japanese in the United States*, Stanford, 1932.

Kent, Percy Horace. *Railway Enterprise in China: An Account of Its Origin and Development*, London, 1907.

Ladd, George Trumbull. *In Korea with Marquis Ito*, New York, 1908.

Luttmer, William Joseph. *Some Aspects of American Press Opinion During the Russo-Japanese War, 1904–05*, Washington, 1950.

McKenzie, Frederick A. *Korea's Fight for Freedom*, New York, 1920.

McLaren, Walter W. *A Political History of Japan During the Meiji Era, 1867–1912*, New York, 1916.

Malozemoff, Andrew. *Russian Far Eastern Policy, 1881–1904: With Special Emphasis on the Causes of the Russo-Japanese War*, Berkeley and Los Angeles, 1958.

Monger, George. *The End of Isolation: British Foreign Policy, 1900–1907*, London, 1963.

Nelson, M. Frederick. *Korea and the Old Orders in Eastern Asia*, Baton Rouge, 1945.

Price, Ernest B. *The Russo-Japanese Treaties of 1907–1916, Concerning Manchuria and Mongolia*, Baltimore, 1933.

Reischauer, Robert Karl. *Japan: Government — Politics*, New York, 1939.

Romanov, Boris Aleksandrovich. *Russia in Manchuria, 1892–1906*, trans. by Susan W. Jones, Ann Arbor, 1952.

Sprout, Harold and Margaret. *The Rise of American Naval Power, 1776–1918*, Princeton, 1946.

Takeuchi, Tatsuji. *War and Diplomacy in the Japanese Empire*, New York, 1935.

Treat, Payson J. *Diplomatic Relations Between the United States and Japan, 1895–1905*, Stanford, 1938.

Vevier, Charles. *The United States and China, 1906–1913: A Study of Finance and Diplomacy*, New Brunswick, 1955.

White, John A. *The Diplomacy of the Russo-Japanese War*, Princeton, 1964.

Young, C. Walter. *The International Relations of Manchuria*, Chicago, 1929.

———. *Japanese Jurisdiction in the South Manchuria Railway Areas*, Baltimore, 1931.

———. *Japan's Special Position in Manchuria: Its Assertion, Legal Interpretation, and Present Meaning*, Baltimore, 1931.

Zabriskie, Edward H. *American-Russian Rivalry in the Far East, 1895–1914*, Philadelphia, 1946.

VI. Articles

Asakawa, Kanichi. "Japan in Manchuria, I," *Yale Review*, XVII (1908–09), 185–214.

———. "Japan in Manchuria, II," *Yale Review*, XVII (1908–09), 268–302.

Bailey, Thomas A. "The Root-Takahira Agreement of 1908," *Pacific Historical Review*, IX (1940), 19–35.

———. "The World Cruise of the American Battleship Fleet, 1907–1909," *Pacific Historical Review*, I (1932), 389–424.

Buell, Raymond Leslie. "The Development of Anti-Japanese Agitation in the United States," *Political Science Quarterly*, XXXVII (1922), 605–638, and XXXVIII (1923), 57–81.

Conroy, Hilary. "Japanese Nationalism and Expansionism," *American Historical Review*, LX (1955), 818–829.

Dennett, Tyler. "President Roosevelt's Secret Pact with Japan," *Current History*, XXI (1924–25), 15–21.

Esthus, Raymond A. "The Changing Concept of the Open Door, 1899–1910," *Mississippi Valley Historical Review*, XLVI (1959–60), 435–454.

———. "The Taft-Katsura Agreement — Reality or Myth," *Journal of Modern History*, XXXI (1959), 46–51.

Godwin, Robert K. "Russia and the Portsmouth Peace Conference," *American Slavic and East European Review*, IX (1950), 279–291.

Gordon, D. C. "Roosevelt's 'Smart Yankee Trick,'" *Pacific Historical Review*, XXX (1961), 351–358.

Hall, Luella J. "The Abortive German-American-Chinese Entente of 1907–08," *Journal of Modern History*, I (1929), 219–235.

———. "A Partnership in Peacemaking: Theodore Roosevelt and Wilhelm II," *Pacific Historical Review*, XIII (1944), 390–411.

Minger, R. E. "Taft's Missions to Japan: A Study in Personal Diplomacy," *Pacific Historical Review*, XXX (1961), 279–294.

Roosevelt, Theodore. "The Japanese Question," *Outlook*, May 8, 1909.

Root, Elihu. "The Real Question Under the Japanese Treaty and the San Francisco School Board Resolution," *American Journal of International Law*, I (1907), 273–286.

Thorson, Winston B. "American Public Opinion and the Portsmouth Peace Conference," *American Historical Review*, LIII (1947–48), 439–464.

Index